A Companion to the Concerto

A Companion to the Concerto

Edited by
Robert Layton

SCHIRMER BOOKS
A Division of Macmillan, Inc.
NEW YORK

© 1988 Nicholas Anderson, H. C. Robbins Landon, Denis Matthews, Robert Simpson, Christopher Headington, Joan Chissell, David Brown, Robert Layton, Lionel Salter, Arnold Whittall, Michael Kennedy, Harold Truscott and Peter Dickinson

Illustrated music examples prepared by Malcolm Lipkin

First American edition published in 1989 by
Schirmer Books
A Division of Macmillan, Inc.

Schirmer Books
A Division of Macmillan, Inc.
866 Third Avenue, New York, N.Y. 10022

First published in Great Britain by
Christopher Helm (Publishers) Ltd.
Imperial House
21–25 North Street
Bromley, Kent BR1 1SD

Library of Congress Catalog Card Number: 88-26417

Library of Congress Cataloging-in-Publication Data:
A Companion to the concerto.
   Includes index.
   1. Concerto. I. Layton, Robert.
ML1263.C64   1989   785.6   88-26417
ISBN 0-02-871961-1

Printed and bound in Great Britain by The Bath Press
Typeset by Cotswold Typesetting Ltd, Gloucester

Printing number
1   2   3   4   5   6   7   8   9   10

CONTENTS

NOTES ON CONTRIBUTORS

NICHOLAS ANDERSON (*b*. Exeter, 1941). After studying at New College, Oxford and the University of Durham, he joined the staff of Decca and then the BBC's Gramophone Department in 1967. He is an authority on eighteenth-century music and in particular Rameau and is shortly to publish a Concise History of Baroque Music. He is a contributor to *Early Music* and the *Gramophone* magazine.

DAVID BROWN (*b*. Gravesend, 1929). Authority on Russian music. After studying at Sheffield, he became music librarian at University of London and subsequently Professor of Music at Southampton. His books include *Weelkes* (1969) and *Wilbye* (1974) but he is best known for his *Glinka* (1974) and his impressive four-volume study of Tchaikovsky.

JOAN CHISSELL (*b*. Cromer, 1919). Pianist and critic, authority on Schumann. She studied piano at the Royal College of Music, London with Kendall Taylor and composition with Herbert Howells. She was a music critic of *The Times* for many years and is a regular contributor to *Gramophone*. She published an important sudy of Schumann in the Master Musician series, as well as biographies of Clara Schumann and Brahms. She has served on the jury of the International Liszt Competition in Budapest and the Leeds Competition.

PETER DICKINSON (*b*. Lytham St. Annes, 1934). Composer and pianist, studied at Queen's College, Cambridge and at the Juilliard School in New York, where he met Cage, Carter, Cowell and Varèse. In 1974 he became Professor of Music at the University of Keele where he founded the Centre of American Music. His output includes a quantity of vocal and instrumental music including concertos for piano, violin and organ.

CHRISTOPHER HEADINGTON (*b*. London, 1930). Composer and pianist. He studied composition with Lennox Berkeley. His output includes a violin concerto, two string quartets, two piano sonatas and a quantity of vocal music. He has written a *History of Western Music* (Bodley Head, 1974) and a valuable study of Benjamin Britten.

Notes on Contributors

MICHAEL KENNEDY (*b.* Chorlton-cum-Hardy, 1926). Critic and author on the staff of the *Daily Telegraph*. Author of *Vaughan Williams, Elgar*, and studies of Mahler, Strauss and Britten in the Master Musicians series, *Elgar's Orchestral Music* and *Strauss Tone Poems* in the BBC Music Guides as well as biographies of Barbirolli and Boult. Editor of the *Oxford Dictionary of Music*. He was made an OBE in 1981.

H. C. ROBBINS LANDON (*b.* Boston, Mass., 1925). Musicologist and broadcaster. After studies at Boston, settled in Vienna where he wrote a magnificent study of the symphonies of Haydn (1955), and edited modern editions of the scores. His later works include *Haydn Chronicle and Works* (5 volumes, 1976–80), and *Mozart's Last Year* (1988). Professor of Music at Cardiff University.

DENIS MATTHEWS (*b.* Coventry, 1919). Pianist and broadcaster. He made his debut at a Prom in 1939 and has played with most leading orchestras, and was a noted Mozart interpreter. He gave the first performance of Edmund Rubbra's Piano Concerto (1956), and was Professor of Music at the University of Newcastle (1972–84). He was made a CBE in 1975. He has written a Master Musician study of Beethoven, and BBC Music Guides on the Beethoven sonatas and the piano music of Brahms.

LIONEL SALTER (*b.* London, 1914). Critic, pianist and conductor. Studied at Cambridge, and at the Royal College of Music with Constant Lambert and Arthur Benjamin. Conductor of the BBC Theatre Orchestra (1945–46), in charge of music on the BBC European Service, Head of BBC TV Music (1956–63), Opera and Assistant Controller of Music and General Editor of the BBC Music Guides (1967–74).

ROBERT SIMPSON (*b.* Leamington, 1921). Composer and author, studied with Herbert Howells, and is the author of the first monograph in English on Carl Nielsen, Bruckner and the Beethoven Symphonies. He was on the staff of BBC Music Division from 1951–80. He has composed nine symphonies, of which Nos. 1 (Boult), 3 (Horenstein), 6, 7 and 9 (Handley) have been commercially recorded, eleven string quartets and concertos for the violin (1959) and piano (1967).

HAROLD TRUSCOTT (*b.* 1914). Composer and writer on music. He is the author of a study of Franz Schmidt, and a prolific contributor to learned periodicals. He has written some orchestral music but as a composer is best known for his impressive cycle of sixteen piano sonatas, many of which have been commercially recorded.

ARNOLD WHITTALL (*b.* Shrewsbury, 1935). Musicologist and authority on twentieth-century music, studied at Emmanuel College, Cambridge. He has held a number of academic appointments (Nottingham, 1964–69; Cardiff, 1969–75) and is now Reader in Music at King's College, London. His publications include studies of the Querelle des Bouffons, the music of Britten and Tippett, and of Romantic Music.

ACKNOWLEDGEMENTS

The music examples from the following works are reproduced with the kind permission of their respective publishers.

PIANO CONCERTO NO. 2—*Rachmaninov*
  © Copyright 1901 by Edition A. Gutheil
  Copyright assigned 1947 to Boosey & Hawkes Inc. for all countries
  Reprinted by permission of Boosey & Hawkes Music Publishers Ltd.

VIOLIN CONCERTO NO. 1—*Prokofiev*
  © Copyright 1921 by Edition A. Gutheil
  Copyright assigned 1947 to Boosey & Hawkes Inc. for all countries
  Reprinted by permission of Boosey & Hawkes Music Publishers Ltd.

VIOLIN CONCERTO NO. 2—*Prokofiev*
  © Copyright 1937 by Edition Russe de Musique
  Copyright assigned 1947 to Boosey & Hawkes Inc. for all countries
  Reprinted by permission of Boosey & Hawkes Music Publishers Ltd.

VIOLIN CONCERTO NO. 1—*Shostakovich*
  © Copyright 1956 by Anglo-Soviet Music Press Ltd., for United Kingdom, the British Commonwealth of Nations (excluding Canada), the Republics of Ireland and South Africa.
  Reprinted by permission of Boosey & Hawkes Music Publishers Ltd.

PIANO CONCERTO—*Copland*
  © Copyright 1929 by Aaron Copland
  Reprinted by permission of Boosey & Hawkes Music Publishers Ltd.

CELLO SYMPHONY—*Britten*
  © Copyright 1963 by Boosey & Hawkes Music Publishers Ltd.
  Reprinted by permission of Boosey & Hawkes Music Publishers Ltd.

VIOLIN CONCERTO NO. 2—*Bartók*
  © Copyright 1941, 1946 by Hawkes and Son (London Ltd.).
  Reprinted by permission of Boosey & Hawkes Music Publishers Ltd.

NIGHTS IN THE GARDENS OF SPAIN—Falla
HARPSICHORD CONCERTO—Falla
CELLO CONCERTO—Lutosławski
Reprinted by permission of Chester Music

VIOLIN CONCERTO—Walton
VIOLA CONCERTO—Walton
Reprinted by permission of Oxford University Press

PETITE SYMPHONIE CONCERTANTE—Martin
Reprinted by permission of Universal Edition (Alfred A. Kalmus Ltd.)

VIOLIN CONCERTO—Schoenberg
VIOLIN CONCERTO—Sessions
CLARINET CONCERTO—Corigliano
Reprinted by permission of G. Schirmer Ltd., London W1

CONCERTO FOR PIANO LEFT HAND—Korngold
CELLO CONCERTO—Hindemith
VIOLIN CONCERTO—Martinon
Reprinted by permission of Schott and Co Ltd.

VIOLIN CONCERTO—Sibelius
Reproduced by permission of Gehrmans Mosikforlag, Stockholm

VIOLIN CONCERTO—Valen
Reproduced by permission of Harold Lyche and Co. A.s, Drammen

VIOLIN CONCERTO—Bax
© Copyright 1946
Reproduced by permission of Chappell Music Ltd.

INTRODUCTION

Put simply the word 'concerto' means to play in concert. Motets by Viadana, madrigals by Monteverdi as well as works by Corelli and Handel were all described by their composers as concertos. So, too were the *Kleine geistliche Konzerte* (1636) of Schütz or the even earlier sacred concertos of Schein (1618). For it was the differentiation of textures, which distinguished the work of the great Venetian masters a the end of the sixteenth century, that inspired the genre. (The very first publication to use the term was the *Concerti di Andrea, et di Gio. Gabrieli* in 1587.) But, as we see in Nicholas Anderson's survey of the Baroque, the concerto soon evolved into something rather different, in which display and virtuosity quickly assumed an ever increasing pre-eminence. These are qualities which explain the consistent popularity of the concerto form: for it is in the integration of contrasting and to some extent combative forces within a coherent artistic framework that its fascination lies. The popularity of the genre in the classical era gave rise to an enormous literature of many thousands of concertos, through whose labyrinths H. C. Robbins Landon has charted an authoritative course.

But from the concerto as a vehicle for display arose what one might call the heroic vision of Mozart and Beethoven in which the individual is pitted against society. As Tovey more elegantly put it, 'Nothing in human life or history is much more thrilling or of more ancient and universal experience than the antithesis of the individual and the crowd; an antithesis which is familiar in every degree from flat opposition to harmonious reconciliation.' And it is the concertos of Mozart and Beethoven that continue to command the central heights of the repertoire. Those of Mozart have only recently come to enjoy wide exposure. Tovey could complain, in 1903 at the time of his essay, 'The Classical Concerto', of 'their neglect and lack of intelligent observation, for which we at the present time are paying dearly', and even as late as the 1950s not all of them were recorded and many were rarely to be heard in the concert hall. Their diversity of form and variety and richness of expression are illustrated by Denis Matthews, a persuasive interpreter of them in the post-war years. Yet, however often one hears the greatest of them, K491, K503 or K595, or any of the Beethoven concertos, there are always new discoveries to be made. Though this is perhaps not an appropriate forum I make no apology for saying that Robert Simpson's writings on Beethoven are to my mind among the most searching since Tovey, and show by what subtle and profound genius these masterpieces are fashioned.

While this book aims to offer a survey of the genre from its beginnings in the seventeenth century to the present day, it is a Companion—not a Compendium nor a History. Reading it from cover to cover will, however, give some idea of the historical evolution of the concerto. There are essays, like Harold Truscott's, designed to excite the music-lover's interest in Reger and Franz Schmidt, whose concertos are rarely performed these days. Others, such as David Brown, cast new light on repertoire with which we all think we are familiar. Christopher Headington, himself the composer of a violin concerto of real eloquence, discusses the development of the virtuoso composers in the wake of Beethoven, while Joan Chissell follows the symphonic strand. With the romantic movement, the emphasis may be said to have shifted from those qualities that we have in common to those which set us apart. The concerto, along with the symphony and the tone-poem, came to concern itself with the composer's more private and inner world, as indeed it had by the time of Mozart's K595 and Clarinet Concerto. During the nineteenth century, the common musical speech of the classical period was invaded by the growth of national self-consciousness and we have followed the fortunes of the genre by national or regional divisions, save only for Arnold Whittall's essay which embraces a diversity of movements. Composers have pushed back the frontiers of what is admissable as the stuff of art (as indeed have their colleagues in other disciplines) and the interior landscape we observe in the concertos of Berg of Henze encompass areas of experience which would have seemed beyond the province of earlier artists.

These essays are addressed to the concert-goer, the radio listener or record collector with an inquiring mind, and our primary ambition in these pages is to bring him or her a little closer to he riches of the concerto repertoire. Of course, there are omissions—otherwise this book would be more than twice its present size, and I am not alone (I imagine) in possessing scores and records of concertos that I like and admire for which we have not been able to find space. (Among them, for obvious reasons, must be numbered the concertos of three of our contributors.)

This book owes much to the encouragement and patience of Richard Wigmore, whose brainchild it was and many of whose burdens he cheerfully bore. To him and all who have contributed within, I am much indebted.

Robert Layton

CHAPTER 1

The Baroque Concerto

Nicholas Anderson

The Baroque period was one in which many styles were formulated. They were influenced by changes in religious thinking and shifts in political attitudes brought about by a fierce string of wars which few, if any, European countries succeeded altogether in avoiding. Baroque music which spanned, let us say, the years between 1580 and 1750, is rich in contrasts and equally rich in contradictions. Thus, the artistic ideals to which one composer aspired would not necessarily be the same as those of another. Nevertheless, there were certain constant values shared by all creative minds. The most important of them, perhaps since it was central to the thinking of a Baroque artist—painter, poet, sculptor or musician—was a declared intent to move the passions. Descartes had laid emphasis on this aspect of artistic communication in the middle of the seventeenth century, but it had been acknowledged much earlier by Giulio Caccini in the celebrated Preface to a collection of songs *Le nuove musiche*, published in 1602. This aim to move an onlooker, a reader or a listener was quick to spread beyond Italy, the fountainhead of Baroque art in all its forms, to become one of the distinguishing features of artistic endeavour throughout the seventeenth and early eighteenth centuries.

A development in music fundamental to the Baroque, and with far-reaching consequences in later periods of music, was that of the *concertato* style in music for mixed groups or choirs of voices and instruments. From this the instrumental concerto of the Baroque period emerged as an independent form towards the end of the seventeenth century. Earlier in the century in Italy the word *concertato* connoted an association of instrument and voices, of sounding together but also hinting at rivalry between disparate elements comprising the full texture of a piece of music. Alternately, a small ensemble might be contrasted with a larger one which, as we shall see, is a characteristic of the Baroque *concerto grosso*. Thus *contrast*, an important concept in all the Baroque arts, may be considered a significant aspect of *concertato* writing.

The development of the *concertato* style can be seen both in the later madrigal books of Claudio Monteverdi and in the church music and madrigals of Venetian composers such as Andrea and Giovanni Gabrieli. The earliest recorded publication to use the word *concerto* was printed in Venice in 1587 with the title *Concerti per voci, & stromenti Musicali*. This contained madrigals, motets and Mass movements by Andrea Gabrieli and his nephew Giovanni. The writing is often colourful and includes pieces for as many as three distinct contrasting groups. Thus *concerto*, in its earliest use in Italy, was not a term for purely instrumental music but rather one for mixed groups of voices and instruments, usually sacred but sometimes secular.

Ten years after the publication of the *Concerti* of the Gabrielis, uncle and nephew, a treatise on another fundamental aspect of Baroque style was published; this was *Del suonare sopra il basso con tutti stromenti & uso loro nel conserto* (1607) in which the author, Agostino Agazzari, explained the use of figures placed above the bass line to indicate the harmonies of the accompanying middle parts. It was, in other words, a treatise on *basso continuo* practice. Whereas in the Renaissance composers wrote polyphonically, that is in equal independent voices, the Baroque placed emphasis on the treble and bass, the outermost strands of a texture. This was the essence of the new monodic style described by Caccini in his preface to *Le nuove musiche*, and with this polarity between treble and bass came a stronger sense of tonality based on the importance of three principal chords (tonic, dominant and subdominant) as well as chromaticism and dissonance. The instruments used for 'realizing' the *basso continuo* were those capable of providing full harmonic support; lute or theorbo, organ or harpsichord, depending on the nature, requirements and function of the music and also, of course, on availability of performers. These instruments might be reinforced by a bass viol, a cello, a violone or a bassoon, all of which are capable of sustaining the bass line. *Basso continuo* did not, of course, have a part to play in solo lute and keyboard repertoire, where all the parts were fully written out and nothing was left to the discretion of the performer. Thus the *basso continuo* ideal is indissolubly linked with all aspects of baroque style and therefore has a direct bearing on all the music under discussion in this chapter.

So far we have seen that the development of vocal and instrumental forms in Italy during the first part of the seventeenth century is closely connected. Instrumental music, however, did not have the aid of a text to sustain it and had to search elsewhere for an eloquent means of expression. This striving for eloquence is reflected in the variety of structures with which composers experimented during the early decades of the century. Frequently, there is no formal distinction between the terms *sonata*, *concerto* and *sinfonia* when applied by Italian composers to their music. Each of these might contain elements of the most important styles of instrumental composition during the early Baroque: the *canzona* which, at the beginning of the seventeenth century, was the leading form of contrapuntal music was often made up of several sections; the theme with variations (ostinato, chaconne, passacaglia); the ricercare, fantasia or capriccio, which were generally pieces of non-sectional counterpoint; and lastly, various types of dances. In each of these types of composition we shall find as often as not the distinguishing characteristic of one of the others. So it is evident that during the first half of the seventeenth century the development of instrumental music is a complex affair with inconsistencies of terminology and forms which were anything but standardized. Often, for example, the terms *sonata* and *canzona* were practically synonymous when applied to music for small ensembles with basso continuo.

It was not until the second half of the seventeenth century that the sonata freed itself from the characteristics of the older canzona. Around this time instrumental sonatas began to fall into two discernible categories, the *sonata da chiesa* and the *sonata da camera*. The *da chiesa* (church sonata) variety, with its four-movement slow-fast-slow-fast pattern, usually excluded movements overtly of a dance character—though dance measures certainly occur in a great many of them—and were generally of serious intent. The *sonata da camera* (chamber sonata) by contrast, contained sequences of movements of a predominantly dance character, often falling into the dance-suite pattern established by way of the keyboard suite. The usual instrumentation for mid- to late-seventeenth-century Italian sonatas was one or two violins with *basso continuo* consisting of a cellist or viola da gamba player and a keyboard player to 'realize' the figured bass. As we shall see, this trio group was to become the standard *concertino* of the *concerto grosso*. The most important centres in the development of the early Baroque sonata, and later the concerto, were the north Italian city states, pre-eminent among them Bologna; later in the century the sphere of activity extended further south to Rome. Here, the techniques of two composers, **Alessandro Stradella** (1644–1682) and **Arcangelo Corelli** (1653–1713) were beginning to have wide influence, not only in Italy but also, gradually, abroad. The earliest instrumental concerto form, that of the *concerto grosso*, emerged at least as early as the 1670s and is of Roman origin. One of the pioneers was Stradella, who experimented with a contrasting, antiphonal scheme between small (concertino) and large (grosso) groups within the instrumental sections of his oratorios; a notable example of it exists in the most famous of them, *San Giovanni Battista*. This work was performed in Rome in 1675 and involved 27 instrumentalists amongst whom, in all probability, was the young Corelli. The precise disposition of players in the *concerto grosso* is not possible to determine, but Stradella almost certainly wrote for violins, divided violas, cellos and a larger bass stringed instrument. The transition to the more modern ensemble of violins in two parts instead of divided violas dates from the late 1670s or early 1680s. Stradella's *sinfonie a più istromenti* reveal a rich diversity of instrumental combinations amongst which we can find what are probably the earliest examples of string concertino contrasted with string *concerto grosso* in a purely instrumental context.

Meanwhile, developments were taking place in the opera sinfonia. Up until the mid-seventeenth century opera sinfonias were usually confined to a single movement; towards the end of the 1640s, however, a two-movement pattern became discernible, the first, a slow measure, usually in common time, the second faster and almost invariably in triple measure. The composer who seems first to have adopted this practice was Francesco Cavalli (1602–1676), a pupil of Monteverdi; but it was the French composer Jean-Baptiste Lully (1632–1687) who established the bi-partite form and gave it wider currency. The earliest of Lully's works to include rhythmic figures in the form which was to become characteristic of the French Overture is the *Ballet d'Alcidiane*, composed in 1658. It was in 1660, however, when Lully inserted ballet music and an overture into Cavalli's *Serse*, that the pattern of the French overture began to crystallize. Here, the fugal second section of the overture is in triple metre and framed by two slow sections in dotted rhythm, the concluding one of which takes up the idiom of the opening, though in a shortened form. By the time that Lully produced his first tragédie-lyrique *Cadmus et Hermione*, in 1673, this pattern was well established, and was not only to remain one of the most popular orchestral forms throughout the Baroque period but was also to permeate other forms too, such as the trio-sonata, concerto, solo keyboard music and even some of the great choral movements of Bach's church cantatas.

Italy

Corelli, the New Orpheus

Corelli's only set of concertos, his Opus 6, containing twelve *concerti grossi* for strings, was published in Amsterdam in 1714, the year after his death. Eight of these fall into the *da chiesa* pattern, while the remaining four are *concerti da camera*. Although printed in 1714 these works are likely to have been composed many years earlier. In 1689 the Italian theorist and composer Angelo Berardi (c. 1636–1694) tells us in his *Miscellanea musicale*, that 'Concertos for violins and other instruments are called symphonies; those of Arcangelo Corelli, the celebrated violinist, called the Bolognese, the new Orpheus of our time, are especially esteemed today'. We cannot be certain that he was referring to music which eventually was included in Corelli's Opus 6; but it seems at least likely, especially if we also take into account the testimony of the German composer Georg Muffat, who was in Rome in 1682 where he met Corelli. There, Muffat recalls, he heard 'with astonishment some symphonies of Signor Arcangelo Corelli, which were very beautiful and very well performed by a good company of musicians'.

Correctness and a sense of order were aspects of baroque thinking which penetrated almost every facet of cultural and social life. The formal structure of Corelli's concertos is clearly and effectively organized, giving what the French writer Marc Pincherle described as a new 'harmonious coherence' to the various voices of the texture. In his organization of concertino and ripieno, in his interest in instrumental sonority, his fine sense of proportion, strong tonal affirmation and modest use of instrumental virtuosity, Corelli created a style which to a greater or lesser extent influenced composers throughout the first half of the following century. Technically, Corelli's writing is cautious compared both with that of some of his Italian contemporaries and with the greater freedom shown by his successors.

Corelli's twelve concertos possess many of the formal and technical features of his sonatas but offer a richer tonal contrast in texture afforded by the alternation between small and larger groups of instruments. The concertino group, confirmed by Corelli's title-page, should consist of two violins and a cello, while the *grosso* or *ripieno* should contain two further violins, viola and bass instruments including, of course, keyboard continuo. While the *grosso* section could be expanded according to taste or circumstance, the *concertino* remained constant in size, perhaps with its own keyboard or plucked string continuo instrument. Although Corelli never diverges from the solo-tutti pattern fundamental to his sonatas and concertos, he uses it imaginatively, seldom failing to create a high level of musical interest. One reason for this is that he achieves variety within the pattern. Alternating sections vary considerably in length, and movements are sometimes made up from units of contrasting speed, yet the impression of spontaneity, even of improvisation generated by these apparent interruptions, is never allowed to fracture the integral virtuosity or the clarity of the whole design. For an account of a first-hand impression which these concertos left upon Corelli's contemporaries we may turn to Georg Muffat, whose foreword to his own *Ausserlesene Instrumental-Musik* (1701) is of considerable interest: 'The twelve concertos which comprise this set are based on Corelli's models', Muffat tells us,

> I present to you . . . this first collection of my instrumental concertos, blending the serious and the gay, entitle of a *more select harmony* because

they contain (in the ballet airs) not only the liveliness and grace drawn intact from the Lullian well, but also certain profound and unusual effects of the Italian manner, various capricious and artful conceits, and alternations of many sorts, interspersed with special diligence between the great choir [concerto grosso] and the trio [concertino] of soloists . . . The idea of this ingenious mixture first occurred to me some time ago in Rome, . . . where I heard, with great pleasure and astonishment, several concertos of this sort, composed by the gifted Signor Arcangelo Corelli, and beautifully performed with the utmost accuracy by a great number of instrumental players. Having observed the considerable variety in these, I composed several of the present concertos, which were tried over at the house of the aforesaid Signor Arcangelo Corelli (to whom I am deeply indebted for many useful observations touching this style, most graciously communicated to me . . .)

In his *concerti grossi* Corelli not only did much to establish orchestral texture but also perfected a style of composition which was universally admired, if not invariably imitated, by composers during the next half-century.

If we came to enquire whence comes this magical power of Corelli's compositions, [wrote Vincenzo Martinelli] we shall very quickly find that their whole secret inheres in their marvellously imitating the most dulcet and pleasing characteristics of the human voice, and their contriving to express, each according to its range, and with regard to the most exact rules of art. (*Lettere familiari e critiche*, London, G. Nourse 1758; pp 377–81).

Torelli

While Corelli was refining the *concerto grosso* in Rome another composer, further north, in Bologna, was contributing towards the development of the form. This was **Giuseppe Torelli** (1658–1709). During his life Torelli had travelled to Germany and Austria, but by 1701 he had returned to Bologna where, towards the end of his career, he prepared his finest concertos for publication. They were printed shortly after his death in 1709 as *Concerti grossi con una pastorale per il Ss Natale* and issued as the composer's Opus 8. The concertos of Torelli's Opus 8, although adhering to the Corellian formula in certain fundamental respects, are significantly different from them. In the first six concertos of the set the concertino group consists only of two violins with a continuo bass which provides harmonic support but seldom takes a solo role as does the cello in Corelli's concertino. The last six concertos provide a stylistic advance on the earlier six in that the alternating sequence of concertino and ripieno becomes one of solo violin and tutti. With the emphasis that Torelli placed on the solo violin passages the Baroque concerto took a decisive step in a direction that was soon to be developed by Vivaldi and many other composers. Like Corelli, Torelli sometimes preferred to begin his movements with solo rather than tutti statements. The opening movements of the first two concertos of the set, for example, begin with the solo violins instead of the full body of strings; Corelli never begins his concertos in this manner but often does so in subsequent movements. Unlike him, Torelli favoured the three-movement pattern, fast-slow-fast, which had become standard in Italian opera sinfonie by the end of the seventeenth century, in all but one work of the set; that exception is the Concerto No. 8 in C minor, where the first of its two *allegros* leads, by way of an incomplete cadence, to a recitative-like *adagio*; the *adagio*, while acting as a middle movement, nevertheless is integrally related to the previous one.

In the concertos of Opus 8, an important landmark in the history and development of the form, Torelli reveals his skill at constructing movements which are both rich in the diversity of their ideas and unified in their structure. In many of the slow movements we can sense the growing influence of the operatic aria on instrumental music. This is, perhaps, most readily apparent in the song-like character of the violin solos, affecting examples of which are afforded by the middle movements of the last two concertos of the set. Torelli's middle movements are also distinctive in their structure; in Opus 8, with three exceptions, they consist of a tripartite pattern of two slow outer sections, similar though not identically constructed, containing a faster central one. Torelli's most significant achievement lies in the organization of the outer movements, where tutti and solo sections occur in clearly defined alternating periods. Tuttis are linked by a common thematic idea, while intervening solo passages are characterized by florid, idiomatic and lively figuration. Thematic relationship between the tuttis and the solo passages is sometimes close as, for example, in the opening movement of the 'Christmas' Concerto in G minor (Opus 8, No. 6); but more often, a much greater degree of thematic independence prevails between the constrasting sections. Many of Torelli's ideas, though comparatively restricted, were to be exploited and expanded by the following generation of Italian composers. Torelli taught foreign musicians such as the Dresden violinist Pisendel, and through contacts such as this the Italian concerto style quickly spread beyond its native boundaries.

Albinoni

The Italian Baroque concerto reached stylistic maturity within a period approximately between 1710 and 1750. Although there were renowned composers of concertos working in many Italian cities, the focal point shifted from Bologna and Rome to Venice. There, four composers above all made significant contributions to the form. Alessandro and Benedetto Marcello, Albinoni and Vivaldi. **Tomaso Albinoni** (1671–1751) termed himself a 'dilettante' early in his career; in other words he did not depend for a living either on the success of his compositions or his prowess as a performer. Nevertheless, from 1709 Albinoni devoted all his time to music, cultivating a fluent technique and a congenial, uncomplicated style in his compositions. Albinoni's earliest concertos are contained in his Opus 2, published in 1700. The set consists of six *Sonatas* or *Sinfonias* and six *Concerti a cinque* for strings. In the sinfonias the parts consist of divided violins and violas with cello and basso continuo, while in the concertos an additional solo violin strand is incorporated. Albinoni adopts the slow-fast-slow-fast pattern of movements in the sinfonias but a fast-slow-fast pattern in the concertos. The set is rich in contrast; the writing in the concertos allows for a modest degree of virtuosity from the solo violin, at least in the outer movements, while the sinfonias glow with melodic and textural warmth. Slow movements are frequently characterized by affecting suspensions and modulations while faster ones, such as those which begin the Sinfonia No. 2 in C major and the Concerto No. 1 in F major, foreshadow a Handelian idiom in their different ways. Two works in this set, the Sinfonias No. 3 in A major and No. 6 in G minor are, perhaps, especially successful and engaging and, deservedly, have been taken up by present-day ensembles.

Albinoni's second set of concertos, his Opus 5, appeared in 1707. These, like the Opus 2, are *concerti a cinque* but show a stylistic advance on the earlier set. They were evidently successful, for in 1710 a second edition was published in Venice, and two further editions were printed in Amsterdam. Surprisingly, perhaps, the solo element in Opus 5 has not significantly gained ground from that occupied in Opus 2, and there are only modest solo violin excursions. All the concertos in Opus 5 adopt the three-movement pattern of his earlier concertos but show a tauter organization of material. The greatest variety of formal pattern is to be found in the middle movements, which range from being little more than a sequence of affecting modulations (Concerto No. 1 in B flat), to lyrical utterances in which the solo violin plays a prominent part (Concerto No. 2 in F major). Finales are fugal, often with engaging subjects and worked out in a craftsman-like manner. Opening movements are notably robust and here, as in two or three of the Opus 2 pieces, we may discern a flavour of what, later on, we have come to term Handelian (Concerto No. 2 in F major, 1st movement).

A distinctive, and indeed novel feature of Albinoni's next two sets of twelve concertos was the inclusion of works for one and two oboes. The earlier of them, Opus 7, was published in 1715 and contains four concertos for one oboe, four for two oboes and four for strings. The string writing throughout is in four parts for divided violins, viola, cello and basso continuo. All twelve concertos adopt the three-movement pattern of the operatic sinfonia. The oboe concertos were amongst the earliest of their kind, for although oboes had played a prominent role in French court music and above all in Lully's opera orchestra since the 1670s, it was not until the turn of the century that they began to appear in Italian ensemble music. Albinoni's oboe concertos may not, in fact, predate Vivaldi's earliest concertos for the instrument, though the manner of writing for them is somewhat different. Albinoni's oboe parts are generally more song-like than those of Vivaldi and are closer both to a vocal idiom and, especially in the works for two oboes, the dialogue trumpet-writing of the Bologna school. Vivaldi is less compromising and keeps fairly strictly to a modified violin idiom in his oboe writing. While in the outer movements of his oboe concertos Albinoni follows the alternating tutti-solo principle, by now well established, he frequently introduces a convention borrowed from the vocal aria: briefly, this consists of a short solo statement by the oboe(s) following the initial tutti and almost invariably based on its material. The tutti then returns, after which the soloist repeats the previous solo quotation this time extending it. This technique of presenting the soloist with an introductory *motto* is called a *Devise*, a German term coined late in the nineteenth century by Hugo Riemann.

In 1722 Albinoni published his Opus 9. Like the Opus 7 this too contained four concertos for one oboe, four for two oboes and four for strings. There is no significant stylistic advance on the previous set except that each of the string concertos contains a solo violin part and that the oboe concertos are more extended. Some commentators have discerned a lack of freshness and invention in Albinoni's Opus 9, yet the set contains one of his finest creations in the Concerto in D minor for oboe and strings (No. 2 of the set). Indeed, its lyrical *adagio*, tinged with pathos, may be considered one of his outstanding achievements. Albinoni published one further set of concertos, his Opus 10, in about 1735. The twelve works, *a cinque* are all for strings: violins in three parts of which one, the *violino principale*, plays sometimes in unison with the first violin but at others, notably in the Concertos No. 8 in G minor and No. 12 in B flat, in a solo capacity, viola, cello and continuo. Apart from the solo violin writing, which is more extended and more virtuosic than we find in the earlier sets, the Opus 10 concertos, although *rococo* in spirit, show no real advance on Albinoni's previous mature concertos. Any lack of invention here, however, is compensated for by the many lyrical gestures, the pleasing melodies and the sheer vitality of the composer's convivial manner. These qualities are present in each work, but above all, perhaps, in the outer movements of the Concerto No. 5 in A major, the menuet-like finale of the Concerto No. 3 in C major and the opening movement of the Concerto No. 10 in F major.

The Marcellos

Two of Albinoni's Venetian contemporaries, who also styled themselves 'dilettante', were the brothers, **Alessandro Marcello** (1684–1750) and **Benedetto Marcello** (1686–1739). Alessandro was not a prolific composer by the standards of his day, but his set of six concertos *La cetra* (The Lyre) published in Augsburg in about 1740, is worthy of mention. Stylistically, it belongs to the final phase of the Venetian Baroque concerto, but it is convenient to discuss them here in the company of his brother's concertos, which appeared at a much earlier date. The concertos of *La cetra* are scored for two flutes or oboes, strings and continuo and adopt a three-movement pattern in each case. There is a wealth of varied musical expression in these concisely constructed works; the style often recalls Vivaldi, as for instance may be seen in the *andante larghetto* of the Concerto No. 3 in B minor, one of the most extended and impressive movements in the set, suggesting in its pathos the opening of Haydn's Symphony No. 49 in F minor, *La Passione*. There is a pleasing individuality about these concertos whose forward-looking idiom draws upon musical ideas current in centres beyond Venice. The work by which Alessandro Marcello is best known, however, does not belong to *La cetra* but was published in about 1718 in a set of twelve concertos by various composers. His Oboe Concerto in D minor was one of several Venetian concertos which fascinated Bach sufficiently for him to make a harpsichord transcription of it (BWV 974). The work is more conventionally oriented round the Venetian late Baroque idiom than those of *La cetra* and is striking for its pathetic utterance. Arthur Hutchings, with characteristic insight and discernment, has described it as a work 'which so remarkably combines romantic pathos with classical integrity and elegance that many must regard it, as Bach evidently did, as one of the supremely beautiful works of the Venetian School'. (Hutchings: *The Baroque Concerto*, London 1961, p. 170). I would add to this that Marcello, perhaps more than any other of his Italian contemporaries, understood the expressive potential of the oboe, exploring it in a manner which suggests that he was very familiar with both its strong and weak technical features.

Benedetto Marcello's only published set of concertos was printed in Venice in 1708 and issued as the composer's Opus 1. These twelve concerti *a cinque* are in certain respects less forward looking than those of Albinoni's

Opus 5, which had appeared in the previous year. Marcello adopts in all but one work a pattern of four or more movements corresponding with that of Corelli's Opus 6. On the other hand, his use of concertino and obbligato instrumentation leans towards the solo as opposed to the group or *grosso* concerto. Marcello's concertino group consists of two instruments, violin and cello, as opposed to Corelli's two violins and cello, for example. The music, as I have implied, looks towards both Roman and Venetian models; nine of the twelve concertos begin with a slow introductory movement followed by a fugal Allegro, and it is not unusual to find Marcello juxtaposing fast and slow sections within a single movement in the manner favoured by Corelli—the Finale of the Concerto No. 2 in E minor is a good example. Yet the obbligato writing for violin and cello is frequently more extended than that found in the Roman concertos and adopts lively idiomatic figurations more in character with the Venetian style. An example of the importance given to solo/obbligato passages occurs in the second movement of the Concerto No. 3 in E major, whilst the fugal second movement of the Concerto No. 2 in E minor vividly foreshadows a style of writing found in Vivaldi's *L'estro armonico*, (Opus 3). The subject of the fugal finale of the Concerto No. 4 in F major, incidentally, bears a close resemblance to the fugal section of the 'Ouverture' which begins Handel's Concerto Grosso in D minor, Opus 6, No. 10. The Finale of the Concerto No. 6 in B flat was clearly also known to Handel, who incorporated its initial melodic idea into his Trio-Sonata, Opus 2, No. 4 (3rd movement), first published in the 1720s. Handel later used the same material in a more brilliant way in the Organ Concerto in B flat, Opus 4, No. 2 (1738). Marcello's later concertos, of which there are but two known to us, show both to what extent he was influenced by Vivaldi's solo violin concertos and his lively feeling for the *galant* style of the mid-eighteenth century.

The term *galant* is one which we shall encounter many times within this chapter and a brief explanation is required. During the first half of the eighteenth century *galant* was used to denote all that was elegant, graceful and unashamedly intended to please the senses. Above all, perhaps, it suggested an antidote to the 'seriousness' which had been such a feature of baroque artistic endeavour. In music, *galant* implied pleasing melodies with simple accompaniments, and graceful dances such as the *minuet*. Many theorists attempted to define *galant*, amongst whom were Johann Mattheson in Hamburg, Johann Adolphe Scheibe in Leipzig and Quantz at Potsdam. It was, to a great extent, new values versus old ones, secular versus sacred, amusement versus seriousness. By the 1770s, however, contrapuntal virtues were being extolled once more and *galant* gestures were assimilated into the mature style of the late eighteenth century.

Vivaldi

The Venetian Baroque concerto reached its apex, both in respect of invention and organization, in the works of **Antonio Vivaldi** (1678–1741). '. . . the most popular composer for the violin, as well as player on that instrument, during these times was Don Antonio Vivaldi . . . maestro di capella of the Conservatorio della Pietà, at Venice . . .', remarked Charles Burney in his *General History of Music.*

> . . . his pieces called Stravaganze . . . among flashy players, whose chief merit was rapid execution, occupied the highest place of favour. His Cuckoo Concerto, during my youth, was the wonder and delight of all frequenters of country concerts . . . If acute and rapid tones are evils, Vivaldi has much of the sin to answer for. 'It is very usual', says Mr Wright in his *Travels through Italy*, from 1720 to 1722, 'to see priests play in the orchestra. The famous Vivaldi, whom they call the Prete Rosso [Red Priest], very well known among us for his concertos, was a topping man among them at Venice'.

Burney is less generous and unreliable in his assessment of the Venetian Baroque concerto later on, but the brief picture given above is attractive, and points to those features of Vivaldi's style which evidently made a particularly strong impression.

Between 1711 and 1729 Vivaldi published nine collections of concertos in the course of which we can discern development both in his skill as a composer and in the form of the concerto. His first set, *L'estro armonico* (Harmonic caprice or inspiration) Opus 3, appeared in 1711 and quickly became known, both via his Amsterdam publisher Estienne Roger and through travelling virtuosi, in northern European countries. The young Bach, at Weimar, had probably seen several if not all the concertos of Vivaldi's Opus 3 before they were published; that they were of the greatest interest to him is beyond question, since he transcribed no less than half of the set—two for solo organ (BWV 593 and 596 from Op. 3, Nos. 8 and 11 respectively), three for solo harpsichord (BWV 972, 976 and 978 from Op. 3, Nos. 9, 6 and 7) and one, a much later transcription, for four harpsichords and string orchestra (BWV 1065 from Op. 3, No. 10). In a sense, Bach's transcriptions—in fact 'arrangements' would be a more suitable term— reflect the sheer variety of techniques on display in *L'estro armonico*, which contains concertos for one, two and four violins arranged in four symmetrical groups. Like Benedetto Marcello's Concertos, Opus 1, Vivaldi's *L'estro armonico* has a foot in both Roman and Venetian camps though not always in similar respects. Corelli may have been Vivaldi's Roman model, for although his opus ultimum was not published until 1714—three years after *L'estro armonico*—its content was, as I have demonstrated, well known through performance. However, as Michael Talbot has pointed out, it may have been the concertos of another Roman composer, Giuseppe Valentini (1681–1753), which served as a model. In one of the twelve concertos of Valentini's Opus 7 (1710) four violin parts are employed similarly to the correspondingly laid-out concertos in Vivaldi's Opus 3 (Nos. 1, 4, 7 and 10).

Notwithstanding certain Roman leanings, notably in the instrumental layout of *concertino* and *ripieno* parts, the predominant character of the music is Venetian; Venetian too is the inclusion of two viola parts—as we have already found in Albinoni's first two concerto collections—and an obbligato cello in five of the works including the Concerto No. 7 in F major, which is outwardly, perhaps, that which most readily evokes the Corellian manner. Two others of the concertos of the set, No. 2 in G minor and No. 11 in D minor, preserve the Corellian concertino of two violins and cello, and three of the twelve adopt a four- rather than a three-movement pattern. The degree of experimentation is such, and the invention so fertile, that it would be difficult to single out any one work especially deserving of attention. Two concertos however, No. 8 in A minor and No. 10 in B minor, are outstandingly effective. Concerto No. 8 is for two solo violins and begins with arresting tutti chords recalling the Italian opera-overture convention of three initial 'hammer strokes' at the head of a ritornello. In this work Vivaldi dispenses with the obbligato cello, concentrating on the two violin parts both in an idiomatic and lyrical manner. The middle movement is a particularly poetic utterance in which the solo lines weave a hauntingly beautiful melody over a *ground* bass. In the Finale we find another typical and effective Vivaldian device where one soloist plays a lyrical cantilena against the accompanying arpeggiated figurations of the other (Ex. 1). The Concerto No. 10 is scored for four concertino violins and a concertino cello. In the concertino passages Vivaldi explores a variety of instrumental combinations in order to achieve contrasts both within the group and between the group and tutti-*ripieno* sections. The slow movement is as effective as it is unusual. There is no melodic pattern, but instead, each of the four solo violins plays broken chords, and these chords change with every bar. Furthermore, each violin plays its arpeggiated chords in a different manner creating, in the words of Marc Pincherle, 'a shimmering kind of harmony'[1] (Ex. 2).

Vivaldi's second published set of concertos, *La stravaganza*, appeared in about 1714. Here we find a further step towards the solo concerto, with seven works for one violin, four for two violins and a fifth for two violins and

1. M. Pincherle, *Vivaldi, Genius of the Baroque*, London, 1958, p. 101.

Ex. 1

cello. As with *L'estro armonico*, we can be fairly sure that some of the concertos of *La stravaganza* had been in circulation before Estienne Roger printed them in Amsterdam; Bach, at least, seems to have encountered two of them in earlier variant forms, since his Concerto in G major (BWV 980) contains only the first movement of Vivaldi's Opus 4, No. 1 in B flat, while the Concerto in G minor (BWV 975) closely follows the opening of Opus 4, No. 6 in G minor, but greatly modifies the second movement and incorporates an entirely different finale. Commentators often find less to admire in *La stravaganza* than in Vivaldi's other published collections of violin concertos; yet although there may be, perhaps, less formal variety than in *L'estro armonico*, both the poetic and the pioneering endeavour is strong. Arthur Hutchings describes the first concerto of the set as 'inferior and merely orderly';[2] orderly, certainly—Vivaldi is seldom wanting in that discipline—but what may appear undistinguished on the printed page certainly comes to life in a brilliant manner in performance. The finale of the Concerto No. 1 in B flat is as exciting in effect as it is unusual in design.

2. A. Hutchings, *The Baroque Concerto*, London, 1961, p. 152.

Ex. 2

Instead of the more usual pattern of four or five solo sections alternating with the tuttis, which characterizes the larger number of Vivaldi's outer movements, this one consists of a single solo section within two tuttis, the first of which comprises almost two thirds of the entire movement.

It is the slow movements of *La stravaganza*, however, which make a more lasting impression. Two of them, perhaps, are especially deserving of mention. One is the *grave e sempre piano* of the Concerto No. 4 in A minor, whose sighing suspensions, ethereal solo violin line and characteristic chromaticisms evoke an air of almost fairy-tale enchantment; moreover, the harmonies in this movement often resolve in unexpected directions (Ex. 3). The other slow movement belongs to the Concerto No. 12 in G major; this *Largo* is anchored to a six-bar *ostinato* bass above which an initial melody, poignant in character and disarmingly simple in conception, is treated to a series of six variations. The movement is just one amongst many whose lyricism is inspired by the operatic airs of the Italian theatre, for which

Ex. 3

Vivaldi composed prolifically. *La stravaganza* is rich both in experiment and in musical fantasy, and we can hardly be surprised that it was the source both of interest and admiration amongst eighteenth-century connoisseurs.

La stravaganza was followed in about 1716 by two further publications of Vivaldi's concertos by Roger in Amsterdam, now under the imprint of his daughter Jeanne; these were Opus 6, consisting of six concertos for solo violin and strings, and Opus 7, containing twelve concertos of which two in B flat (Nos. 1 and 7) are for oboe and strings. Vivaldi's treatment of the oboe in these works is somewhat rudimentary compared with the two included in his Opus 8 and his remaining oboe concertos. The slow movement of the Concerto No. 1 has a simple melody and accompaniment more closely related to Albinoni's idiom than to anything distinctively Vivaldian. In both outer movements there are weak moments in the tuttis, a feeling that the composer was not yet quite on firm ground. There is a greater structural variety in the remaining violin concertos of Opus 7. Slow movements are often notably poetic, with affecting solo violin *cantilenas* floating above a simple though by no means always harmonically predictable accompaniment. Fine examples of Vivaldi's lyrical gifts occur in the *Grave* of the Concerto No. 5 in F major and in that of the Concerto No. 3 in G minor where the wide-ranging freedom of the melody and the expressive intensity foreshadow some of Tartini's slow movements. Fast outer movements follow the *ritornello* form of alternating tuttis and solos, and though perhaps in no particular way remarkable, nevertheless possess an infectious energy and robustness. In the finale of the Concerto No. 2 in C major we can detect melodic and rhythmic patterns which Vivaldi used in his Latin oratorio, *Juditha Triumphans*, composed at approximately the same time as these concertos were printed. The eighth concerto of the set, in G major, attracted the attention of Bach, who arranged it for solo harpsichord in the same key, (BWV 973).

In 1725 the Amsterdam publisher Michele Le Cène issued Vivaldi's Opus 8, *Il cimento dell'armonia e dell'inventione* (The Contest between Harmony and Invention). It contained four concertos which, had the composer written little or nothing else, would have legitimately and deservedly secured for him a niche in posterity. These are *The Four Seasons*, which were soon to enjoy wide currency outside Italy, especially in France. The printed edition was dedicated to a Bohemian Count, Wenzel von Morzin, who was distantly related to Haydn's future patron and whom Vivaldi had nominally served as *Maestro di Musica in Italia*. The publication contained, furthermore, four sonnets, one for each season, as well as specific captions in the scores as additional assistance to performers and audiences in recognizing the programmatic references. While many of Vivaldi's descriptive titles, such as *La tempesta di mare, Il piacere* and *La caccia* (attached to Concertos Nos. 5, 6 and 10 of Opus 8), are no more than generally impressionistic, evoking a mood or colouring an image, *The Four Seasons* can justly claim to be real programme music. The nature images which Vivaldi calls forth in these four concertos are vividly coloured and handled in an original way whilst remaining within the ritornello form with which we are, by now, well acquainted. The pastoral vignettes are not confined to the solo violin episodes but are contained in the tuttis as well. Sometimes they provide an impression as, for instance, we find in the opening movement of *Winter* where the tuttis vividly convey the season's sharp chill with biting dissonances and repeated trills in the violin parts. At other times they are more specific in their portrayal of a particular affect. Such is the case with the Adagio molto of the *Autumn* concerto, where Vivaldi depicts 'sleeping drunkards', and the finale of *Spring*, subtitled *Danza pastorale*. Vivaldi's imitations of nature caught the imagination of succeeding generations; they made an impression on the Swiss philosopher Rousseau, who wrote variations for unaccompanied flute on the *Spring* concerto; but other French composers too, having doubtless heard Vivaldi's *Four Seasons* at the Parisian *Concert Spirituel* or at private gatherings, made arrangements of the music. Michel Corrette based an elaborate *grand motet* for soloists, chorus and orchestra on *Spring* and Nicolas Chédeville arranged music from *Spring* and *Autumn* for musette, two violins and continuo: *Le printems ou Les saisons amusantes: concertos d'Antonio Vivaldy.*

The remaining eight concertos of *Il cimento* are not, perhaps, of uniform interest. In two of them, No. 9 in D minor and No. 12 in C major, Le Cène provides an option between solo violin and solo oboe. Vivaldi, however, clearly conceived them as oboe concertos since there is almost a total absence of the type of violin figurations which characterize the remaining works. Both are well suited to the comparatively confined tessitura of the oboe, and the darkly coloured *Largo* of the D minor work is particularly effective on the instrument. Amongst the non-programmatic violin concertos the eleventh of the set, in D major, is the most impressive. Structurally, the outer movements show an advance on those in Opus 7, for instance, with more ambitious solo sections in which, on occasion, the *ritornello* material is incorporated in the lower strands of the texture. The main theme of the finale offers an attractive proposition for fugal treatment and is introduced by the second violins, followed by the first violins, viola and cello. Other attractive features of the set occur in the finale of the Concerto No. 8 in G minor, in character a robust country dance, and in the many instances of Vivaldi's inventive and animated writing.

One further set of twelve violin concertos was published during Vivaldi's lifetime. This was *La cetra* (The Lyre), printed once again by Le Cène in Amsterdam in 1727. By then Vivaldi's standing as an instrumental composer had long been established both in Italy and in countries abroad including Germany, France and England. *La cetra* was dedicated to the Austrian Emperor Charles VI, whom Vivaldi probably met in Vienna in the mid-1720s. The esteem in which the Emperor held Vivaldi is delightfully illustrated in letters from the Venetian nobleman, the Abbé Conti, to Madame de Caylus. When Charles VI visited the port of Trieste in 1728 Vivaldi travelled to meet him; in a letter of 23 September, the Abbé wrote, 'The Emperor conversed for a long time with Vivaldi about music; they say that he talked longer to him in private in fifteen days than he talks to his ministers in two years.'

All but one of the concertos comprising *La cetra* are for solo violin and strings; the exception is the Concerto No. 9 in B flat, in which Vivaldi writes for two solo violins. In two other works, the Concerto No. 6 in A major and the Concerto No. 12 in B minor, the composer requires *scordatura* (the retuning of the opening strings of the solo violin). This was a practice widely cultivated in Austria by composers of an earlier generation, outstanding amongst whom was the Bohemian Heinrich von Biber (1644–1704). *Scordatura* was used by composers for three principal reasons—to achieve special tonal effects, to extend the conventional compass of the instrument, and to facilitate chordal passages which might otherwise be awkward to bow or to finger. *La cetra* has not enjoyed the popularity granted to *L'estro amonico* or *Il cimento*, yet it is in no musical sense inferior to them, providing clear examples both of the composer's skill in formal design and of his ability to move the passions in a direct and personal manner. There is surely a ready sense of humour in the repeated pattern of emphatic hammer strokes, drawn from a convention of the Venetian opera sinfonia, which dominate the opening movement of the Concerto No. 4 in E major; and his feeling for dance-measures is delightfully captured in the gigue-like finale of the Concerto No. 6 in A major. Lyrical writing abounds but is, perhaps, especially affecting in middle movements such as those of the Concerto No. 2 in A major and the Concerto No. 10 in G major, where a warmly expressive aria for the solo violin is accompanied by pizzicato violins and violas without continuo bass. It is in the opening *Allegro non molto* of the Concerto No. 12 in B minor, however, that Vivaldi provides us with a sustained and characteristic example of his lyrical genius. Here, in the third solo episode, the soloist with arpeggios assumes the role of accompanist whilst a *cantilena* of serene beauty is passed to the first violin line of the tutti. Second violins and violas complete an enchanting effect with a light quaver accompaniment (Ex. 4). *La cetra*, taken as a whole, is plentifully endowed with those qualities which give distinction to Vivaldi's mature concerto style: clarity of form, expressive melodies, rhythmic vitality and contrast, and a lyricism often marked with pathos.

The three remaining sets of concertos published in Vivaldi's lifetime each

Ex. 4

Companion to the Concerto

contain six works only. By and large they are musically less interesting, though there are notable exceptions. Opus 10 was published by Le Cène in about 1728 and contained concertos for flute and strings. The transverse flute began to enjoy popularity in Italy from the mid-1720s, and Vivaldi himself was probably stimulated to write for it after a meeting with Quantz in Venice in 1726. Johann Joachim Quantz (1697–1773) was one of the greatest flautists of his age and an important theorist. His own compositions for the flute, of which there are a great many, contributed both towards its popularity and to the development of its technical resources; we shall encounter him again later in the chapter. All but one of the concertos of Vivaldi's Opus 10 are arrangements of earlier works, chiefly for a treble recorder. First thoughts are often the happiest, and while there is an abundance of effective writing in the Opus 10 version, it is the youthful vitality and subtler instrumental colours of the earlier chamber concertos for mixed woodwind and string ensemble which strike a note of greater originality. Three of them, *La tempesta di mare* (Opus 10, No. 1), *La notte* (Opus 10, No. 2) and *Il gardellino* (Opus 10, No. 3) have a pronounced programmatic element, as their titles suggest. Of these, *La notte* is, perhaps, the most interesting of the three; its affecting modulations, its subheadings such as *Fantasmi* and *Il Sonno* and its varied tempi contribute towards an evocative nocturnal fantasy with a lively sense of theatre. The remaining concertos are more conventional but hardly less engaging; the Concerto No. 6 in G, for example, concludes with a delightful set of variations on a theme initially presented in the previous movement but in a minor key. Vivaldi used the same melody, incidentally, in the middle movement of his Concerto in G minor (Opus 8, No. 7).

The extent to which Vivaldi himself was involved in the printing of Opus 11 and Opus 12 is uncertain; both appeared in 1729 from the publishing house of Le Cène and at the publisher's expense, without either titles or dedicatory notices. The quality of the works in Opus 11 is uneven; the outer movements of the Concerto in D major (Opus 11, No. 1) and the Concerto in A major (Opus 11, No. 3), for instance rely on somewhat predictable arpeggio or scale-wise patterns for effect. The Concerto in E minor, *Il favorito* (Opus 11, No. 2), on the other hand, reveals Vivaldi at the peak of his ability. This work, whose bold first movement triads at once recall the opening movement of Bach's E major Violin Concerto (BWV 1042), and the dramatically charged Concerto in C minor (Opus 11, No. 5), are finely sustained creations, drawing upon a wide range of expressive devices. Both these concertos and another in G minor for oboe and strings (Opus 11, No. 6) exist in different but authentic versions. The Opus 12 set contains no concertos as impressive as these, although there are individual movements of affecting beauty such as the Largo of the Concerto in C major (Opus 12, No. 4) or that of the Concerto in B flat (Opus 12, No. 6) whose pizzicato accompaniment of the solo violin and absence of continuo recalls the Largo cantabile of the Concerto in G major (Opus 9, No. 10). In general terms outer movements adopt well-tried and effective formulae, but although sometimes hinting at fresh pastures, have little new to say.

Vivaldi's published concertos, though plentiful, as we have seen, are nevertheless vastly outnumbered by those which remained in manuscript. Furthermore, while in all but one or two instances the published concertos are representative of his best work, they do not reflect the extraordinary variety of instruments for which he wrote; and we should beware of believing that the finest of the unpublished pieces are in any way inferior to those of the printed sets. The greater number of the manuscript concertos are, like the published ones, for solo violin and string orchestra. Amongst the many jewels which lie hidden in this Aladdin's Cave are a handful which deserve at least a brief mention. The Concerto in E major *L'amoroso* (RV 271), which incidentally Vivaldi included in a manuscript set called *La cetra*, quite distinct from the published Opus 9 of that name, illustrates once again Vivaldi's ability to evoke a particular mood or effect; caressing grace-notes and a key chosen for its warmth are features in the work which bring out the character of 'The Lover' of the subtitle. Similarly effective concertos evoking a particular mood are *L'inquietudine* (RV 234), where in the first movement downward arpeggio patterns create a feeling of restlessness, *Il sospetto* (RV 199) and *Il riposo*, (RV 270). In this last-mentioned piece Vivaldi requires muted strings without harpsichord continuo; the work has a tenderness and an intimacy which relate more closely, perhaps, to another of its descriptive subtitles, *per il Natale*, thus associating it with the Christmas story. A Concerto in D major, *per la Solennità della S. Lingua di S. Antonio in Padua* (RV 212), is interesting for the extended and technically adventurous violin cadenzas which occur in its two outer movements. In its earliest form, dating from 1712, it is amongst the comparatively few concertos in which woodwind instruments—a pair of oboes in this case—augment the string tuttis.

Vivaldi's legacy to the cello and bassoon repertoire is a notably rich one. In the 27 concertos for cello and strings Vivaldi's fertile invention seldom seems to have deserted him. Here, and in the bassoon concertos, of which there are 37, the solo writing is as a rule technically advanced, moving between the bass and tenor registers with frequency and confidence. Slow movements are especially affecting, but the tuttis of outer movements are no less arresting for the freshness and individuality of their melodic and rhythmic ideas. Another striking feature of the outer movements is the varied and elaborate manner in which Vivaldi handles the instruments accompanying the solo episodes, sometimes introducing material from the tuttis. Amongst a wealth of distinctive and invigorating tutti-*ritornelli* are those of the opening movements of the Bassoon Concertos in E minor (RV 484), and F major (RV 485—Vivaldi used this once again in the Oboe Concerto in F major (RV 457)—and of the Cello Concerto in G major (RV 413).

Solo concertos by Vivaldi exist for almost every instrument in current usage in his day: there are seven for viola d'amore and strings, one for mandolin and strings and a colourful assortment of works for two solo instruments, like and unlike. Several of them, like the Concerto in C major for two trumpets (RV 537), the Concertos in F major for two horns (RV 538 and 539), the Concerto in G major for two mandolins (RV 532) and the Concerto in G minor for two cellos (RV 531) are frequently performed nowadays. Others, especially perhaps the concertos for two violins and strings which are not contained in the published sets, are less familiar but deserve wider currency. An attractive example is afforded by the Concerto in G major (RV 516), which Vivaldi also left in a trio-sonata version (RV 71). The solo material is evenly distributed between the two solo violins and there is much effective interplay between them. The opening movement is characterized by an infectiously lively dance-like tutti-*ritornello* interspersed with three well-contrasted solo episodes. The middle movement, in B minor, is a duet for the violins with only continuo support. Lastly comes an animated *allegro* showing off this characteristically Venetian type of concerto in all its finery; vigorous, full-textured tuttis alternate with animated solos which reach a climax in the fourth and last episode, with extended arpeggio figures in the first violin lyrically accompanied by the second.

Vivaldi's interest in orchestral sonority is proclaimed by the immense variety of instrumental combinations for which he wrote. During much of his time at the Venetian orphanage, the *Ospedale della Pietà*, with which he was closely associated for the greater part of his life, its orchestra enjoyed the reputation of being the best disciplined in Italy, and even, perhaps, beyond. In constant touch with an establishment where almost every known musical instrument was taught, and in large measure responsible for the excellence of its executants, Vivaldi had an opportunity, unusual in those days, to experiment with different sounds and techniques. One of Vivaldi's sterling merits was that he was able to write for all these instruments—strings and wind—in an informed and therefore effective way. His range of colour and affect is wide; it embraces, at its most sumptuous, works for a vast array of disparate instruments, such as the Concerto in C major (RV 558), which is scored for recorders, trumpets, chalumeaux (early members of the clarinet family), mandolins, theorbos, concertante violins and cello, strings and continuo. At the opposite end of the scale are works such as the Concerto in D minor for viola d'amore and lute (RV 540), whose muted string tuttis contribute towards a tonal picture of gentle pastel shades tinged with pathos. Vivaldi performed both these works at the Pietà in 1740 in honour of a visit to Venice of Friedrich Christian, Prince Elector of Saxony. His aim, no doubt, was to put on display both the versatility of the performers and the rich diversity of his own music.

Before leaving Vivaldi we should certainly not overlook either his relatively small but significant legacy of 'chamber' concertos, in which each part other than the continuo has an obbligato role, or his *ripieno* concertos, without soloist, where the composer often foreshadows the early symphonists of the next generation. Fine examples in this last-mentioned category are afforded by the Concertos in A major (RV 158) and F major (RV 142).

Bonporti and Durante

Such is the position by Vivaldi in the development of the Baroque concerto that it would be all too easy to ignore the activities of other Italian composers working beyond Venice. A brief mention of the most gifted of them is necessary for our survey. Older than Vivaldi by six years was **Francesco Bonporti** (1672–1749); Bonporti, like Vivaldi, was ordained a priest, but unlike his Venetian contemporary actively served as one throughout his life, preferring the status of *dilettante* where his musical activities were concerned. After a period of study in Rome during the 1690s Bonporti returned to his native Trent where he composed the majority of his surviving works. His ten *Concerti grossi*, Op. 11, were published in Trent some time after 1727. The tuttis of outer movements sometimes recall those of Corelli, with whom he may have studied, but in middle movements— Bonporti usually preferred the three-movement pattern—he strikes a more original note with wonderfully expressive melodies. Fine examples occur in the *Siciliano* of the Concerto in B flat (Opus 11, No. 4) and in the *Adagio assai*, a lyrical, vocally orientated recitative, of the Concerto in F major (Opus 11, No. 5).

Further south, in Naples, **Francesco Durante** (1684–1755), made a significant contribution to concerto repertoire with eight *Concerti per quartetto*, (that is, in four parts) probably composed in the late 1730s or early 1740s. In these works the solo element is less prominent than we might expect from Italian concertos of this period. Durante loosely and irregularly follows the four-movement scheme of the church sonata rather than the fast-slow-fast pattern of Vivaldi; but he further introduces, on occasion, specifically illustrative elements as, for example, we find in a section marked *amoroso* in the Concerto in F minor. Elsewhere too, Durante's instrumental style, though conservative and somtimes austere, is markedly individual, only rarely recalling that of his contemporaries.

Locatelli and Tartini

The form of the mature Italian Baroque concerto was consolidated by composer-virtuosi like **Pietro Antonio Locatelli** (1695–1764) and, above all, **Giuseppe Tartini** (1692–1770). Locatelli published five sets of concertos between 1721 and 1762; the last of these is lost, but those which are preserved show Locatelli to have been influenced both by Roman and Venetian models. His twelve *concerti grossi*, Opus 1, for instance, are clearly Corellian in design, though the *concertino* group includes one or even two violas as well as two violins and cello. Like Corelli's Opus 6, the first eight works follow the church sonata pattern while the remaining four are of the chamber variety with named dance movements. In both sets, furthermore, the eighth work is a 'Christmas' concerto with a pastorale movement whose origins lay in Italian folk tradition. Few Italian Baroque composers of concertos overlooked this delightful reference to a traditional rustic melody with drone bass, and there are 'Christmas' concertos or sinfonias by Torelli (Opus 8, No. 6), Manfredini (Opus 3, No. 12), Giuseppe Valentini (Opus 1, No. 12), Schiassi, Tartini and doubtless others too. In his later concertos, notably, perhaps, those of his Opus 3: *L'arte del violino* (1733)—which also include 24 capriccios—Locatelli looks towards Venice. *Ritornellos* are often more extended than those of Vivaldi and solo episodes, which also penetrate the tuttis, explore a notably wide tessitura. Most of the later concertos follow the fast-slow-fast pattern, but there are exceptions, such as the unusual two-movement scheme of the Concerto in E minor (Opus 3, No. 8).

Tartini is one of the most fascinating composers of the Italian Baroque. In 1728 he founded a school of violinists in Padua which became known as *The School of Nations* because it attracted musicians from all over Europe. Through his playing, his teaching and his compositions Tartini not only brought violin technique to dazzling heights of virtuosity but also extended the expressive vocabulary of the instrument. Fast outer movements are often characterized by well-organized and well-proportioned tuttis, with solo episodes requiring a highly developed technical skill. Celebrated though he is, however, for fiery passagework and brilliant virtuosic gestures, it is, perhaps, to his slow movements that we should look in order to appreciate his outstanding gifts as an expressive composer. Progressively, the central movements of his concertos and the opening slow movements of his sonatas became the focal point of a composition. Here, to a greater extent than either

Vivaldi or Locatelli, the guiding principle is the imitation of the human voice. So much is this the case that amongst Tartini's autograph manuscripts we frequently find the opening of arias from Metastasio's opera libretti, setting the scene or mood, so to speak, of a given slow movement. Other poets too, such as Tasso, were used by Tartini as a specific source of musical inspiration. One such example is afforded by an alternative slow movement—Tartini sometimes included two, one of which he usually regarded as definitive, in his concertos—to the Concerto in A major (D 96). Here, the *Largo andante*, one of his most affecting pieces, is prefaced by the inscription 'A rivi a fonti a fiume—correte amare lagrime—sin tanto che consumi—l'acerbo mio dolor' (like streams, springs, rivers, flow bitter tears until my cruel grief is spent). Although Tartini spent most of his life in Padua his musical style was Venetian. He favoured the Vivaldian three-movement pattern though did not invariably follow it. Though the most lyrical writing occurs in the solo passages of his slow movements, his progressively exceptional gifts at *cantabile* permeated both solo and tutti elements of his fast movements, too. Over 130 concertos for violin have survived, as well as a concerto for cello, another for viola or viola da gamba, and two for flute, though the latter are of doubtful authenticity.

Germany

Muffat and his German Successors

Corelli's reputation, as we have already seen, was such that his compositional style was taken up by imitators both in and beyond Italy. Amongst the very first German composer to do so was **Georg Muffat** (1653–1704). Muffat, of Scottish ancestry through French born, regarded himself as a German. He studied first with Lully in Paris, then later in Rome with Bernardo Pasquini. While there, he had heard Corelli's *concerti grossi*, at that time still unpublished; they made a deep impression on him, and in 1682 Muffat published his *Armonico tributo*, which contained pieces modelled on those of the Roman master. Although Muffat called his works *sonatas* they are in all but name *concerti grossi* after the Corellian model, though containing movements of a markedly French character too. Muffat's formal scheme, like Corelli's, is fairly flexible; it includes elements both of the *church* and *chamber* concerto types with movements, mainly dance oriented, ranging from five to seven in number. The Corellian influence is most readily apparent in the movements without specific dance character where fugal patterns, 'walking' bass parts and contrasts between *concertino* and *ripieno* abound. Muffat's last publication, the *Ausserlesene Instrumental-Musik* (1701), is a collection of twelve *concerti grossi* containing six new works and revised versions of the six *sonatas* of *Armonico tributo*. The publication contains an interesting foreword in which Muffat suggests that the scoring can be adapted to available resources, and as well provides information about bowing and dynamics.

Whilst through Muffat and other apostles of Italian music such as J. K. F. Fischer (*c.* 1670–1746), and Johann Christoph Pez (1664–1716) the Corellian type of concerto became popular in south Germany during the last two decades of the seventeenth century, it did not circulate further north until the second decade or so of the eighteenth century. By then, however, the Venetian concertos of Albinoni and Vivaldi had stolen some of the Corellian thunder and were proving especially popular in northern states such as Saxony, Hesse-Darmstadt and Hanover. All the major German composers of the late Baroque followed, to a greater or lesser extent, the example of the Venetian concerto while at the same time, in various ways and in varying degrees, adding features both of their own culture and of France too. What resulted was an assimilation and fusion of ideas admirably summarized by Quantz in his treatise *On Playing the Flute*:

> If one has the necessary discernment to choose the best from the styles of different countries a mixed style results that, without overstepping the bounds of modesty, could well be called the German style, not only because the Germans came upon it first, but because it has already been established at different places in Germany for many years, flourishes still, and displeases in neither Italy, nor France, nor in other hands.[1]

One of the most important figures in the history of the German Baroque concerto is **Georg Johann Pisendel** (1687–1755). His significance lies not so much in his own compositions—seven violin concertos and four *concerti grossi*, only, are known to us—but in the fact that he studied in Ansbach with Torelli and later in Venice with Vivaldi, acquiring along the way a reputation as one of the foremost German violinists of his generation. Thus, he learned at first hand from two pioneers of the Italian concerto and was able to impart to his fellow German musicians the fruits of these encounters both through his own compositions and, above all, in his performances of Venetian concertos and sonatas. Pisendel joined the Dresden court orchestra in 1712, officially becoming its Konzertmeister (leader/director) in 1730. His reputation as a brilliant violinist is confirmed by the fact that Albinoni, Vivaldi, Telemann and possibly others too, dedicated violin concertos or sonatas to him; it has been suggested furthermore, by C. S. Terry and others,

1. J. J. Quantz, *On Playing the Flute*, London, 1966, p. 341.

that Bach, whom Pisendel had met in Weimar in 1709, intended at least some of his violin concertos for the Dresden maestro.

Apart from Telemann and Handel, who for the purposes of this survey more properly belongs to the section on English concertos, the successful German concerto composers of Bach's generation were **Johann David Heinichen** (1683–1729), **Christoph Graupner** (1683–1760), **Johann Friedrich Fasch** (1688–1758) and **Gottfried Heinrich Stölzel** (1690–1749). Heinichen was not only an important Baroque theorist—his treatise, *Der General-Bass in der Composition* (The Thorough-Bass in Composition) led the eighteenth-century English music historian Charles Burney to describe him as 'the Rameau of Germany'—but also a successful opera composer; and it was opera rather than instrumental music which took Heinichen to Venice in 1710 where he met Vivaldi and other leading musical figures. He, like Graupner and Stölzel, followed Italian models in his concertos, but in common with almost all German concerto composers of the time, shows a lively and imaginative awareness of varied instrumental colours and unusual sonorities.

Graupner, although like Heinichen an opera composer, was much more prolific as a composer of concertos and symphonies. He inclined towards Vivaldi rather than Corelli both in style and form, but his music speaks with an individuality which, if we were able to hear it with the frequency with which we hear Telemann's concertos, for example, would strike us as hardly less distinctive. His most impressive concertos, perhaps, are those which include woodwind instruments. Like Telemann he wrote for a wide variety of these including flute, oboe, oboe d'amore, treble recorder, bassoon and two sizes of chalumeaux. The solo/concertino writing, ranging from one to four instruments features both similar and disparate groupings, and Graupner chooses either a three- or four-movement pattern in almost equal proportion. Graupner, and to a greater extent his pupil Fasch point, more than Telemann, perhaps, towards the early Classical style in many of their concertos. Fasch shows a similar interest in woodwind textures, often using them in pairs episodically within tutti sections of a movement. Stölzel was a less prolific instrumental composer than his contemporaries but he was held in high regard as a musician and as a theorist by Bach and others. Stölzel favoured equally the *concerto grosso* and the solo concerto, and in the former he approaches a manner more closely resembling that of Bach than of his other contemporaries. His *Concerto grosso a quattro Chori* in D major for two groups of trumpets, woodwind and strings affords a fine example of this neglected composer's style, and it is not hard to understand why it made an appeal to Bach, who included his Partita in G minor in *Das Clavier-Büchlein vor Wilhelm Friedemann Bach*.

Telemann

As we have already seen, a degree of eclecticism was an essential ingredient in the concertos of German composers and this is especially true in the works of **Georg Philipp Telemann** (1681–1767). In Telemann's concertos the French idiom is sometimes as well defined as the Italian one, and notably in slow movements. A further stylistic element which gives Telemann's suites and concertos a distinctive character derives from Polish folk-music. In 1705 Telemann took up a position with Count Erdmann II of Promnitz at Sorau in Poland; his employment there was short but it left an indelible mark upon the young composer's musical development. In 1739 he wrote:

> I heard there . . . the Polish and Hanakian music in its true barbaric beauty . . . one would scarcely believe what wonderful ideas the pipers or fiddlers have when they improvise . . . An observer could scoop up from them enough ideas in 8 days to last a lifetime . . . I have, in my time, written various large-scale Concertos and Trios in this manner, which I have clad in an Italian coat with alternating Adagios and Allegros.[1]

Although Telemann himself once claimed that writing concertos did not come easily to him — 'Because it was a pleasant diversion I also began to write concertos. But I must admit that in my heart of hearts I never got on with them . . . .' — he composed a large number of them the finest of which sit comfortably alongside those of his contemporaries, with the exception, perhaps, of Bach and Handel. Telemann's career was a long one, but it is probable that most of his concertos had been written by the time that he arrived in Hamburg in 1721 as Cantor of the Johanneum School and Music Director of the city's five principal churches. Over one hundred are known to us, mostly through contemporary copies, though a handful have survived in autograph. Telemann's concertos belong to three main types—the solo concerto, the concerto for one or more solo instruments, and the *concerto grosso*. A seemingly isolated example of a fourth type exists in a Concerto in A minor for treble recorder, oboe, violin and continuo. This chamber concerto, in which all parts other than that of the continuo fulfil an obbligato role, closely resembles similar works by Vivaldi; both composers reveal their interest in tonal colour in these small-scale pieces for mixed ensembles of strings and woodwind. Telemann himself played a wide variety of instruments, and above all, perhaps, in his music for oboe, flute and treble recorder, wrote for them in an informed manner.

1. Telemann, autobiographical sketch published in Johann Matteson's *Grundlage einer Ehren-Pforte*, Hamburg, 1740.

If we take Telemann's entire concerto output into account we see that there is virtually no type at which he did not try his hand and that his style is correspondingly wide ranging. He recalled in his autobiography that Corelli had served him in his youth as a model for his instrumental writing; yet the Venetian models afforded by Albinoni, Vivaldi and others clearly inspired him no less. Within the Italian concerto types already discussed, however, Telemann offers a rich variety of stylistic features, some of which closely reflect his Italian models, while others show his lively interest in French music and in newer expressive ideas nearer home. Somewhat less than half the number of Telemann's surviving concertos are for a solo instrument with strings; some 20 of these are for violin, eleven for flute, eight for oboe, two for oboe d'amore and a handful for other instruments. The remainder consists of concertos for two or more soloists, and it is here that we often find bolder strokes of originality.

Telemann's violin concertos, though plentiful in number, are variable in quality. He seems in many of them to be writing in the shadow of Vivaldi and other Italian masters. The assimilation and efficient handling of outside influences are not enough in themselves to make a composer's language necessarily an interesting one, and in some of the violin concertos we may sometimes feel that Telemann follows his Italian models too assiduously. Yet few of them are without features which lend them appeal, and the finest examples deserve to be more frequently performed nowadays. The four-movement *sonata da chiesa* pattern slightly exceeds that of the three-movement Italian sinfonia in number but, as Pippa Drummond has remarked, 'if we disregard the opening slow movement of Telemann's *da chiesa* concertos, the remaining movements correspond almost exactly with those of the three-movement works'.[1] Amongst the most interesting of the works for violin and strings are the Concerto in E major and the Concerto in B flat, which Telemann dedicated to Pisendel. Both are cast in four-movement form and both are illustrative of the composer's mature feeling for the medium. Each work begins with an extended slow movement—an *Affettuoso* and *Largo* respectively, in which the soloist is given a lyrical melody over a simple accompaniment. The solo material and *ritornelli* of the fast movements owe much to the Italian style, although Telemann introduces the flavour of a Polish folk-music idiom in some of his rhythmic patterns. The most characteristic gesture, however, is to be found in the *Quasi andante* of the Pisendel work, where Telemann writes a sustained solo violin *cantabile* of great beauty over a rhythmic accompaniment of three (in the first violins) against two (in the seconds and violas (Ex. 5).

1. Drummond, *The German Concerto*, Oxford, 1980, p. 192.

Ex. 5

The concertos for solo woodwind and strings, taken as a whole, offer a more colourful picture of Telemann's style than the violin concertos. Whilst structurally the woodwind concertos offer no advance on the violin concertos, the varied tonal colours of a recorder, flute, oboe or oboe d'amore almost invariably draw striking sonorities from the composer's pen. Although Telemann was a capable violinist, he himself acknowledged his limitations as a performer, and if we use the music itself as evidence, his greater facility and affection lay with wind instruments. In these concertos the four-movement scheme comfortably outnumbers that of three, but even so, Telemann adopts various procedures within that pattern: several movements are in binary form (that is to say in two sections with each half repeated), and four of the concertos (three for flute and one for recorder) end with one or a pair of menuets reflecting the *galant*, courtly status of the recently developed transverse flute. Opening movements—especially those of the *sonata da chiesa* scheme—are often especially interesting; it is here that Telemann usually presents the solo instrument in its most 'affective' attire by writing for it in the idiom and tonal range which suits it best. The Concerto in E minor for oboe, in A major for oboe d'amore and the *moderato* of the five concertos in D major for flute provide splendid examples.

It is in his outstanding ability at blending the disparate sounds of orchestral instruments of his day, however, that Telemann excels. Only Bach, in his Passions, Oratorios and cantatas and, somewhat later, Rameau in his operas, were his equals in this respect. Whether it is in his writing for two or more similar instruments, or for dissimilar groups of two or more, Telemann's imagination seldom disappoints us in matters of colour and texture. The reasons are twofold: first, he had an extraordinarily acute ear for sonority and a pioneering intent to explore hitherto unconsidered possibilities; secondly, as I have already stressed, he knew the capabilities of the instruments—their strong and their weak points—and wrote accordingly. Telemann himself neatly summarized the matter in a little couplet: 'Give each instrument what it can sustain, thus is the player happy and you well entertained.' While in the movements adhering to the *ritornello* principle Telemann offers little in the way of formal innovation, he nevertheless achieves a variety within a set formal structure which makes generalization unhelpful. Rather, perhaps, we should look at a handful of the most successful of his concertos with two or more solo instruments and see what makes them so.

One of his happiest creations of the group-concerto type is the Concerto in E major for flute, oboe d'amore and viola d'amore with string orchestra. In this work of four movements Telemann explores with consummate skill the tonal contrasts of the three solo instruments. He uses the opening movement, an andante in this instance, to acquaint the listener with the expressive voices of his chosen solo group. Here he introduces flute, viola d'amore and oboe d'amore in turn against a gently throbbing accompaniment, an affecting testimony to his extraordinary skill at mixing a palette of gentle, pastel colours (Ex. 6). The two fast movements, both of which in their rhythms owe something to Polish folk influence, contain interestingly varied *concertino* passages between the *ritornelli*; the finale, in particular, creates a sound and rhythmic picture of notable individuality with its syncopations and its curious tentative, halting passages in the initial oboe d'amore statements. In this work and in another comparatively well-known piece, the Concerto in E minor for flute and treble recorder, we find Telemann well able to organize his material, technically conservative though it may seem at times. Both derive interest chiefly from their appealing and effective tonal colours, from the *cantabile* solo writing in the slow movements and from the dance-oriented vigour of the faster ones, of which the finale of the E minor work, closely related to Polish folk-music, is an example, *par excellence*.

Three further interesting concertos for two or more solo instruments are included in Telemann's three-part orchestral and instrumental anthology, published by subscription in Hamburg in 1733. This was the *Musique de Table* which contained examples of his work of which, presumably, he himself thought highly. As proof of his skill in writing concertos Telemann selected three contrasting pieces: a Concerto in A major for flute, violin, cello and strings, another in F major for three violins and strings, and a third in E flat for two horns and strings. All are mature works in the sense that the composer has fully mastered the *ritornello* principle. Problems evident in some other concertos, such as that in E flat for oboe and strings, for example, where the last solo episode of the finale fails to lead into the closing tutti in a convincing manner, have been solved. The concertos from the *Musique de Table* are also mature in their stylistic outlook, and especially, perhaps, in the case of the A major concerto which, though constructed in the older church sonata pattern, nevertheless leans towards the *galant* idiom in the easy gestures of its opening *Largo*. Indeed, in this concerto, as fine as any from his pen, we find not only a stylistic synthesis but also a stylistic range which forges a link with the emerging classical period. Hand-in-hand with these qualities in his music belong his fertile ability as a melodist and his tireless devotion to exploring new orchestral textures. The third movement of the Concerto in E minor for recorder and flute, or the opening movement of the Concerto in A major for oboe d'amore, provide persuasive examples of the validity of the first, while the many unusual instrumental groupings to be found in his concertos—such as, for example, the Concerto in B flat for three oboes, two violins and continuo, the concertos for four violins without

Ex. 6

continuo, or the concertos for two chalumeaux and strings—attest to the second.

J. S. Bach

Hardly less eager to experiment with the almost limitless possibilities inherent in the Italian concerto form was Telemann's contemporary and friend **J. S. Bach** (1685–1750). Bach, as we have already seen, had become acquainted with concertos by Vivaldi and, doubtless, by other composers too while he was serving at the court at Weimar (1708–17). During this period Bach had arranged several of Vivaldi's concertos for solo harpsichord and so, by the time he came to write his own concertos, he was conversant with their structure and fluent in his handling of the material. In 1717 Bach moved to the court at Cöthen; as Kapellmeister to the musically inclined Prince Leopold, he was required not to produce church music but rather to provide the court ensemble, the *Cammer Musici*, with orchestral pieces. It is possible that Bach had already composed concertos before he went to Cöthen—much of the music of the Brandenburg Concerto No. 1 in F major and an earlier version of the Concerto No. 6 in B flat almost certainly predate his arrival—but it was there that he concentrated on concerto composition, and by far the greater amount of his surviving works of this type belong to the Cöthen period (1717–23).

Compared with almost all his successful contemporaries Bach's concerto legacy is a small one: the six Brandenburg Concertos, three violin concertos, seven concertos for harpsichord and strings, three for two harpsichords and strings, two for three harpsichords and strings, one for four harpsichords and strings and one for flute, violin, harpsichord and strings. This list is further reduced when we take into account the fact that three of the harpsichord concertos are Bach's own reworking of the three violin concertos, another a reworking of the Brandenburg Concerto No. 4, and a fifth an arrangement of Vivaldi's Concerto in B minor for four violins, from *L'estro armonico* (Opus 3, No. 10). On the other hand, reconstructions of several of the harpsichord concertos undertaken by Tovey and others in the present century have, perhaps, served to clarify Bach's original intentions concerning instrumentation as well as enlarging and further colouring the repertoire.

Bach's Violin Concertos in A minor (BWV 1041), E major (BWV 1042) and the Concerto for two violins in D minor (BWV 1043) have survived in their original form, but as I have implied, it is at least likely that several of the concertos for one or more harpsichords were originally composed for the violin. These may have been written for Joseph Spiess, the leader of the Cöthen band, though Bach might have had the Dresden virtuoso Pisendel, whom he had already encountered at Weimar, in mind. To a greater or a lesser extent the three works, each in three movements, follow the Vivaldi pattern which Bach had thoroughly explored at Weimar. Closest to that pattern are the A minor and D minor concertos, but although he follows his Italian model in the contrasting alternation of tuttis and solos, the sections are enriched in numerous ways, expanded and treated with greater freedom. The extent to which Bach both enriched and developed the *ritornello* pattern of the outer movements can readily be seen in the E major concerto. In its opening movement, a combination of *ritornello* and *da capo* form, Bach's handling of thematic material is particularly striking. Here there are no less than six solo episodes and seven *ritornelli*, of which the last three with their two intervening solo episodes provide the *da capo*, with a repeat of the opening 52 bars of the movement. The slow movement, an adagio, is subtly expressive; in this Bach provides the soloist with a lyrical *cantilena* over a darkly coloured quasi-*ostinato* bass—a similar pattern prevails in the slow movement of the A minor Violin Concerto—which gives the music an air of pathos. A deeply affecting passage occurs at bar 28, where the *ostinato* is interrupted and the solo violin emerges from C sharp minor to E major in a melody of haunting beauty (Ex. 7). The impact of this section is, in fact, as dependent upon the effect of such a key-change as upon the material itself. The finale of the E major Concerto is a dance-like rondo of a kind which Bach seldom used elsewhere.

Bach's most celebrated concertos have survived in an autograph fair copy which he prepared for Christian Ludwig, Markgraf of Brandenburg, and dated 24 March 1721. He called them *Six Concerts Avec plusieurs Instruments* which, since the last century, have become affectionately known as the Brandenburg Concertos (BWV 1046–51). Although Bach assembled six uniquely diverse concertos in order to fulfil a commission, he undoubtedly intended them to be performed by the court orchestra at Cöthen. Individual dates of composition, however, cover a wider period extending back to the Weimar years, and existing variant versions of music in the first and fifth concertos of the set, for instance, throw useful light on Bach's methods of adaptation, expansion and revision. In these works, once again, we find the composer absorbed in experimentation with the varied possibilities afforded by *concerto grosso* principles. Each work presents a different aspect of the form in which Bach succeeds brilliantly and confidently in achieving the highest peaks of baroque concerto technique. In all of them he adopts the three-movement plan of the Italian sinfonia though, as we shall see, the first concerto contains additional movements as well.

Brandenburg Concerto No. 1 in F, which contains elements both of the concerto and suite forms, has an interesting history. An earlier version, termed *Sinfonia*, consisting of the first two movements, a menuet and two

Ex. 7

wind trios, may have been connected with a birthday cantata (BWV 208) which Bach performed for the Duke of Sachsen-Weissenfels in about 1713. When Bach made the fair copy for the Markgraf of Brandenburg, however, he rescored existing material to include a *violino piccolo* (a small violin whose tuning in this concerto is a minor third above standard violin tuning), added a second *allegro* and inserted a *Polacca* (polonaise) within the alternating movements of the Menuet. The presence of stylized dances gives this concerto a strong French bias of a kind which we can often find amongst the German followers of Lully—composers such as Georg Muffat and J. K. F. Fischer. Amongst the many fascinating details of Bach's tonal palette are the traditional hunting calls of the horns in the opening measures of the first movement. Horn players were not numbered amongst the regular orchestral musicians at Cöthen but visits by horn virtuosi are recorded at around this time. Equally colourful is Bach's wind writing in the Trios; in the first of them (D minor), he follows an instrumentation established in the French operas of Lully, where the standard woodwind trio consisted of two oboes and a bassoon. The second Trio (F major) for two horns and an oboe provides a vivid contrast with the first; this movement, along with the second *allegro* of the concerto reappeared in freshly scored versions in 1726 in one of Bach's Leipzig congratulatory cantatas (BWV 207). In the same year the opening Allegro served once again as a sinfonia to a vocal work, this time a church cantata (BWV 52).

The second Brandenburg Concerto which, like the first, is in F major, is of a kind at which German composers excelled and of which Telemann, Stölzel, Fasch, Graupner and Bach all provided fine examples. This was the *concerto grosso* in which concertante instruments of a disparate tonal character feature prominently. The *concertino* group in this work consists of trumpet, violin, oboe and treble recorder set in contrast with the purely string texture of the *ripieno*. In the two outer movements, the second of which is a fugue, the trumpet plays a dominant role; but partly out of consideration for tonal contrast and, doubtless, partly to give the trumpeter a rest from the demanding technical requirements exacted by Bach, it is excluded from the middle movement, whose gentle lyricism is derived from an initial violin melody taken up and elaborated by the three soloists over a continuo bass of gently moving quavers.

In Brandenburg Concerto No. 3 in G major Bach explores the tonal and contrapuntal possibilities inherent in nine string parts (three violins, three violas, three cellos) with continuo bass. These parts sometimes merge together providing the ripieno, as others play solo or thrust ideas in groups between them. Thus each player has both a concertino and a ripieno function and, consequently, uniform virtuosity is required. There are aspects of this writing related to the older Italian *concertato* manner; but Bach's consummate artistry opens up a whole new world of sound in which he exploits the sonorities of pure string texture in a dazzling and satisfying way. There is no slow movement in this concerto but merely a Phrygian cadence linking the two fast ones. Some performers like to insert a movement from another of Bach's works at this point, but he clearly did not intend that this should be so. Much more likely is that he envisaged a brief solo violin cadenza or, indeed, wished to have the cadence played as it stands in the fair copy.

The fourth concerto of the set, in G major, provides an interesting example of a work in which *solo* and *grosso* elements coexist. The work is scored for violin, two *fiauti d'echo* and strings: the concertino group consists of a solo violin and the two *fiauti d'echo* (Bach almost certainly had treble recorders in mind when he used this curious term, relating it, perhaps, to their 'echoing' role in the middle movement). Bach gives the violin pride of place in the two outer movements, the second of which is an exhilarating fugue with an engagingly melodious subject, while treating the recorders variously as accompanists to it and as soloists but in a more restricted fashion than the violin. In the *Andante* middle movement, however, the recorders assume comparable prominence with the *violino principale.*

In a sense, a similarly uneven division of labour to that which we find in the fourth concerto, exists in the Concerto No. 5 in D major. For, although the work is essentially a *concerto grosso* with a concertino group consisting of flute, violin and harpsichord (which also acts as continuo instrument), it is the harpsichord, with its extended first movement cadenza and shorter solo passages elsewhere, which emerges as the most prominent of the three. The middle movement, however, is quite simply a piece in trio-sonata style for the three soloists. The part writing here is especially satisfying and reveals Bach's rapport with and understanding of both the technical and expressive possibilities inherent in the newly fashionable flute. Nowhere, perhaps, is this more beguiling than in the affecting G major passage between bars 30 and 34 (Ex. 8). This concerto was almost certainly the last of the six Brandenburgs to be composed, though earlier manuscript sources, some of them markedly different from the version which Bach prepared for the Markgraf, should warn us against pinning too late a date to it. Although it is probable that Bach usually led the Cöthen orchestra from his place among the violins or violas, it is likely that in this Concerto he played the harpsichord and, specifically perhaps, a new instrument which had arrived from Berlin in 1719.

In its date of composition the sixth concerto in B flat is probably the earliest of the Brandenburgs. Thurston Dart improbably placed it as early as Bach's years at Arnstadt (1703–7), but more recent German scholarship vacillates between *c.* 1713—one suggestion is that it stems from

Ex. 8

instrumental sinfonias to secular cantatas, and we may recall, for example, Bach's four-part viola scoring in a church cantata, *Gleichwie der Regen* (BWV 18) of the same period—and 1718. The scoring, which somewhat recalls the seventeenth-century English viol consorts, is unusual: two violas, two viole da gamba, cello, violone and harpsichord continuo. Like the third concerto of the set, also for strings only, Bach groups the instruments in accordance with their range; but unlike the other, he confines the melodic and contrapuntal substance of the music to the violas which, with the cello, provide the concertino group of the work. In the *ritornelli* of the outer movements, violas and cello combine with the remaining instruments, but in the middle movement a trio-sonata piece like that of Concertos Nos. 2 and 5, they are accompanied by continuo only. The comparatively uncomplicated writing in the gamba parts may, perhaps, be explained by the fact that Bach's employer, Prince Leopold, an ardent music lover, was also an amateur gambist. We may well imagine, therefore, that he, with his teacher Christian Ferdinand Abel, took part in performances at Cöthen. In its instrumentation and in the way Bach makes use of his resources this concerto, one of the most expressively subtle of the six, is furthest away from its Italian models.

Bach's remaining concertos—those for one or more harpsichords, the *Italian* concerto for harpsichord alone (BWV 971) and, perhaps, the Concerto in A minor for flute, violin, harpsichord and strings (BWV 1044)—belong, at least in the form in which they have been handed down, to the composer's Leipzig years (1723–50). Although Bach's chief musical responsibility at Leipzig lay in the provision of church music, he was both actively and enthusiastically involved in other aspects of the city's musical life. In 1729 he became director of the Collegium Musicum, a largely student society which had been founded in 1701 by Telemann; Bach held the directorship until 1735 but resumed it once more in 1739. The society used to meet on Thursday evenings inside one of Leipzig's newly opened coffee-houses during the winter months, and in the gardens of another during the summer. It was both for these gatherings and also for the musical instruction of his children that Bach wrote his harpsichord concertos, all but one of which (the Concerto in C major for two harpsichords, BWV 1061) almost certainly existed either in earlier versions for violin and orchestra or were drawn from elements within the Leipzig church cantatas.

The model which Bach took for the harpsichord concertos was the three-movement pattern derived from the Italian sinfonia. Five of them have been preserved both in their original versions and in the harpsichord arrangements which Bach made later on: these are the two concertos for violin, the concerto for two violins, the fourth Brandenburg Concerto and Vivaldi's Concerto in B minor for four violins (Opus 3, No. 10), which Bach arranged as the Concerto in A minor for four harpsichords (BWV 1065). Although it seems likely that most of the remaining concertos were originally intended for violin, it has been demonstrated by Tovey and others that three works, at least, may have been written for members of the oboe family. One of these is the Concerto in F minor (BWV 1056), whose lyrical middle movement has survived in an alternative scoring for oboe and strings as the Sinfonia to an Epiphany cantata (BWV 156). Bach's solo writing both here and in the outer movements of the concerto is well suited to the tonal character and technical resources of an oboe, though this fact hardly diminishes its claim to be a violin concerto. Similarly, it seems likely that the Harpsichord Concerto in A major (BWV 1055) and the Concerto for two harpsichords in C minor (BWV 1060), may have been concertos for oboe d'amore and oboe and violin, respectively. Both reconstructions have been published in the *Neue Bach-Ausgabe* with a useful critical commentary.

Recent and largely convincing reconstructions have also been made for three violins of the Concerto in C major for three harpsichords (BWV 1064). This is a work of great invention and the manner in which Bach organizes his solos in contrast with the tuttis is impressive. In the first movement the soloists enter as a group rather than three individual elements, but the finale is an imitative *tour de force* in the form of a six-part fugato. Between the two

Bach placed a powerful, almost abstracted *adagio* with a quasi-*ostinato* bass which provides a sombre foundation for music which strikes a note of profound melancholy. Bach's nineteenth-century biographer Philipp Spitta described this work, in its version for three harpsichords, as 'one of his most impressive instrumental compositions'. Even so, Bach's authorship of the original has been questioned as, indeed, is the case with certain other of the harpsichord concertos.

One further insight to Bach's methods of reworking is afforded by the Concerto in A minor for flute, violin, harpsichord and strings (BWV 1044). Each of its three movements is based on an earlier composition. The first and third are adopted from the Prelude and Fugue in A minor (BWV 894) for harpsichord, which Bach had probably composed in Weimar; the slow movement is an arrangement of the Organ Sonata in D minor (BWV 527). Some modern scholarship, furthermore, inclines towards the view that the outer movements belonged to a lost keyboard concerto in the first instance and that the organ sonata, from which the middle movement comes, itself derived from an earlier instrumental trio. Bach's hand in the arrangement of this concerto has also been questioned, some commentators attributing it to his pupil J. G. Müthel (1728–1788); but the brilliant handling of the concertante parts, of which a parallel may be found in the fifth Brandenburg Concerto, their relationship with the ritornellos, and the remoulding process in general point to a musician of extraordinary ability; nor should the notably *galant* idiom of the music necessarily indicate the hand of a younger musician, for that Bach understood it completely is demonstrated by several works of his maturity such as *The Musical Offering* (BWV 1079) and the bass aria from the wedding cantata, *Dem Gerechten muss das Licht* (BWV 195).

Amongst the most satisfying of Bach's Leipzig concertos are one for solo harpsichord and strings in D minor (BWV 1052) and another for two harpsichords and strings in C major (BWV 1061). Both works provide splendid examples not only of the extent to which Bach developed the *ritornello* principle of his Italian models but also of his inexhaustible eagerness to experiment. The Concerto in D minor was almost certainly based on an earlier violin concerto, and one of which Bach himself evidently thought highly, since its first and second movements became the Sinfonia and opening chorus, respectively, of the cantata, *Wir müssen durch viel Trübsal* (BWV 146) and the finale the opening Sinfonia to *Ich habe meine Zuversicht* (BWV 188). The outer movements have a supple Vivaldian vigour though the harmonic language is much bolder; the middle movement which, in a Baroque concerto is almost invariably in a contrasting mode, remains in the minor—G minor. Here, a modulating ground bass of twelve bars provides the fundament upon which Bach weaves a well-sustained and poignant melody. The Concerto in C major, alone perhaps amongst the harpsichord concertos in being conceived in this form, differs considerably from the others. Bach's chief interest in this work lies in the relationship between the two harpsichords. In both the outer movements the string parts, though adding colour and providing a richer texture, are perfunctory. This was noted by Johann Nikolaus Forkel, Bach's first biographer, in 1802, when he wrote: 'It can be played without string accompaniment and still sounds admirable'. In the slow movement, an intimate and beautifully crafted dialogue of four-part writing takes place between the two harpsichords. Bach dispenses altogether with the strings, a feature which has led some commentators to suppose that he conceived the entire work for solo harpsichords without orchestral support—a corollary, perhaps, to the *Italian Concerto*.

England

English musical life during the first half of the eighteenth century was dominated by the imposing figure of Handel. His influence both upon the cultural milieu of his day and upon his younger English contemporaries can hardly be overstated. During the last decades of the previous century England had learned much about Italian and French musical styles from Purcell; she was, therefore, especially receptive to continental fashions. This was, furthermore, the beginning of the age of the 'Grand Tour', when educated and wealthy citizens embarked on journeys to Italy, France, Germany and the Netherlands. As often as not they returned home full of enthusiasm for the academies, theatres, opera houses and concert life which they had encountered in Europe. England, in short, became a welcoming host to foreign virtuosos, impresarios, singers and composers: 'he who in the present time wants to make a profit out of music betakes himself to England', wrote the German theorist, critic and composer Johann Mattheson in 1713 *(Das Neu-Eröffnete Orchestre)*. In England as, to begin with, in Germany, the chief instrumental model was Corelli, whose music first became known in London towards the end of the seventeenth century. In 1715 John Walsh senior issued Corelli's twelve *concerti grossi*, Opus 6, from which time they were performed, adapted and, from all accounts, universally loved. The English music historian Sir John Hawkins mentions an occasion in 1724 when an enthusiastic group of amateurs, having just acquired Corelli's Opus 6 from a bookseller, 'played the whole twelve concertos through, without rising from their seats'.[1] Not surprisingly, therefore, although concertos by

1. Hawkins, *History of the Science and Practice of Music*, 1776, Dover, New York, 1962, Vol. 2, p. 806.

other Italian composers such as Torelli and Vivaldi were published in England—the novelist Laurence Sterne, author of *Tristram Shandy* and a keen amateur violinist, borrowed music by Vivaldi from the library of the Dean and Chapter at York in 1752—the prevailing taste seems to have remained for the Corellian *concerto grosso*. Many such concertos, by a variety of composers, both English and Italian, were printed in London during the 1730s, bringing the publishers a healthy profit.

One of the first composers to have concertos printed in England was Geminiani. **Francesco Geminiani** (1687–1762) was born in Lucca but came to England in 1714. Apart from visits to Dublin, where he died, Geminiani remained in London, building up a fine reputation as a teacher, theorist and violin virtuoso. He was not a prolific composer but his sonatas and concertos, modelled to a great extent on those of his own teacher Corelli, reveal meticulous craftsmanship. His earliest concertos were a set of twelve, published in two parts in 1726, as arrangements of Corelli's Opus 5 sonatas for violin and basso continuo. In these Geminiani retains Corelli's thematic material and basic harmonic structure while extending the imaginative character of the music through richer textures and the employment of newly developed string techniques. Here too we find a *concertino* group consisting not just of the Corellian two violins and a cello but with an additional strand for viola, thus creating a four- rather than a three-part texture. The practice was to become standard in Geminiani's later concertos. Following this homage to Corelli, Geminiani brought out no further concertos until 1732 when he published six *concerti grossi* as his Opus 2. These were followed in the same year by what may perhaps be regarded as his finest collection, the six *concerti grossi*, Opus 3. Geminiani revised this set later on and issued them in full score in about 1755. In the words of Dr Burney[1]—usually a stern critic of Geminiani—the Opus 3 concertos 'established his character, and placed him at the head of all the masters then living, in this species of composition'. In this set and, above all in the fine third Concerto in E minor, Geminiani proves himself a fluent and imaginative contrapuntist. Elsewhere, as for example in the arresting opening *Largo* of the Concerto No. 4 in D minor, he can be dramatic, and both in this set and in Opus 2 he can frequently surprise us with unexpected harmonic progressions (Concerto in A major, Opus 2, No. 6), or divert us with beguiling *cantabile* melodies (Concerto in B flat, Opus 7, No. 6).

Two further sets of six concertos—one of them arrangements of trios from Corelli's Opus 1 and Opus 3, the other arrangements of violin sonatas from Geminiani's own Opus 4—appeared in 1735 and 1743 respectively,

---

1. Burney, *op. cit.*, Vol. 2, p. 991.

before he published his last set of *concerti grossi* (Opus 7) in 1746. The six works which comprise Opus 7 differ from Geminiani's earlier concertos in an important respect; for here he matches the viola of the *concertino* with a viola in the *ripieno* which normally consisted of two violin parts and basso continuo. Other features, such as the writing for a bassoon with solo passages in the Concerto No. 6 in B flat—a notably grand concerto in terms of design—reveal Geminiani as both less conservative and less limited in vocabulary than is often claimed.

Handel

Whilst Geminiani was establishing his reputation as an instrumental composer, **George Frideric Handel** (1685–1759), who had settled in London in 1712, was chiefly occupied in the production of Italian *opera seria*. Only when his fortunes were on the wane in this particular direction did he begin to interest himself in the assembly and composition of concertos. As Winton Dean[1] has observed, the greater part of Handel's orchestral music is a by-product of his work for the theatre. Many of the movements in his *concerti grossi* and organ concertos derive from vocal and instrumental numbers in his cantatas, operas and oratorios. Handel's first set of concertos was published by Walsh in London in 1734 as the composer's Opus 3. The six works must have appeared without close consultation with Handel himself, for the fourth concerto was almost certainly not by him; when Walsh issued a second edition later in the same year this concerto was replaced by another, whilst the fifth was extended by the addition of three further movements. Much of the music had been composed many years earlier but it loses nothing in its concerto context, furthermore revealing Handel as a colourful and resourceful composer. No two concertos are identically scored and the variety of instrumentation on display is an attractive feature of the set. The Concerto No. 1 in B flat has some unusual features: while the opening movement is in B flat, the remaining two are in G minor in which key the work ends. Handel writes for divided violas, a Venetian characteristic, in this concerto but not in any of the others; the full instrumental body consists of a concertante violin, two oboes, two treble recorders (in the middle movement only), two bassoons, strings and continuo.

The most satisfying work in Handel's Opus 3 is, perhaps, the Concerto No. 2 in B flat. Scored for a concertino group of two oboes, two violins and two cellos, with strings and continuo, it begins with a supple *vivace* in triple-time in which the two solo violins feature prominently with idiomatic Italianate figurations. The *Largo*, which follows, introduces an expressive

1. Dean, *Handel*, in The New Grove, 1980.

oboe melody above a broken-chord accompaniment played by the two concertante cellos. The third movement is a robust unconventional double fugue which leads to two concluding dance movements, a minuet, though not so named, and a gavotte whose theme is treated to engaging variations. For the third concerto, in G major, Handel allowed a choice between transverse flute or oboe with concertino violin, strings and continuo. The Concerto No. 4 in F major offers yet another instrumental combination: two oboes, bassoon, strings and continuo; this is closely allied to the scoring of the fifth concerto, in D minor, which, however, does not call for a bassoon. The Concerto No. 6 in D major stands out from the remaining works in the set in requiring an obbligato organ in addition to a pair of oboes, bassoon, strings and continuo. As with the first concerto, this one too begins in a major key but concludes in a minor one; it is, perhaps, the least satisfying work in Opus 3.

Handel's next set of published concertos were of a very different kind, and were to a great extent his own invention. They were written for solo organ with an orchestra of strings and woodwind and were published by Walsh in 1738 as the composer's Opus 4. For Handel their role was a functional one since they were largely intended for performances in theatres between the acts of his oratorios and odes. Handel played them himself on these occasions, and from the first they seem to have had wide appeal, for a second set appeared in 1740, and in 1761, two years after his death, a third was issued as his Opus 7. Two further organ concertos, one of them in D minor, based on two movements from a sonata in B minor for transverse flute and continuo from Telemann's *Musique de Table* (1733), to which Handel subscribed, were published by Samuel Arnold in 1797. Charles Burney has left a vivid and touching account of Handel's organ playing at oratorios during the last years of his life when he was blind:

> To see him ... led to the organ ... and then conducted towards the audience to make his accustomed obeisance, was a sight so truly afflicting and deplorable to persons of sensibility, as greatly diminished their pleasure, in hearing him perform ... for, after his blindness, he played several of his 'old' organ concertos, which must have been previously impressed on his memory by practice. At last, however, he rather chose to trust to his inventive powers, than those of reminiscence: for, giving the band only the skeleton, or ritornels of each movement, he played all the solo parts extempore, while the other instruments left him, 'ad libitum' ...[1]

1. Burney, *An Account of the Musical Performances in Westminster Abbey and the Pantheon in Commemoration of Handel*, 1785, pp. 29–30.

The music of the organ concertos represents an intricate maze of self-borrowing with occasional borrowing from other composers, notably Telemann, too complex to enter into here; but taken on their own merit they illustrate Handel's brilliant gifts as a composer of solo concertos. in the Opus 4 set the organ solos are mostly written out and the *ad libitum* element, fairly small. The Opus 7 collection, by contrast, offers notably larger scope for improvisation not only in the extemporization of entire movements but also within the body of movements otherwise written out. Such gaps as these can present problems to the performer since Handel's intentions are inevitably unclear. We can be sure, however, that Handel himself would have known exactly what to do, since he had long been celebrated for his ability at keyboard extemporization and his playing seems to have been regarded by his public as a 'high-spot' in the evening's entertainment. All but one of his organ concertos (Opus 7, No. 1 in B flat) are written for an instrument without pedals, for instruments with a pedal-board were a rarity in the England of Handel's day.

A brief glance at some of the music in Handel's Opus 4 and Opus 7 concertos will give us an idea both of its complex history and of the skilful manner in which the composer adapts borrowed material. The first and last concertos of Opus 4 were played at a performance of Handel's ode *Alexander's Feast* in 1736. Handel originally scored the Concerto in B flat (Opus A, No. 6) for harp with two treble recorders and muted strings, and that was how it was performed in *Alexander's Feast*; but it was published as an organ concerto. The second and third concertos were played a year earlier at a revival of his oratorio *Esther*. The fourth concerto, one of the most impressive in the set, was performed with the oratorio *Athalia* in 1735, whilst the fifth—a reworking of an earlier treble recorder sonata (Opus 1, No. 11) was played at a revival of the oratorio *Deborah* in the same year. As an example of the variety of self-borrowing in which Handel indulged we need look no further than the Concerto in B flat (Opus 4, No. 2). The earliest occurrence of its short opening *adagio* is in the Latin motet *Silete venti* which probably dates from the 1720s. For the robust *allegro* which follows, Handel turned to an earlier trio-sonata (Opus 2, No. 3) for material; this movement provides a particularly fine example of the effective way in which he remodelled earlier material. The pattern is much the same with the Opus 7 concertos, all of which derive from premières of odes and oratorios. The self-borrowings here too are plentiful, though hardly more so than his borrowing from other composers, notably Gottlieb Muffat and Telemann. This set contains what is probably Handel's last orchestral composition, the Concerto in B flat (Opus 7, No. 3), and its opening quotation from the *Hallelujah* chorus of *Messiah* (1742)—Handel rewrote this movement in order to accommodate it—can immediately be recognized. This, and the first concerto of the set are impressive works but it is in the Concerto in D minor (Opus 7, No. 4) that Handel strikes what is, perhaps, a more individual note. Its opening movement survives in two forms, one for solo organ with a continuo organ, as well, the other for solo organ, two oboes, two bassoons and strings. This darkly coloured movement, with its divided cellos and bassoons, is one of Handel's most distinctive utterances and is, furthermore, an imaginative and effective contrast with the sparkling character of the D major *allegro* which follows. Handel based it on a particularly striking movement in the French *ouverture* of the second 'Production' of Telemann's *Musique de Table*; but it is Handel's reworking of the material which appeals to our senses with the greater impact. The finale returns to D minor and to music closely allied with the last movement of the Concerto in D major/minor (Opus 3, No. 6).

Handel set to work with a remarkable burst of energy on what was to be his finest collection of concertos in the early autumn of 1739. By the end of October he had finished them, and in the following year Walsh published them, by subscription, as *Twelve Grand Concertos* (Opus 6). These *Grand Concertos*—the title is simply a translation of *concerti grossi*—are scored for string orchestra though optional oboe parts to four of them (Nos. 1, 2, 5, 6) were added sometime later. In the sense that they derive from Corelli's models, with which Handel was thoroughly conversant both from his period in Italy (1707–10) and doubtless, from the fact that they were widely admired in England, the Opus 6 concertos were old-fashioned for the late 1730s. In England, however, this was the taste of the time, and although Handel's technique is often similar to Corelli's—his concertino group consists of two violins and cello rather than the quartet favoured by Geminiani, for instance—in few senses can they be regarded as backward-looking. Indeed, Handel's terms of reference are impressively wide, embracing features both of the suite and of the concerto; but it is, above all, the level of inspiration, the Handelian stamp which is imprinted on every one of these concertos, that assures them of a place alongside Bach's *Brandenburg Concertos*, establishing the high water mark of the baroque concerto.

Hand-in-hand with the wide range of Handel's musical idioms is a rich variety of expressive language developed through his experience in the theatre, and often reflecting his own temperament—sometimes imperious, sometimes witty, often humorous and always diverting. The Concerto No. 1 in G major opens with robust, extrovert gestures which remain the predominant characteristic of the work. In the following three concertos—F major, E minor, A minor—Handel strikes an altogether gentler note, with a strong sense of pathos in the slow movements of the fourth concerto.

Concerto No. 5 in D major is plentifully endowed with humour and high spirits. The two opening bars, almost a call to order, lead into a movement in the style of a French overture with a lively fugal subject. These two sections, together with the graceful concluding minuet, are adapted from the introduction to Handel's *Ode for St Cecilia's Day* which he had completed only shortly before. The third movement *(Presto)*, in binary form, is mischievously built around a common-chord arpeggio which moves upwards in the first half and downward in the second. We can, perhaps, once again sense Handel's humour in the fugal movement of the Concerto No. 7 in B flat. Its first three bars are on a single repeated note—two, four and then eight, notes to a bar. Nothing in the entire set, however, rivals the concluding *hornpipe* of this concerto in its sheer unbridled exuberance; this is a splendid movement, full of vitality and, as Stanley Sadie has remarked,[1] 'boldly shaped lines and teasing rhythms' (Ex. 9). The concerto, incidentally, is not strictly a *concerto grosso* but an orchestral piece with no contrasting concertino and tutti episodes.

Ex. 9

1. Sadie, *Handel Concertos*, London, 1972, p. 49.

The sixth, eighth and twelfth concertos of Handel's Opus 6 each contains a slow movement of affecting beauty. In the Concerto No. 6 in G minor it is an inventive *Musette*, containing a variety of string figurations and rhythms, which provides the focal point of the work. The Concerto No 8 in C minor begins with an *allemande* recalling the *concerti da camera* of his Roman models; but it is the haunting beauty of the brief *adagio* in E flat which draws us into the midst of Handel's world. This piece, in which concertino and ripieno strings unite, opens with a quotation from Cleopatra's aria, *Piangerò la sorte mia* from one of Handel's most successful London operas, *Giulio Cesare* (1724). Handel saves his most beautiful melody for the last concerto in the set, No. 12 in B minor. The movement is a *larghetto* in E major whose serene melody is presented in binary form, each half, that is, repeated; Handel then treats each half, or strain, in turn, to two variations.

Both the ninth and eleventh concertos contain music from two organ concertos of the second set, published in 1740 without an opus number. Nevertheless, there is some new material and much of the old is reworked to advantage. The Concerto No 10 in D minor is one of the most stylistically varied of the set. It begins with an *Ouverture* in the French manner with a lively and well-constructed fugue. An *air* follows which has something of the character of a slow sarabande, giving this movement too a French flavour. Two well-contrasted *allegros*—the second an elaborate and inventive piece suggestive of a concerto movement for two violins—both in D minor, lead us to the finale, a simple and appealing little binary dance in D major, each half of whose melody is played twice and then played in the same manner in a captivating semi-quaver variation.

Apart from the concertos in the sets already discussed, there are a few miscellaneous works which further enrich our picture of Handel's activities in this field of composition. They consist of a *concerto grosso* in C major, (HWV 318) three concerti *a due cori*, a Sonata in B flat major (HWV 288) and three oboe concertos only one of which, however, can be definitely attributed to Handel. The earliest of these is the Sonata in B flat which is, to all intents and purposes, a concerto. It dates from Handel's period in Italy and it has been suggested that the prominent solo violin part, with virtuoso passages in the last of its three movements, was written for Corelli. The *Concerto Grosso* in C major, scored for oboes and strings, was first performed between the acts of Handel's oratorio, *Alexander's Feast* in 1736. Although here Handel adopts the concertino-ripieno pattern of his Italian models, he develops the thematic material in several interesting ways, dividing his loyalties, so to speak, between Venice and Rome; the concertino writing of the opening movement illustrates a fascinating dichotomy between brilliant Vivaldian solo violin writing, on the one hand, and a more fully integrated Corellian concertino writing on the other. The violin writing in the fugally inclined third movement also contains energetic violin figures; the finale is a delightful gavotte whose crisp *Lombard* rhythms, or *Scotch snaps*, give the music a somewhat impish character.

Handel's three Concerti *a due cori* belong to the last creative period of his life, and probably date from the late 1740s when they would almost certainly have been performed in the intervals of his oratorios. Despite the term *due cori* (two choirs), each of the concertos is scored for three choirs of instruments: one choir of strings, and two choirs of two oboes and bassoon to which a pair of horns are added in the second and third of the concertos. Most of the music is adapted from earlier material, which has led one writer to describe them as 'little more than echoes of things Handel has done before'. This is an unfair judgement for, as we know, Handel seldom if ever disappoints us in his borrowings and there is much splendid writing for woodwind and horns. Amongst many delightful movements in these concertos, two of which will be immediately familiar as borrowings from *Messiah*, is a graceful minuet which concludes the Concerto No. 1 in B flat; in this dance, for oboes, bassoon and strings, Handel drew upon material which he had used for a bass aria in the second act of his opera *Lotario* (1729). Although Handel's name is associated with three works for oboe and strings—two, in B flat, were published by Walsh in 1740 whilst a third, in G minor, was published for the first time in 1863—only one of them, the Concerto in B flat (HWV 302a) is indisputably by him. All three, however, are attractive works, and the two of doubtful provenance are idiomatically more suggestive of Handel than of any other baroque composer whose style is recognizably individual.

Handel's English Contemporaries

Handel's concertos, for the most part, are of a stature which somewhat dwarfs the achievements in this field of a handful of indigenous English composers; yet the concertos of men such as Arne, Stanley, Avison, Boyce and a few others are well constructed, often inventive and, at their best, possess individuality of character. The composer seemingly least interested in the form was **William Boyce** (1711–1779). Boyce was a great champion of Handel's music, which he promoted with zeal, but it was in his *Eight Symphonys*—the last of which, in D minor, is in fact termed a *concerto grosso* in some manuscript scores—rather than in some four surviving concertos that Boyce's gifts in orchestral writing are most strikingly apparent. **Thomas Arne** (1710–1778), like Boyce, was foremost a composer for the voice, but around 1787 *Six Favourite concertos* for keyboard and orchestra were posthumously printed; taken as a whole, these concertos reflect a versatility in Arne's style ranging from a Handelian grandeur to a reflective, sometimes melancholy manner.

Charles Avison (1709–1770) was the most active composer of concertos amongst the English-born musicians. Some 50 or so were published during his lifetime, and in many of these Avison inclined towards the example of his teacher Geminiani, both in his preferred four-movement scheme and in his use of a concertino group of two violins, viola and cello as opposed to the two violins and cello of Corelli and Handel. Amongst Avison's concertos are twelve arrangements for string orchestra of harpsichord sonatas by his great contemporary Domenico Scarlatti (1685–1757). Several of these, despite Sterne's[1] disparaging remarks about the tempo markings of the sixth concerto of the set show a lively feeling for orchestration and a boldness of invention which is lacking in some of the concertos of other sets. The set of twelve *concerti grossi* for strings, published in 1758 as the composer's Opus 6—though some of these had previously appeared in his Opus 2 and elsewhere in a different form—seems conservative by comparison with the Scarlatti arrangements; but it contains, in concertos such as the eighth in E minor, what are perhaps the finest examples of his craftsmanship: a well-constructed fugue with a striking chromatic subject, a lyrical movement marked *amoroso* and an appealing gavotte conclusion. This concerto could easily hold its own ground against those in the regularly played Baroque repertoire of the present day.

According to Burney,[1] **John Stanley** (1712–86) lost his sight at the age of two 'by falling on a marble hearth with a china bason in his hand'. Stanley was not a prolific composer and all his concertos are contained in two sets. The first of them, his Opus 2, is a set of six *concerti grossi* for strings, published in 1742. Shortly afterwards, perhaps reflecting the popularity of Handel's example, they were arranged as concertos for organ and strings with the organ taking over the concertino role. They are in the Corellian tradition but owe something to Handel, whom Stanley both admired and imitated. By contrast, the six concertos of Stanley's later set, Opus 10, published in 1775, lean towards the early Classical idiom of the time. Several concertos from these sets deserve to be heard more frequently than they are, and we might single out the Concerto in A minor (Opus 2, No. 5) as representative of Stanley's considerable strength in this direction.

Amongst other composers who published concertos in London during the mid-eighteenth century were the Dutchmen Willem de Fesch and Pieter Hellendaal, the Italian Pietro Castrucci, and two seldom encountered English

1. Sterne, *Tristram Shandy*, Book 3, Ch. 5, London, 1761.
1. Burney, *op. cit.*, p. 494.

musicians, Richard Mudge and Capel Bond. **De Fesch** (1687–1757?) came to live in London during the 1730s, and in 1741 published eight concertos as his Opus 10. Burney considered his concertos 'dry and uninteresting', a criticism which should not apply to Hellendaal's *Six Grand Concertos*, Opus 3. **Hellendaal** (1721–99), a pupil of Tartini, came to England from Holland in 1752 where he lived for the rest of his life. His six *concerti grossi* were published in London first by Walsh in 1758, then by another English publisher, John Johnson, shortly afterwards. Like Geminiani and Avison, Hellendaal's concertino group consists of a quartet: two violins, viola and cello, but he is less consistent than Geminiani in his use of it. These six concertos possess a sureness of style and an expressive individuality which compare favourably with much *concerto grosso* writing at this time; these qualities are present, to a greater of lesser extent, in each of the Opus 3 concertos of which the fourth, in E flat major, is perhaps the most interesting on account of the varied character of its five movements. **Castrucci** (1679–1752) came to England during the second decade of the eighteenth century and led Handel's opera orchestra for over 20 years. Contemporary opinion suggests that he was a brilliant violinist, and Burney, furthermore, thought him a fine composer for his instrument. Castrucci's twelve *concerti grossi* were published in 1736 as his Opus 3. **Mudge** (1718–1763), **Bond** (1730–1790) and a handful of other English composers issued concertos between the 1740s and 1760s: Mudge's only known published collection, *Six Concertos in seven parts . . .* appeared in 1749; the first of these has a part for solo trumpet whilst the last, following the fashion of the time, has a solo part for keyboard. Bond was born in Gloucester and became organist of St Michael's, Coventry—now Coventry Cathedral. His *Six Concertos in Seven Parts* were published by subscription in 1766 and are, like those of Mudge, varied in their instrumentation; four are somewhat conservative *concerti grossi* for strings, but the remaining two, for solo trumpet and solo bassoon with strings, are *galant* in their idiom and show, furthermore, that Bond was effective in the concerto medium.

France

French composers did not begin to write concertos until comparatively late in the period; works such as the *Concerts Royaux* of **François Couperin** (1668–1733) contain elements of the Italian *concertato* principle but, nevertheless, are essentially suites, the instrumental form with which they were most preoccupied—and it was not until the 1720s that concertos conforming with the broad outlines of Italian models began to appear in

France. One of the earliest collections to be printed was by **Joseph Bodin de Boismortier** (1689–1755), whose six *Concertos pour 5 Flûtes traversières ou autres instruments sans basse* were published in 1727 as the composer's Opus 15. As we can see from the title, which probably contains the first instance of the word *concerto* being used by a French composer, these early steps towards the Italian concerto were tentative. Nevertheless, these concertos, for which Boismortier does in fact provide an optional figured bass, are cast in the three-movement pattern of the Italian sinfonia and in other small ways indicate that Boismortier intended to organize his material in the manner of his Italian contemporaries. Several other collections of concertos by Boismortier subsequently were printed, and the music, though technically undemanding and sometimes trivial, seldom lacks either elegance or affecting simplicity. Amongst the most interesting of them is Opus 26 (1729) which contains five sonatas followed by five solo concertos for various instruments including bassoon.

Boismortier's earliest collection of concertos was quickly followed by others. In 1728 **Michel Corrette** (1709–1795) published his Opus 3: six *Concertos pour les Flûtes, Violons ou Hautbois, avec la Basse Chiffrée* [figured bass] *pour le Clavecin*. These conform with the pattern of an Italian *concerto grosso* more closely than Boismortier's earliest publication. All of them adopt the fast-slow-fast pattern and in each the *concertino-ripieno* principle is clearly apparent. Corrette was a lucid theorist, an able performer and notably well informed about the lighter repertoire of the French music of his day. Popular tunes play an important part in a great many of his compositions as we can see from the instrumentation and titles of many of his concertos. Several are based on old French Christmas carols and are scored for instruments such as the musette or the vielle (hurdy-gurdy) with an assortment of other more conventional instruments. Amongst his most attractive collections are those containing 25 *concertos comiques*, whose melodies, drawn from a rich variety of popular repertoire, are effectively arranged into short, simple and appealing concerto movements.

Less familiar composers such as **Jacques Aubert** (1689–1753) and **Jacques Christophe Naudot** (c. 1690–1762), made significant contributions to the French Baroque concerto repertoire. Aubert was a noted violinist whose two sets of six violin concertos (Opus 17, published in 1734, and Opus 26, published in 1739), though uneven in quality, possess movements of strength and individuality. His Opus 17 contained the first violin concertos to be printed in France, and in that set the third concerto, in A major, offers a particularly attractive sample of a Frenchman's conception of a Vivaldian violin concerto. The scoring here, as in all Aubert's concertos, is for four violins, with a cello independent of the continuo; tuttis are clearly modelled on Venetian concertos and solo episodes in fast movements are technically quite advanced, with double-stopping and lively passagework. In slow movements Aubert often preferred the dance measures of his native France—the gavotte or minuet, for instance, in the use of which he achieved a pleasing elegance and an effective contrast with the two flanking movements. Naudot was chiefly a composer of sonatas for his own instrument, the flute. His first collection of concertos, scored for flute and strings, was published in Paris during the mid-1730s as his Opus 11. The music is attractive and, as we should expect, sympathetically written for the flute; but Naudot seemed unable to rise above somewhat bland and trivial invention, and his music, though often diverting, remains slight. Much of it is wearisomely tonic-dominant oriented, a feature which, in his second and last set of concertos (Opus 17, 1742) is dicated by the limited tonal vocabulary of musette and vielle.

Leclair

The concertos of all the French composers whom we have so far discussed, however, are far outstripped by those of Leclair. **Jean-Marie Leclair** (1697–1764) was, after Rameau, the most gifted French composer of the late Baroque. Like Aubert, Leclair was early in his career both dancing master and violinist, adding to these accomplishments, furthermore, that of lace-maker. We know little of his early career, but at one stage he studied in Turin with Giovanni Battista Somis, a pupil of Corelli. He was not a prolific composer and the bulk of his work consists of sonatas for his own instrument, the violin. These are of high quality, but a quality which is matched by two sets of violin concertos and one opera, his tragédie-lyrique, *Scylla et Glaucus.* Leclair's first set of violin concertos were published in 1737 as his Opus 7. It contained six works for solo violin and strings, and was followed in about 1744 by a second set of six, published as his Opus 10. There is not a concerto amongst the twelve which is either weak in construction or dull in invention. Leclair follows a fast-slow-fast pattern in all but one of them (Concerto in D major, Opus 7, No. 2) where he adds an introductory *adagio.* Structurally, they show an advance on most, if not all of their Vivaldian models. By and large he follows the alternating tutti-solo pattern of the Italian concerto, but sometimes, as for instance in the opening movement of the Concerto in A major (Opus 10, No. 2), tuttis are interrupted by solo passages. The movements themselves vary in scale and, in the Concerto in G minor (Opus 10, No. 6) Leclair constructs his outer movements on notably expansive ideas. His solo violin writing, as we might guess from the pen of a celebrated virtuoso, is technically demanding. Double- and treble-stopping is frequently demanded, but Leclair successfully avoids employing the more extravagant devices merely for display, effectively integrating virtuosity with the substance of the music.

Amongst many conspicuously attractive features of Leclair's writing is an abundance of graceful melodies and a notably successful accommodation of French and Italian styles, assimilated, fused or juxtaposed. This appealing blend of native *beau chant* with Italian virtuosity is, as we might say, a hallmark of the composer's style, giving him substantial claim to have achieved, better than any of his French contemporaries, that elusive but much sought-after manner termed by Couperin *les goûts réunis*. Slow movements, particularly, impart a French flavour both in the song-like simplicity of their solo melodies and, occasionally, by the use of dance rhythms; both of these features are present in the tender gavotte-like *aria graziosa* of the Concerto in F major (Opus 10, No. 4), and the menuet-like *aria* of the Concerto in D minor, (Opus 7, No. 1), while further evidence of Leclair's notably lyrical talent is displayed in the slow movements of the Concerto in D major (Opus 7, No. 2) and the Concerto in A minor (Opus 7, No. 5). On the other hand, the G major *largo*, in siciliano rhythm, of the Concerto in E minor (Opus 10, No. 5), is wholly Italian in character, and it is in the finale that we must look to find the composer in his Franco-Italian clothes. Perhaps the most striking of them all is the *adagio* of the Concerto in C major (Opus 7, No. 3), which Leclair scored for a choice between violin, flute and oboe as solo instruments. In this movement the darkly coloured, notably expressive solo part is punctuated by a tutti in dotted rhythm, recalling the opening section of a French overture.

Outer movements in Leclair's concertos are more consistently Italianate in character than the middle ones, often bringing to mind composers of his generation such as Tartini and Locatelli. Yet, although they are organized within the alternating solo-tutti pattern there is a freedom and invention which gives the music a distinctive character of its own. In the opening movement of the Concerto in A major (Opus 10, No. 2), for example, the solo and tutti passages closely intermingle throughout in what must be one of Leclair's most freely constructed pieces. The tonal scheme of the fast movements is similar to that which we have encountered in his Italian contemporaries, but he is often strikingly adventurous in his modulations. Sometimes Leclair introduces a section to a movement in the opposing mode to the prevailing one; an effective example of this occurs in the somewhat quirky finale of the concerto in A minor (Opus 7, No. 5). The solo episodes here are biased towards Italian models until we reach the last one which leads us into the world of the French eighteenth-century dance. This section, distinct from the remainder of the movement both in key (A major) and in character, provides the listener with a focal point in the movement of great charm. At other times Leclair could be more consistently Italian as we find him in the finales of the Concerto in D minor (Opus 7, No. 1) and the Concerto in D major (Opus 7, No. 2). Vivaldi's idiom, with its sequential figuration in the solo part, provides the closest analogy in this instance; indeed, the writing in the D major work suggests that Leclair had Vivaldi's *Four Seasons* in mind; these were concertos which almost certainly would have been known to him and which, in all probability, he would himself have played. Few composers can have achieved such a widely expressive and technical range as that achieved by Leclair in his twelve violin concertos; fugue, chromaticism, modulation, idiomatic figuration, a feeling for dance and a gift for melody all contribute towards Leclair's rich and colourful palette.

CHAPTER 2

The Pre-Classical Concerto and the Concerto Parallel to Mozart

H. C. Robbins Landon

The average musician in London, when Haydn had just left—in the middle of August 1795—would hardly have heard a single Mozart concerto for any kind of instrument unless he had visited Vienna, where Mozart had lived for ten years (1781–91), or been to Germany, where some of Mozart's piano concertos were played by admirers and pupils. But it is safe to say that in 1795 Mozart's greatest innovation in the field of purely instrumental music was awaiting discovery throughout 90 per cent of Europe. Hence a history of the concerto during this period does well to separate Mozart from the mainstream of concerto life simply because he did not yet exist in the minds of his contemporaries and thus had no influence at all on most of Europe's leading writers in the form. Therefore our aim has been to isolate Mozart, both historically and splendidly, and to outline the rest of the Continent's production as follows: first to trace the predecessors of the form in the opening section, then to display, however briefly and inadequately (considering the thousands of extant specimens) the classical concerto 1760–80; and, finally, to discuss what was happening in the world of the concerto parallel to Mozart, until the end of the century (or more exactly until the advent of Beethoven's piano concertos in 1795, though there will be a small overlap in such a work as Haydn's greatest concerto, that for trumpet in E flat, of 1796). It was thought that this seemingly eccentric procedure is the only one to do any kind of justice to the subject from the historical standpoint: moreover it is obvious that Mozart's concertos are so much in a class of their own that they warrant such a special isolation which reflects their position both aesthetically and historically.

The Outgoing Baroque Concerto

By the middle of the eighteenth century the most popular form in instrumental music was, without any question, the concerto. Its popularity had continued for five decades and had indeed began before 1700. There were two principal kinds: the solo concerto and the *concerto grosso* or multiple concerto. There were, in Italian concertos (and the Italians were the originators and principal composers of the form all during the period in question), two further subdivisions which applied both to the solo concerto and the *concerto grosso*: the secular kind and the pieces intended for, and executed in, the church *concerto da chiesa)*. This same subdivision had also existed for the solo and trio sonata, of course, yet it is safe to say that by 1750 the differences in style between the secular and the sacred were, especially abroad, but largely also in the mother-country Italy, becoming blurred to the point of non-existence. In the intervals of theatrical pieces in Protestant England, church sonatas and works like the Corelli Christmas Concerto (a typical *da chiesa* work composed for and first given in the Vatican at Christmas time) were performed years after they had been composed. By 1750 concertos for solo instruments, one or more, had come gradually to replace the *concerto grosso*, which used to have as its characteristic make-up a solo section or *concertino* of two violins and violoncello and an orchestral or *ripieno* (literally, 'full') body of strings; there were often, especially in larger performances, two harpsichords or even more, one for each of the two sections. Although the *concerto grosso* was moribund by 1760, its precepts had not been forgotten. Haydn had taken over its form in many sections of his first symphonies for Eisenstadt (1761), *Le Matin, Le Midi* and *Le Soir*; and there is an interesting theory that the *symphonie concertante*, or multiple concerto, had its origins directly in the old *concerto grosso*.

The popularity of the concerto had been assisted immensely by the now widespread dissemination of music through the printed page. For a time, in the second and third decades of the century, the centre for publication of concertos, especially from Vivaldi's immensely popular and seminal *L'estro armonico* Opus 3 (1712) onwards, had been in Amsterdam with Estienne Roger. It is safe to say that Roger's activities, and those of his associates and successors, paved the way for Amsterdam, and Holland in general, becoming a centre of music publishing altogether. (In the second part of the century, the leading Dutch publisher was J. J. Hummel, who opened a Berlin branch of the firm as well, making it an international operation. Hummel published many of the most popular instrumental concertos in our period.)

By 1750, however, the concerto was losing some of its popularity to the symphony, and in turn the symphony was beginning to exert a fundamental influence on the concerto, just as opera had done a few decades earlier. This influence took several forms: the most obvious was orchestration. Instead of the hitherto string orchestra, the accompaniment now began to be standardized to oboes, horns and strings, from which the previous harpsichord continuo began to disappear. Not that previous concertos and *concerti grossi* were always so conservatively scored: apart from Bach's elaborate orchestra for the 'Brandenburg' Concertos, in far away Edinburgh Frederico Barsanti, a native from Lucca, was composing concertos for equally extravagant combinations, e.g. with a *concertino* or solo group of two horns and timpani, accompanied by the customary string orchestra and harpsichord continuo. Another Barsanti extravagance was a concerto scored for a *concertino* including solo trumpet (with other instruments).

But the symphony was exerting other influences too. The first movements began to move away from what might be called the Vivaldian *ritornello* form to an approximation of what was happening with the symphony: in other words a move towards the tripartite symphonic concept of exposition, development, recapitulation. And there was a steady change towards the new *galant* style, with Italian–Mannheim crescendos, as well as the trappings of the Italian *sinfonia*: repeated quavers (in quicker tempi crotchets or even minims) in the bass line, repeated semiquavers (or whatever) in the violins; in short, the orchestral parts of the concerto began more and more to sound like extracts from symphonies. A clever listener, not knowing the piece being performed, could however guess the form by the middle of the first *ritornello*. If it stayed more or less in the tonic, it was a concerto (though in 1800 he would have been puzzled by Beethoven's Third Piano Concerto, in C minor, which stays so persistently in the relative major that the music begins to sound like a real symphony). The scene was set for the real pre-classical concerto, and throughout Europe. Italy was still the home of the three-movement symphony (an operatic overture in fact), but the Italians were losing their interest in concertos, and other countries—especially Austria, Germany and France—were beginning to be the centre of the new pre-classical concerto form.

The Pre-Classical Concerto 1760–80

The insuperable difficulty in providing a history of the concerto in this period is twofold: first, most concertos were written by composers for their own use, or composed especially for some performer; the performer (whether also the composer or not) usually kept his new concerto in manuscript so that he would have the exclusive right to play it. Hence it is something of a miracle that such a concerto survives at all. The most famous cases of such a slender survival are both by Haydn—the Trumpet Concerto of 1796 which exists only in Haydn's autograph and was not printed until this century, and the Cello Concerto in C, accidently discovered in the Prague National Library in 1961.

ompanion to the Concerto

Secondly, not more than five per cent of eighteenth-century concertos are available in any kind of score. Thus our judgement of the form as a whole is woundingly limited. Are we sure that among all those eighteenth-century manuscript concertos for violin, flute, oboe, horn, organ, harpsichord or cello, now lying in the great Prague library, there are not forgotten masterpieces, like that charming D major Symphony by one of the Miča family which was discovered in an obscure Bohemian church archives after the Second World War? How many supremely beautiful concertos of the period are lost forever? Among all the lost Haydn concertos—for flute, bassoon, horn, two horns, violin, cello and even double bass—were some the equal of the highly popular C major Cello Concerto? We shall never know the answer to the last question, and it will take us another generation before we can know all the unpublished concertos of the period. Any report at present is therefore at best a partial truth.

Still, the situation has improved immeasurably in the last 30 or 40 years. Who in 1950 knew anything about Michael Haydn's concertos? Now, fortunately, almost all of them have been published. And if all this sounds extremely odd to the layman, one might add that, as I write, a major Joseph Haydn concerto, for organ (or harpsichord) in D major (Hob, XVIII: 2) is about to be published for the first time.

Italy

If we start our survey in Italy, the situation is particularly bleak. Most of the concertos written between 1760 and 1780 in Italy have either not survived at all or have never been printed. There are rays of hope, nonetheless. Recently a handsome flute concerto by **Niccola Piccinni** (1728–1800)—of Gluck–Piccinni fame—has been discovered in the composer's dated autograph (Rome, 1769) and is now published. It is scored for oboes, horns and strings and must represent hundreds of similar, lost works of this kind composed in Italy in the 1760s and 1770s. One of the interesting stylistic features of this winning piece is the way in which the *ritornello* and solo sections are scored: when the flute is playing, the orchestra almost always disappears, leaving only the two violins, *and of these the top line is always violin II*. Since this feature occurs throughout the piece, I suggest that it may represent some kind of purely Italian trait.

In northern Italy, and especially in Venice, there was a strong tradition of harpsichord concertos. Even famous opera composers like **Baldassare Galuppi** (1706–1785) wrote them in substantial quantities. Most of them seem to be works of the Baroque period, but one at least, in F major (Editore G. Zanibon 4865), is in the *galant* style and might be from *c.* 1760 (or even later?). The fact that a score is preserved in the Dresden library shows that

Galuppi's harpsichord concertos, like his operas, travelled widely: a German manuscript even attributes to Galuppi the Haydn organ concerto discussed above (which must be Haydn's since the composer entered it in his own private thematic catalogue, known as *Entwurf-Katalog*).

In this particular period musical life in Italy was often financially precarious, and Italian composers liked to seek their livelihood abroad, even as far as Russia (where Catherine The Great welcomed a whole series of Italian opera composers—Galuppi, Sarti, Paisiello, Cimarosa, etc.). Consequently, many of the best 'Italian' concertos were composed abroad. In some cases, such as Luigi Boccherini (1743–1805), the composer settled for good in a foreign country—in Boccherini's case it was Spain. In other cases, such as Paisiello and Cimarosa, the visits were more of a temporary nature. To introduce some kind of logic into the discussion, Boccherini's concertos are discussed under Spain, whereas Cimarosa's Concerto for two flutes (Vienna, 1793) has been placed (as it were) in Italy. In a brief survey such as ours, only the high points can be mentioned, leaving (no doubt unfairly) dozens of good composers and hundreds of concertos by the wayside. But it seemed of little use to be analysing unprinted horn concertos by Hampel and Carl Lau, bassoon concertos by Weinlich or harp concertos by Gera, when we have readily available works by Joseph and Michael Haydn or Viotti which are still (or just?) in the regular repertoire.

Austria: Haydn

After Italy we must move northwards, to Austria and its provinces (Austria was then a huge empire). Vienna had by 1760 become a centre of music north of the Alps and indeed the focus-point of an entire new school. Concerto-writing thrived there, especially for the organ (without pedals) and harpsichord. The young **Joseph Haydn** (1732–1809) had just been engaged by Count Morzin (about 1757) and had already produced an attractive series of organ concertos, as well as a Double Concerto for organ, violin and strings in F. Some of these organ concertos were not published until after the Second World War, but nowdays they have become very popular: they are simple and easy-going, but fun to play. Some have trumpets and timpani in the orchestra (possibly later additions). There are several in C major, one in D and the one in F with obbligato violin: all have been printed and all have been recorded on the organ. Haydn naturally expected players to use the harpsichord if no organ were available, but he also composed a series of real harpsichord concertos, of which the two most celebrated are in G (XVIII: 4) and D (XVIII: 11), the latter probably written about 1780 with the new fortepiano in mind: both are now available for the first time in immaculate editions by the Henle Verlag.

After the Trumpet Concerto the D major keyboard concerto is arguably Haydn's finest work in the form. Though lacking the complexity and richness of interplay between soloist and orchestra of Mozart's great concertos, it is a shapely, compact piece, with a surprising depth of feeling in the *Adagio*, where Haydn draws the most delicate poetry from very simple material. The final rondo, marked *all'ungherese*, is a highly exhilarating movement, with a touch of gypsy wildness that points forward to the famous rondo of the G major piano trio.

There are also delightful organ concertos by Haydn's teacher (**Georg Reutter Jr**, 1708–1772), all alas unpublished, and also by Haydn's colleagues, of which the most interesting are surely those by **F. X. Brixi** (1732–1771), from a Bohemian family of organists. Brixi died of tuberculosis at the age of 39, leaving behind an astonishingly prolific legacy of 105 masses, 263 offertories, 26 litanies, four vespers, five requiems and five organ concertos (one, in D, has splendid trumpet and timpani parts); the organ concertos have been edited by Czech scholars and are readily available. There were also hundreds of harpsichord concertos of the period being composed throughout the Austrian empire; from Vienna were dozens by the Cathedral Chapel-Master of St Stephen's, **Leopold Hofmann** (c. 1730–1793), **J. C. Wagenseil** (1715–1777), who taught music to the royal family at Schönbrunn, and the Bohemian composer **Joseph Anton Steffan** (1726–1800) who was Archduchess Marie Antoinette's teacher and composed interesting keyboard music.

Many of these Viennese composers—Viennese by adoption in many cases—composed concertos for unexpected combinations. Wagenseil wrote flute, violin, organ and cello concertos (the latter published by Doblinger Verlag); some were only discovered after the Second World War, among them a concerto for trombone. One of the most unusual composers of the period was Beethoven's teacher **J. G. Albrechtsberger** (1736–1809), who was in his youth organist at Maria Taferl and Melk Abbey and had assisted in the first performances of Haydn's string quartets at nearby Weinzierl Castle. Albrechtsberger composed harpsichord and organ concertos, but also a trombone concerto (for alto trombone, hence of hideous technical difficulty), several concertos for Jew's harp (recently published and also recorded), and four concertini for harp of 1772 as well as many other works for that instrument (including a concerto in C of 1773). I suggest that these harp pieces may have been composed for the great virtuoso on that instrument **Johann Baptist Krumpholtz** (c. 1745–1790), who was engaged in 1773 to play in Haydn's orchestra at Eszterháza and for whom Haydn seems not to have composed anything whatever. Perhaps Krumpholtz, who later married his pupil and, when she eloped, drowned himself in the Seine

(1790), whiled away the long hours at Eszterháza playing these pretty pieces by Haydn's friend Albrechtsberger.

Another friend of Haydn's was **Carl Ditters** (later **von**) **Dittersdorf** (1739–1799), whose concertos number in the dozen—for violin (i.e. for himself) but also for numerous other instruments, including the double bass (a concerto in E is published by Schott). This pleasant work makes us regret the lost double bass concerto composed by Haydn in 1763—lost, along with other concertos listed above (p. 60). There are, however, several memorable wind and string concertos that Haydn wrote between 1760 and 1780. They include one genuine horn concerto in D of 1762 (VIId: 3), three violin concertos (VIIa: 1, 3, 4)—of which that in C for Haydn's leader Luigi Tomasini has always been the most popular (it has a heavenly slow movement)—and the newly discovered Cello Concerto in C (VIIb: 1) dating from the early 1760s—the single greatest musicological discovery since the Second World War (if we, pehaps, except the emergence of Haydn's *Missa Sunt bona mixta malis* at a Christie auction in 1983). This is a work which—unlike the also newly discovered Violin Concerto in A ('Melk')—has entered the repertoire and become a favourite with the public. Vital in its invention with a graciously lovely slow movement, the concerto shows, particularly in its driving virtuosic finale, what a high level of string playing had been reached even in the Austrian provinces, far from Italy (the performer was Joseph Weigl, first cellist of the Esterházy orchestra in Eisenstadt, then part of Hungary).

Even further away in the Austrian provinces was Grosswardein in Transylvania (now Oradea Mare in Romania), where first **Johann Michael Haydn** (1737–1806) and then Dittersdorf was *Capellmeister.* In the early 1760s Michael was composing a series of concertos for his patron, the Bishop of Grosswardein, which are bolder and more original than those of his brother at the same period: apart from the beautiful Violin Concerto in B flat of 1760, there is an extraordinary Double Concerto in C for organ, viola and strings, which is now frequently played and recorded. The viola writing again shows what an extraordinary standard had been reached in the Austrian provinces by 1760. In 1762 Michael and Joseph Haydn both wrote difficult horn concertos in Vienna for Ignaz Leutgeb, later of Mozartian fame.

Michael Haydn went to Salzburg in 1763 and among the many works he wrote there were two flute concertos in D, which give us an idea of the kind of works being produced at the archiepiscopal court in Mozart's youth. The year 1763 was the one in which Leopold Mozart—who had composed concertos for horn, two horns and trumpet—and his family arrived in Paris, where at the end of the year he could write home to Salzburg that 'my children have taken almost everyone by storm'. Not only Wolfgang and Nannerl, but Austrian-German music had taken Paris by storm. As the centre of the music publishing world, the French capital exerted an influence of extraordinary potence. Many a work of the period has survived only in a rare copy of its French print (the Revolution played havoc with the great aristocratic libraries: many vital editions, even by Haydn, have not survived at all). Paris was, in the truest sense, a market place. It was from here, and not from Mannheim, that the symphonies and concertos of Johann Stamitz (1717–1750), Carl Stamitz (1745–1801), C. J. Toeschi (1732–1788), Anton Filtz (1730–1760) and F. X. Richter (1709–1798) went forth to conquer Europe.

One of the primary moving forces in concerto-writing for wind during these crucial years (and indeed beyond) was the Bohemian school. It was they who supplied not only the wind players who peopled the orchestras of Europe, but also the composers who wrote especially for them and the instrument-makers who perfected the instruments on which they played— especially true of the clarinet and bassoon family. In 1750 it was the flute which by far predominated in concerto-writing, but 20 years later there were almost as many works in the form for other wind instruments. Some of these concertos travelled to Paris, were printed and survived. Others also survived in their native habitat, but by a terrifyingly slender thread. It seems gratuitous to select another D major flute concerto from among thousands of candidates, north German, French, Italian and Austrian (in the larger sense, i.e. including Bohemian); but if we compare a newly discovered Flute Concerto in D by **Anton Filtz** with that by Piccinni mentioned above, it will be seen that the Bohemian work (or Mannheim, depending how you view the matter: Filtz was a pupil of that orchestra's leader, Johann Stamitz) is in another world. Discovered in 1946 in the private archives of a schoolmaster's family in Chornice in Bohemia, the Filtz Concerto is a work of poetic grandeur, a worthy predecessor of Mozart's famous flute concertos. Filtz is altogether an unusual composer, and the extraordinary section in D minor that succeeds the main theme shows us that we may expect something out of the way; indeed, this work shows us that, although earlier than the Piccini of 1769, the Bohemian–Mannheim school was light years away from Italy in technique and inspiration. Another major discovery was the Bassoon Concerto in C major by **J. A. Koželuch** (1738–1814), the uncle of the better-known composer and rival of Mozart's, Leopold Koželuch. This concerto, first played in our times in Prague in 1952, is a magnificent, large-scale work with trumpets and kettledrums in the orchestra and fully the equal of Mozart's in B flat (K191).

These two brilliant resuscitations were never printed in Paris, but they are exceptions in the general output of the Mannheimers, whose principal works were disseminated by French publishers. It is a moot question who invented the most popular type of multiple concerto, the three- or sometimes only two-movement *sinfonia concertante* (usually called by its French equivalent): the French, the Bohemians or indeed the Italians; but it is safe to say that by 1770 it was fast outstripping the concerto in popularity. The second-generation Mannheimers, especially Carl Stamitz and Christian Cannabich (1731–1798) composed dozens of these multiple concertos, often with wind instruments, and it is to Mannheim's influence that Mozart composed his lost *symphonie concertante* (*not* identical with K Anh. 9 = K 297b, a spurious work for wind instruments and orchestra) in 1778. Soon, native French composers—and foreigners settled here—were providing their own variety of multiple concertos, and some of them are very creditable: we might single out those by the **Chevalier de Saint-Georges** (c. 1739–1799), a racy mulatto from Guadeloupe who was a famous swordsman and lady-killer, and who was the go-between in persuading Haydn to compose his 'Paris' Symphonies. One set of Saint-Georges's *symphonies concertantes*, Op. 9, was published the year Mozart went to Paris, 1778, and very pretty they are too. Another gifted Frenchman with many *concertantes* to his credit was **Jean-Baptiste Davaux** (1742–1822), who began publishing multiple concertos about 1772; but the most gifted was surely Simon LeDuc (c. 1745–1777), who wrote one *symphonie concertante* for two violins in G in 1774 with no less than 16 parts. A famous composer of concertos for one or more instruments was **Francois Devienne** 1759–1803), to whose fertile pen has recently (and wrongly) been attributed the spurious Mozart bassoon concerto in B flat (K Anh. 230A). Most of **Giovanni Giuseppe Cambini's** (1746–1825) many concertos and *symphonies concertantes* have been forgotten, but he was a partner in the Italian 'Boccherini' string quartet of the 1760s and was much appreciated for his sinuous melodic lines with pretty chromatic touches. Recently, there has been a revival of concertos by the French organist and composer **Jean François Tapray** (1738–1819), who collected Haydn autographs—perhaps his veneration for the Austrian master led Tapray to compose, in the manner of Haydn's Quartets Op. 20, a *fuga a tre sogetti* in his Organ Concerto Op. 1 No. 1. Tapray composed in that fateful Mozartian year 1778 a *Simphonie concertante* in E flat (Op. 9) for harpsichord, fortepiano, violin and orchestra—a highly original and attractive work with a slow movement of delicate French sentiment.

C. P. E. Bach

Germany was divided then, as it is now, into two widely differing cultural worlds—north and south. In the northern, Protestant part—Catholic

Dresden was an amazing exception, also architecturally—the influence of the Bach family was still paramount. There is a theory that **Carl Philipp Emanuel Bach** (1714–1788) wrote his greatest music when his father was still alive, e.g. the brilliant *Magnificat* of 1749 and the austerely beautiful Concerto in D minor for harpsichord and strings of 1748. But of course, he composed enormously and interestingly after he left for Hamburg in 1767, where he spent the rest of his life.

Emanuel Bach composed over 50 concertos, nearly all for harpsichord, though several of these also exist in versions for flute, oboe or cello. His restless, probing spirit created music of intense originality, characterized by striking, wide-ranging melodic lines, discontinuities of texture, with sudden explosive outbursts and strange harmonic twists, and an unfailingly adventurous approach to form. The concertos he wrote in Berlin during the 1740s and 1750s are rooted in Baroque forms and techniques, particularly the Vivaldian *ritornello* design. But Emanuel Bach's expressive language is always highly personal, with a spiky, nervous vitality in the *allegros* (above all in the magnificent D minor concerto (W23) of 1748) and a deeply affecting vein of sentiment in the slow movements. One of the finest such pieces is the *largo* from the A major concerto (W29) of 1753 (a work later transcribed for both flute and cello), in which sighing appoggiaturas, syncopations, abrupt dynamic contrasts and a high density of chromaticism combine to produce music of searching introspection. The equally intense slow movement of the C minor concerto (W31) is an astonishing conception, with eloquent recitatives for the soloist and extreme fluctuations of tempo, from *adagio* to *presto*.

The concertos Emanuel Bach wrote in Hamburg during the last 20 years of his life owe rather less to Baroque techniques and more to the new sonata style. The orchestration, which in the earlier concertos was usually confined to strings, is now frequently enriched with flutes and/or horns, creating a more 'modern' sonority, while many of the thematic ideas approach a Classical poise and balance. But the later concertos are as bold and exploratory as ever. Particularly fine is the set of six harpsichord concertos (W43) of 1771, which abound in characteristic formal experiment: in the C minor concerto, No. 4, where the first movement breaks off surprisingly and is then resumed after a slow movement and a minuet; in No. 2 in D, where the opening movement alternates a fiery *allegro di molto* and a lyrical *andante*; and in the G major, No 5, where the slow introduction to the capricious opening *presto* later initiates the central *adagio*. Throughout the set, movements run into each other without a break, creating abrupt, sometimes disconcerting changes of mood. Another salient feature of these concertos is the quasi-improvisatory nature of much of the keyboard writing, brilliantly fanciful in the faster pieces, rhapsodic and self-communing in the slow movements.

Emanuel Bach's brothers all composed rewarding concertos: the so-called 'Bückeburg' Bach, **Johann Christoph Friedrich** (1732–1795) composed one amazing concerto for pianoforte and viola with orchestra. His dissolute but gifted brother **Wilhelm Friedmann** (1710–1784) composed several harpsichord concertos, of which certainly one (Falk 43, E minor) was composed during the composer's Halle period (1767–70). But the most influential concertos by the Bach sons were composed by Johann Christian (1735–1782), whose work we shall examine when discussing England.

Frederick The Great was a distinguished amateur flautist, and at his court there was a regular round of flute concertos in the Baroque style composed by the king himself, or by J. J. Quantz (whose theoretical works were mentioned above), and by a whole family of Bohemian musicians called **Benda**—all with immense talents, lasting until the late conductor Hans von Benda, whose pioneer work for the gramophone brought to light many then unknown delights of the classical period (including works by his ancestors). Among the Benda family, the harpsichord concertos by Georg (1722–1795) are far more interesting in their austere, north German way than the more celebrated violin concertos of his elder brother Franz (1709–1786). It is typical that most of Georg's keyboard concertos are in the minor key (there is a particularly stormy one in F minor composed in the late 1770s).

In the softer, more relaxed world of southern Germany, the concerto flourished: it had a centre at a distinguished small court, presided over by the genial Prince Krafft-Ernst von Oettinger-Wallerstein, at whose pretty castle in Wallerstein there was a first-rate orchestra for which Haydn composed symphonies (and in 1790 conducted them too, on the spot). There were two distinguished composers in residence there: **F. A. Rosetti** (actually Rösler, a Bohemian, 1746–1792) and **Friedrich Witt** 1770–1837), a native German. Both wrote many concertos, but their works for one and two horns are especially important because they influenced Mozart, and indeed in the case of Rosetti were direct Mozartian models. They make delightful listening today, and many have been published and recorded: the Romance-like slow movements in tripartite form will be found in Mozart's horn concertos. And Rosetti's finale tunes sound uncannily like Mozart, who took over the type unabashedly.

Spain: Boccherini

In Yves Gérard's catalogue of works of **Luigi Boccherini**[1] (1743–1805), we find no less than ten cello concertos, but the evidence of their collective and

1. *Thematic, Bibliographical and Critical Catalogue of the Works of Luigi Boccherini*, London, 1969, pp. 527–52.

individual authenticity requires further research. We may take as genuine the four works published in Paris in 1770 and 1771 by the Bureau d'Abbonement musical (Gérard 477, 479, 480, 481) where they appeared as 'Concerto I [II, III, IV] per il violoncello obligato', and Gérard 483, which was published by Artaria in Vienna in 1785 as Op. 34 (Boccherini was in direct contact with the firm at this period, as we know from letters). Op. 34 is a much more substantial work, with extended development and a larger orchestra (available in a good modern edition by Ricordi). The famous B flat Cello Concerto (Gérard 482), which may—despite the barbarous arrangement by Friedrich Grützmacher in 1895—be authentic, is published by Eulenburg (using the only known source, a manuscript score in Dresden). On the other hand, the Violin Concerto in D (Gérard 486), with its similarities to Mozart's K 218, is a twentieth-century forgery, while the Flute Concerto in D (Gérard 489) is actually by the Regensburg composer F. X. Pokorny. The Harpsichord Concerto in E flat (Gérard 487), which exists only in a set of manuscript parts (the harpsichord part is supposed to be authentic, but that assertion is doubtful) in Dresden, might be genuine. But despite this maze of problems regarding authenticity, there *is* such a thing as the Boccherini concerto style, and it is very different from that of other masters—the pace is slower, also literally (with leisurely *allegros* that are, in effect, in 8/8 time), the writing for the cello is superbly idiomatic, the orchestration primitive (compared to Haydn or Mozart) but the sensuous melodies often irresistible. Most of these concertos were written in Spain, or in the brief period 1767–9 when Boccherini was touring Italy and France with his fellow-Luccan violinist, Filippo Manfredi.

Boccherini was undoubtedly the leading composer in Spain about 1770, but he was not alone. Recent research in Catalán archives by Josep M. Vilar has revealed a large number of hitherto unknown and unpublished works of the eighteenth century, including many symphonies, *concertanti* and concertos. Another Italian musician working in Spain for the Duke of Alba (who adored Haydn) was **Gaetano Brunetti** (*c.* 1740–1808), whose symphonic work (with many *concertante* elements) has been recently published by his American biographer Newell Jenkins (in the Garland series). There was also one set of concertos by a local Spaniard, Padre **Antonio Soler** (1729–1783). In the Library of El Escorial are preserved the manuscripts of his Six Concertos for two organs, 'for the diversion of SS^{mo} Infante de España Dn. Gabriel de Borbon'—delightful and sophisticated music which has been revived with great success in our time.

England

In England foreigners dominated the scene, as they had done for the whole century. Always a conservative country in its musical tastes, the thriving British concerto tradition stemmed from Handel, whose *concerti grossi* and organ concertos inspired the organ concertos of such local composers as William Felton (1715–1769), Charles Avison (1710–1770) and John Stanley (1713–1786): all very Handelian, as were the sprightly works of William Boyce (1710–1779). But by 1763 the *galant* concerto tradition had arrived in England in the form of J. S. Bach's youngest son, **Johann Christian** (1735–1782); it was in that year that he published his Op. 1, Six Harpsichord Concertos dedicated to the Queen (whose music master he had became the year before). They were very simply scored, with only two violins and a cello, and so could be played either with orchestra or as chamber music. The same scoring appears in his Op. 7, whereas 'A Third Sett of Six Concertos for the Harpsichord or Piano Forte' Op. xiii, uses two oboes and horns *ad libitum*. Here was the graceful and charming *galant* at perhaps its most characteristic. Johann Christian also composed concertos for flute, oboe and violin, and he excelled in the new *symphonie concertante*, scoring them for up to four solo instruments. Bach's great strength was his consummate ability to unite beautiful, singing melodies with the sturdy orchestration and nervous bass lines of the European symphonic tradition. His music was perhaps the most important single influence on the young Mozart, who arrived with his family in London in 1764.

Among the many foreigners in London we might single out the keyboard concertos by **Johann Samuel Schroeter** (1750–1788), whose wife Rebecca later became Haydn's intimate friend. Schroeter's concertos were widely admired—also by Mozart—for their weighty tone and solid craftsmanship.

The Concerto Parallel to Mozart (1781–1800)

As Mozart was composing his now famous violin concertos in Salzburg in the middle 1770s and his epochal piano concertos in Vienna in the 1780s, Europe produced an enormous number of concertos, even a systematic listing of which would fill all the remaining pages of this survey. We do not propose to attempt such a list, but rather to concentrate on a few of the greatest works. What purpose can there be in discussing endless mediocrity?

The Italians continued to lose interest in the concerto. As before, their principal area of activity was the opera; instrumental music was always a dispensable luxury, and usually—but as we shall see, not always—their concertos reflected this attitude. **Muzio Clementi**'s (1752–1832) one known piano concerto (in C, preserved in a manuscript copy by Beethoven's teacher Johann Schenk, dated 1796, in the Gesellschaft der Musikfreunde,

Vienna) is a surprisingly unadventurous work which was soon turned into a piano sonata (Op. 33 No. 3, 1794). And **Domenico Cimarosa**'s (1749–1801) Harpsichord Concerto in B flat (edited by G. C. Ballola), despite its introduction of a whole scene—Recitativo and Aria *(Largo)*—from the world of opera, is a very mediocre composition. If there is any one piece of evidence to show the staggering influence of Mozart, it is in Cimarosa's one great Concerto, that for two flutes in G, composed in 1793 in Vienna where he was producing his operatic masterpiece *Il matrimonio segreto*, and where he was in close proximity with Mozart's music. This ravishingly beautiful Cimarosa Concerto is one of the real musicological finds of our age.

The one great exception to our rule about the opera-loving Italians is in the life and works of **Giovan Battista Viotti** (1753–1824), who left his native province of Turin to settle first in Paris and then in London. Although primarily a violin virtuoso who revolutionized violin technique, Viotti was a very considerable composer, not least of a couple of dozen violin concertos. Forced to flee Italy, J. P. Salomon (Haydn's impresario) offered him a haven in London, where he arrived in 1792 to become a celebrity overnight in the Salomon concerts at Hanover Square in 1793. By 1794 Haydn and Viotti were appearing together, and Viotti was composing his masterpiece, the Violin Concerto No. 22 in A minor, a magnificent work with Romantic, even tragic, overtones, with a rich score including clarinets, trumpets and drums. Although Viotti's great work is now rather less in evidence than it was even a hundred years ago, it is a mountain in the dreary landscape of monotonous third-rate violin concertos with which Europe was filled at this period.

As the century was ending, England was bringing forth another foreign genius—**Johann Ladislaus Dussek** (1760–1812)—a great pianist whose beautiful legato touch and Chopin-like dexterity with passage work made him a major influence, even on Beethoven. His dozen piano concertos, though uneven, are on occasion brilliantly composed and would repay revival (some have been edited in our age). When they were first played during Haydn's initial seasons in London, Dussek's concertos were greatly admired.

One of Haydn's pupils, **Ignaz Pleyel** (1757–1831), became for a time much more popular than his teacher. Pleyel's music had many of Haydn's stylistic characteristics but carried to the point of caricature in Pleyel's later music. He composed a large amount of both concertos and *symphonies concertantes*, whose placid content and flaccid presentation make it astonishing to us that he should have been considered as a potential successor to Haydn; but no less a man than Mozart thought it would be a good thing for music if Pleyel could 'in time replace Haydn'.

Haydn's Later Concertos

Pleyel's *symphonies concertantes* were one of the genres of music he took with him to London in 1792 when the Professional Concert set him up in opposition to his old teacher Haydn. Actually the 'battle' came to nothing because the two opponents did not enter into the fray, but it caused a great deal of pressure to be put on Haydn, who suddenly found he had to compose a large amount of new music. One of the new works was a 'Concertante' in B flat for oboe, bassoon, violin and cello with large orchestra (1: 105), which Haydn composed quickly in 1792 to counter the many popular *symphonies concertantes* which Pleyel brought with him from Paris and with which he flooded the Professional Concert. Haydn's work is, of course, much superior to those of his erstwhile pupil and beautifully written for the four soloists, but it cannot be said that the genial, relaxed 'Concertante' is quite on the level of the very greatest London Symphonies.

There are a number of other concertos by Haydn composed in the 1780s and 1790s which require our attention. The first is the famous Cello Concerto in D of 1783, long thought to be the work of the principal cellist in the Esterházy orchestra of the time, Anton Kraft. Now that Haydn's autograph manuscript has been discovered his authorship is assured, though it is entirely possible that much of the extremely difficult passage-work, flageolet tones, etc., were 'tailor-made' for Kraft, and on the whole the work has always proved more fascinating to cellists than to the public. (The fact that there are no great cello concertos at all, with the exceptions of Dvořák's and Elgar's, must tell us something about the unsatisfactory character of the genre.)

In 1786 Haydn probably completed six delicious concertos for the eccentric King Ferdinand of Naples and the Two Sicilies: five (VIIh: 1–5) have survived and were not printed until 1959. The king played a kind of improved hurdy-gurdy with a small built-in organ called the *lira organizzata*, an obsolete instrument which can be easily replaced by flute or oboe. Haydn wrote the concertos for two *lire organizzate*, and when he composed a similar set of *Notturni* for the king in 1789 and 1790, he later used them in London, substituting two flutes, or flute and oboe, for the two lira parts. Otherwise, the concertos are scored for horns, two violins, two violas and bass line, and hence can be performed either as chamber music or with an orchestra. They are among Haydn's loveliest concertos—music with a real touch of the south wind in them—and he used two in symphonies: one in F (VIIh: 5) in Symphony No. 89 (second and fourth movements); and one in G (VIIh: 3) contained a 'Romance' which Haydn later expanded and reorchestrated as the slow movement of the 'Military' Symphony, No. 100—a piece that turned out to be the biggest success of Haydn's English career. Yet another

Ex. 1

movement—of Concerto No. 2 (VIIh: 2)—was taken from an insertion aria (the Cavatina, 'Sono Alcina', in Gazzaniga's opera *L'isola di Alcina*, Eszterháza 1786). Haydn obviously thought that the King of Naples would like a movement based on an Italian opera, and he was not mistaken; for Ferdinand soon ordered more music from Haydn (the above-mentioned *Notturni*). As an example of this sophisticated music, here is the beginning of Concerto No. 5 in F. We have come a long way from the noisy tuttis of a typical Italian concerto of the 1760s. Here, the solo instruments creep into a panorama of what we would call Mozartian subtlety, though it is quite as characteristic of Haydn too at this period of the 'Paris' Symphonies and 'Tost' Quartets.

Haydn's final Concerto is an extraordinary affair. It is a work for keyed trumpet in E flat, a trumpet with keys which enabled it to play all the chromatic notes of the scale. This 'keyed bugle' had a considerable success after its invention and perfection by the Viennese court trumpeter Anton

Ex. 2

Weidinger. Haydn's was the first known piece of music written for it (1796), but the instrument persisted right up to Bellini's *Norma*, the autograph manuscript of which clearly specifies keyed trumpets.

It took Weidinger four years before he dared to perform Haydn's taxing concerto in public, which he did in the spring of 1800 at the Burgtheater in Vienna, shortly before Beethoven's big benefit concert in the same house (where the First Symphony was performed for the first time, also the Third Piano Concerto in C minor in its first state with the reduced keyboard). J. N. Hummel (1778–1837) also wrote a trumpet concerto for Weidinger in E major, a delightful work, which however already belongs to the budding nineteenth century.

Haydn's Concerto (VIIe: 1) is without any question his greatest, certainly his most popular work in the form. It is music which effortlessly combines novelty, brilliance of orchestration and good tunes; the music is also perfectly suited to the trumpet. It is now an indispensable work for trumpeters, while the public loves its virtuoso gyrations and scintillating finale—an uproarious conclusion to a work of sense and sensibility, whose flamboyance is tempered by the mellow lyricism and chromatic subtlety of Haydn's ripest style. The slow movement is pure poetry; and we cannot resist from quoting the last wistful finale theme appearance, just before the end of the work (Ex. 2). It is the only concerto of the period to be worthy of Mozart's Clarinet Concerto of 1791—and that is the highest compliment an eighteenth-century wind concerto can have.

CHAPTER 3

Mozart and the Concerto

Denis Matthews

Mozart enriched practically every musical form that he encountered, but it is generally agreed that two genres in particular give the most comprehensive views of his genius: opera and concerto. He was drawn to both at all stages of his career. There are, moreover, cross-currents between these very different media. Opera thrived on the development of the Classical style, and the arias and ensembles in *Figaro* and *Don Giovanni* owed much to Mozart's experience as a composer of sonatas and symphonies. The concerto, especially the solo concerto, is in its nature dramatic: the opposition of the individual and the multitude may even be traced back to the Greek tragedies of Aeschylus. Before Mozart's time the vocal aria, whether in opera or oratorio, struck a parallel with the Baroque concerto's alternation of orchestral *ritornello* and solo paragraphs. Even the cadenza, a regular feature of the Classical concerto, could trace its origins to the expansion and embellishment of a singer's final cadence. But the parallels in Mozart's case were strengthened by his keen observation of human emotions and his ability to translate their infinite shades and conflicts into musical terms. His operatic characters live through his craft of composition, and this in turn affected the emotional range and dramatic overtones of his instrumental music. It was once said that 'all Mozart is opera', a gross simplification maybe. Yet many pianists playing his early E flat Concerto, K271, with its premature solo entry must have felt the theatrical humour of the situation, like an operatic character appearing before the curtain after the first bar of the overture.

The evolution of the concerto from its Italian origins to the Classical masterpieces of Mozart and Beethoven has been obscured by the fact that pioneers are not necessarily great composers. The normal concert repertory leaps from Bach and Vivaldi into Mozart, but what of Tartini, Monn, Wagenseil, Vanhal, the Stamitz family and others who bridged the gap between the Baroque and Classical styles? Even the concertos by Bach's sons Carl Philip Emanuel and Johann Christian are hardly repertory works, though Mozart owed much to both. His early experiments in concerto form included arrangements of three sonatas by J. C. Bach, in which he had already grasped the principles of good concerto writing, delaying vital key-changes until the entry of the solo, holding back some secondary material, exploiting antiphony and repartee, and adding cadenzas and cadence-themes. These adaptations are now thought to date from 1772, seven years after the child Mozart's meeting with J. C. Bach in London. Meanwhile, in 1767 at the age of eleven, he compiled four other keyboard concertos from sonata-movements by various composers. His interest in the medium was kept alive by the need for new works to play himself, and it is worth noting that his greatest contemporary, Haydn, as a more modest performer, contributed far less to the history of the form. The advent of the fortepiano was to be a further incentive and it would be a misguided purism to play Mozart's earlier concertos on the harpsichord. His first original one, K175 in D, was composed at Salzburg in 1773, but he revived it in Vienna nine years later, wrote a new rondo for it, and obviously played it on the new instrument.

Although Mozart's concertos for the piano were by far his greatest achievement in this genre, most of his works for other instruments have become fairly firm repertory pieces. They include five for violin, a Concertone for two violins and the Sinfonia Concertante for violin and viola; solo concertos for flute, oboe, clarinet, bassoon and horn, as well as the doubtful Concertante for four wind players dating from Mozart's visit to Paris in 1778; the Concerto for flute and harp also dates from that time; and there are rondos and other alternative or isolated movements as well as lost and fragmentary pieces.

Piano Concertos

The conventional numbering of the piano concertos invites confusion. There are in fact 21 for solo piano with two alternative rondos, one concerto for two pianos and one for three; but the Breitkopf collected edition began its series with the four miscellaneous arrangements already mentioned, making a total of 27 and calling the first original concerto 'No. 5'. This misleading system did not account for the J. C. Bach transcriptions though it is still in common use. The Köchel numbers are the surest means of identification.

First came the transcriptions in which Mozart's father Leopold may or may not have had a hand. Though slight in musical substance they had great value as apprentice works. The handling of the orchestral opening, a legacy from the *ritornello* of the Baroque concerto, was a vital feature. Stability of key was the norm, unlike the exposition of a sonata-form movement where a firm move to the dominant or relative major is awaited. Only one of Mozart's later concertos, K449 in E flat, gave the orchestra its head at this point, but this was exceptional. Meanwhile, it did not require great ingenuity to modify sonata beginnings by J. C. Bach in K107 or Raupach and Honauer in the four composite works K37 and K39–41 and to transplant the crucial bars into the subsequent solo section. Other movements in that earlier series came from C. P. E. Bach, Schobert and Eckard. The modest scoring with the keyboard serving as continuo made both sets ideal as travelling concertos on Mozart's youthful tours; and the range of texture in accompanying passages already shows his instinct for the medium. As a practical musician he wrote dispensable wind parts that added support and colour without disturbing the integrity of the strings who could play on their own if the wind was absent. Back in Salzburg the orchestral forces were more predictable, but even there he generally wrote for safety. A glance at the scores of the piano concertos up to K449 in E flat will show that they are mostly playable with strings alone, a situation that changed radically from K450 onwards with the prevalence of good wind players in Vienna.

Nevertheless, he added trumpets and drums as well as the expected oboes and horns in his first original concerto, K175 in D. It was a key with festive associations and the resonance of orchestral open strings added to the brilliance. In 1773 listeners must have been struck in the outer movements by the unremitting liveliness of the solo part, as much suited to the harpsichord as to the fortepiano. There is great reliance on the Alberti bass and its variants, those busy left-hand patterns that became a standby in the Classical period. They are used more discreetly in the slow movement, which has a tenderness of expression that sets it above such models as J. C. Bach. Although his style and skill were to develop rapidly, Mozart thought highly enough of K175 to revive it in 1782, but discarding the finale in favour of the easy-going Rondo, K382, with its simple variations, a probable reflection of the taste of his Viennese public. The original had been more robust and 'learned', beginning with a stark canon between treble and bass, self-consciously Baroque, evoking a quick response from the natural horns and trumpets, and no doubt approving nods from the Salzburg hierarchy.

The next piano concerto, K238 in B flat, was far more personal and lyrical, the first of three composed in 1776. Its warmth of heart seems to owe something to the violin concertos of the previous year. Even the traditional passage-work, the streams of semiquavers that encourage the player's virtuosity, is primarily melodic, recalling William Glock's remark that 'in Mozart the route is more important than the destination'. The slow movement too has a dreamlike quality, with its muted violins and undercurrent of triplets that soon comes to the surface, looking forward to the better known one in the C major, K467. In his study of the concertos Arthur Hutchings even went so far as to call the finale 'silly'. It serves its purpose in a more conventionally playful way, offsetting the gavotte of the rondo-theme with more rapid triplet figuration. In its middle episode the dramatic move to G minor is again a presage of later and greater things. A month later, in February 1776, there came the curiosity of a concerto for three pianos, the F major, K242, written for the Countess Lodron and her daughters. Mozart often rose to special occasions with works of genius but in this case he was content to please, writing an easier part for the third player and approving a version for two pianos. There was clearly no call for a virtuosic rondo, and the idea of a more leisurely minuet-finale was also followed in the remaining solo concerto of the year, K246 in C. Once again the heart of the music lies in the slow movement with its tenderly shaped melodic line. Elsewhere the moods and methods are more routine. The first movement, for example, has a bright epigrammatic manner that is only partly relieved by a solo second subject with more lyrical aspirations. Yet this theme planted a seed that bore fruit in two later C major concertos at parallel places, as shown in Ex. 1.

Such key associations were strong in Mozart. Three of his most original concertos shared the key of E flat and the first of them, K271, was completed less than a year after the works just discussed. Although still restricted to an orchestra of strings with optional oboes and horns, it was a remarkable breakthrough and his first really great piano concerto. One incentive was the arrival in Salzburg of the French pianist Mlle Jeunehomme, inspiring him to a new maturity of material and resource and a whole series of dramatic surprises, witty and profound, in all three movements. The first comes at the start, with the solo's immediate response to the orchestra's opening phrase, an amusing gesture Mozart never repeated in later works. It does not undermine or supplant the orchestral exposition, any more than do Beethoven's departures from tradition in his Fourth and Fifth concertos, though it established the rivalry earlier. But the piano's next entry is also premature, an impatient trill overlapping the cadence theme and recalled in

Ex. 1—solo second themes, K246, K415, K503

an unexpected re-entry after the cadenza. The first movement also impresses with its profusion of ideas and its rhythmic variety, filling its stage with operatic characters and amusingly reversing the solo and tutti roles at the moment of recapitulation.

In the *Andantino*, his first concerto movement in a minor key, Mozart created a profoundly tragic atmosphere with a low-lying theme in the strings to which the piano adds a counterpoint with stressed dissonances. The close canon between first and second violins is a good reason for separating them to left and right, a seating arrangement usually ignored in modern performances. Yet such antiphonal effects abound in the Classical and Romantic periods. Mozart's expectations seem clear in his enthusiastic letter about the Mannheim orchestra later in 1777: 'On either side there are ten or eleven violins . . .' In this slow movement of K271 the pathos is intensified by the translation of the secondary material from major to minor on the reprise, a feature of Mozart's minor-key sonata movements; and the incorporation of recitative, in the manner of C. P. E. Bach, adds an even more personal expression.

The high degree of invention is carried into the finale, an elaborate *moto perpetuo* interrupted by a spacious minuet. Writing for a visiting artist Mozart embellished the solo part with variants that could have been left to the spur of the moment when playing himself. This seems self-evident from the bare outline notated at a similar episode in the finale of the later E flat Concerto, K482. But the subject of 'bare patches', lead-ins and cadenzas raises special problems in the later concertos. The original cadenzas for K271 are ideal, though the convention remained of leaving such moments to the discretion (or indiscretion) of the player.

In September 1777 Mozart and his mother set out from Salzburg on a lengthy tour to Munich, Augsburg, Mannheim and Paris. The Parisian vogue for concertos for more than one instrument left its mark on him, as will be discussed later, and his next concerto was for two pianos, K365 in E flat, written in 1779 for performance at Salzburg with his sister Nannerl. Although avowedly entertainment music, with little place for the profound emotions of K271's slow movement, it is rewarding for the perfect sharing of interest between the two players. Their brilliant unison entry and subsequent antiphony shows how well Mozart could grasp the essence of an unusual enterprise. The orchestra's role, except in the tuttis, is naturally more subservient than usual though clarinets, trumpets and drums were later added for a Viennese revival. Meanwhile Mozart gave his pair of oboes a glimpse of limelight near the start of the slow movement, phrases that could be transferred to the strings without trouble. In the finale the winning rondo-theme pauses on a humorous, interrupted cadence that later changes the direction of the music twice. The cadenzas for the outer movements are brilliantly distributed.

The three concertos K413–15 were composed in 1782 for Mozart's new Viennese audiences. He expressed his intentions in a letter of 22 December to his father: 'There are passages here and there from which connoisseurs alone can derive satisfaction; but these passages are written in such a way that the less learned cannot fail to be pleased, though without knowing why.' All have optional wind, including the trumpets and drums of K415 in C, and can be played with strings 'a quattro', as Mozart put it. The first, K413 in F, has a wholly intimate manner, introducing the solo with a gentle overlap but relying on standard scale and arpeggio patterns for the passage-work. Even the slow movement, with its touching echoes of phrase-ends, is content with a more or less continuous Alberti bass. Nor does the finale emulate the brilliant rondos of K271 or K365, but its minuet character is no mere reversion to an earlier style. The emergence of its theme from a quiet unison and the delicate ending are subtleties for connoisseurs rather than public display.

A more outgoing melodic warmth pervades the favourite of this group, K414, known as the 'little A major' in deference to K488 in that key. K414 also illustrates the relation between themes, even between movements, that Leopold called *il filo*: the thread that binds a work together without advertising itself. A family likeness pervades the most lyrical themes of the first movement and links the opening of the concerto with the second subject of the slow movement (Ex 2). In the *Andante* Mozart began by quoting, or seeming to quote, four bars from an overture by J. C. Bach, who had recently died. Whether intended as a tribute or not, the piano leaves the phrase unembellished and offers it in an organ-like sonority. The finale, in turn capricious and tender, finds its own *filo* in the undulating unison theme that follows the opening, aptly described by Tovey as 'full of sly resource'.

Ex. 2—K414 (i) b 1–4, (ii) 2nd sub

As with K238 and K246 at Salzburg, Mozart followed a lyrical work with a more impersonal one, K415 in C. It has a grand manner: in the contrapuntal treatment of the opening formula a march rhythm that was to start off four of his six concertos of 1784; in the spacious transitions of the first movement;

and in the extended solo climax at the end of the second subject. The brilliant build-up before handing back to the orchestra in mid-movement, so familiar from Beethoven's concertos, had become a regular feature. The evidence of sketches suggests that Mozart planned a C minor *Adagio* instead of the eventual ornate F major *Andante*, but this has some bearing on the slow episodes in that key that interrupt the otherwise carefree 6/8 rondo that ends, like K413, in a subdued *pianissimo*. Two so-called 'concert' rondos also date from 1782: the D major, K382, a set of variations provided a more relaxed ending for the first concerto K175; while the gently lyrical A major, K386, was possibly intended as the original finale of K414.

Two years later the demand for new works increased. In 1784, an *annus mirabilis* for the piano concerto, Mozart produced half a dozen, to be followed by a further six in 1785 and 1786. In this astonishing output quantity was matched by quality. Mozart wrote to his father about the first four of this series, all completed in the spring of 1784, explaining that only the E flat (K449) would be of much use in Salzburg 'since you rarely have wind-players at your house'. It is, in fact, the only one to retain optional wind parts: Alan Tyson's researches have now shown that Mozart began work on its two years before at the time of the previous group and then set it aside. With or without its oboes and horns, K449's operatic overtones are obvious from the opening tutti, as if he already foresaw the characters and situations in *Figaro*. 'I should dearly like to try my hand at an Italian opera' he had written in the previous May, having just met his future librettist Lorenzo da Ponte. The give-and-take in this lively 3/4 movement is more mercurial than ever, culminating in a vigorous exchange of trills in the development but not excluding moments of tenderness, even mystery. Such was to be Mozart's enhancement of the language of *opera buffa*. After this vitality the *Andantino* unfolds a serene long-breathed melody with richly expressive inner voices: as in K414, Mozart seemed sure of his violas. The key-scheme is rich too, with settlements in F, A flat and E flat before the return home to B flat for an apotheosis of both subjects, rounded off with an inspired postscript based on the simple linking figure that had ushered in the solo (Ex. 3).

Whereas this brief dialogue offers one aspect of true concerto writing, the through-composed nature of the finale invites co-operation rather than antiphony, most of its adventures being taken in the strides of its staccato crotchet subject. Soon after the piano entry the crotchets give way to continous quaver movement: all the rondo-returns are inventively varied, including the start of the 6/8 coda. This concerto, like K453 in G, was written for Babette Ployer, daughter of the Salzburg agent in Vienna for whom Haydn was to compose his F minor Variations nine years later. Although there are calls for bravura as well as delicacy in both K449 and K453, the

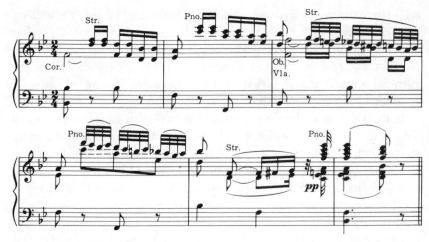

Ex. 3—K449 (ii) b 119–124

intervening concertos, K450 and K451, were the ones, in Mozart's words, 'to make the player perspire', especially the former.

K450 in B flat is a landmark, quite apart from its double thirds in the first movement and the cross-rhythms and rapidly crossing hands in the finale. It was the first piano concerto to bring complete emancipation of the wind, and it is hardly accidental that the superlative Quintet in E flat for piano and wind dates from the same month of March 1784. Mozart was quick to explore these new possibilities of colour and antiphony. Oboes and bassoons have the first word in K450 and the conversational nature of the music would be lost without them. On the other hand, the wind entry in the *Andante* is delayed until mid-movement, where the variation-theme is suddenly taken over with marvellous effect against pizzicato strings and piano arpeggios, while in the finale the first oboe and newly added flute discourse with the piano as soloists in their own right. Apart from the Rondo, K382, the *Andante* was Mozart's first concerto movement in variation-form, to be adopted again in K456 and the finales of K453 and K491; and the final rondo was one of several in a 6/8 'hunting' style. Memories of his recent horn concertos are clinched by the wind fanfares in the closing bars.

If the importance of the wind in K450 leads to special brilliance and technical hurdles in the piano part, the addition of trumpets and drums in the D major, K451, imparts a grandeur to its first movement, in spite of its more conventional keyboard writing. The neglect of this work, usually blamed on its rather trivial finale, was sufficient for its cadenza to be wrongly attributed to the 'Coronation' Concerto in the same key. Considering that it was completed within a week of K450 its finale may be forgiven for being lightweight, and haste may also explain the query from Mozart's sister about the C major solo halfway through the slow movement. 'She is quite right in saying that there is something missing', he wrote, supplying the deficiency by sending a more ornate version, a *locus classicus* for players confronted with similar passages in the later concertos (Ex. 4).

(Variant)

Ex. 4—K451 (ii) b 56–59 (2 versions)

The miracle continued. Three weeks later Mozart finished the G major Concerto, K453, a work of exquisite proportions, light, transparent textures and continuing glory for the wind players. The very first bar picks up the martial rhythm familiar from the openings of K415 and K451 transforming it into a graceful melodic phrase. This lightness of manner does not exclude harmonic audacity, whether the stressed F natural in the fourth bar or the mysterious dissonance that appears during the second subject and after the cadenza. Perhaps the delicacy of the piano writing, after the robuster manner of the two previous concertos, owes something to the talents of Babette Ployer, which players on modern instruments should bear in mind when accompanying woodwind dialogues with traceries of arpeggios. The slow movement, like so many of Mozart's, is unique in structure. A serene but questioning theme, with shades of the 'Et incarnatus est' from the Mass in C minor, pauses after a half-close and calls forth a variety of responses in as many keys—tranquil, dramatic, pathetic, jubilant—until the piano finds its ideal matching phrase in the coda. The wind are again richly expressive; and the key-scheme in this elaborate sonata-form movement is far ranging, with an astonishing return to C major from distant sharp regions at the reprise. For the variation theme of the finale Mozart recorded his debt to a pet starling and in so doing pre-glimpsed the musical character of his bird-catcher Papageno in *The Magic Flute*. The variations, full of rhythmic resource, include a gravely thoughtful one in the minor; but in the end they break off for one of his most entertaining surprises, a pure *opera buffa* finale in which, as Tovey amusingly put it, 'the original theme romps in among the other conspirators as if it had known them all its life'.

Variations of a different kind are the heart of the next concerto, K456 in B flat. Here it is the G minor slow movement, a key Mozart often turned to for expressions of pathos, and in fact the second half of the binary theme expands its expected eight bars to thirteen as though under the pressure of profound emotion. Otherwise K456, despite its spaciousness, is rich in epigrams, and, if the theme of the 'hunting' rondo seems four-square, the finale compensates with a middle episode that moves to the remote key of B minor for an impassioned outburst in which wind and then piano play off in 2/4 against the prevailing 6/8. It was apparently written for the blind Viennese pianist Maria Theresia von Paradis to play in Paris, but Mozart certainly performed it during his father's visit to Vienna in 1785. Leopold wrote home about 'the interplay of the instruments' that brought tears to his eyes, and of the Emperor's shout of 'Bravo Mozart!'. The slow-movement variations had included one in a strongly contrapuntal manner. But the revival of the earlier 'learned' style was to be more wittily displayed in the finale of the last of the 1784 concertos, K459 in F.

Nor is the first movement of K459 without its contrapuntal interest in the strettos and canons that arise from the well-worn yet ever fresh dotted rhythm. If there is less operatic influence it is supplanted by an intellectual delight in economy of material, more typical of Haydn and sometimes described as monothematicism for its tendency to iron out the usual thematic contrasts. There are other themes in abundance, as we expect of a Mozart first movement; but they mostly give way to further developments of the basic idea. In the 6/8 pastoral *Allegretto* too, the opening phrase grows into a canonic 'second subject' with rising woodwind scales as in Susanna's nocturnal aria 'Deh vieni'. Mozart did not begin *Figaro* in earnest until the following autumn, but the influences between opera and instrumental music were reciprocal. The finale in a lower octave could make a lively *buffo* aria until the patter of piano and wind is interrupted by a peremptory exhibition of counterpoint from the full orchestra: the combination of the two ideas is brilliantly exploited in the development.

After the six concertos of 1784 Mozart finished K466 in D minor on 10 February 1785 and K467 in C on 9 March, playing each on the day after completion. One wonders how the orchestra coped with the difficult arpeggios in the finale of the D minor at such short notice, but Leopold reported that Mozart played magnificently. K466, popular with the Romantics, was his first in a minor key. As always, he was quick to explore the art and pathos in turning major-key themes into minor and vice versa, seen already in the slow movement of K271. The drama of the first movement of K466 was also intensified by dynamic contrasts: the subdued agitation of the opening syncopations, the powerful tutti passages, the tender cadence-theme leading to the new subject of the solo entry. The idea of introducing the piano with new material had been tried before, in K450 for example, but never with such an eloquent theme. This theme remains the solo's property, returning in various keys in the development, a procedure followed in the only other minor-key concerto, the C minor, K491. Arthur Hutchings criticized the slow movement for its oft repeated refrain and its stock-in-trade material, but this is to discount the stormy G minor episode and the fact that Mozart undoubtedly decorated the returns of the Romance theme, which provides a needed charm and repose in surroundings of storm and stress. The piano opens the finale with a spectacular 'Mannheim rocket', the arpeggio figure that challenges strings and wind in turn, but the movement also includes a witty subject far removed from the pathos of the first movement. This returns in D major in the wholly sunlit coda with a comic aside from horns and trumpets in the *opera buffa* spirit that had marked the ending of K453.

K467 in C starts in a more delicately poised operatic manner: a quiet march in the strings punctuated by wind and drums. Continuity is to be provided by the dovetailing of the solo entry, a device used only sparingly by Mozart. Then, in the subsequent transition, there is the sudden plunge into G minor, deepening the proceedings with a dramatic gesture that never returns. Something similar happens in the first movement of K482 in E flat, but in K467 the key of G minor produced a remarkable prophecy of the famous symphony of three years later (Ex. 5). This is a passing phase:

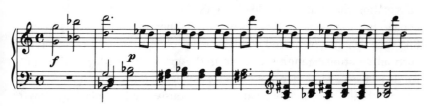

Ex. 5—K467 (i) b 109–114

elsewhere, the mood is bright, with passage-work of purposeful variety, including the bracingly dissonant figuration following in the wake of the solo's radiant second subject. The slow movement has recently acquired an independent popularity which, as with the *Adagio* of the 'Moonlight' Sonata, may lead one to take its sublimity for granted. The gentle triplet motion, the wide leaps in the theme's continuation and the advanced harmonic complexes that cast temporary shadows over its serenity: all these make it another unique experience. In the finale, witty and volatile, it is the motivic development of the opening bars that commands attention, particularly in the fierce exchanges between left-hand octaves and low oboes and bassoons in the middle episode.

In the winter season of 1785–6 Mozart must have been sure of his clarinets. The next three—K482, K488 and K491—were the only solo piano concertos to include them. K482, entered in Mozart's catalogue on 16 December, is notable for the splendour of the wind sonorities in all three movements. The key of E flat was a favoured one for clarinets and the resolute opening another case of key-association: compare the late E flat Symphony, the Sinfonia Concertante, K364, the Wind Serenade, K375. K482 was called the Queen of the concertos by Girdlestone, no doubt referring to the grandeur of the first movement. The recapitulation is particularly rich in combining elements from both orchestral and solo expositions, an unpredictable order of events to be met again in the first movements of K491 and K503. Mozart turned to C minor for the slow movement as he had done in the early E flat Concerto, K271: there is a spiritual affinity between their grave themes, scored with muted violins. But K482's mixture of variations and episodes is again unique in its relations between piano and orchestra. The wind-band, having been silent during the theme and the first solo variation, take over in a self-contained serenade (E flat) in which piano and strings have no part. In the second episode flute and bassoon join the strings for the first time in an ethereal duet (C major) and the piano is again content to listen. All the orchestral forces then gather themselve for a final variation in which their full strength is at last subdued by gentle solo replies, even anticipating the *Andante* of Beethoven's Fourth Concerto. It is left for the coda to tie up these varied events by turning the rustic clarinet duet from the first episode into a piano and wind exchange of pure pathos. In keeping with such an emotional range the finale is the grandest of Mozart's 'hunting' rondos. Like K271, it incorporates a slower *Andantino* section but now with clarinets to the fore, and the piano part obviously needs amplifying from the mere outline noted by Mozart for his own use.

The well-known A major Concerto, K488, has its own structural surprise in the first movement. Much has been made of the orthodox treatment of the solo, which is largely content to follow the material of the opening tutti. The surprise is the delayed arrival of a new theme that dominates the development and is recalled before the cadenza (Ex. 6). This is, moreover, an orchestral proposal—had the solo forgotten its usual extra subject matter?—and the piano follows with a variation, avoiding direct competition with the cantabile of the strings. This simple reporting does not account for the special warmth of heart of all the lyrical themes, including a first subject closely related to the Clarinet Quintet and Clarinet Concerto. The F sharp minor *Adagio*—not *Andante* as in some editions—shows how well

Ex. 6—K488 (i) E major theme

Mozart could differentiate between solo and orchestral material: a piano theme with poignantly wide intervals, and an orchestral sequel in closely woven counterpoint. Whether or not to decorate the bare notes of the solo part towards the end has always been controversial. Arthur Hutchings believed the simple version so striking as to be intended; Tovey, on the other hand, wrote that he claimed to be an absolute purist in *not* confining himself to the text. The finale, full of the spirit of *Figaro*, would again be unthinkable without its woodwind: the D major clarinet and piano duet, the virtuoso bassoon bass later imitated by the solo.

The C minor Concerto, K491, has the richest wind section of all, oboes as well as clarinets, and is arguably the greatest of the series in its range and dramatic force. Its haste of composition is shown in the autograph: the orchestral parts clear and ready for the copyist, the piano part full of crossings-out, alternative passage-work and skeletal outlines. There is an important structural change in the first movement too, affecting the order of events in the opening tutti, and the re-entry of the piano with quietly fluttering arpeggios in the closing bars may have influenced Beethoven's concerto in the same key. The presence of oboes and clarinets enabled Mozart to display each in turn in the wind episodes of the slow movement, a rondo of the Romance type which calls for improvised lead-ins and perhaps embellishments. In the finale variation form enabled Mozart to exploit a wide range of textures. Again, there are two episodes in which the wind lead, lightening the mood with major keys, though unlike the D minor Concerto the work ends in the minor. It was of a recurring Neapolitan phrase in the coda that Beethoven remarked: '*we* shall never get an idea like this'.

For the next season, in December 1786, Mozart composed K503 in C, another work on a grand scale and far removed from the worlds of *Figaro* or *Don Giovanni*. Any operatic influences are those of *opera seria* and the derivation of the rondo theme from a gavotte in the ballet-music to *Idomeneo* seems symbolic. This was the work that the young Czerny played to Beethoven at their first meeting in 1800. Some have found it frigid and austere, but Tovey chose it to illustrate his article 'The Classical Concerto'. Its grandeur is Olympian. Those who expect the lyric grace of K488 may be surprised at the spacious procession of tonic and dominant chords that opens the first movement. There is a ceremonious air about the continuing ideas too, a short Beethovenish motive treated in counterpoint and a formal march in C minor that is bypassed in the piano's second subject but recalled as the sole topic of the development. In these majestic surroundings the tentative first entry of the solo is a surprise in itself, exposing a vein of tenderness that returns in its G major theme, already mentioned as a flowering from Mozart's earlier C major concertos. The spacious time-scale is matched in the profound aria of the slow movement and the gavotte-inspired rondo, notable for the lengthy dominant preparations leading to the returns and the new significance given to fairly neutral triplet figures. But the romantic F major duet between oboe and piano is likely to remain longest in the listener's memory.

After this remarkable outpouring of concertos Mozart gave the form a rest for two years but provided a temporary postscript in the unique concert aria 'Ch'io mi scordi di te'. It was written for Nancy Storace, the first Susanna in *Figaro*, but derived its text from the new material he added for the 1786 revival of *Idomeneo*, thus forming a curious link with the rondo of K503. The aria is unique in its integration of an important piano part, as though Mozart relished the opportunity of weaving arabesques around a singer he admired. Above all it crystallizes the close relation between opera and concerto. His next piano concerto, K537 in D of 1788, was comparatively uneventful, showing the signs of a 'travelling' work with none of the woodwind glories that had elevated the great Viennese series. In fact Mozart played it in Dresden in 1789; and a year later it was apparently performed along with K459 in F at the celebrations for Leopold II in Frankfurt, leading to its popular nickname the 'Coronation'. There are some interesting chromatic touches in the first movement that add a brief 'learned' flavour to the music, and a simple charm in the romance-style *Larghetto*; but after the noble rondo of K503 the lengthy finale seems merely garrulous. The concerto has always had its admirers and was played to the exclusion of most of the greater ones during the nineteenth century, perhaps because of its nickname, perhaps because its easy charm fitted in with the limited view of Mozart as a 'period' composer.

In 1791, the last year of his life, Mozart composed one more piano concerto, K595 in B flat. It is above all an intensely personal work, revelling once more in the freedom of the wind instruments, and of a rare autumnal beauty. Its restraint may mislead those who sense a return to a simpler style, untouched, it seems, by the drama and grandeur of K491 or K503. But its simplicities are deceptive, like those of *The Magic Flute*, and its subtleties run deep. The mixture of comedy and tragedy that lies at the heart of so much of Mozart is expressed through minor-key shadows in a serenely major-key context. In the first movement the predominant lyricism overflows into the brief tuttis that punctuate the solo part, no longer 'the rattling of the dishes at a royal feast', as Wagner described the traditional *ritornelli* of the Classical concerto, but throwing out ideas for development or carrying over the melodic line from the soloist. Although the *Larghetto* cries out for embellishment in places, its main theme has such spiritual beauty that in sensitive hands its repetition does not pall. Even the finale, in the six–eight hunting rhythm so familiar by now, has a tenderly suppressed gaiety with disturbing shifts to the minor-key. There is an underlying sadness in this last piano concerto that led Eric Blom to detect a 'valedictory note'. Was Mozart somehow aware of this when he took the opening of the rondo as the starting-point for the song 'Sehnsucht nach dem Frühlinge', written only a few days after the concerto (Ex. 7)?

Komm, lie - ber Mai, und ma - che die Bäu - me wie - der grün

Ex. 7—(a) K595 (iii) b 1–4

(b) Sehnsucht nach der Frühling, b 1–4

Concertos for Strings

String concertos before Mozart had a longer and more varied history, striking back to the Italian roots of the form. In fact the evolution of the keyboard concerto from the violin concerto is clear enough from the works of J. S. Bach. He may not have invented the former, but his keyboard arrangements of his own violin concertos were the first lasting examples of an art-form that has thrived ever since. Not that Mozart would have been likely to know the Bach concertos, which were still unpublished, except perhaps by hearsay or through his childhood meetings with Johann Christian. But the genealogy of the violin concerto was also shrouded. There is no mention of Corelli or Vivaldi in Mozart's letters, and composers' names are noticeably absent from his father's *Violinschule* of 1756, the historical section being more concerned with Orpheus and Pythagoras. Yet serious musicians of the time must have been well aware of the contrast and conflict between the 'learned' and *galant* manners, nowadays lightly summed up as typical of the late Baroque and early Classical periods. Tartini, Locatelli and Viotti were also important in the development of the eighteenth-century violin concerto. So was the Mannheim school, which left clear imprints on Mozart's orchestral style. His solo violin concertos were, however, written well before his visits to Mannheim on his way to and from Paris in 1778. All five were composed at Salzburg in 1775. Apart from Leopold's paternal care the resources and influences in an oppressively provincial city were limiting; but as a child prodigy Mozart had stayed in London, Paris, Vienna and Rome, and his ears were keen.

In 1930 a Violin Concerto in D was published by Schotts of Mainz and claimed as a long-lost work composed by the ten-year-old Mozart in Versailles and dedicated to Louis XV's daughter Adelaïde. The suggestion was taken seriously by Hindemith, who wrote cadenzas for all three movements, and by the young Yehudi Menuhin, who took it on tour and recorded it. The 'Adelaïde' Concerto has since been written off as a forgery. Two other concertos are considered dubious though they may contain some genuine material. The E flat, K268, is supposed to date from 1780 but descends from acceptable themes to banalities unthinkable from the composer of *Idomeneo*. Then there is the D major Concerto, K271a, thought to be partly authentic because of its foretaste of the ballet-music *Les petits riens* and written in a virtuoso style suitable for Mozart's Paris audiences of 1778; but the manuscript, said to have been owned by the French conductor Habeneck, has disappeared and the work is not generally accepted into the canon.

The earliest 'authentic' work is the Concertone in C, K190, usually described as for two violins but containing other solo parts for oboe and cello. Its title literally means 'large concerto', hence for a group of soloists, a *concerto grosso* or *concertante*. Like the Bassoon Concerto it was composed in the summer of 1774, presumably for some Salzburg festivity, but no details are known. When Mozart played it through on the piano to his Mannheim friends in December 1777 it was declared 'just the thing for Paris', but the treatment of the solos is more conversational than brilliant. It has an amiable serenade-like atmosphere with a warmly melodic *galant* style and much reliance on simple sequences, but it opens in a festive vein and ends with a robust minuet in which the *concertante* element is purely episodic. There seems a distinct *filo* relation between the first violin entry in the *Andantino* and an engaging yodelling theme from the first movement, and there are some phrases that forecast the deeper eloquence of the Sinfonia Concertante, K364. Imitative entries in canon and passages in thirds and sixths are expected of the two violins, with any likeness to Bach's Double Concerto purely fortuitous, but the oboe discourses with them on equal terms and the cello has moments of freedom beyond its duty as a bass to the group.

In the following year Mozart devoted himself to the solo violin concerto. The incentive is uncertain: perhaps he wrote them for himself to play (though he preferred the viola) or for some other Salzburg violinist, or perhaps his father reminded him of an important genre still untouched? In any case the achievement for a 19-year-old is remarkable. The last three of the five are firm repertory works. Part of Mozart's gift was his ability to absorb influences quickly and transcend his models; but he also learnt from himself and it is hardly by chance that these five concertos progress so astonishingly in confidence and invention.

The first of the five, K207 in B flat, has all the feel of an apprentice work. Its short opening tutti, with violas doubling the bass-line throughout, lacks the decisive contrasts expected of the Classical style. Much of it is in two-part writing, harking back to the Baroque and calling for keyboard support, the lingering continuo tradition that had generally outlived its artistic purpose, yet the work's credentials are valid and its date confirmed. Nor does the soloist add much of distinction: a brief transition theme dissolves into ungainly passage-work, arbitrary exercises across the strings, and so it continues when the orchestra vainly throws out the fragment from the introduction that serves as a second subject. The development brings a more promising gesture from the solo but this too is short lived, leading to mechanical sequences of arpeggios that could come from a book of studies. The absence of genuine antiphony surprises and disappoints in view of the vast gulf Mozart was to bridge within so few months. There is more to enjoy in the *Adagio*, a simple essay in the *galant* style, and the finale makes the most of its slender material at a headlong tempo with the wit and antiphony that were missing earlier. Yet its volatile character was, it seems, too much for Gaetano Brunetti, who led the Salzburg orchestra from 1776: Mozart wrote for him the gentler Rondo, K269.

If the first movement of K207 poses a problem, the D major Concerto, K211, of June 1775 offers a solution: an opening tutti with lively textures as well as firm unison passages, and a well-defined subsidiary in the Tyrolese yodelling manner already noticed in the previous year's Concertone. When this emerges as the second subject proper the solo take-over is beautifully prepared. There is a refreshing freedom too in the treatment of the *ritornello*, the bold orchestral re-entries that highlight important points in the structure. The *Andante* also rises above the mundane sequences of its predecessor: an operatic aria recalling Aminta's 'L'amerò sarò costante' from Mozart's recent *Il Rè pastore*, which also includes a violin solo. After an imposing first movement the rondo seems unduly lightweight, a minuet fitting for a set of dances and with episodes that are content to mark time—or so it must strike one in the light of the A major Concerto of only six months later.

The G major Concerto, K216, was completed on 12 September. It seems too obvious to speak of freshness and charm, but these qualities at once raise the work above its earlier neighbours. The opening is no longer an agreeable formula but a delightful invention in which vigour yields to grace, more so in the seven-bar phrase that answers the initial four. Unlike the earlier piano concertos, where the wind were content to add support and colour, the pairs of oboes and horns are quite essential: in the tutti's main second subject with its 'horn fifths' set against a murmuring violin background, and the bridge in oboe thirds that leads to the solo entry in place of the usual rounded cadence. In the development too the first oboe takes over a new theme with soloistic aplomb and a rivalry Mozart was unable to match in the piano concertos until the rondo of K450 in B flat, perhaps because the latter were still designed as all-purpose works, for travelling or even domestic use 'a quattro'? There are elements of parody in K216 too, a moment of mock-recitative before the first-movement reprise calling for a brief filling-in by the soloist, and a change of mood, time and tempo halfway through the rondo. This G minor-major episode seems esoteric, possibly an allusion to popular or rustic music-making not lost on the Salzburg audience and with parallels in the rondos of the next two concertos. The *Adagio* is outstandingly beautiful even by Mozart's later standards and the serene opening phrase more memorable for being unaccompanied until the appoggiatura at the first half-bar. It was another inspiration to end the movement with an unexpected re-entry of the soloist in its celestial register, rounding off this phrase for the first time with a sublime sense of fulfilment.

Mozart finished the second of his D major concertos, K218, in October. The martial opening, played by the full but modest band of strings, oboes and horns in unison, is redolent of absent trumpets and drums, and its eventual elevation to the high register of the solo violin spectacularly exposed. But the immediate sequel to this idea, though a standard enough sequence, is worth comparing with the opening of the Andante and a brief snatch from the 6/8 sections in the rondo (Ex. 8).

Whether contrived or not, this seems another case of the unifying *filo*, woven into all three movements. Leopold would doubtless have noted and

Ex. 8—K218 (i) b 3–8
       (ii) b 1–4
       (iii) b 27–29

approved. Writing from Salzburg to Mozart on his travels two years later he reported on a performance by Brunetti of 'your Strassburg concerto'. As with K216 and K219 the rondo of this D major work has its intruder: a gavotte and musette 'in the Strassburg style' with the open G string providing a drone-bass. Its caprice extends further to the main body of the movement: an unusually stately rondo-theme, combining wit and grace and never completed, alternates with the 6/8 *Allegro* briefly quoted above. The 6/8 expands and allows the virtuoso some brilliant arpeggios and broken thirds, but the ending with its pre-Mannheim decrescendo reflects the tenderness that pervades the work as a whole in spite of its formal opening. In the first movement this showed itself in chromatic touches at the end of phrases, and in the *Andante* with a sustained vocal line, expressive placing of appoggiaturas and well-judged descents from high to low registers on the repeat of themes. The term *cantabile* was fitting here: Mozart nurtured the violin as he did his favourite singers, though without quite attaining the ethereal heights of the *Adagio* in the G major Concerto.

And so to the last of the five, the A major K219, which was ready on 20 December. Here, Mozart built on his experience of the past few months, refining and ordering his ideas with consummate mastery and apparent ease. There is no casual or superfluous note: the *ritornello* themes are brought sharply into focus with no trace of the amiably gangling gait sometimes found in the previous concertos. The little rising arpeggio that ends the first tutti may seem a throw-away line, but it soon provides a new starting-point, and the early stages also involve two innovations, in fact masterstrokes: an orchestral first subject that turns out to be the accompaniment to the real theme, delivered in great style by the solo over its full working compass of three octaves; and the actual solo entry with seven bars of *adagio* that never return. This brief cantilena is moreover supported by an undulating movement in the orchestral violins, reminding one of the evocative texture in the farewell trio in Act 1 of *Così fan tutte*. But the combination of first-subject themes must be quoted (Ex. 9) if only for comparison with a similar contrapuntal revelation at the reprise in the finale of the Mendelssohn Violin Concerto nearly 70 years later.

Ex. 9—K219 (i) b 47–52

It is hard to discuss the second movement without resorting to such catch-phrases as 'melodic warmth' or 'lyrical unfolding'. These qualities may now be taken for granted and the music's special features noted, the short slurs at the opening that give point to the stretto that later brings it back, the seamless melodic line and unity of mood, not precluding a gentle drift to darker and deeper emotions in the development, and a sustained tessitura with less call for the dramatic changes of register observed in the previous concerto. Perhaps for this reason Mozart replaced it in the following year at Brunetti's request with the E major *Adagio*, K261. This alternative, scored with flutes instead of oboes, has not ousted the favourite original but is sometimes heard as a separate piece. In the final minuet-rondo the impression of unhurried ease persists as it moves to the dominant and the relative minor for equally spacious episodes, taking on slight variants for the second return of the theme. The two previous rondos had introduced their galanteries *en route*, and Mozart did not disappoint the Salzburgers. This time it is a 2/4 *Allegro* in A minor in which the soloist throws off passages in the gipsy or 'Turkish' style punctuated by stamping refrains from the orchestra. Tovey called it a contredanse. Such pieces were danced to in Vienna and exotic effects were popular, as Mozart conceded in the 'Alla Turca' finale of his A major Piano Sonata, K331. The key of A minor was a natural one for the violin, with an open-string resonance beloved of the itinerant street-musicians he must have heard on his travels. K219's rondo recovers its minuet and its composure after this episode.

The greatest of the string concertos is the Sinfonia Concertante in E flat for violin and viola, K364, written in Salzburg in 1779. It achieves a new mastery and depth of expression especially in its C minor slow movement, comparable in its pathos with that of the K271 Piano Concerto of two years previously. But whereas the piano concerto was a harbinger of a whole series of later works, the Sinfonia Concertante was a culmination, an early farewell to the string works apart from two isolated movements. We can only imagine the kind of violin concerto Mozart could have produced if a commission or opportunity had materialized in the later 1780s and regret that he abandoned a projected cello concerto, and also two concertante works around the time of his violin-viola masterpiece. The first, a double concerto for piano and violin, dates from his return to Mannheim on the way home from Paris in November 1778 but breaks off, as often happens with Mozart's unfinished works, in the development of the first movement. Alfred Einstein wrote of it as a great loss indeed. The other, contemporary with K364, was a triple concertante for violin, viola and cello, broken off at a similar place. The influence of Parisian taste on these projects seems clear: after his move to Vienna he never returned to the multiple concerto idea.

But the Mannheim influence is also apparent from the opening tutti of the violin–viola concertante: in the abrupt forte-piano effects and the long crescendo of trills. As in his two-piano concerto Mozart introduced the soloists together but in a far subtler way, with a lyrical theme in octaves that emerges almost imperceptibly against a fading orchestral background. Thereafter the players answer each other with a perfectly balanced antiphony, gathering themselves together in preparation for the subsequent tuttis. This antiphony is displayed with the utmost eloquence in the C minor *Andante* and the more straightforward bucolic finale, and extends to the ideal cadenzas Mozart left for the first two movements. To single out an extract from this work is hard enough, but the transition theme from the first movement is quoted for its eternal freshness and seemingly effortless beauty. In this case the viola proposes, the violin disposes, a situation then reversed (Ex. 10).

Although he completed no violin concertos in his Vienna years, Mozart wrote two movements which may have been intended for larger works. In April 1781 he composed the Rondo in C, K373, for the visiting Salzburg violinist Gaetano Brunetti, mentioned in a letter to his father as 'for a concerto' though this may have meant quite simply 'with orchestra'. Four years later, almost to the day, came the lost Andante in A, K470, known from the incipit Mozart recorded in his catalogue. Its background is uncertain.

Ex. 10—K364 (i) b 106–113

Perhaps it was written for another visitor, Heinrich Marchand or Anton Janitsch, and as a substitute slow movement for a revival of the D major Concerto, K218. Such replacements were common, as with arias in operas, but the simple canonic opening that survives is only the slenderest guide to the character of the piece.

Wind Concertos

Discussion of Mozart's wind concertos must also begin with a lost work. On 12 November 1768 his father reported that on their visit to Vienna 'Wolfgang has composed a solemn mass, an offertorium and a trumpet concerto for a boy'. Nothing remains of the last named: it would have been unique in his output and, coming from a 12-year-old, his earliest original essay in concerto-form. His Bassoon Concerto in B flat, K191, is, however, very much alive. Though still youthful, dating from 1774 in Salzburg, it is a repertory work for an instrument not too well endowed between the copious Baroque examples and the Weber Concerto of 1811. As so often with works for solo wind instruments it was written for a specific player, Baron von Dürnitz, an amateur who commissioned other music from Mozart including a Sonata for bassoon and cello, K292, and apparently two more concertos in C and B flat, though the former was lost and a modern edition of the second has been questioned on stylistic grounds. K191 itself is in a pleasant *galant* style, making effective use of the bassoon's registers, its singing qualities and its agility, as in the playful decorations that surround the finale's minuet-theme.

Mozart and the Concerto

An Oboe Concerto, K271k, supposedly written in the summer of 1777, is, however, beset with confusion—another lost score. Was this the work Mozart referred to in a letter from Mannheim the following February as written for Joseph Ferlendis and which was having such success there? Or was he speaking of the oboe version of his still more recent Flute Concerto in D, K314, transposed down a tone into C major? Two flute concertos were composed for the Dutch flautist De Jean shortly after Mozart's arrival in Mannheim, and an Andante in C, K315, in which a graceful cantilena is introduced by pizzicato string chords, may have been an offshoot from the first of them, the G major, K313. Although the flute was not one of his favourite instruments and his heart may not have been in the project, he wrote other works for De Jean including at least two quartets for flute and string trio. Both concertos are in the *galant* Salzburg manner with no place for special Mannheim effects or the structural surprises of his most recent piano concerto, K271, in E flat. There are the expected acrobatics, passage-work with a liberal mixture of slurring and tonguing, wide melodic leaps and rapid skips of a tenth. The first movement of K313 has the more interesting development with both vigorous and expressive minor-key exchanges. Its finale, a minuet with a rather staid rondo theme, is less winning than that of the D major, but the slow movement with its muted strings has a serene beauty akin to that in the G major Violin Concerto of 1775 and is a challenge to the player's command of long phrasing. The D major, K314, has more distinguished outer movements, with a lightness of scoring that throws its rhythmic figures into relief, such as the downward arpeggio that first introduces the solo. The main episode in the finale is quoted for its 'learned' display of counterpoint but it is also clearly derived from the rondo-theme itself (Ex. 11). Was this in fact the oboe concerto of the previous summer, transposed up a tone?

From Mannheim Mozart went on to Paris, where the public events of the Concert Spirituel were organized by a Joseph Le Gros with whom Mozart had chequered dealings. Concertos for two or more soloists were popular and he wrote repeatedly to his father about a Sinfonia Concertante he had composed for flute, oboe, horn and bassoon. Its performance was obstructed by Le Gros for no apparent reason, but the score was left with him and Mozart vowed to write it down again out of his head in due course. There is however, no trace of an autograph, but a nineteenth-century copy with clarinet instead of flute was heralded as authentic, or largely so, and the work (listed as K Anhang-9) is often heard in this form and announced as by Mozart. The bold E flat opening rings true and so does the unison entry of the four soloists. There is so much characteristic beauty in the work that one is inclined to ask the researcher: if not Mozart, who else? The final variations,

Ex. 11—K314 (iii) b 152–159

in which the players parade their agility in turn, are more routine, but if they risk outstaying their welcome the same might be said of some of Mozart's other variation-sets such as the finale of the D major Piano Sonata, K284. These lost-and-found concertantes may in fact be separate works, but if the form of the latter is proved spurious it contains gold as well as dross. The virtuoso horn flourish that opens the ninth variation of the finale seems designed for Mozart's intended player Giovanni Punto, better known as the inspirer of Beethoven's Horn Sonata 22 years later.

Mozart's visit to Paris also produced the Concerto in C for flute and harp, K299, written for the Count of Guines and his daughter. Its charm and brilliance seem clearly geared to the French taste he is known to have despised, though Tovey wittily observed that he expressed his opinion of the harp by writing it an unplayable passage towards the end. Nevertheless, the Count's daughter played 'magnifique'. The possibilities and problems of combining two such instruments on equal terms are endless, but Mozart faced and solved most of them. A cantabile theme will sound thin when transferred from flute to harp: most of the shared ideas are therefore lively, with a tendency to bird-like repetitions already evinced in the opening bars. But the harp can be brilliant in passage-work and is a richly harmonic accompanist, as in the luxuriant sequences that unfold near the start of the slow movement. The liveliness of the final gavotte no doubt pleased the audience that reacted with enthusiasm to the extrovert 'Paris' Symphony of the same time. Perhaps Mozart overdid his treatment of the harp as a piano with Alberti basses and arpeggios that fall naturally under the keyboard player's hand? It was the only time he wrote for the instrument.

The infiltration of concerto elements into other forms was mentioned in connection with the elaborate solo piano part in the aria 'Ch'io mi scordi di te', K505. Haydn exploited solo instruments in symphonies, and in *Die Entführung* Mozart introduced Constanze's 'Martern aller Arten' with a lengthy preamble featuring solos for oboe, flute, violin and cello. In March 1783 he wrote from Vienna about a concert of his works that included 'the short concertante symphonie' from his last 'Finalmusik', actually the third movement and probably the adjacent ones, from the Serenade in D, K320, written at Salzburg in 1779, once again highlighting the wind players. Meanwhile, Mozart had turned his attention to the horn with the Rondo in E flat, K371, and sketches for other concerto movements. In a letter of March 1781 he referred to Ignaz Leutgeb, a Salzburg horn player who set up as a cheesemonger in Vienna with the help of a loan from Mozart's father. Mozart was on bantering terms with him, writing him four concertos and scrawling ribald comments in the margin. All the finales are in six–eight time with the hunting character that spilled over into some of the piano concertos, but the isolated Rondo, K371, was exceptional in being in 2/4: its more sedate tune was to be eclipsed by the best-selling rondos in the completed concertos. First came the E flat, K417, finished on 27 May 1783. Humour and good humour are the expected hallmarks, with an element of risk in quick passages that is lessened when these works are played on the later valve-horn. There may be some loss of character too: the difference in quality between natural and stopped notes was expressive and often humorous. Mozart had the rare gift of turning instrumental (and vocal) limitations to musical ends, and he also anticipated the more Romantic view of the horn in the slow movements. His next horn concerto was probably K447, also in E flat, in which the lyrical side is stressed from the start, enhanced by the warm sonority of clarinets in the orchestra. The Romance movement also has a haunting cadence phrase that is repeatedly woven into the closing bars, while the hunting finale theme is touched with passing 'stopped' chromatics creating an amusing effect on the natural horn. Yet another E flat concerto, K495, dates from June 1786. Its slow movement theme looks forward to that in the finest of the piano-duet sonatas, K497 in F, completed five weeks later, and the rondo is probably the most familiar of the hunting variety, making entertaining use of reiterated pedal-notes. The dating of a fourth concerto in D, K412, thought to have been the first of the series, has recently been corrected from 1782 to 1791 by Alan Tyson's researches. This two-movement work, with its rondo incomplete in the manuscript, thus belongs to the last year of Mozart's life along with the Piano Concerto, K595, and the Clarinet Concerto. Alfred Einstein was convinced that an unfinished E major slow movement was intended for K412, but the choice of key was untypical and unlikely.

Whereas the horn concertos are *pièces d'occasion* of a high order, still retaining their vigour and freshness, Mozart's only Clarinet Concerto, K622, is a masterpiece comparable with the greatest of the piano concertos. It was also a true if unconscious valediction, completed less than two months before his death. As with Leutgeb for the horn, so with Anton Stadler for the clarinet: Stadler was another Salzburg musician who moved to Vienna and for whom Mozart also wrote his Clarinet Quintet in the same key of A. The first movement of the concerto was, however, originally sketched in G major for basset-horn, a tenor clarinet with an extended lower compass, and the work itself has been recently reconstructed for the 'basset clarinet' Stadler is believed to have used. Mozart in any case revelled in the lower reaches of the clarinet, enjoying them in widespread arpeggios or sudden contrasts of register, as in the brief quotation from the first movement (Ex. 12). Analysts

Ex. 12—K622 (i) b 115–119

may comment on the richness of the orchestral contribution in which *ritornello* ideas flourish and develop to an even greater degree than in the last piano concerto. This continuity is assured to the end of the first movement through the absence of the usual cadenza, a break with tradition often credited to Beethoven's 'Emperor'. The many excursions into minor keys and the exclusion of oboes from the scoring help to give the music a tender warmth and compassion: a special quality, as Stanley Sadie remarked in *The New Grove*, 'that it is tempting to regard as autumnal'. The *Adagio*, closely related in theme, texture and spirit to the *Larghetto* of the Quintet, is sublimely statuesque and the slight harmonic changes on the return are infinitely telling. The rondo, in a playful and sometimes parodistic 6/8, is again deepened by its turns to the minor key, and its pathos intensified by sudden pauses; yet on a more superficial level there is plenty to show off the virtuoso's agility.

Mozart's total achievement in the concerto form had no remote parallel. In his greatest examples, and there are many of them, he combined the highest quality of musical thought with an unerring sense of balance and proportion that raised the Classical concerto to the finest realms of art, comparable with the string quartet and the symphony. The nature of the form changed with the Romantics. At its lowest ebb the concerto became a display piece with a glamorous orchestral background, setting the stage but adding little to the subsequent musical argument. The Mendelssohn Violin Concerto and the Schumann Piano Concerto are masterpieces that discovered new ways of unifying their material, but despite Mendelssohn's structural innovations and Schumann's transformations of themes, their forms are far more predictable than Mozart's. Yet in the first hundred years of concerts by the London Philharmonic Society, founded in 1813, the Mendelssohn received 38 and the Schumann 28 performances. During this time the Mozart Clarinet Concerto was played only once. Even the piano concertos were rarities, with the D minor and C minor heading the list, the A major, K488 unheard until 1900, the majority completely neglected. When Busoni described Mozart as 'the greatest example of musical talent that has yet appeared' he may not have foreseen the revival and spread of Mozart appreciation that we now take for granted. Many pianists play the complete concertos as a labour of love, and most of those for other instruments are familiar from concerts and recordings.

The principles of the Classical concerto were inherited by Beethoven and belatedly by Brahms, who was scorned for his conservatism by Hugo Wolf. Both wrote cadenzas for Mozart concertos, Beethoven for the D minor, Brahms for the C minor. Whereas Beethoven talking about Mozart is too good a piece of musical history to miss, the anachronism of the Brahms is hardly acceptable today. Cadenzas that exceed the compass of Mozart's keyboard can have the disastrous effect of reducing the impact of his own writing, though his pupil Hummel ignored this obvious precept. His ornamentations overflow into an age of superficial glitter, though they reflect an area of performance practice that cannot be disregarded by serious Mozart students. Fortunately there are enough original cadenzas and variants to guide the player's taste in such matters.

CHAPTER 4

Beethoven and the Concerto

Robert Simpson

The Classical concerto with large *ritornello* was perfected and developed by Mozart; Beethoven was closely familiar with some of his masterpieces, notably the D minor and C minor concertos, and for the D minor he wrote a famous cadenza. Mozart's concern is mainly to explore the subtleties of the relation between individual and crowd, in terms of both rivalry and co-operation. In some of Mozart's piano concertos (K453 in G and K467 in C, for instance) the orchestra and soloist for the most part keep to their own thematic material, poaching on each other's only for strategic reasons. The balance of power between them constantly fluctuates; a subtlety in K467, for example, is the way the whole orchestra, including trumpets and drum, is playing in the *pianissimo* anticipation of the first movement recapitulation, breathlessly preparing for an abrupt seizure of the initiative. By the time the general pause for the cadenza is reached, honours are even, and the soloist now has to try to gain the upper hand—his cadenza should take advantage of material he has himself held in reserve. Mozart wrote no cadenza for K467, and the pianist must base his on material with which he can 'surprise' the orchestra, material Mozart has deliberately reserved for him. Anyone looking at the movement in the kind of detail from which no performer should be excused will see what Mozart has in mind—so far none of our great Mozartians who has ever recorded this concerto appears even to have glimpsed the nature of the problem.

In creating and mastering this type of concerto as well as the more collaborative kind that lives chiefly on physical contrasts, Mozart achieved unprecedented breadth and scale. Beethoven was aware of this, acutely enough to avoid encroaching on a field already cultivated near to its limit. His instinctive concern was for larger limits, with different effects; a new scope for tonality in a wider fling, and a deeper exploration of the soloist's technical resources against a more trenchant orchestra. This did not involve the playing-off against each other of exclusive material by the protagonists. In Beethoven their relationship is nearly always essentially concurrent, sharing a flow of ideas towards an agreed object, a form differently felt from that created by productive tension between Mozartian rivals. With

Beethoven the preoccupation is with scale and line, with new tonal vistas, with contrasts of broader scope. Using extra techniques and greater natural mobility and range, the soloist acts as an enlivening mentor, like an architect moving quickly in and around a building under construction. The subtleties Beethoven achieves in this way are not more intricate than Mozart's; the scale is greater, and the subtleties have to be different, though no less imponderable.

These questions are already posed in the first-written of his acknowledged concertos, No. 2 in B flat, Op. 19 (if we forget the earliest juvenile E flat piano concerto of 1784). Op. 19 was originally composed in 1795, but is said to have been revised three years later, after the C major concerto he called No. 1 (Op. 15) had been done. Beethoven did not regard the B flat as one of his best works, and this may have led to some misunderstanding. Tovey and other commentators have suggested that in his first three piano concertos Beethoven showed uncertainty about the function of the *ritornello*, that he failed to see that in Mozart its function was to display (a) the tonic key and (b) a certain number of identifiable themes (though they themselves did not see that these themes were often specifically associated with the orchestra alone). In employing apparent surprise modulations in the *ritornello* Beethoven was thought to have confused its nature.

In the first movement of the B flat concerto we find the first of these so-called digressions. Beethoven seems to shift the tonality as if he thought it were a symphonic exposition moving to its second group. The music makes steady and apparently symphonic progress to the dominant of the dominant, where it waits for a reply (bar 40). But instead of a second subject in the expected normal key of F, there is a drastic evasion on D flat (Ex. 1).

And this is no new theme, but a treatment (it seems in D flat) of the second phrase from the first theme. This soon turns naturally to B flat minor, the tonic minor, of which D flat is a close relative, and in no time at all we are back in the tonic major as if nothing had happened. We can call this a digression if we like but it is decidedly humorous and poetic, its proportions are perfect, and it does not disturb the essentially introductory character of the *ritornello*, or the monolithic nature of its tonality. Far from being a 'misunderstanding' of something which Beethoven had already learned to appreciate to the full, it is too deft and abrupt to be anything but a very good (and economical) joke which, moreover, shows a fresh view of the hackneyed Neopolitan ploy.

It makes good long-term sense too. After a full exposition dominated by the piano, in which we get a real second group in a real F major (see bar 127), the abrupt stroke from the *ritornello* is recalled in the development, where it

Ex. 1

now discovers E flat. Most of the development stays around that key, which we realize at length is the home subdominant; it moves to the dominant, and soon there is a regular recapitulation. But the abrupt and therefore memorable stroke has now put E flat, at first rather mysteriously, into our heads, so that the beautiful E flat *Adagio*, when it comes, has a little more significance than its subdominant key would normally give it. This device is much less subtle than those (sometimes regarded as equally blameworthy) in the two concertos that followed, but it is far from being the inexperienced mistake Tovey's authority has made many believe. The immense and powerful cadenza Beethoven added during the period of the late sonatas renders amusingly bland the simple orchestral close of the movement.

The *Adagio* is a deeply tranquil and notably concentrated movement; despite its great spaciousness, it is very terse. It is in full sonata form, with a development that gives the impression of magnificent breadth while being only six bars long. Here Beethoven perhaps learned something from the slow movement of Mozart's C major concerto, K503; if so we must beware all the more of treating some of his other strokes of genius as evidence of inexperience or misunderstanding. This marvellous economy wins the composer time for a deeply poetic expansion in the coda, where the piano, using the sustaining pedal, drops notes through the still air like dew from a leaf. Before endorsing too readily Beethoven's verdict on this concerto we must ask ourselves where in Mozart can we find a passage like this.

The brilliant final rondo is one of the most delightful of Beethoven's early finales, effervescent and zestful in a way difficult to reconcile with the story that he was suffering a severe attack of colic while composing it. Yet it could be true—Beethoven's music is always splendidly detached from personal woes. A few years later his growing deafness prompted the harrowing Heiligenstadt Testament and the possibility of suicide—at which time he was composing the gloriously confident Second Symphony. The lively displacement of accents in this concerto-finale's main theme gives rise to some exhilarating syncopations in the central episode, and are wittily reversed into 'normality' when the main tune appears in the bright key of G major at the start of the coda (bar 261). This finale is probably a substitute for the Rondo in B flat (WoO 6; *c.* 1795) which may at first have been intended for this concerto, and which now exists only in a somewhat adulterated edition by Czerny.

By the time Beethoven came to write the C major concerto in 1797–8 his perception of the possibilities had considerably sharpened; his awareness of this caused him to issue the C major first, as No. 1. Although he was undoubtedly too harsh towards the other work, we can easily see that the muscular compactness of the C major concerto must have been preferred by him as more obviously expressing the confidence of a young master in his own strength; he had found a discipline holding the seeds of a new power, a kind of severity and rigour that became fully exerted only later. No early work shows more clearly what crisp and potent use he could make of mere formulae. Most of the themes of the first movement are made of formal tags that mean little in themselves. It is the force that infuses them that brings them to life, Beethoven's already remarkable power of momentum; so finely articulated is his progression from one theme, one sentence, one paragraph to another that we are carried on an irresistible current. Passage-work that might have been by Czerny is swept into the general momentum by a continuously and perfectly defined sense of reassurance. In many ways the first movement of this concerto anticipates its much greater counterpart in the so-called 'Emperor'—there are figurations that eventually generated vaster paragraphs in the later work.

In Op. 15 Beethoven commits the second of his 'blunders', which can be much more dangerously misinterpreted than the stroke already referred to in the B flat concerto. Here the ramifications are more far reaching, and if understood will seem even less to be any kind of error. These subtleties do not seem to have been generally noticed, and it is important to draw attention to them, and to further impressive consequences resulting from another 'mistake' in the *ritornello* of the C minor concerto.

The C major's *ritornello* begins with a militant opening paragraph, which halts grandly on the home dominant. By Mozartian standards this is normal, though perhaps more aggressively expansive than usual. Nevertheless we expect another theme in the tonic, maybe gentler. We get a contrasted theme, but abruptly in the unexpected key of E flat (Ex. 2).

This is the 'blunder', so it is said, that now compels Beethoven to spend precious time imaginatively repairing, by somehow getting back to C major before the damage becomes irreparable. He does get back, but how? No one seems to have seen the significance of his way of doing this. He moves from E flat (bar 47) in upward steps, up a tone to F minor (bar 56), and up another tone to G minor (bar 63); the G minor then turns to major and becomes the dominant of C. Soon we are back in C major with a new theme that sounds as if it is going to be 'The British Grenadiers' (bar 86). This stepwise progression of tones (really extended harmonies, not proper keys), E flat, F, G, becomes very important in the movement. The whole development is based on these successive pitches, beginning with a knowingly drastic change to E flat (see bars 257 to 266) even more striking than the one in the *ritornello*. Then follows a drifting process through F minor (bar 288) to G, the dominant of C (bar 304). There the music stays for a long time, descending into a deep hush with no more than a subdued throbbing rhythm, commandingly interrupted by an exultant sweep from the soloist, perhaps the most dramatic return in all Beethoven's earlier works. So there is method in Beethoven's 'blundering'! Curiously enough, the first of the three cadenzas he wrote for this movement also reflects the stepwise progression of E flat, F, and G; for some reason he left this very apt cadenza unfinished (though not by much) and did not return

Allegro con brio

Ex. 2

to the scheme in the other two. In his magnificent recording of this concerto Claudio Arrau plays a splendid completion of this first cadenza.

Distinguished though it is by beautiful clarinet writing, the slow movement *(Largo)* is surpassed by its more nearly sublime counterpart in the B flat concerto. The solo part is elegant and decorative, and the orchestration translucent, with the clarinet a ready foil to the piano. The movement is a sonata form in A flat, with the recapitulation of the second group replaced by a long coda that makes sustained and inventive use of cadential matter in a way that, at least in method, looks forward to the coda of the slow movement of the Ninth Symphony. But the music does not hint at such depths, which are more than glimpsed in the *Adagio* of the B flat concerto.

No reference is made in the *Largo* to the stepwise progressions of the first movement, but these reappear in the bubblingly energetic final rondo. Its first tonal twist is into E flat (bar 39) and the return to C major is through D flat, E flat, F minor, and G (bars 130–51), another striking stepwise process. The impetus is not slackened in the A minor central episode, where a persistent leaping figure alternates with smoother polyphonic material. This is one of Beethoven's most vigorously humorous early pieces, delighting in irregular rhythmic invention, subtle and powerful in its muscular movements.

With the C minor concerto, No. 3, Op. 37, we are at the threshold of Beethoven's 'second period'. It is often said to have been influenced by Mozart's concerto in the same key (K491) which Beethoven greatly admired (he is said to have remarked to his pupil Ries, 'The likes of us will never do anything like that!'). But the only resemblances lie in the key and in the unison of the first theme; even here Beethoven's square-cut, direct subject is like Mozart's tortuously chromatic theme only in its first two notes (Ex. 3).

Ex. 3

But it is one thing to note connections of this kind, tenuous though they are; it is another to treat Beethoven's work as a blunted attempt to rival his great predecessor. This has been done with other early works by Beethoven—the E flat string trio, Op. 3 (in relation to Mozart's famous Divertimento, K563) and the Quintet for piano and wind, Op. 16 (as a failure to compete with Mozart's K452); Beethoven revered these Mozart works, but we can understand his early masterpieces only by allowing them their own terms, in which they are seen to be independent. With the Third Piano Concerto, however, we are on more clearly established Beethoven territory, a fact that makes comparisons the more hazardous. Such hazards are compounded by yet another so-called 'mistake' in the *ritornello*. By now we should be getting used to the idea that Beethoven wants a productive incident in the course of what would otherwise be a plain-sailing monotonal *ritornello*. We should also not need warning that the history of music criticism swarms with real mistakes, especially in relation to strokes of genius, the more so when they are characteristic and persistent in a composer's work: Schubert's 'digressions' in sonata expositions, Bruckner's 'clumsy sonata-form', Max Reger's 'eternal modulating', none of which exist in objective fact when these composers are in full control (far more often than not)—such intrepid generalizations are still common usage in some quarters. The idea that Beethoven needed the 'mistakes' of three concertos to discover how to write a *ritornello* still dies hard, and its currency seems to be reinforced, paradoxically, by the sheer weight of so impressive a work as his No. 3.

Impressive it is, a work of deathless genius and an original achievement beyond all but the highest powers. This much is agreed even by those who perpetuate the 'mistake' theory, who tend to treat the work as a transition to something even greater. It is certainly that, but we must also observe that it is a culminative work, the climax of an unorthodox process started in the two previous concertos. It does not restate their mistakes—it advances on their discoveries.

In No. 3, we find the most drastic example of the phenomenon. After the C minor opening the *ritornello* moves grandly and rather abruptly into E flat major and its first sustained tutti is an E flat counterstatement of the main theme (bar 24). This is early for the solid establishment of a new key, so we can accept it as an environ of C minor, not necessarily disturbing the proper equilibrium of a *ritornello*. But Beethoven then turns it to E flat minor, a disconcertingly sure way of misleading the ear into regarding it as a tonic in its own right. When the mass subsides and a new, very memorable tune follows in E flat major, no one is likely to be surprised (Ex. 4).

It is of course this that has been regarded as a mistake—as if Beethoven has not seen the difference between a symphonic exposition and a concerto

Ex. 4

ritornello. On the face of it, this resembles the conventional symphonic opening much more than the two earlier concertos—or it would were it not for the fact that the 'second subject' sounds merely like a change from minor to major, not like the result of a real modulation to a new key. Beethoven's first change to E flat, at bar 24, is merely harmonic, not tonal. The subsequent turn into the minor creates the illusion that E flat was a real key, so that the supposed 'second subject' in E flat (bar 50) sustains for the moment this illusion that the composer thinks he is writing a symphony. So it is no surprise that some observers have been misled into supposing that Beethoven's subsequent abrupt return to the tonic constitutes a guilty attempt at correcting and obscuring a mistake. We should know enough about Beethoven to realize that if he were conscious of having turned in a wrong direction he would recompose the entire thing so that no suspicion of uncertainty remained. The apparent 'correction' in this case must be accepted for the time being, just in case Beethoven turns out to be a great composer after all! The 'second subject' tune is now heard in C major, but the gleam of its E natural (bar 62) is too bright and it soon fades into C minor, where the *ritornello* ends in preparation for the solo entry.

We should hear clearly the difference when in the exposition Beethoven makes a proper modulation, making crucial use of the soloist, to E flat for the second group. Ex. 4 is now in a real E flat (bar 164), and this is no tautological fault. Events will prove it to have been part of a stroke of genius emphasizing in a new way the soloist's right to command the shape of the exposition. The orchestra's anticipation in the *ritornello*, drastically checking itself, is deference in advance. Beethoven is sharply aware of the difference between a concerto and a symphony, and equally sharply he prompts our hindsight.

This is not the end of the matter. When Ex. 4 comes back in the recapitulation it is in a fully prepared C major for the first time in the work (bar 340), establishing properly the E natural that was only a bright though memorable gleam in the *ritornello*; the splendid effect of this would have been turned into hapless tautology if Beethoven had stuck to convention in the *ritornello* and delivered it plainly in nothing but C major. And we must be very careful what we say about the younger Beethoven who, in his cadenza, comments further on the situation by producing the same theme for the first time in G major, the home dominant!

In the first movement the note E natural (as opposed to E flat) has been subtly emphasized by means of long-term strategy. It becomes the tonality of the beautiful E major *Largo*, the largest and noblest of Beethoven's early slow movements, its gravity worthy of Gluck and its depth purely its own. There is enormous breadth and calm, a profound, unusually sustained maturity of feeling that Beethoven seems always to have possessed. As the first movement made a point of E flat versus E natural, resulting in the E natural tonality of the slow movement, so the *Largo* makes the most of the contrast between its own major and minor thirds, G sharp and G natural. The serene main theme descends into G major harmony in its ninth bar, and the first modulation of the development is to G major, a deep lake of sound after the luminous B major it follows. We remember it when Beethoven begins the finale with the notes G and A flat (i.e. G and G sharp). The wrenching effect is both humorous and irascible, but also profound in view of all that has happened.

The construction of the brilliant and weightily powerful final rondo is fully prepared by the previous subtleties. The first of the central episodes is in A flat (G sharp) (bar 182) and a propulsive *fugato* then leads to a vivacious reversion to E major, the key of the slow movement, of which G sharp is the major third (bar 264). This generates an air of suppressed excitement, in which argument between G natural and A flat brings about the C minor recapitulation (bar 298). The restatement of the second subject in a bright C major (bar 331) has the same effect as the corresponding event in the first movement, and for a similar reason—this is the first time in the movement that we have heard a fully prepared C major, with its E natural. But it darkens towards the minor; the orchestra pauses on the dominant, and the soloist swings upwards in a cadenza, stopping gently on the note G (bar 407). The G turns to G sharp and becomes a quick upbeat to A natural; this time there is no more confusion between G sharp and A flat—it was decidedly G sharp this time, and must go upwards, and the A natural is in a C major that can at last stand its ground. The tempo is *presto*, the coda exuberant and certain, the freshness of C major guaranteed by all the associations of its past and the many subtle inflexions of major and minor thirds throughout the work, none of which would have been half as successful without Beethoven's 'mistake' in the *ritornello* of the first movement. So this is after all a great and deep masterwork, in no need to fear irrelevant comparison with Mozart or anybody else. None of its critics could have attempted anything like it, for Beethoven himself could not have achieved it without fully understanding what their misunderstanding suggested he did not know.

The next stage in Beethoven's thinking about the concerto problem is crucially embodied in the Triple Concerto in C major Op. 56, for violin, cello and piano. Sketches for it are found among those for the *Eroica* in 1803, a context significantly concerned with expansion. The concerto was probably completed in 1804, and it was first performed by the young Archduke Rudolph at the piano, with Seidler and Kraft playing the violin and cello parts. This no doubt explains why the piano part is the easiest and the cello the most difficult—Kraft was a player of exceptional powers. Despite Rudolph's involvement, the work is dedicated to Count Lobkowitz, and its actual *raison d'être* is unknown. Whatever the truth, its very constitution was suitable for this stage of Beethoven's exploration of the concerto—the presence of three solo instruments made it necessary at once to achieve spaciousness and (to prevent the prolixity threatened by such a group, each soloist needing ample treatment) maximum terseness. The *Eroica* sought the expansion of the symphonic horizon; the expansive process in the Triple Concerto was subject to another, more physical discipline, the accommodation of three soloists. In its solution of this artistic problem the work is a masterpiece, and if it does not represent Beethoven's very greatest heights, it is still far beyond any but a composer of his calibre. Its first movement is a masterly and characteristic demonstration that terseness and spaciousness are not contradictory terms, the short slow movement consists of one of the greatest melodies ever given to the cello, and the finale is the grandest and most comprehensive of all polonaises. These are reasons enough not to neglect the work, without which the greater last three concertos might not have been achieved.

The *ritornello* of the first movement eschews the productive and provocative 'incidents' or 'blunders' that mark the first three piano concertos. But it is far from orthodox. The beginning, on unharmonized cellos and basses, is unusual, its very plainness invoking a sense of mystery (Ex. 5). Has any earlier work, by Beethoven or anyone else, begun like this?

A piled-up *crescendo* fixes C major, only to culminate in a massive subdominant, which has to be pulled weightily over on to the dominant (bars 21–33). Here there is a hush, and the mere dominant harmony seems to be treated in the old-fashioned way as if it had been a key, with a new theme (Ex. 6).

Soon, however (bar 40), it acknowledges that the G major is no key and sets its feet once more on the solid ground of C; this is an example of an old device being used for the purposes of a new kind of expansive terseness. The space created by it is immediately filled by an exquisite 'purple patch' of foreign harmony that leaves the tonality entirely undisturbed. Beethoven uses this device again in the *ritornello* of the Fourth Piano Concerto, and something like it in the Violin Concerto, in each case with a different function. As the Triple Concerto's *ritornello* proceeds, it again tends to rise

Ex. 5

Ex. 6

into the dominant, so much so that it has to be 'corrected' by its final cadence (Ex. 7).

Considering its variety this *ritornello* is very compact, to make room for the enormous expanse of three successive solo entries, all in the tonic. The ensuing exposition manages to be both economical and incalculable, even finding space for a completely new orchestral theme (bar 114) (Ex. 8).

Ex. 7

Ex. 8

Ex. 8 is taken up by the cello with piano accompaniment, adorned by a fresh continuation, then decorated by the violin, as if there were all the time in the world. This is what Tovey would have called sublime effrontery. A broad transition, through yet another new theme around the dominant of A minor (bar 138) brings about the second group, with Ex. 6 basking in the fascinating sunlight of A major (bar 156).

The use of this bright submediant major to begin the second group serves a double purpose; as its remoteness enhances the sense of spaciousness it also makes unnecessary the proportionate physical expansiveness required for a second group in an unmysteriously related key. Beethoven was often concerned to try second-group keys other than the dominant, and the use of the radiant submediant major occurred to him for similar reasons in the magnificent neglected C major string quintet, Op. 29, the 'Archduke' Trio, and the 'Hammerklavier' Sonata. Physical space can be saved by the power of suggestion gained from judicious mystification, and Beethoven consistently demonstrated this throughout his career in a thousand different ways.

Then the 'purple patch' reappears, and turns the A major to minor, more at home in a C major work. There is a new energetic theme in dotted rhythm (cello, bar 182). In due time the exposition seems to be coming to an immensely spacious quiet end when the orchestra breaks in with Ex. 8, unexpectedly in F (bar 225). Is this the development? But no—the key swings back to A minor, and the exposition ends there with the cadential Ex. 7, now unequivocal (bar 241).

When the development starts we see the reason for the orchestra's interruption in F: Beethoven now wants to enhance the sense of vastness by persisting for a long time in the key of A, restored to major. If the exposition had come to an uneventful quiet close in A, minor or major, at say around bar 230, uninterrupted by the orchestral F major outbreak, the persistence of A at the opening of the development would soon have seemed excessive, and the intended spaciousness would have been prolixity. The dramatic injection by the orchestra of F major harmony at bar 225 insures against this danger, and Beethoven is now able to give no less than the three initial entries of the soloists more or less as they originally appeared, but now in a luminous A major. You cannot have sublime effrontery without knowing the sublime.

So this great movement (and it is a great movement) unfolds itself as

Beethoven teaches himself (and us) lesson after lesson, not by dry machination, but by fine poetry. There is reserve in the use of harmonic colour and a certain plainness in the themes; these are offset by the rich possibilities of the solo group, and made significant by the amplitude of the architecture. This is not the place for a complete, detailed analysis, and perhaps we have gone far enough to give clues for the rest of the movement. At all times we can be amazed, here and in the finale, by the ingenuity and imagination with which Beethoven has deployed the three instruments, circumventing their physical, while satisfying their poetic demands.

What is to be expected after this first movement? A fully developed slow movement giving wide scope to all three soloists would probably be unwieldy, and here, as in the G major piano concerto, Beethoven opts for something of spacious but introductory character. If the opening melody of the A flat major *Largo* had been only the first subject of a full sonata scheme the scale would have gigantic, perhaps equal to that of the slow movement of the 'Hammerklavier' Sonata. But the composer, perhaps to our regret, decides on caution; in recompense he gives the cello, after a grave preludial phrase in the strings, one of his most serious and beautiful melodies. As the other soloists enter we have no idea how expansive this movement is going to be, and the truth becomes apparent only when the A flat key, by settling down on the dominant of C in preparation for the last movement, proves to have been a vast Neapolitan cloud. Again Beethoven has saved an immense amount of space; we may be sorry not to have had 20 minutes of this, but we cannot aver that the physical fact would have been greater than the composer's power of suggestion.

The finale takes advantage of the space-saving by being the greatest and most expansive polonaise ever written. Its first theme has the leisure to slip into a glowing E major (of all keys!) in the middle (Ex. 9).

Ex. 9

This is an anticipation of the stroke of genius at the start of the Fourth Piano Concerto (B major harmony in G major, recovering the tonic by the same route).

Space is all, and it is a polonaise danced by multitudes. Like most concerto finales it is a rondo, and the central episodes are around A minor, so reflecting a salient tendency in the first movement. We must not underestimate the Triple Concerto because Beethoven subsequently wrote more wonderful works. This is like ignoring the marvellous Mass in C major because the composer overshadowed it with one of the supreme achievements of the human mind.

Beethoven is now ready to reach the summit; the last three concertos show how his comprehensive mastery can encompass widely different achievements, each free of the others. The G major piano concerto Op. 58, universally and justly loved, is perhaps the most subtly articulated of the three. Composers who suffer neglect might care to console themselves with the thought that this beautiful masterpiece was heard no more than once in Beethoven's lifetime—when he himself gave the first performance in 1807. It was published in the following year but lay on the shelf for another 20 years, and Beethoven was dead before it was heard again. The period from 1803 to 1808 was one of the most astonishingly prolific in his life. His habit of voluminous sketching gave the impression that he was a slow worker, but this could not always have been so. He often worked on several compositions at once, so that it is difficult to disentangle their chronology; during this process things would move fast. The list of opus numbers in this five and a half years is bewildering—53, the 'Waldstein' Sonata; 54, Piano Sonata in F major; 55, the *Eroica* Symphony; 56, the Triple Concerto; 57, the 'Appassionata' Sonata; 58, Piano Concerto No. 4; 59, the three Rasumovsky quartets; 60, the Fourth Symphony; 61, the Violin Concerto; 62, *Coriolan* Overture; 63–6, publication of earlier works; 67, the Fifth Symphony; 68, the Sixth Symphony; 69, Cello Sonata in A major; 70, two piano trios; 71, early wind sextet; 72, *Leonora* (first version of *Fidelio*). Every work in this list that was composed in these years is a seminal masterpiece, and every one breaks new ground. The scale, scope and originality are unprecedented, constituting a miracle of dispatch equal to the record-breaking feats of Mozart or Schubert, and surpassing them in density of thought. It is more than surprising that there are so few cross-connections between the works, and where these exist they emphasize differences more than similarities. Not many listeners, for instance, stop to notice that the exquisitely gentle and sensitive main theme of the Fourth Piano Concerto is founded on the same rhythm as the fierce opening of the Fifth Symphony.

Beethoven begins the concerto, unusually, with the piano alone, which gives out the first phrase of the main theme. In *The Monthly Musical Record* of May–June 1958 Harold Truscott observed:

> The orchestra completes it . . . The piano phrase ends on the dominant; the orchestra . . . quietly continues it from the major mediant, the brightest and most unexpected harmony Beethoven could have chosen for the purpose . . . His sketches for this work proceed for some time before they show that he had any idea of allowing the soloist to begin. If he had pursued what was probably his first intention, to begin with the orchestra . . . what could he have begun with that would have set off that B major harmony as the piano does? Not strings; that would have spoiled the whole point. Not wind; that would have been too heavy and clumsy for the soft murmur of the strings that was to answer the opening phrase. It had to be something quiet and firm, suggestive without a trace of wavering, without a mixture of colour that could introduce the murmur as a contrast and yet as part of itself. This is a fair description of a piano . . .

I also had made a similar point, later but independently, in a record sleeve note, and there can be no doubt that Beethoven is using the only instrument present that will serve his purpose. Truscott goes further, to suggest that anyone listening without preconceptions will be 'quite unconscious of the fact that he is listening to the solo instrument in those five opening bars, for the simple reason that he is not the solo instrument'. Well, we can see him sitting there, in front of the orchestra, and the programme says it is a piano concerto! Be this as it may, Truscott is certainly right in saying that this beginning is 'Beethoven's only possible solution to the orchestral problem which faced him in his material'. The material itself decides the instrumentation. This is a very different phenomenon from Mozart's joke in starting the early E flat piano concerto, K271, with the solo piano. That is a delightful witticism; Beethoven's stroke is the highest order of poetry, and we should note, first, that his magical chord of B major, the major mediant, is only the dominant of the relative minor, E minor, and second, that it leads to a marvellous chord of E *major* in bar 8, which must then go through harmonies of A major, D major, and a subdominant C major to regain G. Was the main theme of the finale of the Triple Concerto behind this stroke of genius?

Beethoven of course has not 'abolished' or even lessened the importance of the *ritornello*; many later composers, following the lead of Mendelssohn's Violin Concerto, were only too happy to be relieved of much tiresome composition, tiresome to them and no doubt even more tiresome to us had they undertaken it. We cannot accuse Mendelssohn of taking the easy way out; he understood and respected perfectly well the power of the classical *ritornello* and the combined effect of it and the exposition on subsequent events in the recapitulation. His Violin Concerto, a smaller but perfect conception with less scope, is a special case, depending ultimately on the subtleties of an exceptionally sensitive instrumental imagination, as also is his unprecedented placing of the cadenza before the recapitulation. But this is another matter that has nothing to do with the lazy virtuosi who, not understanding Mendelssohn's innovation, used it as excuse for concertos to show off their own prowess as players.

During Beethoven's *ritornello* his tonal sensitivity is further shown. At bar 29, after the tonic G has been thoroughly confirmed, he comes upon a fine new theme, it may seem in A minor (Ex. 10).

Ex. 10

Is this another Beethovenian textbook 'deliberate mistake'? But A minor proves to be no key at all, only a harmony. It moves into the sound of C major and then back to G at bar 37, with the tonic still as secure as if nothing had happened. It cannot be disturbed even by another shift, towards B minor and a beautiful 'purple patch' on the dominant of that key. The effect of these changes is like that of clouds moving across the sun, which remains in the sky. Beethoven decrees that whereas the *ritornello* is normally regarded as the part of the movement where the tonality is least obscured, this concerto makes Ex. 10 appear in much more solidly prepared keys in exposition and recapitulation, respectively D minor (bar 134) and G minor (bar 299). These are real tonalities, in each case part of a firmly based procession of second-group themes. In the exposition he introduces a beautiful new theme in the orchestra, clearly the influence of Mozart's A major concerto, K488 (Ex. 11).

The development moves determinedly to the remotest possible region, C sharp minor, all the time transforming the material into shapes recognizable only by tracing the process back in stages; this anticipates a procedure in the 'Archduke' Trio and in Sibelius's Sixth Symphony. Thematic metamorphosis in Vagn Holmboe's music has a similar basis. By bar 231 the piano is playing what sounds like an entirely new theme, and we leave the reader to seek its provenance. Here C sharp minor is the remote key, and sounds like it. But soon the music drifts to, of all places, G major (bar 239) which seems, not like the tonic but like another very remote key. This is because it is heard so soon

Ex. 11

after its polar opposite C sharp minor, with shifting harmony in between. But when the recapitulation comes emphatically at bar 253 we know we must be at home, not only because of its clear dominant preparation but because of the subtle piece of 'subliminal advertising' at bar 239. This device on an even greater scale is to be found in the first movement of the *Eroica* Symphony. In the concerto Beethoven's strategy is so successful that he can now get away even with recapitulating the miracle of the opening, the piano still playing the first phrase, but *fortissimo.* The soloist can now decorate with lacy figuration the magical soft major mediant answer (bar 258).

Beethoven wrote two cadenzas for this movement, the second of which (the less often played) is notable for an anticipation of some of the piano writing in the last sonata, Op. 111.

The famous slow movement with its dialogue between piano and strings has been likened to Orpheus taming the Furies. It is in E minor, the key suggested by that B major chord in the main theme of the first movement, and the soloist's first instinct in gently replying to the strings' rough E minor is to move quietly back towards the G major they have disrupted (a good reason for a minimum break between the movements, which Beethoven supports by actually joining the last two movements together). The soloist's soft asides become increasingly impassioned, reaching an intense climax on a C trill against chromatic runs below (A to D sharp) and a persistent G sharp-A above (bar 56 *et seq.*). This amounts to the dominant of E minor, confirmed by a cadence, and the movement closes in mystery, with the cellos and basses sounding as if Beethoven had heard a Bruckner symphony.

But perhaps there was after all a touch of ambiguity in the C trill of the previous climax, containing a D natural, persisted with in the little piano cadenza before the E minor cadence. In any event the finale starts in a C major hard to interpret at once as the home subdominant. We may recall the much less ambiguous opening of the finale of the early G major cello sonata,

Op. 5, No. 2, and Beethoven himself may have been aware of the sonata when he came to compose the coda of the concerto finale. In this inexhaustible rondo trumpets and drums appear for the first time, adding brilliance and weight without aggression. The air is crystalline and sparkling with joy—so much so that the second subject, especially when we hear it in D major in the orchestra following bar 92, strongly anticipates the great tune in the finale of the Ninth Symphony. The chief glory of the splendid rondo is its magnificently expansive, vigorous yet leisurely coda, for which a shortened recapitulation makes room. It can be said to begin with the sudden turn to E flat at bar 353, and before incorporating the previously omitted recapitulation of the main theme in its literal shape and proper key, it produces a new and beautiful transformation of it in B flat (violas, bar 269). Later this recurs, but in canon and in the home key, and here Beethoven is perhaps thinking of the last movement of the early cello sonata, where there is a remarkably similar transformation, of a theme that starts, moreover, on the subdominant.

The Fourth Piano Concerto and the Violin Concerto in D, Op. 61, were both finished in the same year, 1806, the year of the first version of *Fidelio (Leonora).* The two concertos share a certain calm, a serene joy in unassertive mastery. Yet both show exceptional boldness, and the Violin Concerto is at the same time one of the quietest and most firmly determined of Beethoven's 'middle period' works; mastery no longer needs to be displayed. So apparently relaxed is this concerto that it has been criticized for its very quietism; one sometimes encounters the objection that both the first two movements are slow, followed by an easy-going rondo, and that Beethoven has not sufficiently exerted himself. This stance would also dismiss the Pastoral Symphony as a product of indolence, but that is to confuse cause and effect. A sense of relaxation may be one of the effects, but it is never a cause with Beethoven, whose music in such works has the indestructible strength that comes from vast tensions exquisitely extended and balanced against each other, within the form of a mighty but tranquilly outlined structure. The G major piano concerto is never accused of undue relaxation, because it has so much animation of detail (at its first performance it was remarked that such rapidity of passage-work had never before been known), but the Violin Concerto dispenses with all but the calmest livelinesss, even in its finale, and finds an effortless sublimity that unfortunately escapes the impatient. It is, in fact, not true that the work has two slow movements; this impression is often created in performance, when the steady *allegro* of the first movement is not permitted its natural momentum. If we compare the modes of motion in the first two movements we see that the *Larghetto* is truly slow, at times almost static, a purposive contrast damaged by laxity in the tempo of the first movement. The rhythm of the five soft drum-taps at the beginning of the first movement marks a tempo that must never be slackened to the point of rendering the device barely recognizable. This often happens, especially in the extended singing passage in the latter half of the development, where soloists succumb to an all too obvious temptation. Here the underlying rhythm must remain potent.

The opening of the concerto, the remote timpani punctuating calm woodwind phrases, is one of Beethoven's most unobtrusively original, made quietly astonishing when the violins deliver the drum-rhythm on D sharp, answered only by a plain dominant seventh (Ex. 12).

Ex. 12

In this context which is the more astonishing—the D sharp or the ordinary dominant seventh? The D sharp is seemingly ignored as the music proceeds in a serene D major, with a new rising scale that forms another theme (bar 18). A *fortissimo* tutti (bar 28) on a B flat chord brings the dominant of D minor, but the music relaxes again into the major with a new woodwind theme, as calm as the first, with the same gentle, rhythmic punctuation (Ex. 13).

Ex. 13

Horns and trumpets adopt the rhythm, softly deepening the solemnity as the mode becomes minor once more. The tension rises—and then we hear the D sharps again as part of a brief 'purple patch', now wonderfully explained away by harmony, and a grand tutti confirms a clear D major, culminating in one of Beethoven's noblest ideas (Ex. 14).

Something like it is found at the start of the *Leonora No. 1* overture, and it is not the only apparent connection between the concerto and *Fidelio* (Ex. 15).

The solo entry sweeps serenely across a vast space, and in the ensuing exposition Ex. 13 begins the second subject in A major, without the intervention of a loud tutti as before. This tutti is reserved for a different interruptive purpose, at the end of the exposition (bar 224), when the soloist appears to be bringing matters to a conventional A major close. The interruption (on a chord of F) now brings about the sublimest piece of effrontery in the whole of Beethoven's 'middle period'. This tutti (its continuation transposed now into the A major of its context) seems to evoke in the orchestra a conditioned reflex, causing it to revert back to the music of the *ritornello*, which it now delivers *in toto* from that point! The boldness of

Ex. 14

Ex. 15

this is remarkable enough (and, to use another Toveyism, will already be causing the enemy to blaspheme) but its purpose is all at once made clear by a drastic modulation, causing Ex. 14 to flow majestically out in C major. As if by another conditioned reflex, the soloist then follows with his introductory sweep, now on the dominant of C. But the expected continuation in C major is mysteriously diverted on to the dominant of B minor, then through E minor, A minor, D major, to G minor—down through the dominants. As the music becomes increasingly contemplative, G minor remains, but then gives way to other harmonies till the home dominant is peacefully reached. A spacious preparation brings in the main theme, *fortissimo*, in a grand recapitulatory statement by the full orchestra. Like the exposition, the end of the recapitulation is brusquely interrupted by the powerful tutti on a foreign chord, now B flat as at first; this time it leads to the pause on the home dominant before the cadenza, after which the movement ends in sublime calm. So disconcertingly unorthodox a plan, executed with such serenity on such a scale, is something totally new in the history of the concerto. Beethoven's somewhat hasty arrangement of it as a piano concerto has as its most interesting feature a written cadenza with drum accompaniment, in which a march-like episode irresistibly recalls the march in *Fidelio*.

The first movement, which must never seem anything but a calm *allegro*, establishes a profound tranquillity from which the *Larghetto* can poise itself above all human strife. Its stillness naturally accommodates variations, and a simple theme is calmly decorated by the soloist. After two variations the orchestra gives out a stronger assertion of the theme, to which the soloist replies with an indication that, for the time being at least, he prefers an even greater composure than variations can afford, and after a small, floating cadenza, gives out a new theme of the deepest humanity (Ex. 16).

Is there a significant, perhaps intentional kinship between this and Florestan's gratitude for refreshment in the dungeon? Thematic resemblances between Beethoven's works are not frequent, even when they have been written together, and should not pass unnoticed (Ex. 17).

Ex. 16

Moderato

Florestan

Euch wer - de Lohn in bes - sern — Wel - ten

Ex. 17

Ex. 16 proliferates, soon merging into another variation of the main theme, then back to itself again, through yet another new idea. At length the orchestra rouses itself, there is a cadenza, and the pellucid final rondo begins, the dancing of angels.

The *Larghetto* is in G, a tonality prominent in the first movement. G minor also controls the central episode of the finale. In this buoyant but always dignified movement, spaciousness is all, from which an overall calm is felt. In a just performance, the unity of this extraordinary work depends on a perception of this, with the realization that the first movement must be played with a sense of motion consistently kept somewhere between those of the last two. Only in this way can the fine balance of the greatest of violin concertos be revealed.

In December 1808 Beethoven put on one of his occasional marathon concerts, at which he confronted the public with an astounding barrage of new works. This one contained the Fifth and Sixth symphonies, the Fourth Piano Concerto, the aria 'Ah perfido!', and three movements from the Mass in C major. As if this were short change, he then decided to compose specially a 'brilliant finale' to end the concert—a piece for solo piano, orchestra, and chorus. This was the so-called 'Choral Fantasia', Op. 80. Since it is a *concertante* work that is, in the words of Willy Hess, 'considerable and beautiful', it must be included here. It has sometimes been dismissed as unimportant, and this illusion is the more likely to persist if we follow the usual line of treating it as a naïve and rather primitive anticipation of the finale of the Ninth Symphony. Admittedly Beethoven himself suggested a connection when offering the symphony to a publisher, saying that its finale was 'in the manner of my piano fantasy with chorus, though on a far larger scale'. But this comment was nothing more than an attempt to use some handy means of describing the shape of a new kind of symphonic finale. The 'Joy' theme in the symphony bears some likeness to the simple melody in praise of music that is the subject of the Fantasia's variations, and to this extent there is perhaps an embryonic element in the earlier work. But we must not allow it to divert our attention from the true nature of the piece, more closely related in spirit to *Die Zauberflöte* than to the monumental paean in the symphony. If we allow it to speak its own message it is plainly a piece of high originality and sunny poetry, and what happens in it cannot be predicted in terms of any familiar pattern. Naïve it may seem, but so does Papageno, and a sometimes Mozartian subtlety helps Beethoven find an idyllic world which (to quote Willy Hess again) 'is like a beautiful spring day full of flowers and sunshine, even if a little summer lightning is introduced by way of artistic contrast'. We must also remember that this was a work composed by Beethoven spontaneously, without commission; it was written in two weeks, but the deadline was of his own making.

It begins with what is probably one of the two finest examples of music Beethoven probably improvised and wrote down afterwards (the other is the wonderful and still neglected Fantasia, Op. 77, for piano alone, written in the following year, and formally modelled on Op. 80, which suggests that the composer took the matter seriously). There is evidence in the shape of some string parts (with second violin missing) that he afterwards thought of providing an orchestral accompaniment to the opening solo, but we can be happy that its improvisatory character has been preserved. It asserts the key of C minor in the style of a *toccata* (a piece in which an improviser will test the responses of an instrument with a variety of styles or 'touches'). This is a powerful stretch of spontaneous *bravura* with gentler elements, and at length the orchestra makes an entry with a conspiratorial little march, starting on unharmonized cellos and basses, the more effective because the piano has been without accompaniment. Its air of expectancy leads to a change to the major—then the piano gives out a simple melody in C major that immediately becomes the basis of five cheerful variations in the same key, the fourth with string quartet accompaniment and the last left to the amiable bluster of the full orchestra. This the piano interrupts by initiating a *codetta*, in which the orchestra concurs, and we are under the impression that the variation scheme has been abandoned. What next?

The soloist now runs into an accelerating cadenza, and surprisingly rips into another variation, *Allegro molto*, in a fierce C minor, still the tonic. The orchestra joins the stampede, but the piano leads it astray, into the remote key of B major with what sounds like the start of yet another variation, still in the quick tempo. But this modulates in the manner of a lively development until it eventually pauses on the dominant of A minor. Now follows a beautiful and regular slow variation in a radiant A major, elegantly adorned by the piano, which arrives at a long trill, during which the key shifts again, this time to F major, where a vivacious little variation in march tempo appears in the orchestra. The piano makes no more than a couple of fragmentary contributions to it before pointing out to the orchestra that F is only the home subdominant, working out a nice, imaginatively roundabout route back to the tonic. The orchestra responds by referring to the conspiratorial march of its first entry (we are after all still in march-tempo);

this of course is in C minor. But why the gloom? There is a chorus waiting at the back there, and this is supposed to be a 'brilliant finale'; let's go back into the major with the main tune and let the chorus finish with some more variations, on a poem in praise of music, with the piano now content to be brilliantly decorative. Towards the end we can expand into a broad coda, and the soloist can reassert himself again individually in the midst of the general rejoicing. The poem, incidentally, is supposed to be by Christopher Kuffner, who was asked by Beethoven to supply it for the occasion. But it does not appear in Kuffner's works, and it is not impossible that the final upshot was a mixture of his and Beethoven's own words. Their fresh naïvety, however, admirably suits the spirit of the music.

Attempts have been made to describe this work as an amalgam of sonata and variation form, but it is best analysed from moment to moment, when a delightfully individual form becomes apparent, as it does similarly in Op. 77. The modulating 'development' in the middle serves no such purpose as normally in a sonata movement, where its vital function is to pass from the key of the second group back to the tonic. But here it follows a solidly established tonic, and its only purpose is to break open what looked like a formal set of variations, a purpose already anticipated by the *codetta* at bar 156. The overall form is an introduction followed by set of variations that gets broken into from time to time, reforms itself, then finally expands into a coda. Such a description is truer to the facts than anything more ingenious or pretentious. The impromptu spontaneity of the whole scheme, with the eventual delighted introduction of the chorus, reflects something of the spirit of *Die Zauberflöte*, with its underlying childlike solemnity, while it foreshadows the kind of impulsive farrago that sometimes attracted Berlioz. We should welcome the powerful Beethoven when he is in this mood; even here his formidable bent for organization does not let him down, but produces something entirely new.

1809 might be thought of as Beethoven's E flat year—it produced the so-called 'Harp' Quartet, Op. 74, the piano sonata *Les Adieux*, Op. 81a, and the Fifth Piano Concerto, whose pompous nickname 'Emperor' was certainly not the composer's. These were the major works of that year, which also saw the piano sonatas, Op. 78 and 79 (the beautiful two-movement one in F sharp and the spirited little work in G) and the six songs of Op. 75. A rich year indeed—the old myth that Beethoven was a slow composer dies hard, and a few statistics from time to time are a useful corrective. In the finale of *Les Adieux* we find clear points of contact with the last movement of the concerto; they share similar passage-work, an unusual phenomenon in Beethoven works. In the first movement of the concerto we also find keyboard writing that recalls the C major piano concerto of a dozen years earlier, now raised to a higher power. Beethoven was usually conscious of such resemblances and in some cases went to some length to minimize them, as in the *Namensfeier* Overture, where he altered a rhythm throughout the work, probably because it was too close to the scherzo of the Seventh Symphony.

There is a tendency to associate keys with character, and Beethoven himself was apt to indulge in such fancies—he said Klopstock's ponderous manner was 'D flat major', B minor was 'a black key', and F minor was 'barbarous', as well as describing the colour of people's clothing in terms of tonalities. In practice, however, we cannot find such consistencies in his own use of keys; the three important E flat works of 1809 are of different natures, and although Beethoven's famous 'C minor mood' is often spoken of, the works he wrote in this key are surprisingly diverse. The key of E flat, with its richly sonorous use of the open G string of the violin, can of course easily be majestic, and it is not surprising that this very grand Fifth Concerto shares the tonality with the *Eroica* Symphony.

Heroism, however, is not the concern of this concerto; it expresses the calm consciousness of achievement rather than heroic endeavour. That Beethoven's music had little to do with passing moods or sensations is well attested by the fact that while the unfortunate man was trying to save the remnants of his hearing by burying his head in pillows during the bombardment of Vienna, he was also working on the serenely confident E flat concerto. Here is another objection to the nickname 'Emperor'; in view of his reaction six years before to Napoleon's declaring himself emperor, this is a title he would certainly have rejected for any of his works at this time. Whatever the distractions, this concerto must rank among his most unmistakeably objective creations. It expresses with majestic joy a calm knowledge of its own vigour, a poetic appreciation of its own superb athletic form.

The first movement is the broadest and most massive he achieved in the concerto field. Like its predecessor in No. 4, it deploys the piano from the outset, but where the G major concerto uses the device with delicate poetry, here the opening has an architectural effect not unlike that to come later, and on a still larger scale, in the introduction to the Seventh Symphony. The *ritornello* is again not dispensed with; the opening chords, illuminated by the soloist, establish the key of E flat like a great portico, through which a commanding view is visible. Over this the orchestra alone sweeps its attention in a great *ritornello*, over broad plains, dramatic outcrops of rock, and mysterious dark places. The use of the piano in the introduction, with its cadenza-like freedom of time, serves also to create from the start a sense of freedom for the soloist, who in this movement is to be denied the usual culmination of a cadenza. This is the most solidly symphonic of Beethoven's concerto movements. The *ritornello* has remarkable range and variety, from its opening strong assertiveness to the magical mystery of a *pianissimo* march in E flat minor and major (bar 41). In the exposition this predictably begins the second group, but unpredictably in B minor (a black key!—but really C flat minor in a more convenient notation—what would Beethoven have said about that?), turning to the major before a magnificently drastic stroke (it can hardly be called a modulation) whips the music mightily into B flat, the orthodox dominant (bar 166).

This dramatic event is powerfully transformed in the recapitulation by a different juxtaposition of harmony—C sharp (= D flat) minor and major brusquely supplanted by E flat—a rise of a tone instead of the descent of a semitone. This is indeed something to listen for; it gives renewed vitality to what would otherwise be a mechanical reproduction of the original incident. The vast breadth of the development culminates in a famous passage of massive piano octaves against a rising, then falling bass; when this subsides the restatement is approached in a spirit of calm deliberation that nevertheless creates considerable tension. At the end of the recapitulation we perceive what sounds like the beginning of a great cadenza; but the horns join in, then more instruments, and astonishingly promote yet another recapitulation from the second group onwards. This expands into a grand coda to end the giant movement. The device of a second recapitulation was to interest Beethoven again, in the finale of the Eighth Symphony and the first movement of the late A minor string quartet, Op. 132.

The beautiful and mysterious *Adagio* follows the hint of the first movement's second subject by emerging in C flat (written as B major), so that it likewise can fall a semitone to the home dominant in a famous hushed preparation for the finale. The form is variations broken into by improvisatory matter, a mutation from the slow movement of the Violin Concerto and the main body of the 'Choral Fantasia', and the mood is of felicitous contemplation. Here it is possible to give the soloist the extempore air purposely denied him after the opening of the first movement.

When the finale comes, it is the most spacious of all Beethoven's concerto rondos. Its main theme is dimly adumbrated in the mysterious link from the *Adagio*, with its softly arresting drop of a semitone; then it leaps out with a sweeping enthusiasm that causes it to catch its breath before the orchestra fierily bears the music up again. The rondo is of extraordinary range, able even to feign indolence by producing a contrasting theme (such as might be mistaken for a 'second subject') in the tonic (bar 51). The real second group starts at bar 74 on the dominant of B flat, soon bringing about the rondo-return of the main theme. This movement is a vast sonata-rondo, and the development displays three immensely spacious treatments of the main subject, beginning in C major, A flat, and E major (gigantic steps of major thirds, the same three keys juxtaposed by Bruckner in the finale of his Seventh Symphony, certainly without allusive intent!). The consummate power and breadth of this movement is an apt conclusion to this peerless concerto, itself the inevitable climax to an adventure of a scope incomparable in only seven works.

Here he stopped, and to try to imagine what kind of concertos Beethoven would have written in the period of the late quartets can be no more than frustrating. Perhaps he was no longer interested in works with elements of display—yet who knows? If someone had commissioned a concerto, how might he have responded? There can at least be no doubt that he would have explored new and profound aspects of the relationship between the individual and the mass, and that no-one since has moved into the regions he alone knew. Perhaps nobody ever will, especially in our time, even if the human species survives its own ingenious folly, an unlikely achievement now that its violence, which seems ineradicable, has inevitably produced and continues to proliferate the means of certain self-destruction. But that is something Beethoven in his time could never have imagined or, if he had lived in ours, countenanced. Such a profoundly positive search would now need not only supreme genius but resolution of the highest and most obdurate order.

CHAPTER 5

The Concerto after Beethoven

(i) The Virtuoso Concerto
Christopher Headington

The calls for social change and freedom of personal conscience associated with the end of the eighteenth century were inevitably reflected in the art of the time. In the concerto too, it seems that the time was now ripe for a development of a Classical form that would parallel such trends by affording the soloist opportunities both for inventive display and for dialogue, even disputation, with the orchestra. Beethoven showed the way with such passages as the expressive exchanges between the piano and orchestra in the *Andante con moto* of his Fourth Concerto (often likened to Orpheus taming the wild beasts) and the imperious solo flourishes that begin its successor the 'Emperor'; and we may compare the latter with the opening of Liszt's First Concerto, a work that shares the same key. But Beethoven too was part of a movement that had begun well before him. The element of soloistic self-assertion in the concerto characterized by elaborate flourishes had been foreshadowed in Baroque times by the ornamented reprises which star opera singers gave to *da capo* arias, while the *concerto grosso* with its ensemble work had been superseded by solo concertos. A soloist could also assert his dominant role by invention, as when (as Alfred Brendel has written of Mozart) the notes required 'piecing out at times; by filling . . .; by variants . . .; by embellishments . . .; and by cadenzas'. The time was ripe for the emergence of the virtuoso concerto which was designed solely as a showpiece for a master performer.

The German School

Among Beethoven's contemporaries, one whose piano concertos fit clearly into this category is **Johann Nepomuk Hummel** (1778–1837); and like nearly all composers of virtuoso pieces he was himself a master of the instrument. As a young boy he studied with Mozart and even lived in that composer's household in the late 1780s; and like Mozart, he was taken on lengthy tours as a performing pianist by his father. In London (1792) he was described as the most surprising visiting performer since Mozart himself.

Later he settled in Vienna and studied with Haydn, Albrechtsberger and Salieri, and though Beethoven's presence in the city endangered his growing reputation as a performer, composer and teacher, the two men struck up a lasting if at times stormy friendship. As Beethoven became increasingly isolated by his deafness and changing style, Hummel's reputation grew; he was a pallbearer at Beethoven's funeral (together with Schubert, who dedicated his last three piano sonatas to Hummel) and played at Beethoven's memorial concert. Because of his essential conservatism, his own death ten years later seems to mark the passing of the Viennese classical era.

Hummel has been described as 'fundamentally a warm and simple person . . . [looking] so arch-bourgeois that one hardly expected to find an artist'. His six piano concertos are highly idiomatic in their solo writing, though it is possible to feel that the A minor and B minor Concertos (Nos 2 and 3, dating from 1816 and 1819 respectively) stretch their material a little too far. Nevertheless, the orchestral exposition of both works contain much attractive melody, while the soloist embellishes the material in a flow of elegant and sparkling pianism. In the A minor the soloist makes his entry with an almost improvisatory decoration of the orchestral cadence as in the Beethoven Violin Concerto. Imaginative though the entries both here and in the B minor Concerto are, real poetic depth is to be found in the central *Larghettos* of both concertos, that of the B minor being the more extended. The orchestra plays a subordinate role throughout, as it does in the two Chopin concertos, for which Hummel was a model. (Other models were Ignaz Moscheles (1794–1870) whose G minor Concerto, Op. 58, Chopin admired and Friedrich Kalkbrenner (1785–1849) who left his mark on the E minor concerto.) Chopin was much flattered in 1830 when a friend thought his new F minor Piano Concerto 'finer than Hummel's A flat, Op. 113, which Haslinger has just published'.

Besides the works designated as concertos, Hummel also wrote a double concerto in G major for violin, piano and orchestra, Op. 17, probably modelled on the Mozart Sinfonia concertante in E flat, K364, and whose first movement owes much to the F major Concerto, K459. There are also concertos for mandolin and trumpet. The latter, in E major, is one of his best-known pieces, and though obviously modelled on the Haydn E flat it owes its place in the repertoire to its fresh and resourceful invention.

Spohr

Louis Spohr (1784–1859) contributed to the violin concerto repertory in a way that has some parallels with Hummel's achievement in that of the piano, but was perhaps a more imaginative artist. Besides being a violinist he was a conductor and opera composer, and this helps to ensure the interest of his orchestral writing. The imaginative and even dramatic nature of his art found successful expression in his 15 violin concertos of 1802–44; indeed, No. 8 in A minor (1816) is subtitled *in modo di scena cantante* (or *Gesangszene*) and takes the form of a lyrical scene or soliloquy in which the soloist provides a rich flow of melody against a subtle orchestral background, the whole being in a distinctively chromatic style. The Concerto has three linked movements marked *Allegro molto*, *Adagio* and *Andante-Allegro moderato*. In the first two movements taken together, after a march-like orchestral prelude in A minor a violin recitative flowers into aria style and a change to F major and triple time. The final bar in this example, its first subject, is harmonized with an A major chord, the dominant of D minor, and the modulatory freedom is typical of this composer (Ex. 1).

Ex. 1

The finale, also preceded by recitative, is elaborately developed from an opening theme whose compass is instrumental rather than vocal. A more relaxed second idea dances in semiquavers and a further episode in E flat major is thoughtfully lyrical. Spohr's use of form here is not dissimilar to the operatic cavatina-cabaletta construction developed at this time by Rossini, and his subtitle makes it almost certain that this was intentional. Such a chosen blend of concerto and opera is probably explicable by the fact that this concerto was intended for the Milan audience to whom Spohr gave its première at La Scala, but it was undoubtedly also congenial to him. However, in forming his concerto style his first models were not Italian but French, notably the violin concertos of **Pierre Rode** (1774–1830), and from them he learned to balance lyrical sensitivity with bravura. He was the author of a *Violinschule* (1832), and naturally his music for the instrument displays a wide technical range, such as the use of on-string staccato played with an up-bow as here in his Ninth Concerto (Ex. 2).

This bowing is difficult, and Spohr himself said that its execution was 'to some extent a natural gift'; when Mendelssohn heard him play he was

Ex. 2

delighted by this particular technique. But for all the skill needed by a soloist, Spohr's concertos are more remarkable for their thoughtfulness than for their extrovert brilliance. It has rightly been said that he stood against the trivialization that always threatens the virtuoso concerto, and that his concertos are a bridge between Beethoven and Mendelssohn. Wagner was to praise him as 'worthy of the highest honour'; while Tovey wrote that 'his sense of beauty is such as only an unhealthy taste will despise'. His other concertos include four for clarinet, works stimulated by the skill of Johann Simon Hermstedt who was the soloist in each of their premières.

Weber

Carl Maria von Weber (1786–1826), himself an admirer of Spohr, also wrote a clarinet concertino and two concertos, all three of which date from the year 1811, as does his Bassoon Concerto; in his case the virtuoso who inspired these was Heinrich Baermann. The Concertino begins with a variation set and ends with a vivid *Allegro*; in such music as this brilliant finale the composer's fluency is characteristic and effortless, but the most personal music in all these works comes in their slower sections. The soloist's style at times suggests recitative, and instrumentation is a strong point also, with individual touches in the slow movements of both the First Clarinet Concerto and the Bassoon Concerto, where in each case the soloist is accompanied by horns.

Weber's own instrument was the piano, for which he composed two concertos, the First (1810) being in C major and the Second (1812) in E flat major. These are notable for their elegant passagework and for a spontaneity that anticipates Chopin—who was interested in Weber and as a boy in 1826 noted the 'extraordinary *recherché* harmony' of *Der Freischütz*. As elsewhere, the instrumentation is inventive, and especially so in the slow movements; indeed in the *Adagio* of the Second Concerto we are reminded of the colourist who was to create the *Oberon* Overture. Nevertheless, in these relatively early works, preceding by some years Weber's operas, it is the pianism that impresses most of all, and notably in the finales. Even so, we know that Weber distrusted virtuosity *per se*, writing in his unfinished novel *Tonkünstlers Leben* (*c.* 1820) of those 'damned piano fingers which through endless practising take on a kind of independence and mind of their own [and] are unconscious tyrants and despots of the creative art'. His own large hands allowed him 'to play tenths as easily as octaves', but his command of fine sonority including *cantabile* tone was equally remarkable. According to his friend Hinrich Lichtenstein, he wished as a pianist to communicate feeling rather than to impress as a virtuoso.

Weber's dramatic flair is evident in his *Konzertstück* for piano and orchestra

(1821). This has an elaborate programme in which a medieval lady awaits her husband's return from the Crusades, fearing his death on the battlefield. At his appearance 'she sinks into his arms [upward glissando for the soloist]; love is triumphant, happiness unbounded; the very woods and waves sing the song of love; a thousand voices proclaim his victory'. It is the final march that marks the return of the husband, in C major after the preceding tense F minor, and if the melody is somewhat crude, its directness has an impact akin to that which we often find in Beethoven (Ex. 3).

Ex. 3

Mendelssohn

Among the early Romantic German-speaking concerto composers discussed here, the one with the strongest claim to have written an unflawed masterpiece is **Felix Mendelssohn** (1809–1847). The late Hans Keller used to call his Violin Concerto in E minor (1844) 'the only violin concerto', and certainly it has the firmest place in the repertory of all the works discussed here. Yet although Mendelssohn was a skilled string player, he was more so as a pianist and organist, and thus the work belies the general rule that a virtuoso concerto must be written by a master of the chosen instrument. Belying the popular image of Mendelssohn as an effortlessly fluent craftsman, the concerto, composed for Ferdinand David (who also advised on technical matters), was not written quickly; Mendelssohn began to sketch it in 1838, and although doing the bulk of the work while on holiday near Frankfurt in September 1844, he then tinkered with the score for six months between its completion and the première in March 1845. The soloist plunges immediately into the main theme—and what an inspired idea it is! In doing so he breaks new ground, as he does in both the piano concertos by omitting the orchestral exposition.

The long-arching melody, set mainly in the octave above the treble stave, grows in energy and momentum and leads to lively passage-work for the soloist, after which it is repeated forcefully but more briefly by the orchestra. A lengthy transition initially in flowing crotchets leads to a calmer mood and the relative major, G for the second subject. And here we have something quite special: the soloist sustains G, the lowest note of his instrument, and over this pedal, the clarinet sings the theme. It is an extraordinarily imaginative stroke of the kind that separates genius from talent. The theme is then replayed by the violin and considerably extended, the mood being thoughtful and intimate and the pace gradually relaxing. An unusual reference to the first subject in the major mode marks the start of a long codetta to the exposition that builds to a big climax with—again unusually—orchestral trills and *tremolando*. The development explores a range of keys, with the solo part marked alternately *agitato* and *tranquillo*; after a haunting lull in the music, so characteristic of Mendelssohn at this point in a movement, a timpani roll on B, the dominant of the home key of E minor, brings a sudden orchestral crescendo. But here, instead of the expected recapitulation, Mendelssohn gives us a short but effective cadenza that ends in rapid arpeggios which continue through the quiet orchestral restatement of the first subject that begins the recapitulation. The tranquil depth of the second theme is here intensified, and once again leads to the orchestral trills, while the cadenza's arpeggio figurations are heard again in the *Presto* coda, where the music attains a heightened virtuosity and urgency.

From the final E minor chord of the first movement emerges a soft tenor B held by the first bassoon. This begins a brief introduction to the *Andante*, a movement in which the solo violin sings persuasively in a clear, calm C major; an agitated A minor middle section leads us back to the opening, its serenity now slightly disturbed by the restless string figuration from the A minor section. The finale is also connected to the preceding movement, and approached by a linking passage of 14 bars (*Allegretto non troppo*) that has been called 'wistful' and shows a kinship with the opening theme of the whole work. Then, the ebullient principal theme, marked *scherzando* and *leggiero*, dances forth. This effervescent movement, the last evocation of the fairyland Mendelssohn so often conjured up in his youth, is in sonata form: the first subject dances along irrepressibly, while the second is march-like and introduced by the orchestra *fortissimo*; there is also a flowing third theme (first heard softly in G major from the soloist) designed as a countersubject to the first subject and played with it by the orchestral strings in the recapitulation.

The E minor Violin Concerto is unique but not alone in Mendelssohn's catalogue, for as a boy of 13 he composed a Violin Concerto in D minor (with string orchestra) for which the model was evidently Mozart. Although he must have thought of it as an example of juvenilia since he left it unpublished, it appeared in 1952 in an edition by Yehudi Menuhin and proves to be a skilful piece that bears remarkable witness to the early development of the composer's craft, but only the energetic finale is really striking in its invention. There is also a Piano Concerto in A minor from the same year that again displays charm and skill. More important than either are the two numbered piano concertos, in G minor and D minor, works of Mendelssohn's early maturity which date respectively from 1831 and 1837.

Although the G minor Concerto was 'a thing quickly thrown off', according to the composer in a letter to his father, it is an exuberant work conceived on tour in Italy and then set down in Munich, where he played it in 1832. Both here and in the D minor Concerto, composed on his honeymoon in the Black Forest and elsewhere in Germany, he wrote with evident joy in thematic inventiveness and keyboard dexterity, as well as a sensitivity that stops just short of sentimentality. Schumann called the D minor Concerto 'a fleeting, carefree gift'. Possibly the slow movements of both concertos offer the most subtle writing; that of the G minor is in the remote key of E major, with a nocturne-like melody marked *tranquillo*, while the *Adagio* of the Second Concerto is in part a dialogue between soloist and orchestra, with quite lengthy passages for the pianist alone. The three movements of the G minor are played with little or no break, the first being fairly terse with its lack of an orchestral exposition and a compressed recapitulation, while the *Presto* finale is distinctly free in its deployment of themes; the *Adagio* of the D minor also goes *attacca* into the witty *Presto scherzando* finale. Two boyhood concertos for two pianos and orchestra in E minor (1823) and A flat major (1824), together with the effective *Rondo brillant* of a decade later make up the tally of Mendelssohn's works for solo instrument(s) and orchestra.

Joachim

Joseph Joachim (1831–1907) was the outstanding violinist of his generation as well as a composer of some distinction. Born in what is now Hungary, he became a pupil and protégé of Mendelssohn at Leipzig, and made his début there in 1843 in a concert in which that composer and Clara Schumann also participated. He was the dedicatee of the Brahms, Schumann and Dvořák concertos as well as the Bruch G minor. Like Spohr, Joachim was schooled in the tradition of Rode, which in turn owed much to Italian *bel canto*; in other words his playing was predominantly lyrical. Thus, he was a near-ideal exponent of the Beethoven Concerto, his performance of which as a young man was described as 'artistic perfection which put all bravura behind it'. In this respect, both Joachim and Spohr may be seen as representing a school of musical thought somewhat opposed to that symbolized by Paganini's dazzling dexterity; and this is evident in their compositions, where virtuosity is to be found less in agility than in an unbounded expressive resource coupled with a full identification of a solo instrument and performer with the music.

Joachim's works for solo instrument and orchestra are all for violin, the principal ones being a Concerto in One Movement (*c.* 1855), a Concerto in Hungarian Style (1861), a set of Variations (1882) and a Concerto in G major (1899). None survives in the concert hall though the Hungarian Concerto has been recorded. It has been said that their relatively conservative style (Joachim was once close to Liszt but later repudiated the ideals of the new German school) lacks impact and that they 'present players with considerable difficulties without being particularly rewarding either musically or as display pieces' (Roger Thomas Oliver in the *New Grove*). But one may hope that this judgement is too harsh. Tovey, writing over half a century ago of an artist who was also his friend, thought that the interest of Joachim's works would 'grow with the passage of time; for it depends on ideas that stand on their own musical merits without regard to fashion'; he also declared that in Joachim's violin works 'not a note is there for display'. Tovey also considered that 'Joachim never wrote a bar that did not aim instinctively for clearness and completeness in the presentation of true musical ideas'—a remark which seems bland for this normally penetrating critic. Moreover, Tovey declared, wrongly, that all Joachim's compositions were early works; even the Variations which he discussed in his *Essays in Musical Analysis* date from the composer's early fifties. These have a somewhat Brahmsian theme in E minor which is meticulously marked with articulation and dynamics but is rather square and uninteresting save as a vehicle for classical variation procedures of increasingly elaborate figuration, as well as a hunting-rhythm version with horns (Variation 6) under the soloist's scales and arpeggios and another 'hunting chorus' in Variation 17, and a final brilliant rondo ending in the major. Only the solo Variation 8 (violin chords) and its full orchestral echo in Variation 9 provide anything really new.

Bruch

Max Bruch (1838–1920) was in many respects a typical though unusually able Kapellmeister in the German tradition. Unlike Joachim, he was not a skilled performer, save on the conductor's rostrum; and though he studied the piano in his youth all but one of his four concertos are for violin. By far the best known is the First Violin Concerto in G minor (1866). He called its first movement a *Vorspiel* (Prelude); but like the Prelude to *Parsifal* it is too substantial to be regarded as merely introductory. It begins quietly and poetically with a series of exchanges between the solo violin and the orchestra; then the soloist has a declamatory theme against *tremolando* strings and a long-short-long-short rhythm which will recur, while a flattened leading note lends a slightly Bohemian flavour. A change to B flat major (the relative key) brings a gentler second subject that has the soloist accompanied by the orchestral strings; then the first theme and its accompanying rhythm returns and the tempo increases towards a powerful tutti in which the same rhythmic figure takes on a disturbing force. The music now calms to a return of the opening idea, but instead of proceeding to an expected recapitulation Bruch brings us *via* a sustained B flat, the dominant of E flat major, to the *Adagio* in that key. Its theme, stated by the soloist, is strikingly Mendelssohnian but no less memorable for that. This movement develops and flowers in a lyrical manner that seems to foreshadow the slower music of Elgar's Violin Concerto of 40 years later, and as a violinist himself Elgar probably knew Bruch's work. Quiet timpani lead to an orchestral-then-solo return of the main theme in G flat major about halfway through the *Adagio*, and after this a big climax is built which gradually dies away to the ending.

The finale is an *Allegro energico*. Its *pianissimo* start in E flat major is merely the introduction to a brilliant Hungarian-style theme (possibly intended as a compliment to Joachim) announced by the violin in double-stopping thirds and sixths. The key is now G major, the time *alla breve* and the structure sonata form: triplet figures for the soloist lead after extended passage-work to a D major second subject with leaping intervals, first presented triumphantly by the orchestra and then taken over by the solo violin. The return of the 'Hungarian' theme marks the beginning of a short development which is followed by a conventional reprise. The composer reserves the most exciting music for a coda which accelerates to a dizzy *Presto*.

The Bruch G minor Concerto will always be popular with violinists who appreciate its idiomatic writing for their instrument (doubtless Joachim helped on the technical side) and its lyricism; but the skill and resource of the orchestral writing also deserve notice, the richness of the instrumentation being akin to that of Brahms. His other two violin concertos (1878, 1891) rather surprisingly share the same key of D minor: though No. 2 also has a romantic atmosphere, it is perhaps only in the big first movement that it quite matches up to its predecessor. Bruch was nervous about the work and made several revisions of it after its première with Sarasate as the soloist. Two other works for violin and orchestra, the Third Violin Concerto and the *Konzertstück* in F sharp minor (1911), were neglected until Salvatore Accardo took them up in the 1970s, but a decade later they are no nearer finding a place alongside the popular G minor Concerto. Nor are the Romance in A minor, Op. 42 (1874) or the *Adagio appassionato*, Op. 57 of 1891, but one other piece for violin and orchestra, the melodious if episodic *Scottish Fantasy* on folk melodies (1880), is popular with violinists, and in the hands of a Heifetz, Chung, Lin or Perlman it can take on a stature and appeal comparable with that of the First Concerto. A work for cello and orchestra, the *'adagio* on Hebrew melodies' called *Kol Nidrei* (1881), has also found a secure place in the repertory. Its form is superficially similar to that of the

Scottish Fantasy, but it is more introverted in style as befits its devotional nature.

Master Performers: Paganini and Liszt

The Italian word 'virtuoso', as used in the sixteenth and seventeenth centuries, merely meant a person of intellectual or artistic distinction. But by the late eighteenth century it referred more often to a solo performer of especial personality, in whose art a display element was pre-eminent, or nearly so. Franz Liszt, himself the greatest piano virtuoso of his time, declared that 'virtuosity is not an outgrowth but an indispensable element of music'.

Liszt's first model was the Italian violinist **Nicolò Paganini** (1782–1840), whom he first heard at the age of 19 in Paris. Like everyone else, he was bowled over. In fact Paganini's unique skill owed much to day-long childhood practice. And as it happens, he too had had his model to inspire him: for when he was about twelve he had noted with delight the 'multitude of technical tricks' in the violin playing of the Polish performer August Duranowski (*c.* 1770–1834) who visited Paganini's native Genoa, later admitting that it was Duranowski who had shown him what the violin could do and inspired him to go further.

Paganini's early training in composition allowed him to create skilfully in the larger forms. He wrote numerous works for violin and orchestra, including six concertos which follow established classical outlines and, for all their remarkable pyrotechnics, never deteriorate into mere showpieces. Yet in each of them the solo violin dominates and dazzles. The opening solo in the First Concerto is typical, and in the characteristic violin key of D major (so suited to the instrument because of the tuning of the strings), we immediately meet brilliance and authority (Ex. 4).

We notice here the crisp and somewhat marchlike *maestoso* rhythm, the

Ex. 4

use in a mere eight bars of the whole compass of the instrument from its lowest G to the E nearly two octaves above the treble stave, the triple- and quadruple-stopping, the effective arpeggios which link one register with another, the carefully marked accents and articulation (in other words the use of the bow) and finally the rhetorical pause in the fourth bar.

Yet Paganini offers another kind of virtuosity too that is less obvious. You cannot make a whole concerto out of one mood, and his second subject in this movement is a simple A major tune marked *dolce*. But in the hands of a master violinist, the way a gentler and more lyrical theme such as this can be shaped and shaded in its dynamics, articulation, vibrato and even pitch can also thrill. Another example of this is the opening solo melody in the second movement of the same concerto. Given Paganini's background, it is hardly surprising that the melodic style owes much to the *bel canto* of Italian opera. The entry occurs after six bars of a chordal pattern from the orchestra (Ex. 5).

Ex. 5

Paganini's technical innovations and demands include left-hand pizzicato and occasional retuning upwards of one or more of the violin strings. He was particularly fond of bouncing (ricochet) bowing and of harmonics, obtained by lightly touching an open or stopped string at a suitable point (node) with a left-hand finger while bowing, and sounding as high and somewhat flute-like notes, and liked to use thinner strings than the norm so as to facilitate these. There are whole passages of stratospheric melody played in harmonics in the finale of the First Concerto and also (after letter D) harmonics in thirds by means of complex fingerings indicated in the score. It has been said (by Boris Schwarz) that Paganini's tone 'had infinite shadings . . . he displayed a phenomenal command of the fingerboard . . . [his] technique had a dare-devil character, tailored to his own style of playing; he took enormous risks in performing works that demanded superhuman control.'

What, then, of the pianist **Franz (Ferenc) Liszt** (1811–1886)?

> For the past fortnight my mind and fingers have been working away like two lost souls . . . I practise four to five hours of exercises (thirds, sixths, octaves, tremolos, repeated notes, cadenzas etc) . . . Ah! provided I don't go mad, you will find in me an artist.

Thus the young Liszt, after hearing Paganini in 1831. He was to compose two piano concertos, with ideas for both dating from the 1830s. However, neither reached its final form until much later, after undergoing several revisions. The First Concerto, in E flat major, was originally completed in 1849 with some assistance from the composer's protégé Joachim Raff and was then revised in 1853 and 1856; but its première took place before the final revision at Weimar in 1855, with Berlioz conducting and the composer himself as the soloist. It has an unusual structure for a concerto, evidently borrowed from that of Schubert's *Wanderer Fantasy* for piano solo. It has been described as having a 'four-movements-in-one' form, though this is a little misleading in that there is a clear stop before the *Quasi adagio* section in B major which is the second of the four; and the other novel feature is the use of thematic transformation, which links the movements much more effectively than mere continuity. Schubert may have shown the way, but Liszt went further with the technique, which he also employed in such works as his 'Faust' Symphony and the symphonic poem *Les Préludes.* Thus the opening four-bar orchestral statement also occurs altered later in the first section and again in the third *(Allegretto vivace)* providing also the material for the Concerto's coda, while the Bellini-like floating melody of the *Quasi adagio* is turned into a march for the first subject of the finale, marked *Allegro marziale animato* (see Ex. 6).

Even the opening cadenza for the soloist returns in a modified form to lead to the trills that link the scherzo with the finale. But for all its vigour, the first section is mainly lyrical and eloquent, almost improvisatory. Without a

Quasi adagio

Ex. 6a

Allegro marziale animato

Ex. 6b

classical development it is hardly in sonata form, and its 'second subject' is a drooping melody featuring a triplet (or dotted) rhythm played first by the soloist and in the same key as the opening. The E flat/D sharp link between this section and the *Quasi adagio* is well managed, as is the gradual modulation back to E flat major and minor for the scherzo. This has the piano marked *capriccioso scherzando* and a solo part for triangle that Hanslick thought vulgar but which lends a fine glitter to this already brilliant score. In the sense that the finale introduces no significant new material, it may be thought of as a kind of recapitulation or summing-up of the whole story.

Liszt's Second Concerto in A major is also played without a break, but falls into three fairly clearly defined sections. It has been called 'less brilliant and more poetical', but this may mislead a little since the First Concerto has its poetry also, while there is ample brilliance here in the Second as well as the poetry of such passages as the solo cello's playing of the initial theme over a quiet piano accompaniment in the first section. The gentle chordal opening, scored for woodwind, proves rich in thematic possibilities, and the hushed mood is maintained by the piano, entering *dolce armonioso*. But a short cadenza leads to a martial passage that ushers in an *Allegro agitato assai* in B flat minor that is later actually marked *violente*. A very brief cadenza leads to an *Allegro moderato* which is more relaxed in mood, with a tune in E major for the soloist (alone) which is a gentle variant of the preceding one, now in 4/4 instead of 6/8. The cello solo mentioned above now gives us the theme of the concerto's opening bars, its chromaticism having a strongly Italian flavour. A gradual increase in momentum leads in due course to the *Allegro deciso* beginning in D flat major which may be seen as a development section to the whole work. Yet the piano's thunderous chords here are accompanimental, and so are the filigree scales and arpeggios that follow; after this, passages in double octaves give the soloist further scope for bravura. In due course the triple *forte* of the *Marziale, un poco meno Allegro* is reached, and—as in the First Concerto—the feeling of a recapitulation–finale: the theme is of course that of the very opening, now transformed from its quiet triple time into a triumphal march. A quieter section for the soloist alone *(appassionato)* brings us to the *Allegro animato* coda with its four white-key glissandos boldly set against A major harmonies in the orchestra. This Second Concerto was first played by Liszt's pupil Hans von Bronsart, the dedicatee, under the composer's baton.

Liszt wrote a few other works for piano and orchestra, of which the strangely-named *Malédiction* (c. 1840) for piano and strings and the *Totentanz* (1859) are the most important and familiar. The former was originally a youthful concerto of a programmatic kind, the title applying to its first theme and other themes being labelled 'Pride', 'Tears-Anguish-

Dreams' and 'Raillery'. The other work was inspired by Orcagna's fourteenth-century fresco in Pisa depicting the Day of Judgement, with Death as a female figure holding a scythe. It consists of thirty continuous variations on the plainchant *Dies Irae* theme and is a notable example of the composer's gift for demonic brilliance—here, indeed, is what Gregorovius called Liszt, 'Mephistopheles dressed as an abbé'. It features glissandos and the chromatic runs for alternate-hand octaves, which were Liszt's own invention, and are still called 'Liszt octaves' today.

Field and Chopin

If Liszt owed much to Beethoven in authoritative vein, his contemporary Chopin derived more from rather gentler predecessors whose virtuoso writing emphasized elegance rather than emotional and physical force. There are piano concertos by the Bohemian composer **Jan Ladislav Dussek** (1760–1812) of which at least one (in E flat major) anticipates Chopin in its decorative slow movement and vivid bravura. Passages of octaves and thirds are frequent, and definite pedal indications appear as early as his 'Military' Concerto in B flat major of 1798. One oddity about some of these Dussek concertos is their published designation 'for piano or harp', immediately suggesting a gentler style than that of most other composers. **Ignaz Moscheles** (1794–1870) composed eight piano concertos between 1819 and 1838 and knew Chopin, who played with him in a Paris performance of his Grande Sonate for piano duet, Op. 47, in 1839. But his style is only overtly Romantic in such places as the slow movement of his Concerto No. 2 in E flat major (1825) and his Seventh ('Pathétique') Concerto in C minor (1836). **Friedrich Kalkbrenner** (1785–1849), was a virtuoso pianist who wrote four concertos for his instrument. Chopin nearly studied with him but decided against it; however, he remained on good terms with the older man and dedicated his E minor Concerto to him. Schumann found only 'contrived pathos . . . artificial profundities' in Kalkbrenner's concertos, but there are striking parallels between him and the Polish master, as comparison of the Kalkbrenner D minor Concerto, Op. 61, his first, with the Chopin E minor and F minor concertos shows.

Possibly more important than any of these figures, not only as a Chopin predecessor but in his own right, is **John Field** (1782–1837), the composer of seven piano concertos written over the period 1799–1832. This well-travelled Irishman was born in Dublin and died in Moscow, his Russian residence from about 1803 arising from his travels as a demonstator pianist for the musician and manufacturer Clementi. After Field played his First

Concerto in St Petersburg in 1804, he was established in society and 'not to have heard Field was regarded as a sin against art and good taste'. His own playing style was subtle, and as early as 1799 critics noted its 'characteristic musical expression'. Later he was praised for 'his touch on the keys, the way his melodies sang, the easy, heavely "floating" of his scales and passagework, the nobility of interpretation'. A Parisian observer, Alphonse Marmontel, remarked on his 'exquisite colour ... singing phrases [and] a sweet and tender feeling that few virtuosi were able to achieve'.

The Field piano style was reflected not only in his nocturnes which provided Chopin with an evident model, but also in his concertos. The first solo entry of the Second Concerto (1816) provides a case in point, though one is tempted to add that drawing attention to the resemblance to Chopin cannot fail to emphasize the somewhat less adroit handling of the keyboard by the older composer (Ex. 7).

Field's First Concerto follows a fashionable taste for national colour by including a set of variations on a Scottish air with a typical 'Scotch snap' rhythm *(Within a mile of Edinboro' town)* as its slow movement; and his ostensibly programmatic Fifth Concerto, subtitled *L'incendie par l'orage*

Ex. 7

(1817) may represent a similar attempt to keep up with the romantic-pictorial times. However, Nicholas Temperley considers that the title of the latter work 'has no obvious connection with the music' although David Branson finds a storm 'in full blast' in some C minor passagework. This Fifth Concerto has a polonaise-style theme early in its first movement, but the piano's entry is a merely conventional declamation in C major and the second subject is no more interesting. More striking is Field's use of nocturnes as slow movements or sections in these concertos, for example in the Second, Fifth, Sixth and Seventh. The pianist and Field scholar David Branson has argued persuasively from the internal evidence in his book *John Field and Chopin* (London, 1972) that Chopin was directly influenced by various passages in these concertos, and regards Field's Second as the composer's 'most considerable achievement ... this concerto is a "key" romantic one, with probably more influence on later romantic piano writers than any other'. We know that Chopin was flattered by comparisons of his music with that of Field. He wrote proudly to his family on 21 November 1830 that his playing had reminded a German musician (Augustus Klengel) of Field's, while a year later he was pleased that Kalkbrenner thought he had 'the touch of Field' and that in Paris many people 'set my name next to Field's; indeed if I were a bigger fool than I am, I might think I had reached the peak of my career'.

Yet by this time **Frédéric Chopin** (1810–1849) had already composed his two concertos, both for the piano, the instrument of which he was himself a master. Like Beethoven's first two concertos, they are numbered in the wrong order: the reason here is that the E minor which is now called No. 1 was published first. In fact they both date from 1830, the F minor having been finished early in the year and the E minor in August. It looks as if the composer began work on the E minor Concerto immediately on completing the F minor, if not actually before. In the circumstances, including the composer's youth, it is unsurprising that they resemble each other fairly strongly in general approach. We cannot find here the individuality and invention displayed in his piano studies composed at the same time or even earlier. But perhaps the young composer was merely being practical: the dedication of the E minor Concerto to Kalkbrenner suggests that he had no intention at the time of moving outside the musical realms understood by an older generation.

Chopin's 'First' Concerto in E minor, Op. 11, was first heard at a private performance on 22 September 1830 in Warsaw: 'our house will witness the event, I'm doing it as a rare treat', he wrote to a friend. But he also said of it: 'I feel like a novice, just as I felt before knowing anything of the keyboard—it's far too original and I'll end up by being unable to learn it myself'. The first of the three movements, *Allegro maestoso*, starts with a stern *risoluto* theme from the full orchestra and continues with a gentler one marked *cantabile* in E major. Its resemblance to the Kalkbrenner D minor and especially the Hummel A minor has often been noted. The entry of the soloist leads to freer writing of greater individuality. The development brings the gentler second strand of the first subject on the piano, in C major, and flurries of semiquavers lead to a shortened recapitulation. The *Larghetto* is in the tonic, E major, and labelled a Romance, but the title may have been an afterthought since at the time of the first performance Chopin referred only to 'my *Adagio*'. This is in effect a nocturne in which the strings are muted (an effect without which, he declared, the movement would fail), and after eleven bars of *pianissimo* orchestral introduction the piano enters with a characteristic lyrical idea. This flowers in a series of improvisatory paragraphs modulating to A flat major for one passage; the soloist plays throughout while the orchestra supports him. As if to disguise the fact that all three movements share the same tonic, the final Rondo begins in the relative minor, C sharp minor, but after a few bars the sprightly piano entry (*scherzando*) confirms E major. The vigour and momentum of this movement in quick duple time suggest a Polish *krakowiak*. An attractive episode over gentle but alert repeated chords from the orchestra begins in A major and then moves through B minor and F major (it is sometimes taken a little slower in performance) and the main rondo theme returns also *dolcissimo* in the remote key of E flat major. But the dancing piano triplets that have already become a feature of the movement return, as does the modulating episode, now starting in B major; after this comes a coda based on a new rhythmic figure and marked *brillante* for the soloist.

Chopin's F minor Piano Concerto, the 'Second', was written when he was approaching his twentieth birthday, and he gave its première at his home two days after that occasion on 3 March 1830 with Karol Kurpiński conducting; the public first heard it two weeks later in the Warsaw National Theatre. Like that of the E minor Concerto, its first movement is marked to be played *maestoso*. The orchestral exposition has the conventional two themes, the *dolce*, *legato* second subject featuring dotted rhythm like the first, but easily distinguished from it by the change to A flat major. The orchestra's subordinate role after the soloist enters caused Berlioz to scorn it as 'frigid and practically superfluous'; and although good performances disguise this to some extent, the very brilliance of the piano writing exposes a lack of character elsewhere: the solo entry with the first subject is far more vital than what went before, and the rather neutral second theme comes to life only with the decorated version the piano provides. The orchestra introduces both the development and recapitulation, making the form easy to follow. Neither this work nor the E minor Concerto has a cadenza, perhaps because the piano writing is so naturally florid throughout.

We know from a letter of Chopin's dated 3 October 1829 that the *Larghetto* was inspired by his attraction to the young singer Konstancja Gładkowska, whom he called 'my ideal, whom I've served faithfully for six months without saying a word to her'. This is an outpouring of melody, decorated in the pianistic equivalent of the vocal *bel canto* style which the composer enjoyed; the soloist is instructed to play 'with the greatest delicacy'. It is dissimilar to the *Larghetto* of the E minor Concerto in that the tender mood is broken here by an agitated middle section with piano recitative over *tremolando* strings: here the solo part is marked *appassionato*. (A resemblance between this movement and that of Moscheles's Third Piano Concerto has been noted, and the suggestion made that the young Chopin used this work as a model.) The finale is an *Allegro vivace*, beginning with a lilting piano theme marked 'simply yet gracefully'. Some commentators have related this theme to the mazurka, but the one-in-a-bar effect is different; the later *scherzando* section in A flat major with its triplet figures and tapping string accompaniment is closer to that dance style.

Violin Virtuosi—De Bériot, Vieuxtemps, Ernst, Wieniawski, Sarasate

Several violin virtuoso-composers succeeded Paganini. The Belgian **Charles-Auguste de Bériot** (1802–1870) performed a Viotti concerto at the age of nine and was later encouraged by that artist; he became principal violinist to the Netherlands court and married the celebrated singer Maria Malibran with whom he gave joint concerts, and after she died, Heine commented that it was as if her soul sang through his violin. Spohr also praised his playing, though had reservations about his compositions. He ended his career as head of the violin faculty at the Brussels Conservatoire. De Bériot's mainly graceful style is already a feature of early works, while his Second Violin Concerto (1835) also incorporates many Paganini devices such as harmonics and left-hand pizzicato. He left ten violin concertos in all (Nos 7 and 9 are still used for teaching) as well as two treatises on violin playing. It has been claimed that his 'elegance and elfin grace' influenced Mendelssohn in his E minor Concerto.

De Bériot's best-known pupil was another Belgian, **Henri Vieuxtemps** (1820–1881). Vieuxtemps was thrilled by Paganini in London as a boy in 1834 and in due course produced his own First Concerto in 1840, combining display elements with Gallic elegance. The solo entry in the first movement, *Allegro moderato*, resembles that of the Paganini First Concerto with its use of arpeggios covering the whole compass and in following *forte* after eight bars by *dolce*, thus presenting the violin in imperious and coaxing mood by turns. The second subject is also marked *dolce*. However, Vieuxtemps marks a triple *forte* where Paganini goes only as far as *fortissimo* (the octaves at bar 196 of the first movement); after this longish first movement, a brief *Adagio* leads into a playful rondo finale.

Vieuxtemps wrote seven violin concertos, characterized often by a certain richness and dignity beyond what is to be expected in a virtuoso work. The Fourth (in D minor) was acclaimed by Berlioz as a 'magnificent symphony with principal violin'; it attempts a larger utterance by adding a scherzo third movement to a declamatory first movement, slow movement and finale. The Fifth Concerto, in A minor, again breaks new ground structurally and is effectively in a single big movement. Here an *Allegro non troppo* with a second subject *semplice* in C major leads to an eloquent *Adagio* and a final *Allegro con fuoco*; the composer provided alternative cadenzas for the close of the first movement.

Heinrich Wilhelm Ernst (1814–1865), born in Brno, also heard Paganini as a boy and was so captivated that he set about following the great Italian on tour, playing his unpublished music 'with a degree of fidelity that astonished the composer'. He made his own début in 1831 in Paris and in due course commenced tours that resulted in his being acclaimed as the equal of Paganini. Joachim said 'he towered above all others' as a violinist, and Berlioz called him a great musician as well as a great player. His *Concerto pathétique* (1844) in F sharp minor is in a single movement. Its technical demands may be gauged from such a passage as this, occurring near the end (Ex. 8).

Ernst's works featured in the repertory of the Polish violinist **Henryk Wieniawski** (1835–1880), who studied in Paris and soon commenced a travelling virtuoso's career. His First Violin Concerto (1853) possibly owes its tonality (F sharp minor) and much of its style to Ernst's *Concerto pathétique*. Here too we find what has been called a 'tone of theatrical pathos', and the

Ex. 8

brilliant use of multiple-stopping, as in this passage from the *Allegro moderato* first movement (Ex. 9).

The first solo entry (at bar 73) is in tenths, and the compass is demanding also, rising to the A two octaves above the treble clef in the first-movement cadenza. But the music also reflects Wieniawski's more sensitive side. The 'warm, rich tone, his glowing temperament . . . his captivating élan' which were admired in his playing are to be gauged in the lilting *poco più lento* second subject of the first movement, as well as the *Larghetto* second movement subtitled *Preghiera* or Prayer. The finale of this First Concerto is a rondo with an expressive yet rhythmical main theme: it refers back at one point *(Maestoso)* to the first solo entry of the first movement.

Ex. 9

Wienawski's Second Concerto, in D minor (1862), is often called his finest work. It begins quietly, and the entry of the soloist (after some while) is likewise gentle and persuasive. Despite passages of brilliance in what follows, one never feels that virtuosity is the *raison d'être* of the work. The poetic element is apparent also in the central Romance, which follows without a break. The final *Allegro moderato, alla Zingara*—in other words, in gipsy style—is energetic but again not excessive in display.

Pablo Sarasate y Navascuez (1844–1908) was an outstanding Spanish player of his time to whom many works were dedicated, including some already mentioned. Joachim dedicated his variations for violin and orchestra to him, but the two men were different in temperament, and Sarasate was displeased when his account of the Beethoven Concerto was compared unfavourably with Joachim's. As a player he had excellent intonation and dexterity, but his music reflects his small hand, that made certain things such as tenths impossible. Of his many works for violin and piano several also exist in orchestral versions. The *Zigeunerweisen* or *Gipsy Airs* (1878) are a group of traditional Hungarian melodies presented in dazzling sequence beginning in C minor and ending in A minor: one of them is otherwise known as *Hearts and Flowers*. The *Carmen Fantasy* (c. 1883) is a similar series of melodies from Bizet's 'Spanish' opera, then still a fairly new work; here too we find a loose but satisfying sequence of themes instead of the traditional structures of concerto form.

(ii) The Symphonic Concerto: Schumann, Brahms and Dvořák

Joan Chissell

Schumann

As early as 1827, when still only 17, **Robert Schumann** (1810–1856) recorded in his diary 'beginnings of a piano concerto in F minor'. His Leipzig notebooks for 1831–2, shortly after he had renounced law to study music in earnest, contain sketches for another such work in F major. As his own dreams of a pianist's career slowly faded, his growing involvement with Clara Wieck, his erstwhile teacher's brilliant young pianist daughter, continued to fan a secret desire to combine piano and orchestra. He was interested enough in an A minor concerto composed in 1833–4 by Clara to undertake much of its orchestration for her, besides making another abortive attempt at a D minor *Concertstück* of his own as late as 1839.

But as the 1830s increased his distaste for meretricious showmanship no less than anything savouring of the academically prescribed, so Schumann came to realize that it was the keyboard miniature, not the concerto, that offered the most spontaneous outlet for his romantically hypercharged, youthful imagination. For close on a decade he devoted himself largely to works for solo piano, rejecting the note-spinning bravura of the fashionable virtuoso-composer school for a more intimately poetic, personally confiding style of his own. Much of this music grew direct from love and longing for Clara in the years when her father forbade them to meet. In time he came to feel the need of words to make feeling more explicit, hence the miraculous outpouring of song in 1840 as hopes of marriage dawned anew.

It was Schubert's 'Great' C major symphony, discovered by Schumann in Vienna among a pile of unpublished manuscripts, that proved the eventual catalyst: hearing its première in Vienna in 1839 under Mendelssohn (whose own effortless craftsmanship he had grown to idolize) made him 'tingle to be at work on a symphony . . . and I believe something will come of it once I am happily married to Clara'. Significantly, it was on 13 October 1840, a month and a day after their wedding, that his *Haushaltbuch* first records 'symphonic attempts'. The floodgates opened soon after, with an orchestral outpouring in 1841 including not only his B flat major and D minor (in its first version) symphonies, but also, to his very great joy, a *Phantasie* for piano and orchestra for Clara, completed between 4 and 20 May. But though tried out by her at a private Gewandhaus rehearsal on 13 August, just 17 days before the birth of their first child Marie, it was not until June–July 1845, soon after their move from Leipzig to Dresden, that Schumann expanded it into the A minor concerto, Op. 54, first writing the 'Rondo', as he refers to the finale in his *Haushaltbuch*, and then the central Intermezzo. He also amended certain details of orchestration in the first movement. Clara herself gave the Dresden première under Ferdinand Hiller, the dedicatee, on 4 December 1845, before introducing it to Leipzig under Niels Gade on 1 January 1846.

Schumann subsequently combined piano and orchestra in the *Introduction und Allegro appassionata*, Op. 92, and the *Concert Allegro mit Introduction*, Op. 134, besides writing a daringly brilliant three-movement *Concertstück* for four horns, Op. 86, and a *Phantasie* for violin and orchestra, Op. 131. But only twice again did he ever use the title 'concerto' for this genre of composition. Both these works date from after his appointment in September 1850 as Director of Music in Düsseldorf, where having an orchestra of his own for the first time inevitably resulted in a great new surge of creative energy. The Cello Concerto in A minor, Op. 129, written between 11 and 24 October, was among its first fruits. This time the challenge seems to have come more from the instrument itself than any particular artist. Just before leaving Dresden he had in fact composed a suite of miniatures for cello and piano, alongside similar pieces for horn, clarinet and oboe, as if bemused anew by instrumental timbre *per se*. Subsequent revision delayed the concerto's publication until 1854, and it was never played in public in the composer's lifetime. A performance by Ludwig Ebert at the Leipzig Conservatoire on 9 June 1860 is customarily acknowledged as the official première.

At that time Schumann had been dead only four years. But the musical world had to wait no less than 84 years to make the acquaintance of his Violin Concerto, written between 21 September and 3 October 1853, for the 22-year-old Joseph Joachim (first encountered by Schumann as a prodigy of 13), whose performance of Beethoven's Violin Concerto had been one of the unforgettable glories of Düsseldorf's recent Whitsuntide festival. The story of its suppression and curious eventual unearthing before introduction to Germany by George Kulenkampf on 26 November 1937, must wait till the end of this chapter.

With as fine a player as Clara Schumann destined to be the Piano Concerto's prime protagonist, the solo part naturally calls for technical assurance of a high order, not least in the exuberant finale. But Schumann had long renounced all interest in virtuosity *per se*. For the most part piano and orchestra are close partners in a romantic adventure conditioned by the same dedicated pursuit of unity and continuity, through thematic metamorphosis, found in all his main symphonic undertakings of 1841—and much else to follow. From this viewpoint nothing in his output is more remarkable than the limitless fertility of the concerto's yearning opening theme, in itself a subtle A minor variant of the falling five-note motto in which Schumann had so often enshrined Clara's image in his solo piano music (Ex. 1).

Perhaps because it was first envisaged as an independent *Phantasie*, the initial *Allegro affettuoso* dispenses with opening classical formalities. After a peremptory keyboard call-to-attention, the all-important Clara-inspired main theme is introduced by the wind before taken over by the soloist. And

Ex. 1

it is the solo piano, which after a freely evolving shared transition, emerges to present that theme in a glowing C major transformation as the movement's second subject. Its opening phrase, together with a fragment from the transition, carry the exposition to a sturdy orchestral climax in the same relative major key. Academic development would have ill-become ideas so lyrical. Instead, Schumann resorts to quasi variation, first allowing piano and orchestra to woo each other in a ruminative *Andante espressivo* interlude in A flat major, reached not by modulation but a typically Schumannesque, side-slipping short-cut. The idyll is rudely interrupted by recalls of the movement's peremptory opening challenge, with both piano and orchestra in high dudgeon before the piano embarks on an animated variation of the main theme. The recapitulation is regular until an *accelerando*, culminating in an arresting dominant seventh arpeggio on the flat sixth (F natural), leads into the composer's own increasingly urgent but never exhibitionist cadenza. The coda unites all forces in an excitable 2/4 *allegro molto* transformation of the main theme.

Casting aside A minor nostalgia for an unclouded F major, the ternary-shaped Intermezzo *(Andantino grazioso)* at once enters a magical new world of spring-like radiance and grace. But its parentage in what has gone before is unmistakable: the uprising semiquaver motif generating the opening and closing sections grows direct from the ascending quavers in the second bar of the concerto's leading theme (Ex. 2). The skilful interweaving of piano and orchestra ('making it impossible to think of one without the other') that so delighted Clara at her Gewandhaus try-out of the first movement, now acquires an even more delicate, chamber-music-like intimacy, not only in the

Andante grazioso

Ex. 2

shy, short-breathed phrases of the opening section but equally in the central episode in C, whose glowing, low-lying song can be recognized as an inspired metamorphosis of a keyboard figure introduced only in passing in the movement's seventh bar. The way soaring violins carry the melody into the heights just before the reprise is a further stroke of genius belying the familiar charge that Schumann had no ear for orchestral colour.

Not for nothing has the merging of slow movement into the *Allegro vivace* finale been hailed as one of the most subtle of his often essayed inter-movement transitions, both retrospective and forward-looking in one. After a swift resurgence of orchestral energy it is in fact the soloist who plunges headlong into the fray, with a bold, 3/4 A major transformation of the concerto's leading theme as first subject of the sonata–rondo argument (Ex. 3). The second subject in E, entirely new, comes as a reminder of

Allegro vivace

Ex. 3

Schumann's lifelong love of rhythmic teasing, here turning the basic three–four into something the ear eventually comes to accept as 3/2. The central episode, starting with a stern fugato development of the main theme, soon dissolves into a smiling new tune (introduced by the oboe) that elicits a further surging stream of animated keyboard comment. Recapitulation of the first subject in the subdominant key of D enables the second to be reached in the expected A major by straightforward transposition rather than recomposition. But the music's impulse is unflagging, with yet a new stream of dancing quavers for the piano, and one further rhythmic transformation of the apparently inexhaustible, Clara-inspired leading theme for the orchestra, to carry the work to a triumphant end.

It is perhaps pertinent to add that the concerto's often questioned metronome markings are traceable to the autograph score, in the first movement in Clara Schumann's handwriting and in the Intermezzo and Finale in the composer's own.

In a letter to his mother of 6 November 1832, soon after the traumatic realization that his lamed right hand had put paid to all hopes of a pianist's career, Schumann wrote: 'At Zwickau I shall take up the violoncello again—for which one only wants the left hand, as it will always be very useful in orchestral composition'. Whether or not he at any time very seriously 'took up' this problematically low-voiced instrument remains a moot point. So it was scarcely surprising that his A minor Cello Concerto of 1850 was much revised before its long delayed publication in 1854. Entries in the *Haushaltbuch* suggest that Düsseldorf's newly arrived cellist, Christian Reimers, tried it out at a rehearsal under the orchestra's leader Wasielewski in March 1851, and that Schumann went through it again in private with Robert Bockmüll, a fine local player, in December 1852. The effort was not in vain: for while totally eschewing all meretricious virtuoso display, the solo cello emerges as the leading voice in a discerningly scored work (with limited use of trumpets and drums) unified by unbroken transition from one movement to the next, as well as the composer's customary thematic interquotation.

The three introductory wind chords of the *Nicht zu schnell* can be recognized as the germ begetting the soaring A minor theme with which the cello makes its entry, a theme whose own opening motif in fact haunts the whole concerto. After a robust orchestral transition, the soloist is also entrusted with the beguilingly lyrical second subject in the relative major key of C, from which two brief snippets, including an ominous triplet figure, are detached for development in a conflict heightened by pleading returns of the first subject—and not just from the solo cello. Two recalls of its opening motif are eloquently scored for the new valve-horn recently discovered by Schumann in Dresden, before orchestral strings sing it out in confident major tonality to herald the recapitulation. Conflict returns in the forceful orchestral coda, with its agitated references both to the opening motif of the first subject and the triplet figure from the continuation of the second. But a magical *Etwas zurückhaltend* transformation of the movement's opening chords suddenly dissolves all strife so that a benedictory four-bar phrase for solo cello can lead direct into the slow movement.

This ternary-shaped *Langsam*, headed *mit Ausdruck*, enters a dream-world all Schumann's own. Its ruminative F major song, as full of *Innigkeit* as many a love-song of old, is entirely sustained by the solo cello with an intimate *dolce* interlude in double-stopping midway through. Trumpets and drums are silenced. The light accompaniment is mainly supplied by the strings, with occasional echoes of this or that turn of phrase in the solo part from the woodwind as well as one or two veiled references to the concerto's opening chords. It is nevertheless not until after the brief reprise that Schumann overtly recalls the concerto's leading theme to launch his transition to the finale; here, in a passage of accompanied quasi-recitative for the cello, it is effortlessly enough merged with the opening phrase of the *Langsam* itself to leave no doubt as to the underlying unity of the whole conception.

For the concluding *Sehr lebhaft*, back in the home key of A minor, Schumann reverts to clear-cut sonata-form, but now with the addition of a cadenza in compensation for the absence of any such outlet for the soloist in the opening movement. Both first and second subjects are characterized by a certain droll humour—of the kind found in the course of the *Fünf Stücke im Volkston* for cello and piano of 1849. But the argument is not sustained without effort. The rhythmic tag launching the cello's entry is over persistent, even working its way into the accompaniment of the second subject as well as dominating the development. This central section does nevertheless bring significant recalls of the concerto's opening theme before heightened activity in the solo part leads to a robust orchestral recapitulation. In the cadenza Schumann breaks new ground by not giving it exclusively to the soloist: gleams of light from strings and wind in fact do much to offset the darkness of the cello's continuously favoured lower strings. Deeming it ineffective, Tovey admitted to 'some hankering' to supply an alternative exploiting the cello's higher register, as Jacobi had already done and several distinguished champions of the work continue to do. But in this day and age Schumann's cause is surely far better served by strict observance, for better or worse, of what he himself actually wrote.

Nothing did more to lighten the darkness of Schumann's last months of illness before total mental breakdown than his friendship with two outstanding young musicians still in their early twenties, the violinist Joseph Joachim, and Johannes Brahms—sent to him by Joachim on the last day of September 1853. At that moment Schumann was just finishing his violin concerto. But having only cursorily studied violin technique during early symphonic forays in 1841, he was counting on collaboration with Joachim if adjustments should prove necessary in the solo part—a hope tragically cut short by his removal to a private asylum in March 1854. After a private run-through with the Gewandhaus orchestra the year following Schumann's death, Joachim himself felt unable to comply with Clara Schumann's request (she is said to have wept when hearing music so indicative of failing powers) to replace the original finale with 'a great last movement' of his own. It was eventually decided by Clara, Brahms and Joachim (who rated the immediately preceding *Phantasie* for violin and orchestra so much better a work) not to include the concerto in the supplementary volume of the Breitkopf *Gesamtausgabe* currently being prepared by Brahms—indeed never to publish it at all. After Joachim's death the manuscript was sold by his son to the Prussian State Library, where it remained undisturbed until Joachim's great-niece Jelly d'Arányi secured its publication in 1937—justifying herself to those who disapproved (including Clara's only surviving daughter Eugenie) with the claim that she had received strange, supernatural guidance from the composer himself spelt out, in a circle of letters, by a glass on which she and friends had only lightly laid their fingers. Jelly d'Arányi introduced the concerto to England at a BBC Symphony Concert at Queen's Hall on 16 February 1938, some three months after Georg Kulenkampf's German première.

For the opening *In kräftigem, nicht zu schnellem tempo*, scored for his usual classical orchestra, Schumann uses traditional concerto form. The orchestra alone contrasts the dramatically arresting first theme in D minor with a more intimately songful, essentially Schumannesque second subject in the relative major, before both are taken over by the soloist in proliferating figuration not always too comfortably disposed in later double-stopping. The brief central development brings no startling thematic transmogrification, even if poignant new light is thrown on the second subject when carried into minor tonality. Its undulating opening phrase, expanded in a crescendo over a dominant pedal, eventually leads to a formal recapitulation. There is no cadenza; but a final recall of the assuaging second subject prepares the way for an affirmative end.

Predictably, the gem of the concerto is the central *Langsam* in B flat. Perhaps Brahms remembered the cello's serene opening song when writing the *Andante* of his second piano concerto nearly 30 years later. As for the heartfelt melody, marked *ausdrucksvoll*, with which the soloist enters, it haunted Schumann enough, just before his mental breakdown, to write it down during the night of 17 February 1854 as a theme for a set of piano variations in the belief that it had just been sent to him by the angels. Both ideas are unfolded with subtle solo and orchestral interchangings before passing C minor stress heralds the reprise and the most moving moment of all when the soloist's opening theme returns a third lower in G minor like a memory of 'old, unhappy far-off things' (Exs 4a and 4b).

The concluding *Lebhaft, doch nicht schnell* in D major owes as much to sonata as to rondo form, contrasting a polonaise-like main theme with a lighter, more playful second subject in A. That Schumann's old pursuit of continuity and unity was by no means a forgotten ideal is clear not only in the somewhat abrupt, four-bar transition linking second and third movements, but also in the recall of the slow movement's opening cello

Ex. 4a

Ex. 4b

theme as accompaniment to the soloist's song in the course of the central development. But this section brings little true thematic growth or cumulative excitement of any kind. Even the violin's last demonstrative lead-back to the recapitulation was once dismissed by Joachim as consisting of 'figures intended to be brilliant which force the solo violin to great but ineffective work'. As he and Clara both at once sadly recognized, the finale is in fact as contrived as it is laboured. But the concerto as a whole presents so revealing a portrait of the composer in his last few heart-rending months that no Schumann-lover today would wish to be without it.

Brahms

Like Schumann, **Johannes Brahms** (1833–1897) was an exceptional pianist in earlier days: at ten his playing was outstanding enough for a visiting impresario to propose an immediate American tour. Discouraging such exploitation, his wise teacher, Friedrich Cossel, chose to hand him over to the eminent Eduard Marxsen so that early attempts at composition could be fostered too. And it was Marxsen who imbued the young Johannes with that profound respect for classical tradition, which disciplining his ardent romantic impulse, prompted Schumann in 1853 to hail him at 20 as 'a genius'. In her own diary Clara was more explicit about their young visitor from Hamburg:

> He played us sonatas, scherzos etc of his own, all of them showing exuberant imagination, depth of feeling, and mastery of form . . . It is really moving to see him sitting at the piano, with his interesting young face, which becomes transfigured when he plays, his beautiful hands, which overcome the greatest difficulties with perfect ease (his things are very difficult), and in addition these remarkable compositions . . . He has a great future before him, for he will first find the true field for his genius when he begins to write for the orchestra.

Ironically, it was Schumann's own breakdown, coupled with Brahms's growing love for Clara, that barely six months later proved the catalyst. Uncertain as to whether to canalize emotional trauma into a symphony (he had just heard Beethoven's 'Choral' in D minor for the first time) or a sonata for two pianos, he sketched a large part of both before realizing that only by throwing piano up against orchestra could the music's full conflict be revealed (the projected symphony's 'slow scherzo in sarabande tempo' was eventually recast as 'Behold, all flesh is as the grass' in his *German Requiem*). Though ostensibly finishing the concerto by October 1856, Brahms extensively revised the finale before the work's politely received Hanover première on 22 January 1859, with himself as soloist under the baton of his close young violinist friend Joseph Joachim, the dedicatee. But when he introduced it to Leipzig just five days later under Julius Rietz, it was hissed. Not until a Mannheim performance under Herman Levi in 1865 did the German public at large cease to condemn it as too symphonic.

In the circumstances Brahms's 20-year delay before returning to this genre was hardly surprising. But his appointment in 1872 as conductor of Vienna's *Gesellschaft der Musikfreunde* eventually rekindled old fires. And with the *St Anthony Variations* and his first two symphonies leaving the world in no further doubt as to his true stature, at last in the course of 1878 he felt ready to begin the violin concerto for which Joachim had so long waited, temporarily setting aside sketches for a second piano concerto in order to do so. Though consulting Joachim about details of solo figuration, Brahms by no means accepted his every suggestion. But he entrusted Joachim with the writing of a cadenza, and it was Joachim, again the dedicatee, who not only gave the Leipzig première on New Year's Day 1879, but who also did more than any of his contemporaries to gain the work acceptance as the true successor to Beethoven's violin concerto in the same key of D major. The Second Piano Concerto in B flat, dedicated 'to my dear friend and teacher, Eduard Marxsen', eventually emerged in 1881. Though no longer the pianist he once was, Brahms gave the Budapest première on 9 November before introducing it to a large number of cities in a very short time as soloist with the Meiningen Court Orchestra (one of the first in Germany to undertake regular tours) under the distinguished Hans von Bülow, who was only too happy when the composer could accept the Duke's invitation to use Meiningen's facilities to try out new works. While again more symphonic than virtuosic in conception, the concerto's glowing inner serenity and close interweaving of piano and orchestra won it the immediate, widepsread acclaim denied its storm-tossed D minor predecessor. Only Leipzig at first remained doubtful.

It was not until after completing his last two symphonies that Brahms, at 54, took up the concerto challenge for the fourth time — in a work designed as an olive-branch for Joachim after a rift occasioned by his sympathy for Joachim's wife at the time of their divorce. Instead of a solo concerto, he now chose to combine violin with the low-voiced cello, in the process playing for safety to an extent which caused even as staunch an admirer as Clara Schumann to express doubts about the work's future because of lack of brilliance in the solo parts. Her diary entry after the official Cologne première on 18 October 1887 under the composer's own baton, nevertheless conceded that Joachim and Robert Hausmann (the cellist in his Quartet) 'could not have played more beautifully'. Posterity, of course, has accepted the work as *echt* Brahms—a composer always to be honoured more for his contribution to the sum than the development of art, in the genre of the concerto no less than most others. As for Brahms himself, with Joachim once more his friend he was content enough to take his leave of the concerto, as indeed of all orchestral activity, for ever.

Perhaps it was no coincidence that Brahms chose D minor for his First Piano Concerto, Op. 15: Schumann's Violin Concerto, written only a few months before his attempted suicide, had embarked from the same key. The *Maestoso* first movement's stark opening theme, hurled out without preliminaries by the strings over a threatening drum-roll, at once presages storm and stress. As in his later C minor and F major symphonies, already Brahms uses a wide compass to convey an impression of elemental power, here as if to suggest the mighty forces of fate against which man pits his own little strength in vain. Apart from two momentary gleams of major tonality, not even this theme's smoother continuation eases the tension. The piano enters unobtrusively with a sadly resigned theme of its own in flowing thirds and sixths before also getting swept into the tumult. And it is to the piano that Brahms entrusts the chordal second subject in the relative major key of F—a subject which, though sounding a new note of assuagement, is clearly derived from the rising fourth in the fanfare-like challenge introduced towards the end of the orchestral exposition. The development, marked by a peremptory return to the opening tempo, leaves no doubt as to Brahms's own formidable keyboard technique in youth: such music could only have been conceived through uncommonly big, powerful hands. Yet never does he resort to virtuoso display. A strictly thematic argument reveals a mind as alert as his fingers, with one particularly arresting diminution of a phrase more expansively expressed in the exposition. The recapitulation also presents opening material in new keys and textures, culminating in an impassioned *poco più animato* coda. In so expansively dramatic a discourse, Brahms rightly recognized there was no place for a cadenza.

For the slow movement Brahms moves into D major, silencing lower horns and trumpets from his traditional rather than 'New German School' orchestra, and reserving drums for just the last two bars. When published, the movement carried only the heading *Adagio*; but in Joachim's manuscript copy of the score Brahms is known to have written the words 'Benedictus qui venit in nomine Domini' as a clue to the music's content (he often addressed Schumann as 'Domine'). To Clara he even once admitted that the music was her portrait. Its 'lofty, devotional atmosphere', to quote Joachim, suggests that it could perhaps have been inspired by memories of Clara at her husband's burial. Certainly in the B minor middle section (the movement is ternary shaped) clarinets, then oboes, tug at the heart-strings with a brief phrase whose tender pathos evokes the sentiment of Bach's 'Herr Jesu, gute Nacht' in the *St Matthew Passion*. For the most part the undercurrent of feeling runs so deep that the tranquil surface is scarcely ruffled. But the recapitulation brings one great swell of fervour, underpinned by a rock-like tonic pedal, also a brief, intimately valedictory keyboard solo marked *cadenza ad lib*, before the veiled orchestral leave-taking.

As first projected, the concluding Rondo neither satisfied the intensely self-critical Brahms nor Joachim, whose opinion was so frequently sought in earlier days of their friendship. It was not in fact until May 1857, some seven months after the concerto's official completion, that it emerged in a revision both of them deemed able to counterbalance the 'passionate breadth' of the first movement and the 'lofty devotional atmosphere' of the second, to requote Joachim. Though dark-hued, the main rondo theme has a sturdy drive: it suggests resolve to 'take fate by the throat'. The contrasting episodes even bring glimmers of sunshine, the first in F through echoes of the Hungarian dance-music Brahms always loved so well. The lyrical elation of the second in B flat is nevertheless soon cut short by fugal development in minor tonality. Always the sections are skilfully dovetailed, and there is yet further proof of precocious technical mastery in the way Brahms develops, instead of merely restating, the rondo theme itself, not least in the movement's D major coda. In the course of its mounting excitement he even includes 20 bars marked *cadenza ad lib accelerando* as a brief concession to the bravura traditionally expected from a soloist at this point. The homecoming, held on a tight rhythmic rein, is heroic, even jubilant.

Like the radiantly lyrical Second Symphony in D of the previous year, the Violin Concerto, Op. 77, was completed at Pörtschach, on the Wörthersee, a holiday resort dear to Brahms's heart where, as he once put it, 'so many melodies fly about that one must be careful not to tread on them'. Though his rejection of many of Joachim's simplifications resulted in a taxing solo part, early criticism of the concerto as a work written against, rather than for, the violin is hard to understand in view of its unending stream of song. But every bar reveals the underlying hand of a mature master-craftsman. Not for nothing did the late Hubert Foss describe it as 'a song for the violin on a symphonic scale', a work showing 'in the highest degree of perfection the reconciling of the two opposite sides of Brahms's mind, the lyrical and the constructive'.

The orchestra at once announces the leading them of the *Allegro non troppo*, a quintessentially Brahmsian melody growing from the notes of the common chord of D. Canonically developed, it serves as transition to not one but a group of second subjects—later to be still more extended and enriched by the violin. Whereas in the D minor piano concerto the soloist's entry was subdued, here it is arrestingly lordly, with freely evolving elaboration of the main theme (over tonic and then dominant orchestral pedals) before its official return as first introduced. This time a new violin chordal challenge leads into the second subject group, which, after beautiful embroidery of its own opening theme (not forgetting its pregnant falling three-note motif) (Ex. 5) now includes a joyous song for the soloist not heard in the orchestral introduction. Growing from the exposition with a seamless continuity, the development in its turn brings startling surprises of key with its many subtle thematic burgeonings, none of them more haunting than the passage of C minor brooding (introduced and subsequently pointedly

Allegro non troppo

Ex. 5

accompanied by the solo violin) over the falling three-note motif from the second subject's opening (Ex. 6). With mounting bravura, the soloist rekindles orchestral fires for a blazing start to the recapitulation. Brahms's recall of the canonic orchestral transition, first heard in the 27th bar, as a final means of heightening tension is a masterstroke that makes any cadenza sound inevitable (countless musicians including Busoni, Tovey and Kreisler have provided alternatives to Joachim's). Perhaps in salute to Beethoven the coda starts *tranquillo* before the *animato* homecoming.

Ex. 6

The move from D to F major for the central *Adagio* coupled with the silencing of trumpets and drums, at once conjures an atmosphere of Elysian purity and calm. Whether Brahms was consciously recalling his youthful FAF motto (*frei aber froh*, free but happy) at the start of the opening theme remains a moot point. But its common-chord derivation, and still more important, the ensuing motif of three falling notes (so intimately cherished by oboe, then flute, over a dominant pedal from the horns at the end of the orchestral introduction) suggests an underlying kinship with the first movement. The soloist enters with a delicately decorated version of this theme before leaving its F major calm for the unexpected tonality of F sharp minor. With the violin still much the leader in intricately spun cantilena, the central section of this ternary-shaped movement is entirely generated by motifs from the main theme, now revealing unsuspected undertones of intense, nostalgic longing. But calm returns in the reprise, where further embellishment of the solo line without the slightest trace of patterning remains one of the movement's miracles.

As Joachim himself was half Hungarian, the Hungary-inspired finale came as no surprise. Brahms had always loved the popular music of this land ever since playing it in his teens with Eduard Reményi, the flamboyant, itinerant Hungarian violinist to whom he in fact owed his initial introduction to Joachim. Cast in rondo form, the movement is launched by the soloist with a rollicking main theme in double-stops (though wholly new in spirit, it, too, has links in letter with the first movement). Ascending *ff energicamente* octaves for the soloist announce the arrival of the cumulatively exciting first episode in E. Though starting with a suave new melody of its own introduced by the violin, the central episode grows into something far more akin to a sonata-form development as earlier ideas increasingly take command. After a resplendent tutti recall of the main theme, the *poco più presto* coda brings further reminders of the composer's limitless invention as rhythmically transformed motifs from both the main theme and the first episode sweep the movement home in the style of an increasingly triumphant march.

Even if not as directly autobiographical a work as its early storm-tossed predecessor in D minor, the Second Piano Concerto in B flat, Op. 83, nevertheless presents as revealing a portrait of its composer in his later 40s as anything to come from his pen. In its warmth and noble strength the music testifies to a mind that had wrestled with pain and conquered, to a spirit at peace with itself and the world. Increasing recognition in its turn had brought many new friends, including the great surgeon Theodor Billroth, who at the time of the concerto's inception had just introduced Brahms to the riches of Italy. The work was in fact completed at Pressbaum, just outside Vienna, in the early summer of 1881 shortly after a second Italian journey embracing Sicily and its sweeping panoramas too.

The breadth and grandeur of the *Allegro non troppo* is presaged in the imposing opening shared by horns and piano, a dialogue also intimating that keyboard and orchestra (again classically constituted) are to be close collaborators rather than rivals throughout. Nothing proves more fecund than the motif of three rising notes at the start of this two-limbed first subject, which is rhapsodically expanded by the piano before being swept into an orchestral tutti. A modulation to F major (and its relative minor) brings the more winsome second subject from the violins; this in turn leads direct to a third theme of strongly marked rhythm played staccato by wind and strings to round off the condensed orchestral exposition. Though the ensuing argument is underpinned by the scaffolding of traditional first-movement form, its unfolding is more in the nature of continuously self-generating development of these and subsidiary ideas, all of it accomplished with a mastery of invention and far-seeing imaginative vision defying description in a limited space. As in the D minor concerto, the solo part demands an exceptionally powerful technique while eschewing all extraneous virtuoso display. There is no cadenza, but instead an extended, urgently motivated coda in which the soloist plays a leading part.

Perhaps it was to emphasize the symphonic character of the work that Brahms next introduced a Scherzo, a movement traditionally conspicuous by its absence in concertos. 'A tiny tiny wisp of a scherzo' was his teasing description of it in a letter to his erstwhile pupil Elisabeth von Herzogenberg, for he knew it to be an extremely high-powered *Allegro appassionato* in D minor. Its urgent, chordal opening theme even seems to hark back to the First Concerto's drama, though assuagement comes in the more lyrical second subject. Brahms's teeming invention in this movement is plain not only in his 81-bar development of opening material as a lead into the proudly confident D major trio, but also in his recomposition of the opening section at the end instead of resorting to a mere *da capo* restatement.

Few movements in his entire output are more rapt than the *Andante*, back in the home key of B flat. To Billroth, remembering their recent travels, it immediately evoked 'a full-moon night in Taormina'. A solo cello is entrusted with the serene main theme both at the start and in the reprise, and it is mainly on this theme that soloist and orchestra rhapsodize with mounting ardour in the middle section of the movement, where modulation carries the music as far away in tonality as F sharp major. But the phrase with which the piano enters this section, stealing its way in bare octaves from the depths to the heights, contributes a hypnotic magic of its own. The way Brahms continues its pattern in the left hand below right hand tracery woven out of the cello theme is just one more instance of the inspired craftsmanship underpinning the concerto's musical beauty (Ex. 7).

The *Allegretto grazioso* finale in B flat reveals the composer at his most ingratiating. Crystalline keyboard texture and light scoring (as in the preceding movement he silences trumpets and drums) help to keep the music on its toes, not least the dancing main theme. The second subject group even brings echoes of the Hungarian popular music he had so long loved. In

Ex. 7

design the movement is a compromise between sonata and sonata-rondo form, with development of the main theme, rather than anything new, taking possession of the central episode. The *poco più presto* coda, again reached without recourse to a cadenza, brings another characteristically Brahmsian rhythmic transformation of the main theme to carry the work to an exuberant finish.

The Double Concerto in A minor, Op. 102, for violin and cello was completed during the second of the three consecutive summer escapes made by Brahms, now just 54, to the Bernese Oberland, where at his water-side retreat near Thun, the snow-capped Jungfrau, Eiger and Mönch provided a rugged backcloth beyond the lake. 'A work of reconciliation . . . Joachim and Brahms have spoken again for the first time in many years', so wrote Clara in her diary after a preliminary try-out with Baden's Kursaal Orchestra a few weeks before the Cologne première. But ready as he was to accept Joachim's criticism, strongly upheld by Clara herself, that the solo parts needed greater brilliance, Brahms characteristically rejected his old violinist friend's suggested amendments in favour of solutions of his own. The manuscript reveals many alterations designed to please, though at heart he must have known that his dark-hued but discreet scoring, with the orchestra rarely called out at full strength unless on its own, was never really likely to obscure either solo instrument.

After a peremptory orchestral call-to-attention (containing the germ of the first subject), solo cello and violin introduce themselves at first individually, then together, *in modo d'un recitativo ma sempre in tempo.* This is Brahms's only concession to self-display in the opening *Allegro*; for the rest, both soloists join the orchestra in a discourse as concentrated as any found in his four symphonies. Announced in full by the orchestra, the commanding A minor first subject is linked to the more lyrically relaxed and sunny second in C by an urgent syncopated transitional theme of considerable later importance. In fact nothing in the development of the traditionally planned sonata-form argument (with double exposition) is more breathtaking than this theme's transformation into a wide-sweeping rising phrase played in turn by cello and violin in the course of the lead back to the recapitulation. Here, the second subject, reintroduced by the violin in soaring song, swells into a rich A major orchestral climax. But victory is not yet won: unpredictably, the coda swings back into the movement's opening minor key.

The warmly glowing, low-lying melody introduced by violin and cello in octaves as the main theme of the ternary-shaped *Andante* in D could only have come from Brahms: its continuation, after the first eight bars, grows from an inversion of its opening phrase. In the central section, marked by an unprepared plunge into F major, the soloists embroider a smooth-flowing new theme introduced *dolce* by woodwind over a subdued dominant pedal for trumpets and then horns. The main theme's initial rising fourth, detached to serve as a two-bar introduction to the movement from horns and woodwind, is subtly recalled by both soloists after the reprise, in the course of a gracious homecoming.

Though the concluding *Vivace non troppo* in A minor is by no means as overt a salute to Joachim's Hungary as is the finale of the Violin Concerto, the music's forthright vigour nevertheless suggests that it was to this same source that Brahms was subconsciously drawn. The movement is planned as a sonata-rondo, with a drolly patterned leading theme in A minor yet again (as so often in the concerto) first given not to Joachim's violin but to Hausmann's cello. And it is to the cello that Brahms also first entrusts the confident, double-stopped second subject in C. Instead of development, as often favoured in earlier rondos, here Brahms opts for an extended central episode bringing arresting new challenges; its first Magyar-tinged idea introduced by the two soloists together is warmly expanded by the orchestra after a contrasting middle section whose syncopations bring reminders of the first movement. After an unusually formal launching of the recapitulation by both solo instruments in turn as before, the second subject makes a jubilant return in A major. And this time Brahms seizes on its major tonality and does not let it go. The concerto ends in triumph.

Dvořák

For his launching into the wider musical world, **Antonín Dvořák** (1841–1904) owed scarcely less to Brahms than Brahms himself did to Schumann. But there was a difference. Dvořák was already 34 when in 1875 he first arrested Brahms's attention in a competition for a state stipend. Nor could Brahms, when introducing his protégé to the publisher Simrock in 1878, have exactly described him as an 'Athena, springing fully armed from the head of Zeus', as he himself at 20 had been hailed by Schumann. For while an intuitive creator for whom music was as natural an outlet as speech, Dvořák took time to master his craft, both as architect and orchestrator, and also to find his own, unmistakable personal vioce. His four concertos alone, written over a span of 30 years, make this very plain.

He was not quite 24 when in 1865 essaying the first, a cello concerto in A to which, though sketching its three movements fairly completely with piano accompaniment, he never returned to revise, orchestrate or publish in any form. The work remained buried until the middle 1920s when Günther Raphael prepared an orchestral performing edition too refurbished to present a faithful portrait of its immature young composer—then, after prematurely curtailed studies at the Prague Organ School, struggling to earn a living as organist, teacher and most important, as viola player in the orchestra of the newly founded Czech National Theatre.

As the son of a village innkeeper-cum-butcher, Dvořák had always loved the Czech countryside and its rustic music-making. But the experience of playing in national opera like Smetana's *Bartered Bride* and *Dalibor*, often under the composer's own baton, was his first full awakening to all that could be drawn from native soil. By the time he returned to the concerto genre in 1876 he had already composed several fatherland-inspired operas himself besides turning to nationalist sources in various other works too. Certainly the finale of his second concerto, this time for piano, in G minor, sounds this new note. He wrote it for his compatriot Karelze Slavkovský (renowned for his championship of contemporary Czech music), who gave the première under Adolf Čech at a 'Slavonic Concert' in Prague on 24 March 1878. Though aware he had not exploited the keyboard's full Romantic potential, Dvořák never found time to fulfill his wish to revise the solo part. That task was subsequently officially delegated to Wilém Kurz, whose version is published under the composer's own in the Complete Edition of Dvořák's works. But not even Kurz's richer textures have won this generously stocked but still somewhat eclectic work a regular place in the repertory.

Thanks, perhaps, to Brahms, some of Dvořák's chamber works had found an immediate German champion in Joachim. So it was perhaps not surprising that like Brahms himself, and Schumann before him, Dvořák should sooner or later have wanted to write a concerto for the great German violinist. The violin, moreover, had been the instrument he had first begged to learn himself as a small boy bewitched by rural fiddlers in his father's inn. After tireless, protracted revision carried out at Joachim's behest ('even though the whole work proves that you know the violin very well, it is clear that you have not played yourself for some for some time' was one of the several charges he had to face), it must have pained him deeply that Joachim never publicly played the work, even though the possibility of a London performance was briefly discussed. The première was eventually given in Prague by the Czech violinist, František Ondříček under Mořic Anger on 14 October 1883, some four years after the work's initial conception.

Like the Piano Concerto, much helped in recent years by artists like Rudolf Firkusný and Sviatoslav Richter, so the Violin Concerto too has found its dedicated advocates (the composer's great-grandson Josef Suk is one of the foremost) without wholly establishing itself as a repertory work. But the cello concerto, written in America between 8 November 1894 and 9 February 1895, with all the habitual immediacy and fluency of the now 53-year-old composer, was at once acclaimed a masterpiece. Shortly before taking up his appointment as director of the National Conservatory of Music in New York, Dvořák had undertaken a farewell chamber-music tour of his beloved homeland in company with the violinist Ferdinand Lachner and the cellist Hanuš Wihan, and it was to Wihan that he dedicated the work as well as consulting him about details of solo figuration. Owing to confusion over dates, the première at a Philharmonic Society concert in London on 19 March 1896 was nevertheless not given by Wihan but the English cellist Leo Stern, enthusiastic enough to have travelled to Prague at considerable personal expense to study the concerto with Dvořák shortly beforehand. It was also Stern, again with the composer as conductor, who introduced it to Prague a few days later. Apart from a minor symphonic poem, the Cello Concerto was to prove Dvořák's last work for the orchestra, and as Robert Layton once put it, 'in no other piece does he give more perfect expression to classical ideals and musical intuition'. Certainly few composers ever bade the concerto farewell with a more consummate blend of mind and heart.

During the eleven years separating the abandoned early cello concerto from its successor for piano, Dvořák wrote no fewer than five symphonies; naturally by 1876 he was a vastly more assured architect and orchestrator. Yet his many revisions in the manuscript of the G minor Piano Concerto, Op. 33, betray self-doubts just as clearly as the ideas themselves testify to a continued search for a personal identity. That identity nevertheless progressively emerges. Echoes of Beethoven and Brahms in the first movement, and even of Chopin in the second, eventually cede in the finale to strains of Bohemian dance never heard in any piano concerto before. Even the much criticized keyboard writing itself draws a new sparkle from fresh country air, as can be noted in the fewer changes made by Kurz in this movement (they are mainly restricted to octave doublings to reinforce the melodic line) than in the preceding two. Dispensing with preliminaries, the *Allegro agitato* opens with the resigned, classically succinct G minor theme that dominates the sonata-form argument. Whether or not Dvořák was emulating Brahms in the D minor concerto when allowing the piano so unobtrusive an entry, with both hands playing the same rising sequence of thirds an octave apart, remains a moot point: only after 43 exploratory bars does it settle down with the main subject in the home key. The second subject is in two parts both in the expected relative major key of B flat. The first, introduced by the soloist, has a smiling lilt; the second is a suaver, chorale-like melody sung by strings before enrichment in fuller scoring, with dancing interjections and decorations from the piano *en route*. Repetitive, sequential-type development of the second subject's first idea mounts to a *grandioso* return of the first subject in B flat. But the lead back to the recapitulation, with the soloist increasingly to the fore, is a less academically contrived, more cumulatively exciting, point of climax. The cadenza, again marked *grandioso*, is of near Brahmsian weight before a demonstratively turbulent coda.

Trumpets and drums are silenced in the *Andante sostenuto*, a tranquil meditation for which Dvořák moves into the dominant key of D. Romantically introduced by solo horn, the first of its two themes ends with a five-note uprising figure echoed by flutes in Dvořák's own inimitable woodland vein. The nostalgic second them comes from the piano in texture evoking memories of Chopin, not least when subsequently delicately embellishing the solo bassoon's simpler repetition of the tune. A recall of the first theme in D flat leads to free development of its once flute-echoed last three notes, at times with the initial phrase of the Chopinesque theme woven into the texture too. For his two big climaxes Dvořák turns to the opening phrase of the first theme before finally allowing this freely unfolding movement to regain its calm. Significantly, Kurz made no changes in the delicately fanciful keyboard figuration at the end.

The concluding *Allegro con fuoco*, an extended sonata-rondo, is launched by a recurrent main theme in two strikingly different yet complementary parts both introduced by the soloist. Whereas the first in the home key of G minor could easily have served as the subject of a fugue, the second is a dancing tune more redolent of the nationalist Dvořák than anything else in the work. Though soon restored to G minor, the dancing theme makes its first appearance in the teasingly unexpected key of F sharp minor, which helps to explain why the piano goes on to introduce the second subject in the still more sharp-laden key of B major before eventually returning it, after its appropriation by the strings, to an anchorage in D. Borrowed from his G major string quintet of the previous year, this melody derives its seductively oriental note from emphasis of the augmented second of the near-Eastern scale. Again, as in the first movement, the development mounts to an impressively grand moment of recapitulation, here cunningly combining the first subject's fugal and dance elements in a *fortissimo* tutti. After an otherwise orthodox recapitulation, with eight bars of spread *pianissimo* chords (and how much more romantically Kurz spreads them) serving as quasi cadenza, the happy G major coda sweeps even the movement's sterner fugal motif into the spirit of the dance—at last revealing that it too stems from a nationalist source, this time a popular Czech song.

It was in the summer of 1879 while staying in the country with his friend Alois Göbl, secretary to Prince Rohan of Sychrov castle, that Dvořák sketched his A minor Violin Concerto, Op. 33, breaking off in its early stages to discuss the project with Joachim—to whom he dedicated the work on its completion that November. On Joachim's advice he willingly made extensive revisions. As he informed his publisher in May 1880: 'The whole concerto has been transformed . . . the harmonisation, the instrumentation, the rhythm, the whole course of the work is new'. But it was not until the autumn of 1882 that Dvořák found time for a private run-through with the Berlin Hochschule orchestra, having already himself modified some uncomfortable figuration in the solo part. On the strength of this try-out Dvořák made further revisions, including some lightening of orchestration and cuts in the finale. But he firmly refused to separate the first two movements as his publisher proposed. That Joachim himself never publicly performed the concerto is commonly attributed to doubts about the work's shape—and most notably the *Adagio*'s uninterrupted flow from an opening movement rejecting classical principles (such as Joachim was currently so ardently championing in Brahms's recent Violin Concerto) in favour of an experimentally condensed argument possibly inspired (as the late Roger Fiske perceptively suggested) by the *Vorspiel* of Max Bruch's Violin Concerto of 1866.

The first of Dvořák's exclusions in this opening A minor *Allegro ma non troppo* is the traditional orchestral exposition. After only four bars the solo violin makes its entry, answering the orchestra's opening challenge with a more rhapsodic, nostalgically tinged reply of its own. Repetitions and developments of both, linked by two suaver transitional ideas, gradually lead to C major and the benignly flowing second subject introduced and subsequently playfully decorated by the rarely idle soloist. Nowhere in the work is the composer's love of Brahms more apparent than in this heart-warming theme. But it never returns. Dispensing with the customary orchestral codetta at this point, Dvořák plunges at once into development of motifs from the first subject alone, after a mere 46 bars recalling it in full might first from the orchestra, then *grandioso ff* from the soloist, as if to launch a full-scale recapitulation. Instead, an unpredictable change to *quasi moderato* after only 36 bars brings a tender transformation of the violin's opening theme so that the first movement can melt imperceptibly into the ruminative lyricism of the second.

For the ternary-shaped *Adagio ma non troppo* Dvořák moves into the key of F, just as Brahms had done in his Violin Concerto. The long-drawn, deep-breathed melody sung by the soloist is imbued with the peace he always found in the world of nature while remaining as unpredictable in contour as in harmonization—such as the heart-tugging fall from C to the G flat of E flat minor towards the end of the first section. A plunge into F minor, *poco più mosso*, presages a central storm. But after developing the motif of three ascending notes from the opening theme, he restores calm in a warm C major melody more like a continuation of that same opening theme than anything new. Trumpets, like drums, previously silenced in this movement, are recalled to herald a free reprise starting from the unexpected key of A flat: its climax comes in a *pesante* return of the C major theme from the middle section before an idyllically tranquil farewell from duetting horns delicately embroidered by the solo violin.

Planned as a sonata-rondo, the concluding A major *Allegro giocoso ma non troppo* stems direct from the village green. Not for nothing had Dvořák recently been immersed in Slavonic Dances and Rhapsodies and a Czech Suite: never before had the folk spirit proved more vitalizing. The main theme is a *furiant*, a lively Czech dance with duple cross-currents in its triple rhythm. On each return it is arrestingly rescored, never more so than when recalled in sounds evoking the *dudy*, or Czech bagpipes, with their characteristic drone. The first episode is no less colourful, not least when finally burgeoning into a rustic E major waltz. For the central D minor episode Dvořák resorts to a *dumka*, a folk-ballad vacillating between the grave and the gay. Translated into A major gaiety, it is the *dumka* theme that launches the coda of a movement never to be forgotten for local colour achieved without recourse to folk quotation: every note is the composer's own. As in the two preceding movements, the soloist enjoys so much of the limelight throughout that Dvořák dispenses with a cadenza.

'Why on earth didn't I know one could write a violoncello concerto like this? If I had only known I would have written one long ago.' So Brahms, with less than a month left to live, confessed to a friend after first hearing Dvořák's Cello Concerto at a Vienna Philharmonic concert in March 1897. Perhaps remembering his early failure in this field, even Dvořák himself expressed surprise at his achievement: while admiring the cello's eloquent middle register he is known to have expressed doubts about its 'nasal' upper register and 'mumbling' bass. Nearly a century later many musicians still claim it as the greatest cello concerto ever written, not only revealing Dvořák at the height of his powers as a craftsman, but also laying bare his heart to a degree unprecedented even for so vulnerable an artist as he.

Whereas a normal classical orchestra had sufficed for its predecessors, here Dvořák adds a piccolo and triangle as well as three trombones and a tuba—the deeper instruments possibly in consequence of his recent hearing of Victor Herbert's Second Cello Concerto, with its own three trombones. While basically adhering to traditional principles, the form of the work creates an impression of spontaneous generation by the ideas themselves, nearly all of them suffused with a nostalgia springing not just from a natural longing for his beloved homeland, but also, more personally, from remembrance of his wife's younger sister Josefina Kaunitzová (*née* Cermáková), who as a teen-age actress taking piano lessons from him, had been his first, never-to-be-forgotten great love and 'onlie begetter' of his early set of unpublished (though subsequently variously metamorphosed) songs entitled *Cypresses*. On learning in America of her serious illness he was moved enough to introduce the opening of her favourite, later to re-emerge in his Op. 82 as 'Leave me alone' (Ex. 8a) in the central section of the slow movement. And when news of her death reached him soon after his return, he completely rewrote the concerto's ending so as to reintroduce this song in more ethereal guise. Discovering that Hanuš Wihan, consulted about details of figuration, had not only proposed but actually composed a cadenza for insertion at this point, Dvořák was incensed enough to threaten to withold the work altogether unless his publisher, Simrock, guaranteed not to allow anyone, not even 'friend Wihan', to alter a single note.

Ex. 8a

After the much criticized liberties of the Violin Concerto, the Cello Concerto's opening *Allegro* starts with a full-scale, traditional orchestral exposition: the regretful yet resolute B minor first subject swells into a *grandioso* tutti before dissolving into the bitter-sweet nostalgia of the second subject in D introduced, hauntingly, by solo horn and then taken over by clarinet and oboe. New light is thrown on both ideas with the entry of the solo cello, setting out, *quasi improvisando*, from E minor before a tautly compressed, spiccato continuation of the first in the home key. The cello's plangent voice also allows the second to speak more personally; Dvořák himself is known to have been particularly pleased with the transitional theme it generates, imaginatively scored for woodwind and *pizzicato* strings with *staccato* semiquaver embroidery of the tune by the cello. Yet another *grandioso* tutti merges exposition into development, where after a swift sinking into the depths, the soloist reintroduces the first subject in A flat minor, *molto espressivo e sostenuto*, like a sudden poignant vision of all things loved and lost. The first subject in fact so monopolizes the central development that the great moment of recapitulation comes in a sweeping *ff* recall of the second subject in the tonic major key of B—and nothing in the work more strongly testifies to the mature Dvořák's wholly unacademic, self-determining master-craftsmanship. The first subject he reserves for the movement's triumphant coda, characteristically marked *grandioso*.

The ternary-shaped slow movement, *Adagio ma non troppo*, opens with a tranquil G major theme introduced by woodwind before taken over by the soloist. But already in its continuation (and, as Lionel Salter once observed, 'as so often with Dvořák the phrases which grow out of the subject are almost as important as the subject itself') there are pre-echoes of anguish to come. With trombones and tuba adding their depth and weight to the plunge into G minor, the middle section brings a dramatically transformed, protesting recall of the song 'Leave me alone', once so dear to the now critically ill Josefina, followed by yet more heartfelt, halting phrases from the cello-like pleas against the inexorability of fate (Ex. 8b). The reprise, launched by three horns, is a freely unfolding sunset-glow meditation on things past, in its course bringing the concerto's one and only brief, totally undemonstrative cadenza.

Ex. 8b

The *Allegro moderato* finale is an unpredictable, self-generating rondo. After a triangle-enlivened orchestral call-to-attention, the recurrent B minor main theme is introduced by the soloist in a spirit of determination to 'take fate by the throat'. the first brief episode of good cheer is never heard again. The second, in contrast, is extended into a self-contained, ternary-shaped interlude, now peremptory, now cajoling, the heart of it contained in its gently rocking *poco meno mosso* middle section in D bringing soloist and reduced orchestra into intimate accord. The third episode is yet more laden: introduced *moderato*, it focuses attention on the work's frequently stressed interval of the rising fourth, now warmly confident in the assuaging major tonality of G. And it is this theme, gleaming in the radiance of B major, *tranquillo e molto espressivo*, that heralds what was originally a victorious ending. But all was changed with the news of Josefina's death. Nothing in the concerto is more poignant than the return of her favourite song from a solo violin in the heights, like a voice from Elysium, before the cello, discreetly upheld by trombones and tuba) takes its own intimately personal, lingering farewell (Ex. 8c). Though still in B major, the brief orchestral homecoming is not triumphant but stormily defiant.

Ex. 8c

CHAPTER 6

The Concerto in Pre-Revolutionary Russia

David Brown

Anton Rubinstein

Anton Rubinstein (1829–1894) was a very remarkable man. The eldest son of a family of Polish-German-Jewish extraction, he received private piano tuition in Moscow and toured Europe as an infant prodigy before being taken to Berlin for two years of composition study with Siegfried Dehn. During the 1850s Anton went on to dazzle Europe with his keyboard virtuosity and to beguile the Tsar's sister-in-law with his personality. Enjoying the support of this formidable lady, in 1859 he founded the Russian Musical Society (RMS), whose concerts he conducted and whose classes in music he directed. So successful were the latter that by 1862 they could provide the foundation for the St Petersburg Conservatoire, of which Anton was to be the very active first principal. Meanwhile, in Moscow an equally talented younger brother, Nikolay, had been following this lead, establishing a branch of the RMS and himself becoming the director of the Moscow Conservatoire which in 1866 grew out of the Society's classes in that city.

Within this biographical summary are pointers to the problems which had faced any Russian musician before these two indefatigable pioneers effected their radical transformation of musical life in their native land. In the eighteenth century Italian composers had colonized Russia as an outpost of their country's musical empire, and for most of the nineteenth century's first half foreign opera remained dominant. Though there were good opera companies, there were no established professional orchestras, nor any music-school teaching advanced performance or composition, and as long as such skills could only be gained abroad, high-quality performers and composers of Russian stock would be few or even non-existent.

It is no surprise, therefore, that composition of serious instrumental music simply did not exist in Russia during the first decades of the nineteenth century. And when in the 1830s and 1840s, while the Rubinstein brothers were being prepared for their professional careers, an even more gifted amateur composer was transforming the prospects for a truly Russian tradition of composition, it was within opera and song that he achieved his finest work. Mikhail Glinka was an extraordinary phenomenon—a dilettante blessed with an imagination which, given the right stimuli, could respond with bursts of striking, often very original music. But while such promptings were abundant in drama and poetry, there were fewer external stimuli applicable to instrumental forms, and when Glinka later turned to orchestral composition it was only to produce brief evocations of his two-year stay in Spain (in his two *Spanish Overtures*), and to allow his fertile musical fantasy to exercise itself around two Russian folk-tunes (in his scherzo, *Kamarinskaya*). True, he thrice attempted symphonies, but all three were abandoned. Once he even began a concerto. What survives is actually scored—but we do not know whether it was for some unspecified solo instrument or, as seems more likely, a precocious concerto for orchestra, for after 71 bars of *ritornello* it suddenly breaks off. And so it was to be yet another of Anton Rubinstein's achievements to give Russia its first concerto.

Despite all his other commitments, Rubinstein was a prodigiously prolific composer, with a catalogue of works including eight concertos (five for piano, two for cello, and one for violin). His enormous facility was unhindered by originality, and he was unashamedly eclectic and conservative. Yet among Russian composers before Tchaikovsky he had by far the best technique. Both as pianist and teacher he was noted for following impulse; equally as a composer he was capable of taking a turn that was not quite predictable, and such surprises sometimes animate music which might otherwise seem wholly routine. His First Piano Concerto dates from 1850, two more following within the next four years. The work of a phenomenally talented young man bursting with ideas, it is an especially Mendelssohnian piece, but lacks that composer's structural neatness. The Third Concerto (1853–4) is a great advance, the spirit of the waltz, which seems to take possession of the first movement, drawing from Rubinstein some of his most engaging melody. The whole concerto demonstrates that the lesson of conciseness has been well learned.

Yet the Fourth and Fifth Concertos, which followed the Third at ten-year intervals, are more interesting, though for widely differing reasons. In the decade since the Third Concerto Rubinstein's expressive world had broadened, and the first movement of No. 4 in D minor (1864) is an impressive piece, displaying a little of the nobility which marks Brahms's concerto in the same key, and a tautness of structure which ensures that none of its modestly memorable ideas outstays its welcome. Though the slow movement's cantabile themes have charm rather than substance, spreading themselves with that leisureliness which came all too easily to Rubinstein, the finale does much to restore any lost ground, and the Fourth Concerto remains worth the occasional hearing.

But the E flat concerto (No. 5, 1874) is the most ambitious of the series.

Here, Rubinstein sought to create a work of epic scale, and the choice of key is revealing; his fifth was also to be his 'Emperor', with thematic, harmonic and textural worlds close to those of its model. Most significant of all, he appropriated the special harmonic and tonal practices of Beethoven's great piece. There is the same primacy of the tonic and dominant, both as chords and keys, the same pregnant moves to the minor which abruptly give birth to deep-flat regions. Beethoven had employed this tension between two distant tonal areas as a massive brace for his whole concerto, C flat (and closely related keys) confronting the tonic E flat in the first movement, claiming the slow movement for its own (though it is written as B major), then yielding again to E flat in the finale. Rubinstein was accepting a superhuman challenge in daring to vie with Beethoven in this kind of achievement, yet he begins well. The trouble was that he had grasped only the externals of what Beethoven had done—merely the expressive effect of moves to remote keys, not the profounder structural purpose—and as the piano enters the second half of the development the tonal moves become less like critical stages on a broadly planned journey than local events in a casual ramble. With the slow movement placed conventionally in the relative minor, his failure to comprehend the main objective of Beethoven's tonal strategy is fully uncovered. As for the finale, conscious of its obligation to match the time-scale of the first movement yet deprived of any real purpose for so doing, it finally degenerates into a disjointed jumble, if judged by the Beethovenian standards Rubinstein had unwittingly set himself.

Yet while the Fifth Concerto is a merciless exposé of Rubinstein's limitations, it is also a warning not to be contemptuous of his abilities. Perhaps his gift to Russia lay less in what he wrote than in what he did; all the same, his view of form was in no way timid, and the example of this forceful yet kindly, difficult yet generous man probably encouraged that structural enterprise which is a striking feature of many later Russian concertos.

Balakirev

In a land where awareness of national culture had for decades been growing stronger, the Western style of Rubinstein's compositions and of the methods his conservatoire would propagate aroused alarm and anger among those resolved to follow the path Glinka had indicated. A leader of this opposition emerged in **Mily Balakirev** (1837–1910). Born in Nizhni-Novgorod, he had come under the patronage of a wealthy amateur and writer on music, Alexander Ulïbïshev, acquiring a serviceable musical education which had made him an able pianist and a better-than-average amateur composer. In 1855 Ulïbïshev brought Balakirev to St Petersburg where he deeply impressed Glinka, who entrusted him with continuing his work. After

Glinka's death in 1857 Balakirev entered into his inheritance with vigour, gathering around himself a group of equally amateur musicians whom he proposed to turn into major composers. The names of these men—Borodin, Mussorgsky, Rimsky-Korsakov and Cui—are evidence enough of the remarkable success of his teaching. Dismayed at Rubinstein's proposals for a conservatoire, Balakirev collaborated in setting up a Free Music School which both promoted concerts and taught attitudes and methods favourable to the evolution of a national style in composition.

Despite the demands all such things made upon his energies, during the late 1850s and 1860s Balakirev began to investigate for himself ways and forms of composing which would permit his natural Russian creativity to be fully exercised. Already, when only 15, he had written a *Grande fantaisie* for piano and orchestra, based on Russian folk-songs, and three years later had embarked on a Piano Concerto in F sharp minor, finishing a single movement. In 1861 he began another piano concerto, completed the first movement and sketched the second the following year, and had the finale sufficiently in his head to play it over to friends. Then he laid it all aside, returning to it over 40 years later, but still leaving only sketches and directions for the finale when he died. From these Liapounov completed the work.

While the F sharp minor concerto had copied the style and rigid sequence of events set out in Chopin's concertos so faithfully that it might almost pass for the first movement of a third concerto by the Polish master, that in E flat contains some relatively novel features, and to approach it solely with conventional Western expectations, taking no account of what a creator of Russian stock may have perceived as his objectives, is to risk misjudging it. A charge frequently levelled at nineteenth-century Russian symphonic works, and one to which this concerto is patently open, is that they rely excessively upon repetition and sequence to fill out the musical space. The listener may attribute Balakirev's very repetitive thematic method to the example of Schumann, certainly a powerful and not always wholesome influence within the Russian musical scene, and blame his inexperience for the somewhat unvarying relationship between soloist and orchestra. All this is fair to a degree, but it ignores one fundamental point: that while German creativity is organic, Russian is decorative. It was the incompatibility between Glinka's Russian urges and the requirements of traditional German symphonic thought that made him drop all three of his attempts at a symphony; his three late orchestral pieces, especially the prodigiously seminal *Kamarinskaya*, were experiments in solving this problem of matching content with form. In all these pieces his solution was to use national material (two employ Spanish, one Russian), then fill out the structure partly through continuous variation, but especially with changing backgrounds—that is, retaining the themes intact, but imaginatively reworking their accompaniments. In fact, decoration/variation is perhaps the very foundation of Russian creativity, and it will be noted that variation of some kind is a factor in all four musical examples in this chapter, whether it involves changing a theme's character, or inserting a pitch contour into different themes while varying the rhythmic structure.

Balakirev grew up in the shadow of these three pieces, and something of Glinka's approach conditions especially the second movement of this concerto, which is little more than a trail of orchestral repetitions of two thematic elements (one a chant from the Russian Requiem), the soloist providing decorative accompaniment. This *Adagio* is a curious conception, easy to censure for lacking any convincing shape, its key shifts sometimes highly uncomfortable, its 'backgrounds' impoverished when compared to the inventiveness of Glinka's at their best. As for the first movement, though sonata-structured, even this tends to build similarly from statements of its three concise themes (or parts of them), usually presented by the orchestra with the piano providing mainly background figuration, as in the slow movement. Though the whole concerto is perhaps more intriguing as a case history from the post-Glinka years than as an experience for the twentieth-century listener, it would be wrong to dismiss it simply because it is sometimes unpolished, even gauche. It is a sturdy, stylistically insecure piece, but engaging for its honest—and successful—determination to be itself. How responsibility for the finale should be apportioned remains uncertain, but Liapounov seems to have done his job scrupulously. In character it is rather like a tumbler's dance of the sort popular in Russian operas, based on a small fund of racy ideas. The opening theme of the first movement had linked the slow movement to this finale, and it recurs twice near the end of the latter.

Tchaikovsky

With two such clearly defined parties, each led by a forceful, energetic personality, each possessing its own resources, high patronage, and institution through which its ideals and practices could be disseminated, it might reasonably be expected that the continuing story of Russian music would be of two irreconcilable traditions growing ever farther apart. But instead, within a very few years, many of the personalities whose postures had seemed so mutually hostile in the early 1860s developed associations with the opposite camp. In 1867, when Anton Rubinstein resigned as conductor of the RMS concerts, his successor was, on Rubinstein's own recommendation, Balakirev. At the same time Rubinstein himself suddenly entered his 'Russian' period, composing a series of works with a national character which won some admiration from Balakirev's associates. In 1871 Rimsky-Korsakov became a professor at the St Petersburg Conservatoire, and in 1874 Borodin began his first string quartet (to Mussorgsky's disgust). Meanwhile, Nikolay Rubinstein had shown much partiality towards Balakirev's work, giving the first performance of his piano fantasia, *Islamey*, in 1869. And **Pyotr Ilyich Tchaikovsky** (1840–1893), having received his composer's training in Rubinstein's conservatoire, soon produced *Romeo and Juliet* under the personal guidance of Balakirev, then in the early 1870s entered his own brief 'nationalist' phase. In fact, the interaction between the high professionalism which Rubinstein promoted and the vital Russianness (in its broadest sense) which Balakirev proclaimed produced some of the finest works of the late nineteenth--century Russian repertoire. Nowhere is this more clearly demonstrated than in the first and greatest of Tchaikovsky's concertos, that in B flat minor for piano (1874–5). The piece is in line from Rubinstein's concertos as regards general character (particularly that of the piano writing), while its employment of two Ukrainian folk-songs explicitly signals its national ancestry. Yet it also declares its Russian provenance in other deeper respects. A decorative art which creates by ever varied invention around a repeated proposition (as in *Kamarinskaya*) points to a mind whose workings are reflective rather than evolutionary. In fact, reflective thinking is another fundamental of Russian creativity. In music it enables the Russian to conceive self-contained but often magnificently broad themes, yet presents him with great problems when he wishes to evolve to the next stage of a piece. And just as that special process of thematic development, which came so readily to the German symphonic composer, was thoroughly alien to Russian creative thought, so also was tonal evolution. Tchaikovsky's natural way of handling tonality in a symphonic piece was in large, single-key areas (though there might be vigorous tonal shifts in the centres of these). The average twentieth-century listener may be barely, if at all, conscious that the first subject of this concerto's first movement ends, not only in theme but in key, precisely where it had began 76 bars before; but what he cannot fail to sense is that, while Tchaikovsky has been ruminating upon the little Ukrainian folk-tune that is his material (Ex. 1a), he has had no longer-term destination in his sound-sights. This section ended, a very calculated shift to a new stage in the work is unavoidable.

It is inevitable that a large-scale work shaped by such a composer will be highly compartmented. Yet while this denied Tchaikovsky's symphonic movements the smooth inevitability of their best German counterparts, his resourcefulness in disguising, even circumventing, this problem was very considerable. In this concerto, for instance: though the wind theme (Ex. 1c) that now enters is still in B flat minor, its very nature is modulatory, and the transition function can therefore be performed within this first limb of the second subject itself. By contrast, its companion, a quiet tune on muted strings (Ex. 1d), is tonally rock-like and firmly establishes A flat as the unconventional key of the second subject. This whole procedure is then repeated, much amplified both in scale and forcefulness, to round off the exposition.

Even such a bare account of this highly successful exposition is enough to indicate that it is also highly unconventional. Such observations help to explain what happened on that distressing occasion when Tchaikovsky played the concerto to Nikolay Rubinstein, whom he hoped would introduce it to the public, only to hear his friend and champion brutally denounce it as ill-composed and unplayable. Rubinstein was wildly wrong,

Ex. 1

of course, and soon perceived this. Yet for a man whose first views on the proprieties of composition had been formed in Germany and whose conception of the Russian piano concerto had been shaped by his brother's five examples, there were other features which would also have been found initially disconcerting—such as the huge introduction set mostly in the wrong key, with a grand tune which never returns. But in fact this tune (Ex. 1b) is a highly original compendium of crucial fragments from which the two subjects will be built, and thus subtly prepares for things to come without revealing the key in which the movement will get down to its main business.

The substantial *ritornello* which introduces the development is a more conventional feature—but not the procedures it brings with it. Just as the movement up to this point has been notable for thematic unity, what now follows is marked by thematic mutation, for during this *ritornello*, and even more in the close dialogue between soloist and orchestra which follows, themes are deftly made to change their character, or even their identity. Equally deft is the recapitulation. Little is changed except the order of some events and the keys; the stable string theme is excluded from the second subject, thus ensuring that this stretch of the movement is tonally restless, and to prolong this tension a written-out cadenza is added. Only then does the second theme enter to assert B flat and prepare the way for the coda.

Neither of its companions attempts to match the scale or expressive achievement of this magnificent movement, quite certainly the finest of all Russian concertos. As in Balakirev's slow movement, so in Tchaikovsky's an heir to Glinka can be detected in the repetitions of the flute theme against modestly varied backgrounds. These provide the flanks; in sharp contrast the fleet centre contains a French chansonette (Ex. 1e) which seems to have helped form the second theme of the first movement's second subject (Ex. 1d). At first hearing the slow movement may seem to be ternary, but the *prestissimo*'s opening has already occurred in slow motion in the centre of the first section where it had prefaced a brief subsidiary idea; thus a simple rondo structure is also detectable. The finale, too, begins like a simple rondo. But after its two themes, the first another Ukrainian folk-tune (Ex. 1f), have run their ABABA alternation, the second (Ex. 1g) is again taken up, built up, and is finally delivered *fortissimo* by both soloist and orchestra. As a conclusion, and as a symmetrical balance to the equally broad theme which had opened the concerto, it is an effective gesture, but it scarcely provides the extra substance this *Allegro con fuoco* really requires after such an imposing and weighty first movement.

Tchaikovsky composed his Second Piano Concerto in 1879–80. Though the quality of the material in the first movement is inferior to that of its predecessor, this *Allegro brillante*'s sequence of events provides an unusual and stimulating journey, starting from when, after the first subject has spread itself expansively and, like its counterpart in the First Concerto, ended tonally unmoved, the first theme of the second subject erupts in E flat. This new, distant key has, of course, the same relationship to the tonic G as C flat had to the tonic E flat in Beethoven's Fifth Concerto. But whereas the German composer had used his C flat as a challenge which would achieve temporary victory in the slow movement, Tchaikovsky employed his two keys as the boundaries of his tonal field—that is, there is scarcely a passage in the whole movement where use is made of more than one sharp or three flats. Key usage, therefore, does not produce structural tension, as in Beethoven, but instead maps out an exclusion zone. For Tchaikovsky it provided an effective control over his tonal resources; for the listener it is the more extreme moves that are made within this deliberately confined world that are most important—as when Tchaikovsky continues nearly all his second subject in this three-flat area, then opens into a blaze of C major sound to begin the development's first *ritornello*.

Strangely, in view of the number of pieces he wrote for the medium, Tchaikovsky insisted he disliked the sound of piano with orchestra, and already in this exposition he has separated his soloist from the orchestra to a marked degree. In the development such segregation is almost total, and results in the movement's most novel stretch: two *ritornelli*, the second particularly extensive, each followed by a grandiloquent piano cadenza. All this makes for a huge and most original central section; by contrast, the recapitulation is little more than a truncated review of the exposition's three thematic elements.

The slow movement is also a substantial piece, very different from that in the First Concerto. Tchaikovsky himself had persisting doubts about the structure of this G major concerto, and in 1888 he made cuts in the first two movements.[1] Yet though their original forms still remain preferable, Tchaikovsky was right to feel the slow movement was not entirely satisfactory. It has also been criticized for its employment of violin and cello soli on equal terms with the official soloist. Yet in a movement so filled with expansive lyrical melody the services of these two interlopers have much value. Most striking about the main theme is the breadth it develops after its modest opening phrase—which is precisely what the tediously sequential theme at the movement's centre fails to do. But the coda is particularly lovely.

1. Probably the cut in the central *ritornello* of the first movement (bars 319–42), and two in the *Andante non troppo* (bars 247–81 and 310–26; in orchestra bar 327).

After two such extended movements, the finale sounds even more diminutive than the B flat minor's. It is similarly built from clearly defined sections, though these are shuffled and tonally organized so as to leave a teasing doubt whether an idiosyncratic view of sonata structure was *really* the background against which Tchaikovsky devised it. Like the slow movement of the First Concerto, there is rather more to this *Allegro con fuoco* than one might at first suspect.

Tchaikovsky's Violin Concerto in D (1878), composed after quitting his native land following his disastrous marriage the previous year, was inspired by Josef Kotek, a young violinist and former pupil to whom the composer had once felt an homosexual attraction, and who had now briefly joined him. The concerto owed nothing to Rubinstein's in G (1857), its only predecessor from a significant Russian composer, for while that had been a thoroughly Western-rooted piece, ambitious in scale, Tchaikovsky's was wholly characteristic and concise. True, except for its introduction, the first movement's pattern has much in common with that of Mendelssohn's concerto, with its written-out cadenza before the recapitulation. But into this mould Tchaikovsky poured a flow of melody entirely his own, and there can be little doubt that it was the promptings of an old passion which stirred to life his inspiration. Yet the remaining two movements uncover a second yearning: for the land he had fled. The Canzonetta, composed in a single day after he had decided his first attempt at a slow movement was unsatisfactory,[1] might be heard as an exile's song of longing, the immensely spirited finale as a projection of Russian vitality, conjuring images of a folk festival. Be these visions as they may, Tchaikovsky's Russianness is more consistently evident in this concerto than in any of his others. For some early listeners it made for discomfort, even distress, especially for the Viennese critic Eduard Hanslick, who was blistering when the concerto was given its première in Vienna in 1881. The work's technical demands account for the delaying of its first performance, Kotek clearly feeling inadequate and Leopold Auer (Tchaikovsky's second choice as soloist) shying away from it. Thus it was left to Adolf Brodsky to undertake the task—and receive the dedication in gratitude.

Except for Rubinstein, Tchaikovsky was the most productive among pre-Revolution Russian composers of concerted music, for besides these three concertos he left a half-dozen miscellaneous pieces. The most substantial is the *Concert Fantasia* for piano and orchestra (1884), a curious two-movement work, like the Second Piano Concerto irremediably handicapped by

---

1. The rejected movement became *Méditation*, the first of three violin/piano pieces published as *Souvenir d'un lieu cher.*

containing scarcely one really strong melodic idea, and in the development of its first movement carrying the segregation of piano from orchestra to its ultimate point by making the entire section a written-out cadenza. The second movement, entitled *Contrasts*, had originally been intended for the Third Suite for orchestra. The two vastly differing themes which prompted this title are made respectively the bases of extensive *Andante cantabile* and *Molto vivace* sections suggesting the slow movement and finale of a conventional concerto. During the second of these the two themes are combined, and the coda echoes the whole work's opening. The *Concert Fantasia* is an unusual conception justifying the occasional performance. However, Tchaikovsky developed doubts about its total effect and provided an alternative ending to the first movement so that this might be performed separately.

Nine years later he took a similar decision with what he had planned should be the first movement of a third piano concerto. In 1892 he began a symphony in E flat, then abandoned it, and the next year employed the sketches of the first movement for a sonata-structured *Allegro brillante* for piano and orchestra. Despite its being no longer than its counterparts in the earlier concertos, Tchaikovsky at first felt it had come out over-large for a first movement and decided it should stand by itself as an *Allegro de Concert*—though it was to be published after his death as the Third Piano Concerto.[1] There is no earthly reason why music which had already been rejected as too uninteresting for a symphony should sound any better in a concerto; far more engaging are the two much shorter pieces with a violin as soloist. The *Sérénade mélancolique* (1875) followed hard upon the First Piano Concerto, employed the same key, and seems to have borrowed something from the chansonette of the concerto's slow movement to condition the character of its own faster central section. The brooding melody from which the flanks of this ternary structure grow is in the sharpest contrast to the stream of sparkling ideas which make the even more slender *Valse-scherzo* (1877) so beguiling. Both pieces are unpretentious yet distinctive.

Sadly though not surprisingly, the *Pezzo capriccioso* for cello and orchestra, composed in 1887 while Tchaikovsky was keeping a harrowing vigil over a dying friend, lacks such engaging freshness. Far more important—and attractive—is the earlier work for cello and orchestra, the *Variations on a Rococo Theme*, composed at the end of 1876 in the wake of *Francesca da Rimini* and in a manner so removed from that of this tempestuous symphonic fantasia as to sound like the work of a different composer from a different

1. At the time of his death Tchaikovsky was working on an *Andante* and *Finale* which were clearly intended as the residual movements of a complete concerto. Taneyev subsequently completed these.

century. Which is precisely what Tchaikovsky intended. All his mature life he was deeply troubled by what he felt were the expressive excesses he could not avoid in his most characteristic music. Mozart was his ideal, and as his own most personal music became increasingly tormented, a corresponding yearning to escape into the pure world of his idol became more irresistible. Tchaikovsky's rococo pastiches were the result, and this cello piece is the finest of them. But Tchaikovsky allowed Wilhelm Fitzenhagen, for whom they were written, to reorder the variations, even to delete one, and the set was issued in this deplorably mutilated form; the cellists who are increasingly using the vastly superior original version cannot be commended too highly. For all his reverence of Mozart, Tchaikovsky's view of the variation form was fundamentally different from the Austrian composer's, and he quickly abandoned the harmonic and periodic structure of his gracious theme, concentrating instead upon the melody itself, not only expanding it but even dismantling and redistributing its constituent parts. Above all, he contrived to admit his own personality in places, especially in the gentle Slav melancholy of the D minor variation and in the pensiveness of the the *valse triste* in C major.

Rimsky-Korsakov

Tchaikovsky was the towering giant of the pre-Revolution composers. Of Balakirev's associates the only one to compose concerted works was **Nikolay Rimsky-Korsakov** (1844–1908). One result of his appointment as Inspector of Naval Bands in 1873 was three pieces for wind soloist and military band. Though the first, for trombone (1877), is dubbed 'concerto', the cheerful virtuosity and amiable cantilenas in its three diminutive movements add up to nothing more high minded than what is offered in the even briefer piece for clarinet (1878), more modestly labelled *Konzertstück*. The oboe variations (1878), based upon one of Glinka's folk-song stylizations, *Why do you cry, young beauty?*, provided the opportunity for some attractive character variations. But Rimsky's Piano Concerto, despite running as one continuous movement and for less than 15 minutes, is very different both in intention and stature. It is based on a Russian folk-song (Ex. 2a), and though composed in 1882–3, was not published till 1886; hence

Ex. 2a

its dedication to the memory of Liszt. The tribute was not merely pious—yet it is the Glinka of *Kamarinskaya* who really stood present at its conception, the opening (Ex. 2b) being bluntly modelled on that piece. But whereas Glinka had used two folk-tunes for continuous variations, Rimsky used one to provide two fragments from which, with great inventiveness, he generated all the material of his four-section piece. Already the figuration of the piano entry derives from *a* in Ex. 2a, the string figuration which provides part of the background the fifth time the folk-tune is heard is from *b*, while the piano tune (Ex. 2c), which ushers in the *Allegretto quasi polacca* second section, exploits the theme's imitative possibilities. An extended portion of the opening (*c* in Ex. 2a) converts itself felicitously into a more cantabile phrase (Ex. 2d) before the third section *(Andante mosso)* returns to the concerto's first sounds (Ex. 2b), though also borrowing a later stretch of the

Ex. 2b

Ex. 2c

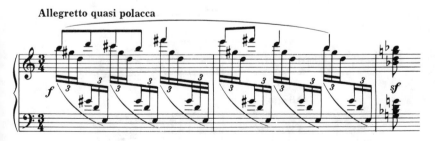

Ex. 2d

folk-tune (*d* in Ex. 2a) to shape the overall contour of its phrase (Ex. 2e). The final section *(Allegro)* also quotes the work's opening theme (Ex. 2b) complete, then presents new thematic formations as well as reminding us of old ones. Yet equally important is the second bar to the piano accompaniment which had opened the *Andante mosso* (Ex. 2f). Though it seems no more than a casual reversal of the folk-song-derived shape in bar one, it is soon to become a theme in its own right (Ex. 2g), and later in two rhythmically restructured forms, it will contribute to the pianist's final cadenza (Ex. 2h), then provide the substance of the brief coda (Ex. 2i).

Common to all these thematic variants is contour, not rhythmic structure (in German motivic technique, the opposite applies). Indeed, the method may be seen as a distant but very real extension of the technique by which countless Russian folk-songs are generated—that is, by variations upon a basic protoshape (Ex. 2a is a brief but excellent instance; note how shape *b* has been prefigured in each of the preceding two bars). Rimsky's Piano Concerto is perhaps the most intrinsically Russian concerted piece ever

Ex. 2e

Ex. 2f

Ex.2g,h,i

composed, a reflective rather than an evolving piece, having no need of tonal dynamism and, despite the local keyshifts, only once displacing C sharp minor by another crucial tonality (F major for the third section). The economical time scale, as in *Kamarinskaya*, is absolutely right for such music. Not surprisingly, this piano concerto, in returning to a world of earlier Russian music, delighted Balakirev. But equally, it seems, it had gifts for later composers, for though none of them attempted its kind of intensive thematic concentration, there followed a number of concerted pieces based on folk material; at the same time the three-movement concerto lost its monopoly, a whole series of one-movement pieces also later appearing. Significantly, perhaps, both Tchaikovsky's E flat concerto movement and his single-movement alternative to his *Concert Fantasia* postdate this concerto.

In concerted music Tchaikovsky had dominated the 1870s and early 1880s, and now Rimsky's Piano Concerto had set one possible direction for the future. But the latter's two pieces with solo violin made no attempt to capitalize on this. They are counterparts to Tchaikovsky's two short pieces of some dozen years earlier. The *Souvenir de trois chants polonais* (1888), like Tchaikovsky's *Valse-scherzo*, is a string of dance tunes, this time mazurkas which Rimsky remembered from his mother's singing. Like Tchaikovsky's *Sérénade mélancolique*, the *Fantasia on two Russian themes* (1886–7) is a more serious-minded piece, as long as the concerto, with some haunting moments, but adding to Rimsky's stature no more than do the two late concerted pieces with piano to Tchaikovsky's.

Tchaikovsky's successors

The period of the great pioneers was over. Rubinstein, Tchaikovsky and Rimsky-Korsakov had established the Russian concerto tradition, given it some of its finest ornaments, and pointed ways to the future. This future now passed into the custody of a younger generation comprising two groups, the first of four composers, Sergey Taneyev, Sergey Liapounov (Lyapunov), Anton Arensky and Alexander Glazunov, all born between 1856 and 1865, who first made their mark in the late 1870s and 1880s, the second of three, Alexander Scriabin (Skryabin), Sergey Rachmaninov (Rakhmaninov) and Nikolay Medtner (Metner), all born between 1872 and 1880, who emerged a decade later. All were professionally trained: Taneyev, Liapounov, Scriabin and Medtner at the Moscow Conservatoire, Arensky at the St Petersburg. Rachmaninov began at the latter, then moved to the former, while Glazunov studied privately with Rimsky-Korsakov. All but Glazunov were also pianists. None of these seven was as gifted as Tchaikovsky or even Rimsky; most are, frankly, no more than minor figures, yet none should be ignored completely.

The oldest was **Sergey Taneyev** (1856–1915). First Tchaikovsky's pupil, then one his closest friends, Taneyev was also the soloist at the premières of all his teacher's works for piano and orchestra except the first. In 1878 he replaced Tchaikovsky at the Moscow Conservatoire, and for the next 27 years was a distinguished teacher there (Liapounov, Scriabin, Rachmaninov and Medtner were among his pupils). As a composer Taneyev was unique among Russians, planning each work in detail before beginning composition. But though by instinct a contrapuntist, he was no pedant, simply a very careful man whose personal existence was also well regulated (most unusual of all for a Russian, he was a teetotaller). Being so fine a performer himself, it may seem surprising that he should have completed no piece for piano and orchestra, but except for a brief and agreeable *Canzona* for clarinet and strings (1883), his only concerted piece was his *Suite de Concert* for violin and orchestra (1908–9). The main ancestral line of this very substantial work runs from Tchaikovsky's orchestral suites, above all the first, for just as that had sandwiched between a fugue and a gavotte movements that would have adapted comfortably into one of Tchaikovsky's own ballets, so Taneyev's suite passes from Prelude and Gavotte into a Fairy Tale, then via a set of variations to a Tarantella. If it had been possible to command sustained attention through thoughtfulness and skill, without either individuality or temperament, then Taneyev might have become as popular a composer as his teacher. But he was an eclectic by necessity for, just as he lacked true temperament and a real instinct for drama (hence, perhaps, his failure to complete the piano concerto he began in 1876), so he lacked that individuality which might here have effected a compelling stylistic fusion. Yet for those with a taste for excellently made music, thoughtful without being ponderous, inventive enough to sustain interest over a 40-minute span, this *Suite de Concert* is well worth investigation.

While in character **Anton Arensky** (1867–1906) was the opposite of Taneyev, he too was to be accepted into Tchaikovsky's closest circle of friends. In his Piano Concerto, completed in 1882, Arensky took Chopin as his main model, though far less slavishly than Balakirev in his F sharp minor movement, adding a much heavier rhetoric in the first movement, but in the finale presenting a more individual, Russian world with five-beat bars that provide some of the earliest evidence of Arensky's penchant for unusual metres. The original ancestor of his remaining work for piano and orchestra, his *Fantasia on themes of Ryabinin* (1899)[1] is *Kamarinskaya* even more than Rimsky's concerto, for the fantasia is based on two closely related folk-tunes, between them heard 15 times, with intervening passages founded upon

---

1. Ivan Ryabinin was a famed exponent of Russian bĭlinĭ, or epic songs.

chains of separate phrases. Despite its small scale and patches of conventional grandiloquence, the fantasia is an arresting piece, gently permeated by an elegiac quality revealed most touchingly in the simple yet telling harmonization which the piano offers at the dying end. The Violin Concerto (1891) is cast as a single movement, an exposition giving way to two self-contained sections, the first slow, the second a waltz. The only hint of development is in the brief passage which links these, and the work's symmetry is completed by a recapitulation incorporating a cadenza. This concerto is the most completely satisfactory of Arensky's concerted pieces, its clear and concise structure designed to allow his greatest single gift, his formidable capacity for attractive melody, to be freely exercised.

Arensky's music has distinctiveness if not originality, personality if not individuality. This becomes clearer still when his work is set beside that of **Sergey Liapounov**, whose initial route was the very opposite: from Moscow to St Petersburg, whither Liapounov was irresistibly drawn by the appeal of the continuing nationalist tradition, and specifically of Balakirev himself. But Liapounov's nature was too eclectic for Balakirev alone to retain hold of him, and it is Rimsky's single-movement concerto which lies behind his four concerted pieces, even though all three of Liapounov's concertos employ an overall sonata pattern. From his First Piano Concerto (1890) he showed a commitment to Lisztian transformation techniques, and Arensky's *Ryabinin fantasia* was a clear influence upon his *Rhapsody on Ukrainian Themes* (1907), similarly based upon folk-melodies, though organized in the slow-fast-slow-fast scheme of Rimsky's concerto. Liapounov was often at his best when at his most lyrical, and the opening of this rhapsody, like the similarly gentle beginning of the Second Piano Concerto (1909), is touchingly beautiful, with some lovely (and very Balakirevian) harmonic touches. The Violin Concerto (1915), clearly conditioned by both Arensky's and Glazunov's examples, interpolates before the recapitulation a substantial slow section, though not, as in the two central sections of Arensky's concerto, founded on new themes, but on existing material.

Yet, engaging as Liapounov can be, his melodies are often too faceless to mark a work with that clear character which will ensure it remains in the memory. It is not that the themes of **Alexander Scriabin**'s Piano Concerto (1896–7) are notable for personality, but many of them have a charming lyrical freshness and a capacity, where necessary, to unfold and develop the spaciousness which may be required of them. As in Balakirev's E flat concerto, melody affords the main thread of continuity, and the soloist is likewise occupied in almost every bar. Yet the composers who, like Scriabin, emerged in the 1890s had no interest in the nationalist tradition of which Balakirev was by now the sole true custodian. Chopin and Scriabin's close friend Rachmaninov, whose First Concerto (also in F sharp minor) was already some five years old, contribute audibly to some passages, but otherwise this early work is very much Scriabin's own, even though its design is thoroughly traditional, the first movement being a neat sonata structure, the finale a sonata rondo, while the central movement is a theme and four variations. Even the designing of these variations is conventional, the structure of the beautiful theme for muted strings being clearly retained and not progressively dismantled, as in Tchaikovsky's cello variations. Nor does anything in the concerto's musical content foretell the highly personal direction Scriabin's creative researches were to lead him. What it does already reveal, however, is his fastidious ear, and though there are weighty passages, the scoring often shows exemplary restraint, and the piano figurations, though luxuriant, are often very delicate. The clear but unaffected return at the concerto's end to first subject material from the opening movement is an enhancing touch. Of late nineteenth-century Russian concertos this is one of the most tasteful and attractive.

Glazunov

By 1917, when revolution overthrew tsardom and Russia moved towards the civil war from which emerged communist rule, Arensky, Taneyev and Scriabin were dead. Faced with such social turmoil Rachmaninov was quick to leave, and in 1918 settled in the USA, dying there 25 years later. The other survivors all followed. Medtner left in 1921, headed for Germany, finding havens in Paris and then London. **Alexander Glazunov** (1865–1936) slipped away in 1928; eight years later he died in Paris where in 1923 Liapounov had made his home for the last year of his life. Liapounov's creative work was done before his departure, but the others all composed their final concerted works abroad. Thus the pre-Revolutionary tradition, like its last composers, ended its days in exile.

Lacking that imaginative insight which we call genius, Glazunov nevertheless commanded an inventiveness from which he fashioned an anonymously individual style with power both to please and to stir. He came to the concerto late. His Violin Concerto (1904), like two of his three remaining concertos, employs a single movement scheme, the first half of this one much like that of Arensky's, with a concise exposition leading into a slow section on a new theme, followed by a development of the exposition material. But then the pattern changes; the development slides seamlessly into a recapitulation, and after the cadenza a lively trumpet tune introduces, in effect, a finale. Though this is to be manipulated with all that craftsman's facility which Glazunov commanded so consummately, there is a glibness about the themes in this simple rondo that scarcely matches the thoughtful thematicism of the concerto's earlier stages. Glazunov had remarkable skill in drawing out long melodic lines, as the two richly lyrical subjects (Ex. 3a and 3b) and the slow section's sweetly expressive theme (Ex. 3d) manifestly demonstrate. But what is also apparent is not only the neat thematic integration effected by the contour of chained thirds in both subjects, but also the use of the five-pitch figure *x* to form a separate thematic particle (Ex. 3c) as well as to provide a nucleus in important supporting figuration (Ex. 3b; in its semiquaver form it has already appeared as an independent melodic line). The figure also momentarily infiltrates the slow section's theme (Ex. 3d). Thus very different thematic elements are related through (literally) a family profile.

Ex. 3a

Ex. 3b

Ex. 3c

Ex. 3d

This quintessentially Russian procedure, already observed in Rimsky's concerto and to be seen in Rachmaninov's Second Piano Concerto, of subjecting a pitch contour to rhythmic restructuring is more fundamental still to the Second Piano Concerto (1917). The model for the two-movement design of the First Piano Concerto (1910–11), with its concluding set of variations, was less Beethoven's last piano sonata than Tchaikovsky's Piano Trio, with its quota of character variations—though that work's recall of first movement material at the finale's end was less comprehensive than Glazunov's. The lavish attention to harmonic and chromatic detail in these variations is proof enough of Glazunov's serious intent. But the piano was not as congenial to him as the violin; it favoured far less the long-drawn lyrical melody which had been the Violin Concerto's greatest strength, and much of the material of this concerto is nondescript. The single-movement Second Concerto opens in leisurely fashion with two sections set a tritone apart, then builds the remainder of the piece somewhat riotously from the two themes on which these are founded, using their contours rhythmically changed, linked, set against each other, accelerated, generating counterpoints, passage-work, even whole sections of differing speeds and character. It is an enterprising venture, in effect becoming a string of variations, but finally too disorientated to make a coherent impression.

It is ironic, perhaps, that a composer who at 16 had made such a precocious debut with his First Symphony should have concluded his last major work 52 years later with a celebration of traditional contrapuntal expertise. Certainly, the extended fugato of the Saxophone Concerto (1934)—though it is more a contrapuntal fantasia around memories of what has gone before—provides that cogency which the end of the Second Piano Concerto had so lacked. Yet it is some of the earlier passages in this one-movement piece which haunt the memory: the dignified opening theme which the soloist sweetly embellishes, the main theme of the *Andante* central section—above all, the whole paragraph which follows this theme's return, where it transmutes itself into what seems an echo from the first movement of Tchaikovsky's Manfred Symphony. Manfred, like Glazunov, was a man living in isolation; there is a sadness and nostalgia in this concerto which surely betrays something of the loneliness of the exile. But Glazunov skirts the temptations to mawkishness which his choice of soloist might have presented, and what could so easily have become glutinous is instead rather touching.

Rachmaninov

Of all these later composers of concerted music **Sergey Rachmaninov** (1873–1943) was the most important and productive. His five large-scale pieces, the last two from his American years, all employ the piano as soloist, and span nearly half a century. Yet despite the shift in style and intention, the composer of the *Rhapsody on a theme of Paganini* (1934) is still recognizably he who in 1890–1 had created the F sharp minor concerto. For Rachmaninov was a true creative individual, if not a great one. His spiritual father was Tchaikovsky, whom Rachmaninov alone could approach in conceiving grand tunes, and these were initially the main weapon in his compositional armoury. His compositions, like Tchaikovsky's, are often bluntly sectional. Yet though the experience they offer accumulates rather than grows, there is nevertheless an expressive totality to his finest works that belies the verdicts of those who would still have us believe him no more than a simpleton with a flair for embarrassingly affecting tunes.

All these qualities are already there in the First Concerto. The structure is unambiguous and mostly traditional—after an orchestra-then-soloist flourish, which proves to be more than a mere introduction, come two melodic paragraphs, clearly profiled and structured, separated by a stretch of brilliant passage work whose function is not to afford a smooth join, but more a punctuation mark. A substantial *ritornello* opens the development, the recapitulation re-runs the exposition with the minimum of adjustment, and there is a written-out cadenza. The *Andante* is matchingly concise—a haunting introduction which searches for the new key, then a simple ternary form whose first theme is alluringly re-presented on its return. The high-spirited last movement is as explicitly sectional as the first, yet novel, for at the end of the exposition, the most savage of tonal wrenches (from A to E flat) introduces a totally new cantabile theme in place of a development.

This unpretentious concerto, as we know it today, requires little apology. Its youthful freshness has disarming honesty, and the exemplary neatness of its form is the result of the mature composer's drastic revision of 1917. As Geoffrey Norris has made clear,[1] while slimming and in part recomposing

1. See G. Norris, *Rachmaninov* (London, 1976), pp. 110ff.

the piece, Rachmaninov also enhanced much of the detail. It is this very inventive, sometimes highly sophisticated refinement in the piano writing especially which contributes so much to the richness and individuality of these concerted pieces. The pupil of Taneyev knew well how to embellish an harmonic progression or texture with contrapuntal details or decorative chromatic lines, how to devise counterphrases to the main tunes. He knew, too, how to use chromatic manoeuvres to enrich strong diatonic progressions. Such things were fully present from the first in the Second Concerto (second and third movements, 1900; first movement, 1901). Yet in no other work did Rachmaninov exploit more vigorously his purely melodic gifts, nor ever create a piece more coherent, either expressively or thematically (the two families of themes in Ex. 4 are by no means exhaustively traced). Those who doubt Rachmaninov's thoughtful approach should observe the unfolding behaviour of the tiny motif (Ex. 4j) which appears early in the first movement's development (also recurring in the finale), then assumes equal status with both subjects in the recapitulation. In fact, since this thematic process is the very basis of the movement's strategy, all that was required was an exposition in which two melodic propositions, one heavily masculine (Ex. 4i), the other more gently feminine (Ex. 4d), could be introduced, a development in which portions of these would be matched and mingled while this new melodic being was discovering itself, and a recapitulation in which this new being might first challenge one subject in powerful counterpoint, then woo and dispossess the other, first in crotchets, then gentle minims.

As in Beethoven's C minor concerto, the second movement is set remotely in E major, and the introduction is concerned to effect the tonal shift, just as that in the finale will return the music to C minor. The piano figuration (Ex. 4a) deceptively divides the twelve-quaver pattern into three groups of four quavers, while the flute tune opts for a three-quavers-in-four metre, with intriguing consequences. Since the clarinet's extension (Ex. 4e) merely continues the tune, the movement is virtually monothematic. However, the easy plasticity of this extension enables Rachmaninov to twist the music in a new direction (Ex. 4f), building through a brief scherzo section to a climax before returning to the quiet opening.

Though the brightly effective finale is scarcely a match for these two highly impressive and original conceptions, there are still some deft touches in this sonata structure, especially the chameleon-like transformation of the main theme (Ex. 4g and h) and the fleet fugato in the development. During the storming final statement of the second subject, the piano supplies echoes from the first subject.

As a realization of a consistent experience embracing all three

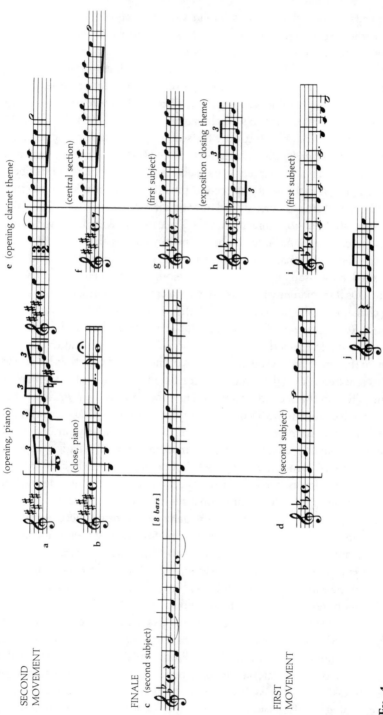

Ex. 4

movements, only Tchaikovsky's Violin Concerto equals 'Rach 2' among these earlier Russian concertos. Yet it is customary to rate the Third Concerto more highly. This is questionable, for though larger and structurally more ambitious, it lacks the surefootedness with which the thematic engagements of its predecessor's first movement are pursued, and its slow movement is far less satisfactory. Though the finale's form is much like that of the First Concerto's, Rachmaninov has capitalized on nearly 20 years' experience, for only slyly does the seemingly new tune of the central E flat section *(Scherzando)* disclose that its progenitor is the *first* movement's second subject. That movement's first subject recurs not only in this finale but also twice in the *Adagio*, the second time (in the quicker section before the orchestra returns to where it had opened the movement) so rhythmically disguised as to be almost unrecognizable. The care that went into the making of this concerto cannot be in doubt; its main weakness lies in its thematic material. The 'big' romantic theme—strong in outline, plain yet broad, and unabashed in its assault on the listener—belongs above all to youth, and by his later 30s Rachmaninov had passed his peak for inventing such things—as had Tchaikovsky (the horn tune of the Fifth Symphony is inferior to the love theme of *Romeo and Juliet*, for instance). But Tchaikovsky had further creative reserves to exploit to a degree that Rachmaninov did not, and the second theme of this finale has to ape the manners of the Second Concerto to extend itself as required. Nor is the cantabile second subject of the first movement as strong as that in the Second Concerto. The other fault is over-writing in the piano part, for what in the Second Concerto had been textural enhancement too often here becomes congestion, most conspicuously in the slow movement. Like its predecessor, this Intermezzo is monothematic except for the two interventions of the concerto's opening theme, but its slender melodic foundation is less able to sustain the expanse of music dependent upon it, despite the wide-ranging tonal route it is made to follow.

Yet, this said, the Third Concerto remains an imposing piece, especially the first movement. For all its engaging simplicity, the first theme discharges its initial duties at considerable length, and this manifest weightiness of purpose is prolonged into the transition, not a burst of sparkling passage work as in the earlier concertos, but a purely orchestral join which ruminates initially upon the first subject. The second subject is heard in two forms, the first crisply rhythmic, the second cantabile—exactly as the second subject of the finale is to be. The development returns to the movement's opening, then dissects portions of the theme for lively discussion. But at this stage thematic relationships to earlier materials are only tenuous, for a more exact review of these is to take place at great length in the huge cadenza. The idea of placing such crucial responsibility solely upon the soloist may have come from observing Tchaikovsky's work—but not the decision to enlist the services of four wind soloists to conclude the scrutiny of first subject matters[1] before the soloist alone attends to the second subject. By now the material has been so exhaustively displayed that a full recapitulation would be otiose, and the very brief recall of both subjects, now in the tonic, is admirably judged.

It would be temptingly neat to conclude that while exile had enabled Glazunov to discover within himself new shoots of personal feeling, Rachmaninov's creative roots had withered in alien ground. Certainly the Fourth Concerto (1926: revised 1941), for all its surface sparkle, is a very uneven piece, its two best ideas salvaged from earlier *Etudes-tableaux*, its greatest virtue its relative textural clarity. Though a degree of cultural disorientation was clearly a factor in determining its elusive, frankly weaker character, Rachmaninov's creative aims had themselves shifted radically. No longer interested in relying upon supercharged urges (even if such were still available to him), he was to discover, as Glinka had nearly a century earlier, that the right theme could trigger in him a series of lively, very precise responses, and when eight years later he applied his new creative attitudes in the 24 variations of the *Paganini Rhapsody*, they faced a challenge to which they were perfectly matched. Some variations are content with dazzling exploitation of the theme's capriciousness. But just as Tchaikovsky had devised his most successful variations not from a musical scrutiny of a theme but from observing it from diverse stylistic and expressive viewpoints, so the character variations in this *Rhapsody* are among the most successful. And just as Glinka in *Kamarinskaya* had found powerful stimulus in a perceived relationship between two otherwise dissimilar tunes, so Rachmaninov discovered a bizarre compatibility between Paganini's playful jingle and the sombre *Dies Irae*. The orchestra used is the largest in all his concerted pieces, yet the scoring is the most selective, for his new wit and brilliance were of the most pointed, even brittle kind—which makes yet more affecting that celebrated eighteenth variation where, inverting another man's tune, he briefly looks back towards that heightened expressive world in which he had ranged so freely years before in his native Russia.

Medtner

Like Rachmaninov before him, **Nikolay Medtner** (1880–1951) was a pupil of both Arensky and Taneyev, and the two were later to become firm friends, even though as personalities they were vastly different. Medtner's music lacks the allure of Rachmaninov's; his sober piano writing, as close to Schumann and Brahms as to Rachmaninov, reflects his German ancestry, his

---

1. Rachmaninov provided alternative versions for the first part of this cadenza.

melody is mostly unglamorous, his textures studiously engineered, with counterpoint sometimes a significant element. Piano music and songs were his métier; his only encounters with the orchestra were in his three very substantial piano concertos. Conspicuously absent in these is any obvious Russian idiom; even the First Concerto (1914–18), though another one-movement design and completed in Medtner's native land, has few externals that point blatantly to its creator's country of origin. Medtner's style is elusive and constantly shifting—yet he was capable of building an experience whose ambitious proportions seem justified, despite the inconsistencies of the music from which they are constructed. The First Concerto is just such a piece—less convincing in its slabs of rhetoric than in its more intimately reflective passages, yet adding up to an impressive achievement. But expatriation seems to have unsettled Medtner; the Second Concerto (1920–7), worthy piece that it is, has a more overtly Teutonic streak, and though the finale is engagingly capricious, the material of the first two movements is rather lacklustre, the stylistic mix more uncomfortable. A deliberate and painstaking worker, Medtner did not complete his Third (1940–3) until he had lived some years in England. Perhaps a little of the tradition which now surrounded him is to be detected in the leisurely reflectiveness of its opening pages, and in the unhurried unfolding of the far more uneven music that follows. It is the most lyrical and immediately appealing of the three; it is also the most dilute, the most amorphous in regional personality. Yet penetrate beneath the surface to what controls events, and again a growth-principle much like that behind the rough yet novel *Adagio* of Balakirev's E flat concerto of some 80 years earlier is revealed, for present in almost every bar of the first movement, for instance, is one of some half-dozen clear themes, and upon this thematic chain, with a diversity of 'backgrounds', the movement unwinds. The distant heir to Glinka still carried some faint family traits.

On 28 March 1943 Rachmaninov died in Beverley Hills. A year later, before an English audience in the Victorian aura of the Royal Albert Hall, Medtner's Third Piano Concerto received its first performance with the composer as soloist and Sir Adrian Boult conducting the London Philharmonic Orchestra. The last rite of a once major tradition had been enacted in an alien land. Seven years later, on 13 November 1951 at 69 Wentworth Road, London NW11, that pre-Revolutionary tradition passed for ever.

CHAPTER 7

Russia after 1917

Robert Layton

During the war years when interest in Soviet music reached fever pitch, Gerald Abraham[1] published a study of some of the then major composers, many of them unknown in the West. Some, like **Lev Knipper** (1898–1974), who has two cello concertos to his credit; and **Vissarion Shebalin** (1902–1963), whose concertos for violin (1940) and cello (1950) remain neglected; while others, like Reinhold Glière or Nikolay Miaskovsky, have established only a peripheral hold on the repertoire. Records appeared of violin concertos by Nikolay Rakov (*b.* 1908), Miaskovsky and Khachaturian—his Piano Concerto enjoyed considerable great wartime popularity—but for the most part, the Russians who commanded most attention then, as now, were Prokofiev and Shostakovich—and, of course, Stravinsky.

At first the Revolution occasioned an exodus of artistic talent from the Soviet Union. Prokofiev, still in his mid-20s, was, of course, to return in the 1930s, but Stravinsky, Rachmaninov and Medtner, all in their mid-30s and 40s in 1917, spent the rest of their lives as globe-trotting émigrés. Their musical personalities already possessed a tangible identity: their stylistic development had been well under way before the outbreak of the First World War. Shostakovich, on the other hand, was only eleven when the Kerensky Government fell and did not experience the conflict of backgrounds and values that faced émigré artists a decade or so older: he was a child of the Revolution. Glière and Miaskovsky adjusted themselves to the new regime and remained in Russia without any loss of integrity. **Reinhold Glière** (1875–1956), with whom Prokofiev had studied, was by this time in his 40s, an influential figure with his *Ilya Mourametz* Symphony behind him, but turned to the concerto rather late in life: there is a Harp Concerto, Op. 74 (1938), the celebrated Concerto for coloratura and orchestra, Op. 82 (1942), and concertos for the cello (1948) and the horn (1951). In the Concerto for coloratura he returns, as it were, to the origins of the concerto, while the Horn Concerto could have been written in the 1890s. It is a brilliant virtuoso showpiece of some 24 minutes written for Valeri Polekh, then solo horn of

---

1. Gerald Abraham, *Eight Soviet Composers*, London, 1943.

the Bolshoi, and treats the instrument almost like a violin, its unlikely model, particularly in the finale, being the Tchaikovsky Violin Concerto. The end of the slow movement is quite striking, the horn sustaining a muted high E flat rather like a flageolet on the violin. It is as unlikely as its companion to gain more than a precarious foothold on the repertoire. Far more substantial are the two concertos of **Nikolay Miaskovsky** (1881–1950), whose reputation largely rests on his 27 symphonies and, albeit to a lesser extent, his 13 string quartets.

Miaskovsky has had a respectful rather than an enthusiastic press in the West; he gets pretty short shrift from Stanley Dale Krebs[1] who speaks of his 'almost total lack of feeling for originality' and as 'a manipulator not a master of form'. The late Boris Schwarz, on the other hand, comes nearer the mark when he writes of 'the depth of Miaskovsky'.[2] His two concertos, for violin (1938) and cello (1944–5), should certainly not be underestimated. Their very 'accessibility' poses problems. He is 'rooted in Russian classicism' (Schwarz) and on first hearing, the Violin Concerto, Op. 44, seems to have some of the Imperial St Petersburg sweetness of the Glazunov or Arensky concertos. The ideas are strong in profile and immediately memorable; yet there is more pain in this music than at first appears. In the Cello Concerto, Op. 66, there is an all-pervasive nostalgia, a longing for a world lost beyond recall. In sensibility, though not achievement, this concerto comes close to the world of the Elgar and its elegiac sentiment is not skin-deep. By the side of Shostakovich's First Violin Concerto, written only three years later, Miaskovsky seems born out of his time, but both concertos have an authenticity of feeling which step outside their immediate circumstances. The working-out may not be innovative formally and the idiom is hardly more 'advanced' than Glazunov, but in its very simplicity lies its poignancy (Ex. 1).

Prokofiev

In sheer fertility of melodic invention, Miaskovsky is not the equal of his friend **Sergey Prokofiev** (1891–1953), but then few twentieth-century composers are! True, his melodic ideas tend to fall into easily recognizable patterns with astringent harmonic spicing and sly modulatory touches, but they always have a totally distinctive profile. In matters of form, Prokofiev was no iconoclast, and the appearance he presented to some of the more sheltered academics of pre-First World War Russia of being an *enfant terrible*

1. Stanley Dale Krebs, *Soviet Composers and the Development of Soviet Music*, London, 1970, pp. 117–8.
2. Boris Schwarz, *Music and Musical Life in Soviet Russia, 1917–1970*, London, 1972, p. 83.

Ex. 1

was deceptive. It was the presentation of the material rather than the material itself that was new. Even in such a brilliant (and underrated) score as the *Scythian Suite*, the harmonic vocabulary does not, for all its individuality, extend much further than Ravel, and it is surely its orchestral complexity, density of sound, and sheer decibel content that gained it notoriety. Prokofiev himself regarded the First Piano Concerto as his first 'more or less mature composition' both as regards its conception and fulfilment. It began life as a concertino in 1911 but the solo part was of unusual virtuosity and the work rapidly grew into a full-scale, albeit short concerto. Prokofiev was only 21 when he first played it in Moscow with Nikolay Tcherepnin and two years later when he graduated from the St Petersburg Conservatoire, he chose his own rather than the prescribed classical concerto as his examination piece. Not only is the relationship between piano and orchestra expertly judged, but the formal layout of the score shows the original quality of mind that the young Prokofiev possessed. We are plunged immediately by both soloist and orchestra into the exultant main theme which returns at the end of the exposition and again at the close of the work. The overall form could be described thus: main theme—*allegro* section corresponding to the exposition in sonata form—the main theme returns—a short *andante* leads to—development in the form of scherzo and cadenza—restatement—theme. Unlike the Second Concerto, also a student work, the First was not retouched or revised to any major extent in later years.

No sooner had his First Concerto been successfully launched in the summer of 1912 than Prokofiev embarked on a successor. While the new concerto did not perhaps have the bravura and glitter of the First, the writing for the keyboard was already assuming greater individuality. The difference between the first two piano sonatas had been striking enough: the world of Medtner, Rachmaninov and Scriabin was firmly behind him. However, when Prokofiev left Russia for the United States in 1918 he lost the concerto and had to reconstruct it from memory. The first movement steals in softly with descending thirds—a figure that appears to have no immediate signifi-cance—and introduces a broad lyrical theme on the piano. It is marked 'narrante' and is a discursive idea full of Prokofiev's deft modulatory sleights-of-hand. Nestyev thinks that it 'suggests a quiet, serious tale in the vein of a romantic legend'[1] and like much of Prokofiev's writing at this time (such as the Second Sonata, Op. 14) seems to have a narrative feel to it. When the strings enter in unison in G minor with a broad singing melody, one feels that the example of Rachmaninov has not gone altogether unheeded. The second theme looks forward to its counterpart in the Third Piano Concerto: there is no mistaking its slightly flippant character. The development section embraces an extensive cadenza for the soloist—marvellously sustained writing it is too—and the movement ends with the first theme combined with the descending thirds that had unobtrusively opened the movement. The scherzo is as high spirited and as tautly held together as any of Prokofiev ebullient essays in this genre: it has an unrelenting sense of forward movement, and the pianist has not a bar's rest from his semiquavers. He resembles some virtuoso footballer who retains the initiative while the opposing team (the orchestra) all charge after him. Having given us a broadly paced first movement and a short but brilliant scherzo, Prokofiev replaces the slow movement with an Intermezzo which is in some ways the most highly characterized of all four movements, with its flashes of sardonic wit and forward-looking harmonies. The finale is full of fleet-fingered brilliance on the part of pianist and orchestra.

The Third Piano Concerto (1921) was written in Brittany, although Prokofiev had already sketched it in 1917, before he left Russia. However,

1. Israel Nestyev, *Prokofiev*, London, 1960, p. 73.

many of the ideas are of even earlier provenance: the E minor theme of the second movement dates from 1913, while the two themes that open the finale were taken from an unfinished quartet (*Quatuor blanc*). The main ideas of the first movement were also conceived before 1917. Prokofiev first played it in Chicago on his 1921 American tour. For many years and to Prokofiev's regret, the Third completely overshadowed its companions in the concert hall (and to some extent still does): it was the only one he was invited to record. The first movement opens with a haunting clarinet melody, which is immediately taken up by the strings which lead into a bustling toccata-like figure. The piano introduces itself with an important idea that generates a great deal of activity until the second subject, a well-spiced thoroughly Prokofievian idea, is introduced by oboe and pizzicato violins over an accompaniment of wind and strings. In the soloist's hands the tune is wittily transformed. The movement follows a course normal in sonata procedure and its invention is consistently arresting.

The slow movement is one of the composer's most delightful creations and its theme has an enchanting blend of simplicity and piquancy. In all there are five variations. The piano, having been silent during the theme itself, is allowed to redress the balance in its somewhat chromatic first variation. The second is brilliant and toccata-like, while the third makes effective use of cross-rhythms between the soloist in triplets and the duple rhythms of the orchestral part to produce an effect of ebullience and high spirits. The fourth is a reflective, poignant variation, the most magical of the five, while the last is more earthy and outgoing with a strong element of the dance. The exuberant finale opens with a burlesque theme on the bassoons and in the second, the piano, as Poulenc once put it, 'literally slaps the strings in the face'. There are two other ideas to look out for: a touching lyrical theme on the orchestra, which is dismissed by a dry, sarcastic idea full of character.

The Fourth Concerto, Op. 53 (1931), was commissioned by the one-armed pianist Paul Wittgenstein, for whom both Ravel and Strauss wrote pieces. Wittgenstein's oft-quoted response on receipt of the score was nothing if not straightforward, 'Thank you very much, but I do not understand a single note of it and I shall not play it'. (Just as well, one might say, after hearing the records he made of the Ravel Left-Hand Concerto!) Prokofiev had planned to rework the score for two hands but never did so, and the score remained unperformed until after his death and was not published until 1966. The same *toccata*-like patter that begins the concerto returns to open the short finale, which is not wholly convincing. Yet there are subtleties too; the relationship between the opening idea and the apparently wholly different idea of the third movement, *Moderato*, and the piano writing has much of Prokofiev's wit (Ex. 2).

Ex. 2

The slow movement is a thoughtful reverie in the pastoral style of *The Prodigal Son*, with some wonderfully inventive decorative writing. If neither this nor the Fifth Concerto, Op. 55 (1931–2) are the equal of the Third, there is still no lack of brilliance and sparkle. The Fifth began life as a work called 'Music for piano and orchestra', which he had planned as unpretentious yet effective. However, it changed course to become a more ambitious display piece, and as far as the piano writing is concerned has dazzling brilliance. The Russian Establishment never much cared for this piece and Nestyev sounds a censorious note, finding that the concerto 'once again revealed Prokofiev's proclivity for experiments in virtuoso writing. The piano virtuosity, which he had neglected since the Third Concerto now acquired meaningless, complicated forms'[1] All the same, though the work is full of stimulus and sparkle, it does lack the strong melodic profile and the feeling of the Third.

Although Prokofiev had perhaps the most original keyboard style of any twentieth-century composer after Ravel and Bartók, yet perhaps his greatest concertos are for stringed instruments. The First Violin Concerto (1917) inhabits a totally different world from the first two piano concertos. There is poetry, great tenderness and a fairy-tale quality that immediately draws the listener into its world. In its exotic luxuriance and sense of ecstasy it calls to

1. Israel Nestyev, *op. cit.*, p. 239.

mind another concerto written in 1917, the First of Szymanowski. There is the same heightened awareness of colour and glowing, luminous textures; oddly enough, Paul Kochański, who wrote the cadenzas for both the Szymanowski concertos, advised Prokofiev on bowing and other technical matters, and the original intention was that he should give the first performance. It is more formally conventional than the Szymanowski—indeed so much so that it in some respects it served as a model for Walton in his Viola Concerto of 1929, even down to the sarcasm of the quirky bassoon tune in the finale. The violin writing is every bit as original as the keyboard writing—varying from the biting sardonic *moto perpetuo* of the *vivacissimo* centrepiece with its phantasmagoric vision, to the extraordinary high-lying cantilena of the opening (Ex. 3).

Ex. 3

This first movement is a sonata design, as easily followed as it is masterly in layout; the return at the restatement to the theme quoted above is pure magic. Briefly, it is as if one is perceiving the world in a dreamlike state which, while it lasts, seems more real than reality, another quality it has in common with Szymanowski's glorious concerto. There is less of the tension between solo instrument and orchestra—he is not *primus inter pares* as Nestyev and others suggest, but more of a leader urging (or in the scherzo movement, daring) the orchestra to follow him.

If the First Violin Concerto sprang from a world close in sensibility, harmonic sophistication and childlike innocence to Ravel, the Second, in G minor, Op. 35 (1935) is more classical in feeling. The concerto was the last work Prokofiev composed before settling in the Soviet Union; it began life as a 'concert sonata' for violin and orchestra and was written for the French violinist Robert Soetens, who gave its first performance in Madrid. 'Where if not in polyphony can one find the path to the new?', Prokofiev once asked, and the concerto certainly has a greater contrapuntal density than its predecessor and a more severe profile. The Second Concerto is particularly strong in architecture though there are no formal innovations. Though its finale has a strong flavour of the dance (the work was composed at the same time as the ballet, *Romeo and Juliet*), there is nothing balletic about the first movement. Its gravity is immediately proclaimed by the soloist who is echoed by the orchestra—and then canonically (Ex. 4).

Ex. 4

In later years Prokofiev became troubled by the layout of a number of his earlier works, including the Fourth Symphony, the Fifth Piano Sonata, and the Cello Concerto in E minor, Op. 58, that he had conceived but not completed while he was living in the West in the early 1930s. Its first performance with the cellist Beryozovsky in 1938 was disastrous: the Moscow critics and Prokofiev's colleagues were hostile. These second thoughts were no doubt fuelled by the prevalent artistic climate and his depressed state following his illness in 1945. In the case of the symphony his afterthoughts are not wholly an improvement and it is possible to argue that the same holds true of the Cello Concerto. In 1947 he heard the young Rostropovich play the Cello Concerto and decided that it was unsatisfactory. At first he called the new work that arose from the ashes of the old, Concerto No. 2, changing it subsequently to Sinfonia concertante for cello and orchestra, Op. 125, but even so some element of uncertainty must have persisted in his mind, since he did not reject or disown the earlier concerto but described the new piece as 'a reworking' of the material of the first, made in collaboration with Mstislav Rostropovich. The first movement is unhurried and lyrical even though there are dramatic elements. The development of the two main ideas involves the soloist nearly all the time but the texture is never too thick, as it was in some of Prokofiev's earlier work, and the cello always comes through. The scherzo is greatly extended and gives the soloist much opportunity for virtuoso display, while Prokofiev expands on the Theme and Variations of the earlier concerto.

Much of the Sinfonia concertante is too close to the earlier work for it to be regarded as completely separate from the Cello Concerto No. 1; one must regret one change in the second movement, but the third movement undoubtedly has greater coherence in its revised and extended form. Inspired by his work with Rostropovich, Prokofiev was engaged on a Concertino for cello and orchestra, Op. 132, which he had nearly completed before his death and which was completed and orchestrated by Rostropovich and Kabalevsky.

Stravinsky

If Prokofiev was conditioned by balletic habits of mind, so to an even greater extent was **Igor Stravinsky** (1882–1971). His thinking is totally suffused by the dance and scarcely any musical idea that he conceived escaped Terpsichore's stamp. While both spent the 1920s in Paris, Prokofiev returned to face the bleak winter of Stalin's Russia, and Stravinsky stayed in the West until circumstances forced him to settle in America. Although he remained Russian at heart, as witness the emotion he exhibited on his visit to Russia in 1962, Stravinsky remains a universal phenomenon who was stimulated by his environment whether it was Paris or California. They are unmusical feet indeed that do not respond on hearing the Violin Concerto. One is tempted to say that were originality the sole criterion of greatness, Stravinsky would be the greatest composer of all. Vaughan Williams once said of Sibelius that he had the capacity to make a simple chord of C major entirely his own, and the same must be said of Stravinsky. With Prokofiev one need only hear a phrase to place the composer; with Stravinsky only a chord. Stravinsky's output of concerted music is relatively meagre but far from unimportant. There are a handful of 'concertato' pieces like the *Ebony Concerto* (1945), written for Woody Hermann, *Dumbarton Oaks* (1938) and the Concerto in D for strings (1946), all predominantly cosmopolitan in outlook. His solo concertos are relatively few: there is the exhilarating Concerto for piano and wind (1923–4), the Capriccio for piano and orchestra (1929) and the Violin Concerto (1931).

Like the better-known *Capriccio*, the Concerto for piano and wind (or 'Concert pour piano suivi d'orchestre d'harmonie' as he calls it on the score) finds him at the height of his neo-Classical (or more properly neo-Baroque) phase, but its sonorities are made particulary rich by the addition of double basses. The work comes from a period when he was fascinated by wind sonorities to which the Symphonies of wind instruments (1920) and the Octet (1923) bear witness. Its eclecticism is as obvious as its originality: the pomp and gravity of Handel are evoked in the opening *Largo*, while the first movement draws together elements of Bach, Scarlatti and jazz. Unusually for Stravinsky, this movement has a strong feeling of ternary form thanks to the fact that he repeats a whole section of the exposition. In the middle of the second movement the piano seems (as the Italian composer, Roman Vlad puts it)[1] 'suddenly hypnotized à la Erik Satie'. Stravinsky had recently heard *Parade* with admiration. Yet this work, like the *Capriccio*, is far more than the musings of a clever pasticheur; it has disturbing overtones for the stylized cardboard cut-outs of past techniques fade to reveal sudden moments of depth. The only flaw is the finale, which seems disproportionately lightweight. Koussevitzky had persuaded Stravinsky to give the first performance of the concerto himself, and this led to a brief period of a decade in which he made concert appearances in his own works. Something of the dry, incisive quality of his playing can be heard in the records he made of the *Capriccio* with Ansermet in 1930, only a year after its completion. In the *Chroniques de ma vie*, Stravinsky speaks of using *Capriccio* in the same sense as Praetorius, 'a synonym of the fantasia which is a free form made up of fugato instrumental passages'. He also speaks of Weber as a model, and in particular the celebrated *Konzertstück* in F minor. Yet there is much discipline here and an even more effective and individual deployment of the keyboard. The repeated notes we find in the mock serious opening of the *Andante rapsodico* movement of the *Capriccio* (and more particularly in its cadenza) is a device carried over from the cimbalom which sustains its tone by this means. But the piano has a more decorative than combative role, and though the *Capriccio* does not touch the depths at which the Concerto for piano and wind hints, it has the same keen, fertile intelligence.

The Violin Concerto came into being only two years later. Stravinsky had been approached by Willy Strecker, then the director of the publishing house of Schott, who wanted him to write a concerto for his young friend Samuel Dushkin. Up to this point Stravinsky's experience of writing for the violin as a solo instrument was limited to *The Soldier's Tale* and he felt ill-equipped to tackle a concerto, but fortunately he took to Dushkin both as a man and an artist when they were brought together. And just as he immersed himself in Czerny before tackling the Concerto for piano and wind, he studied all the major classical concertos before starting work on his own. Yet the work

1. Roman Vlad, *Stravinsky*, London, 1960, p. 85.

which emerged is more directly related to the *Capriccio*, though in vitality of invention and imagination it is superior. Dushkin, who not only gave the first performance of the concerto but made its première recording with the composer conducting, tells how one day when he was lunching with him in a restaurant, Stravinsky showed him the chord D (a tone above middle C), the E a ninth above and the A, an eleventh above that, and asked if it was playable. Dushkin at first said 'No', as he had never seen a chord with such a wide stretch, but on trying it later at home found it relatively easy to play. Each of the four movements begins with this chord. Original as always, Stravinsky replaces the single slow movement of the *Capriccio* with two Arias, the second of which recalls Bach. The outer movements bear Baroque titles: Toccata and Capriccio. In a sense, as Stravinsky himself put it, the Violin Concerto is as much an orchestral as a solo piece, the latter playing more of a concertante role. Similarly the dazzling and effervescent Concerto for two pianos (1931–5) written for himself and his son Soulima, is as much a sonata as concerto with the two instruments on an equal footing and with much of the thematic material shared between them. There is also the Movements (1958–9) for piano and orchestra, a product of his late interest in post-serial techniques, one of the most hermetic of all his works (to quote Eric Walter White).[1] It lasts only ten minutes in performance, but 'has the specific gravity of a tonal work of three times that duration'. Though he originally planned it as 'Concerto for piano and groups of instruments', it is not a concerto in the normal sense of the word, but rather the piano is a participant in various chamber groupings instead of the strong independent personality we find in the earlier concertos. If the concertos constitute a small part of Stravinsky's output, their quality is in inverse proportion to their number.

Among the others who left Russia after the Revolution was **Alexander Tcherepnin** (1899–1977). He grew up in the musical atmosphere of prewar St Petersburg where the family home was the meeting-place for many of the most illustrious names of the day, among them Glazunov, Stravinsky, Prokofiev and Liadov. After spending some time in Tiflis (1917–21), the family left Georgia to settle in Paris. In 1923 he composed his Second Piano Concerto, first performed on two pianos, the composer playing the solo part and Nadia Boulanger at the second piano. His youthful First Concerto, Op. 12, written in 1919–20 when he was still in Tiflis, had been primarily a virtuoso showpiece: the Second, Op. 26 (1923) has more ambitious concerns, a Prokofievian wit and the kind of simplicity for which *Les Six* also

---

1. Eric Walter White, *Stravinsky*, London 2nd edn 1979, p. 504.

strove. The invention is colourful and the work leaves no doubt as to the expertise and confidence of the young Tcherepnin's craftsmanship. Its feeling for structure shows that Tcherepnin's head was not turned by the iconoclasm of the immediate post-war period. When one hears the opening of the Second Piano Concerto it is the sense of momentum that is immediately striking. The motoric rhythms, but not the texture or the language, recall Prokofiev or Roussel. There are six concertos in all—the piano writing of the Fifth, Op. 96, (1963) is a good example of his effective use of an albeit limited range of keyboard devices.

Four years younger and many times better known to the wider public is **Aram Khachaturyan** (1903–1978), whose popular concertos for the piano and the violin hardly call for exegesis. It is tempting but perhaps too glib to dismiss them as kitsch. They are colourful pieces in the tradition of Russian orientalism and have no higher aim than to entertain, which they do effectively. The Piano Concerto (1936), and the rather more rewarding Violin Concerto (1940) are still heard, though not as frequently as in the 1940s and 1950s, while the less inventive Cello Concerto (1946) appears to have fallen from view. Another composer of great facility is **Dmitri Kabalevsky** (1904–1987) who has three piano concertos, two cello concertos and a violin concerto to his credit. The Cello Concerto No. 1 in G minor, Op. 49 (1949) is reckoned to be his finest. It is expertly crafted, and there is a vein of elegiac feeling in the fine slow movement as indeed there is in the opening of the No. 2 (1964). Like so much of Kabalevsky, it is compact in design and straightforward in idiom: its finale uses a theme to which Prokofiev had recourse in his Concertino for cello, Op. 132 (1953), in whose scoring Kabalevsky had a hand.

Shostakovich

While **Dmitri Shostakovich** (1906–1975) composed 15 symphonies and as many string quartets, his interest in the concerto has been less keen. He has written two concertos each for violin, cello and piano. The violin concertos were both inspired by and written for David Oistrakh (as were the two violin sonatas). Likewise, the cello concertos share a common dedicatee, Mstislav Rostropovich. All four come from the post-war years: the violin concertos in 1947–8 and 1968, those for cello in 1959 and 1967 respectively. As a youth Shostakovich was active as a pianist—one of his very first works, the *Three Fantastic Dances*, Op. 5, was for the piano, and he was a good enough player to be accepted as a competitor in the 1922 Warsaw Chopin Competition. His early scores like *The Age of Gold* (1929–30) and *The Bolt* (1930–1) reflect a taste for the grotesque and a mordant (sometimes crude) sense of humour that did not always find favour in the USSR. In the Concerto for piano, trumpet and strings (1933), the wit is more pointed, more sharply focused and more subtle. It was written the year after the completion of the opera *The Lady Macbeth of the Mtsensk District*. As Ivan Martynov[1] pointed out, 'the neo-classicism of the concerto is related to such contemporaries as Hindemith and Poulenc' (particularly the latter), though in feeling it is undeniably Slav. Under its light-hearted surface and its extravagant satirical gestures, there is a quiet but potent streak of melancholy in the slow movement. The first movement kicks off with a characterful flourish—it sums up the pert gamin-like character of the whole work. It is a sonata-form piece with bold, well-delineated ideas of strong personality; it has a well-poised sense of irony and the musical argument is firmly shaped. The sonority that Shostakovich secures from the piano is highly individual—for he eschews the full range of nineteenth-century pianistic effects in favour of cleanly drawn lines and transparent, often sparse textures. The second movement opens with a slow, languid waltz-like idea which at first seems uncertain whether or not to take its troubles seriously. But the gentle self-mockery hides a genuine vein of poetic feeling. Its structure is simple: A-B-A. The *Moderato* that constitutes the third movement comprises only 29 bars and serves as a link into the high-spirited knock-about finale, delightful and inventive with a touch of audacity that remains as fresh now as it was in the 1930s.

More than two decades separate the Second Piano Concerto from its predecessor. It was composed in 1956–7 for his son Maxim, who gave the work its first performance on 10 May 1957, the occasion of his nineteenth birthday. The concerto can be seen as a relaxation from more serious preoccupations such as the Eleventh Symphony and the Sixth Quartet, and like the earlier Concerto for piano, trumpet and strings, its mood is light-hearted and gay, though its humour is gentler and more subtle than that of its predecessor. Its ideas are firmly drawn and plentiful. The first movement opens with a perky bassoon idea which paves the way for the soloist's entry with a delightful tongue-in-cheek theme. The movement has a tremendous sense of momentum and its progress unfolds organically and with a natural sense of flow. As is often the case, Shostakovich exploits the extremities of the keyboard and indulges his penchant for doubling a melodic line in both hands two or three octaves apart, while the writing for the wind is brilliant and characteristic. The slow movement is a dreamy *Andante* as direct in appeal as it is poetic in utterance. Like the companion movements, it is wholly straightforward in structure and uncomplex in language. At times it even comes close to toying with kitsch but successfully maintains it at arms's

---

1. Ivan Martynov, *Dmitri Shostakovich*, New York, 1947, p. 51.

length. The finale returns to the mood of the opening and its youthful exuberance and effervescent high spirits are infectious. Although its dedicatee was on the threshold of manhood, this concerto is obviously addressed to youth, but there are no patronizing overtones.

The somewhat earlier Violin Concerto No. 1 is a different matter. Both violin concertos eschew trumpets or trombones, though the first is scored for larger forces, triple woodwind instead of double, a full complement of strings as opposed to the reduced forces of the second, tuba, xylophone, celeste and two harps. The Nocturne is the most reflective and searching of the four movements. It does not strike the epic stance of the great symphonic *adagios* that open the Sixth, Eighth and Tenth symphonies: its mood is dreamy and inward looking. The movement has moments of rapt tranquillity and a poetic intensity that Shostakovich has rarely surpassed. Although the music gives the appearance of a rhapsodic, improvisatory flow, its development is thoroughly cogent and beautifully controlled. It arises naturally from the opening figure on cellos and double basses, and the soloist's entry that follows immediately (Ex. 5).

A secondary idea (fig. 7), in which the soloist gradually soars over a static harmonic support, leads (fig. 11) into one of the most poignant passages Shostakovich has ever penned. A climax returns us to the second idea (19) and a coda of great fantasy. The scherzo that follows suggests the Tenth Symphony (1953) in two respects: first, its scherzo releases a torrent of pent-up energy that has lain dormant during the long *adagio*, and seems to command unlimited reserves of power; secondly, the opening specifically alludes to the third movement of the symphony. Its contrapuntal ingenuity is as self-evident as its vitality, and the woodwind writing has an astringency that makes a splendid foil to the preceding movement. Then, Shostakovich turns to the *passacaglia*—a form to which he had recourse in some of his most anguished and painful utterances such as the Piano Trio (1944) and the Eighth Symphony. The cellos and double basses together with the horns adumbrate the theme of the *passacaglia*: the woodwind invest it (fig. 70) with a chorale-like character, the soloist making his entry on the next statement of the theme (fig. 71). Succeeding statements of the *passacaglia* theme work the music up to a climax at the height of which there is a long cadenza. The work ends with a lively finale, full of power and energy during which the theme of the *passacaglia* is quoted. The Second Violin Concerto, in C sharp minor, Op. 129, is the Cinderella of the set, and an even greater rarity in the concert hall than the Second Cello Concerto. It is a severe work and its first movement is among the most powerfully integrated and concentrated of all Shostakovich's sonata structures. There is no spare flesh here, and the colours are all dark.

Ex. 5

The First Cello Concerto, Op. 109, is lightly scored, but unlike its companion or the First Violin concerto, its first movement is taut, lithe and concentrated. Its driving force resides in the opening four-note cell (G, E, B, B flat) announced by the soloist to pert woodwind comment. This idea and its associated material dominates the scene for some time until the second group in which the variant of the DSCH motive is heard (C, B, E flat, D). A solo horn assumes a vital (and virtuosic) role in the proceedings and the momentum is unremittingly maintained. The second movement, *Moderato*, is predominantly lyrical in mood and opens with a string melody succeeded by an idea featuring the solo horn. The third is a cadenza which begins by ruminating on some of the material of the slow movement before gradually gaining speed: it makes fleeting reference to the main theme, before launching us into the last movement. The main theme of the finale alternates with contrasting material in the manner of a rondo, more accurately perhaps a sonata-rondo, since the first contrasting figure of importance returns. Towards the end, the opening idea of the whole work returns and its various elements are ingeniously combined with the first subject of the finale. The First Cello Concerto was composed in the wake of the Eleventh Symphony while its successor comes in between the Thirteenth and Fourteenth symphonies, works which did not find immediate favour with the Soviet Establishment. By this time the 'Thaw' which had followed Stalin's death had given way to a harsher climate. The much underrated Second Concerto (1966) has not established itself in the repertoire to anywhere near the same extent as its predecessor, perhaps because it offers fewer overt opportunities for display. The concerto calls for double wind with an additional double bassoon, two horns, a large percussion section, two harps and strings, and in its economy and resource is a model of its kind. The cello line always comes through the orchestra. It is a work of grave beauty, inward in feeling and spare in its textures. The opening *Largo* could hardly be in stronger contrast to the corresponding movement of No. 1. It is pensive and withdrawn in feeling; and on first encounter its ideas seem fugitive and shadowy, though the sonorities have a characteristic asperity. The second and third movements are played without a break, the latter opening with an arresting fanfare for horns. There are moments of great tenderness and melancholy in this movement that resonate in the mind.

Tikhon Khrennikov (*b*. 1913) has earned opprobium for his part in the 1948 Zhdanov Congress, when he denounced Shostakovich, Prokofiev, Mias-kovsky and others, and is an easy target for vilification. However, even had he played an heroic role, it would be impossible to accord him much of a place in the pantheon. His First Piano Concerto is a student work; he has composed a Cello Concerto (1964) and a Second Piano Concerto in C major (1974) of less than slender merit. **Moshei Vainberg** (*b*. 1919) is an altogether different matter. He has composed ten symphonies, few of which have reached the concert hall outside the USSR, His Violin Concerto (1962) is a finely crafted and thoughtful work, rather indebted to Shostakovich, but none the worse for that! **Rhodion Shchedrin** (*b*. 1932) is nothing if not a master of effect and a cunningly expert orchestrator. His First Piano Concerto is an early work, written when he was 21 and to be frank, neither it nor the Second Piano Concerto composed in the mid-1960s is as imaginative or atmospheric as his *Anna Karenina*. Writing in *Sovetskaya Muzyka*, Nestyev[1] said:

Listening to the Second Concerto of Shchedrin, it came to my mind that,

1. Quoted in Schwarz, *op. cit.*; p. 478.

lately, our composers are trying to resurrect the style that during the 1920s was called *Sachliche Musik* in Germany [objective, matter-of-fact music]—a style represented in those days in the scores of Křenek, Hindemith and Kurt Weill, and others. It is a style of 'workman-like' intellectualism, harsh linear combinations, swift *perpetuum mobile* with elements of atonal anarchy, cleverly planned dynamic construction, behind which one does not always feel a diversity of emotion and wealth of soul.

This response strikes a sympathetic resonance, for this concerto seems to me thoroughly manufactured and calculated as does the Cello Concerto in one movement (1963) of **Boris Tishchenko** (*b*. 1939), an ingenious but (to my mind) arid piece, scored for wind, brass, percussion and organ. Both are evidence of a less inhibited artistic climate and testify to the death of 'socialist realism'. So too does the Violin Concerto (1968) of **Kara Karayev** (*b*. 1918), which builds on a tone-row announced at the outset, though as in the Alban Berg Concerto, the row (G B E D sharp F sharp A sharp A C D F G sharp C sharp) is so organized as to make the most of tonal implications. **Alfred Schnittke** (*b*. 1934) has become a cult figure in the West and has attracted impressive advocacy. After studies with Rakov he composed a number of works of a more traditional character before interesting himself in newer Western techniques, including serialism and 'sonorism', in which dynamic gradations assume a motivic significance. There is a Piano Concerto (1960), a Concerto for piano and strings (1978), a Concerto for oboe, harp and strings (1977); there are two *concerti grossi* for various instrumental groupings. But the most important are the four violin concertos, the most first dating from 1957 when he was still studying with Rakov, and the most recent in 1982. The Second (1966) is a one-movement piece, which makes use of note-rows and controlled aleotoric elements. There is something of the aural sophistication of Lutosławski; the work is full of musical incident and there is an underlying feeling of purpose that distinguishes him from much avant-garde music. One senses that this music has meaning even if its language and syntactical rules are not immediately grasped.

CHAPTER 8

The Concerto in France

Lionel Salter

The main focus of musical attention in France during the late eighteenth and early nineteenth centuries was the lyric theatre: writing concertos was an activity almost entirely confined to virtuoso violinists, for whom the creation of vehicles in which to display their own talents was a necessary part of their self-promotion. The traditions of Leclair and his pupil the Chevalier Saint-Georges, of Gaviniès (the first professor of violin at the Paris Conservatoire) and Vachon, were continued in the new century not so much by Baillot and Rode, whose style was of greater depth and dignity, as by the Belgians de Bériot, Léonard and Vieuxtemps, who built upon the spectacular technical advances with which Paganini was then dazzling audiences throughout Europe.

Paganini commissioned **Hector Berlioz** (1803–1869) to write a viola concerto for him, but decided against playing it after seeing the first part, as the solo instrument was not used continuously enough to satisfy him. What finally emerged in 1830 was *Harold in Italy*, described as a 'symphony with solo viola'. It aimed to portray the impressions, amid various Italian scenes, of Byron's romantic hero (a thin disguise for the composer himself), represented by an *idée fixe*, though in fact some of its material had been taken from Berlioz's rejected *Rob Roy* overture. That same year also saw the publication of two piano concertos—a genre for which almost no tradition existed in France—by **Charles Henri Valentin Alkan** (1813–1888), still only 21 but already an established virtuoso (he had been so precocious that he had been admitted to the Conservatoire at the age of six). Each of these works (both labelled Op. 10) is called a *Concerto da camera*, sets formidable challenges to the soloist, and is most unusual in form. The three sections of each are linked but in No. 1 (in A minor) the themes of the initial *ritornello* are never heard again, and the solo piano's themes are not developed before a short *Adagio* intervenes, in turn leading to a loose rondo in which the polka-like second half of the refrain is predominant: No. 2 (in C sharp minor) has a central 6/8 *Adagio*, its simple lulling theme subjected to fantastic elaborations of hair-raising virtuosity, separating the main *Allegro moderato*'s exposition and recapitulation (where the *Adagio* theme is ingeniously worked into the 4/4 texture). Alkan's predilection for bravura octave passage-work almost pales into insignificance, however, when set beside the demands of his immense Concerto for solo piano of 1887 (made up of three of his *Études dans tous les tons mineurs*), a work of prodigious difficulty, even more transcendental than the music of his contemporary and friend Liszt, and containing an element of the diabolic which was later to earn him the sobriquet of 'the Berlioz of the piano'.

A precocious virtuoso in another field, **Jacques Offenbach** (1819–1880) (born in Cologne but brought to Paris in his youth), composed a one-movement *Concerto militaire* for cello in 1848: it owes its title to its trumpet fanfares and a side-drum that introduces and interrupts the jaunty main subject—which might well have come from one of the operettas for which he was shortly to become famous—and reappears at the end of the work. The concerto makes extensive use of the extreme high register of the cello (often sounding more like violin writing), descending to its bottom octave only in the second of two lyrical interludes.

Saint-Saëns

The first major figure in the story of the concerto in France is **Camille Saint-Saëns** (1835–1921), who over a period of almost half a century wrote, besides some dozen shorter display pieces (several with a Spanish flavour) such as the *Introduction et Rondo capriccioso* and *Havanaise* for violin and the *Wedding-cake Caprice* for piano, ten full-scale works, of which four remain in the repertory—Nos 2 and 4 for piano, No. 1 for cello and No. 3 for violin. Possessed of great fluency, elegance, consummate craftsmanship and an ear for effective orchestration, he turned his back on Romantic emotionalism and preserved a sober classical clarity which has often been misconstrued as dryness. He himself explained his credo:

> For me, art is *form*. Expression and passion seduce the amateur above all: for the artist it is different. An artist who is not fully satisfied by elegant lines, harmonious colours and beautiful harmonic progressions has no understanding of art.

His first essay, at the age of 22, was the Violin Concerto published as No. 2, notable only for its linking of the slow movement (in which octaves abound for the soloist) with the finale: his First Piano Concerto opens, somewhat surprisingly, with romantic horn-calls (which return at the end), contains some Chopinesque filigree in its meditative slow movement, and has a jubilant finale which for some time attempts to keep a chorale-like subject at bay. The Violin Concerto No. 1 in A major, a single-movement work of greater individuality and melodic charm written (like all Saint-Saëns's later violin works) for the Spanish virtuoso Sarasate, has a cantabile slow episode instead of a development section, and makes the soloist dominate from the very first bars' vigorous quadruple-stop chords: the orchestra is allowed scarcely any say, and in only two dozen bars does the violin not play.

The Second Piano Concerto (in G minor) of 1868, though written at speed in 17 days (which may help to explain why Saint-Saëns took the first subject from a misconceived exercise by his pupil Fauré), and despite its conspicuous diversity of style, won Liszt's admiration, and has always been popular with the public. It begins with an improvisatory piano prelude rather in the style of a Bach fantasia, proceeds through Fauré's nocturne-like theme, a Schumannesque second subject (which never reappears) and some sparkling bravura to a climactic restatement of the first subject before returning, via a cadenza, to an almost identical reprise of the introduction. A scherzo in Mendelssohn's most airy vein, set in motion by a soft timpani rhythm, is delectable, though its gossamer wit gives way to more rollicking humour in the middle. The busy *tarantella* with which the work ends, though something of an anti-climax, does not really justify the jibe that the concerto 'begins with Bach and ends with Offenbach'.

The Third Piano Concerto of the following year is a disappointment, with too much empty passage-work. The influence of Liszt is discernible in the rippling piano arpeggios at the beginning (which were intended 'to reproduce the murmur of Alpine waterfalls') as well as in the first cadenza, in the audacious harmonies heralding the tenderly chromatic second movement (where the strings are muted), and in the linking of this with the finale. Two points of incidental interest are the allocation of a subject in the slow movement to the pianist's left hand alone, and the surprising appearance in the first movement (whose initial theme resembles that of Schubert's 'Great' C major Symphony) of a Falla-like Iberian cadence.

Perhaps the most popular of all Saint-Saëns's concertos is that in A minor for cello (1873), a work not only of verve and urbanity but often of great intensity. As in most of his concertos, the soloist enters immediately, in this case with a circling-and-swooping theme (Ex. 1a) that provides the source for much that follows. The integrated structure telescopes three movements: the first contains a sonata-form exposition with a short development; the key changes to B flat for a curiously 'olde-worlde' intermezzo (like a minuet) on muted strings, against which the cello adds a high-register counter-

Ex. 1a

melody, with a cadenza *en route*; and only then does the delayed recapitulation appear, much modified and with fully treated fresh material of a serious nature, though the concerto ends gaily in the major. The C minor Piano Concerto (No. 4) of two years later is another three-in-one work, this time adopting Liszt's procedure of thematic transformation. The first movement expounds an initial binary theme (Ex. 1b) on strings, each half of which is echoed by the piano, and this is immediately followed by two more elaborate variations, after which the key drops to A flat major for the appearance of an Elysian chorale. This, however, is succeeded by an entirely

Ex. 1b

new theme that is richly, even passionately, developed at length before the arrival of the scherzo, which first presents an impudent version of the concerto's initial subject and then switches to 6/8 for a playful tune in E flat. Later, the first movement's last theme becomes the subject of a short fugue: a cadenza leads in the finale, which is based on the chorale heard earlier but now transformed in bucolic triple-time guise.

Six years were to elapse before Saint-Saëns composed his Third Violin Concerto in B minor, a well-loved but less adventurous work in orthodox three-movement form. The *Allegro*'s emphatic opening theme (Ex. 1c) again includes the semitonal appoggiaturas which had already featured in the First Cello Concerto and the Fourth Piano Concerto; the *Andantino (quasi Allegretto)* is a lighter-weight barcarolle in the remote key of B flat; and the finale, after a declamatory accompanied cadenza, launches an impassioned gypsy theme (clearly with Sarasate in mind) but also includes a *Lohengrin*-like chorale which eventually reappears triumphantly on the brass before a brilliantly affirmative coda. Fondness for the interval of the minor second becomes almost obsessional in what may have been intended as the first movement of a further violin concerto, the Op. 62 *Morceau de concert* (Ex. 1d), a well-written piece with Mendelssohnian overtones that does not deserve its present neglect.

Ex. 1c

Ex. 1d

Two late concertos remain to be mentioned. No. 5 for piano was written in 1896 in Luxor: exotic Egyptian colour is thickly laid on in the central movement, which quotes a Nile boatman's song and includes an imitation of the rasping of cicadas, and the finale represents 'the joy of a sea voyage', with a suggestion of a ship's propellers (though the joy is presumably marred by having to weather a squall on the way); but in general the work is shallow in thought, facile virtuosity failing to conceal thematic weakness. Copycat commentators have been unfairly dismissive of Saint-Saëns's last (1902) concerto, No. 2 in D minor for cello, ever since one critic branded it as 'de la mauvaise musique bien écrite': in fact the *Andante* (in the unexpected key of E flat) into which the first movement modulates is tenderly poetic. The energetic final *moto perpetuo* (with much cross-string chordal scrubbing for the soloist) brings back from the opening *Allegro moderato* both the vigorously rhythmic first subject and the ceremonial second.

Two of Saint-Saëns's friends were led to follow his example in the 1870s. The Vicomte **Alexis de Castillon** (1838–1873), a gifted Franck pupil with whom he had just founded the *Société Nationale de Musique* (for the encouragement of symphonic music) was unfortunate with his piano concerto: its often improvisatory character—there is a long rhapsodic piano solo at the very start and another in the elegiac *Quasi rimembranza* slow movement—its Schumannesque idiom (suspect just after the outbreak of the Franco-Prussian war) and the length of its stormy finale caused it to be violently hissed at its first performance. On the other hand, **Edouard Lalo**, a less original but more experienced composer, enjoyed instant success with a Violin Concerto in F and with his *Symphonie espagnole*, both owing much to Sarasate's advocacy. The former has dropped out of the repertoire, but the melodiousness, brilliance and subtle scoring of the latter (whose first theme anticipates that of the finale of Saint-Saëns's B minor Violin Concerto) have endeared it to succeeding generations of players. (His own Spanish ancestry made this more convincing than two other nationally flavoured works—a *Fantaisie norvégienne* and a *Concerto russe*.) Perhaps the most characteristically Iberian movements are the second (a scherzo beginning with string pizzicatos) and the *Intermezzo* (a later addition to the work), which features a $3 + 2$ rhythm; but by far the most popular is the finale, a sparkling rondo whose refrain (with a delightful off-beat kick) first appears over an *ostinato*-figure introduction. Lalo followed this up first with a Cello Concerto, notable chiefly for its rhetorical first movement and the combination of slow movement and scherzo in its *Intermezzo*, and then, at the end of the following decade, an overblown and repetitive Piano Concerto whose epic gesturing only highlights the poverty of the material.

This last work was dedicated to Louis Diémer, to whom, four years earlier, **César Franck** (1822–1890) had dedicated his masterly *Variations symphoniques* after Diémer had played the piano part in his symphonic poem *Les Djinns*. The appeal of the *Variations symphoniques* lies in its combination of an ingenious and novel design with a sensuous Romanticism. Taking its cue from the slow movement of Beethoven's Fourth Piano Concerto, it begins with an alternation of brusque orchestral challenge (in the rhythm of 2a) and piano pleading (2b). The piano states a new theme (2c) which has hitherto only been hinted at, and on this six organically connected variations follow, the fourth incorporating the rhythm of 2a, the much slower sixth dreamily in the major, with a magically poetic change to the minor; a lengthy final section largely based on a diatonic major version of 2b brings the work to an end in an atmosphere of radiant happiness.

Ex. 2a

Ex. 2b

Ex. 2c

The last quarter and the turn of the century saw concertos for piano and cello and a piano *Fantaisie*—all rather prosaic, with material that outstays its interest—by **Charles Widor** (1844–1937) (who was to succeed Franck as organ professor at the Paris Conservatoire), a thematically feeble, sloppily constructed piano concerto full of fustian gestures that **Jules Massenet** had sketched as a student and misguidedly exhumed 40 years later, and compositions by two Franck pupils—**Vincent d'Indy** (1842–1912) (his chief disciple) and Gabriel Pierné—and by Claude Debussy, though only one of these was actually called a concerto. The title of d'Indy's work, *Symphonie sur un chant montagnard français*, makes it clear that this is not a true concerto: it could be better described as a symphonic poem based on a folktune (Ex. 3) from d'Indy's native region of the Cévennes, with a technically ambitious but intrinsically merely decorative piano obbligato. The Franckian influence

Ex. 3

is obvious in its chromatic rising sequences and fondness for ostinato figures, as well as in its cyclic form, elements of the basic folktune constantly reappearing in all three movements; but at many points—such as the great climax of the first movement or the viola solo under shimmering trills at the end of the second—a sensitive nature-poet can be discerned behind such academic contrivances. The Piano Concerto by **Gabriel Pierné** (1863–1937), written in the following year (1887), is one that for its vitality and inventiveness should not be allowed to drop out of sight. Its finale owes much to Saint-Saëns: even more does its scherzo to that of his senior's Second Concerto—this has a similar elfin buoyancy and witty orchestral touches (here delicate trumpet fanfares); but most remarkable is the broad sweep of a romantic melody, expounded in the first movement and modified in the last, which sounds astonishingly like an anticipation of Rachmaninov. Pierné's erstwhile fellow-student **Claude Debussy** (1862–1918), who had only recently returned from winning the Prix de Rome, produced a three movement *Fantaisie* (treating the piano much as d'Indy had done) which he withdrew from performance at the last moment as being unrepresentative of the style he wished to pursue. Published posthumously and not performed until 1919, it nevertheless reveals fluency, voluptuous orchestration, and in the *Lento* (for which the key subtly turns to F sharp from the first movement's G) a feeling of sensuous beauty. There is occasional use of the whole-tone scale, and though generally more diatonic than Debussy's mature compositions it already contains many characteristic harmonies and turns of phrase.

Also noteworthy in this period are a few shorter *concertante* works. **Gabriel Fauré**'s *Ballade* (dedicated to his teacher, Saint-Saëns) had originally been conceived as a piano solo, in which form Liszt had, puzzlingly, declared it 'too difficult'; a light orchestral accompaniment was added in 1881, since when its graceful lyricism and limpid texture have won the appreciation of discerning music-lovers. The prevailing mood is one of elegant calm, with echoes in the last section, it has been claimed, of the 'forest murmurs' of *Siegfried*. Equally aristocratic and disdainful of mere display, but of far greater emotional intensity, and revealing the influence of Wagner (particularly in its sombre introduction) as well as of his teacher Franck, is **Ernest Chausson**'s haunting *Poème* (1896) for violin and orchestra, which is imbued throughout with a sense of deep melancholy. Pierné wrote three one-movement works for piano and orchestra before enriching the harp repertoire in 1901 with a *Concertstück*: the surprising employment of a German title may have been intended as a warning that this was no shallow salon piece but a serious symphonic work. As always with Pierné, the taste is impeccable and the structure well integrated (themes being effectively combined in the final section); and in the central *Andante* he again shows his ability to write long-breathed romantic melodies. In striking contrast to Fauré's *Ballade*, already mentioned, is the much less well-known *Fantaisie* he composed 38 years later in 1919. Though it does not succumb to the new idioms of Debussy and Ravel, it seems clear, alike from the astringency of its material, its muscular texture, its sometimes elusive tonality (as at the start of the agitated central section, with its obsessive rhythmic figure) and above all its freely elliptical harmony, that a new century had arrived.

The Twentieth Century

The first quarter of the twentieth century was singularly devoid of new concertos by French composers—a longer gap than is explicable merely by the incidence of the First World War; but as if in compensation, the period from the mid-1920s to the outbreak of the Second World War was one of unprecedented abundance in this field: some 30 works appeared. The language of music, however, had changed along with the changing world. The Classicism of Saint-Saëns, the structured Romanticism of Franck (who had noted down the complete intended tonal scheme of his Symphony before writing a note of it), the once all-pervasive influence of Wagner, the extended harmonic freedom and impressionist techniques of Debussy, had been all but superseded by a deliberately anti-emotional wave of concise, clean-cut, cynically 'amusing' brittle writing—often, indeed, approaching triviality. Major influences were those of the music-hall, early jazz and Stravinskian neo-classicism, and the style was particularly associated with the composers whom Henri Collet dubbed 'Les Six', though in reality this group had only a brief existence and very little cohesion; its members, though friends, differed widely both in their personalities and in their evolution (itself often far from consistent).

Arthur Honegger (1892–1955) (of Swiss parentage but born in France), though out of sympathy with the music of Les Six's father-figure Erik Satie, seemed to exemplify the new frivolous and heartless style in his mechanically busy Piano Concertino of 1924: of its three linked movements the first is based on a short-winded syncopated subject, the *Larghetto* includes atmospheric glissandos for strings, clarinet and trombone, and the

---

angular finale proceeds over a steady bass beat as from an early jazz-band. There is considerably more thematic substance and serious intent in his Cello Concerto of five years later (again in one continuous movement). Its main ingredients are a splendidly expressive cantilena for the soloist which winds its way slowly down through three octaves to his bottom C, and the blues-y Gershwinesque theme to which it passes; a central *Largo* heavy with menace leads to a vehement final section (whose theme is first cousin to a figure in the Piano Concertino's opening movement—itself deriving from the finale of Honegger's Clarinet Sonatina) which lovingly recalls the two initial subjects before ending vigorously.

Honegger's junior by only a month, **Germaine Tailleferre** (1892–1983), the only woman member of Les Six, seems to have had particular problems in deciding on a style (and was later to drift into serialism). She too wrote a Piano Concerto in 1924—a bright-eyed neo-Classical work in D major: its first movement insouciantly adopts a figure from Bach's D minor keyboard concerto, the *Adagio* is even more Bachian, and only in the busy finale is the diatonic idiom stretched. But her earlier *Ballade* for piano and orchestra is very different, owing its sophisticated harmonic language and florid piano writing to the example of Ravel (with whom she had studied): the work is largely in 5/4 time—even the less elaborate later part marked *Mouvement de valse*. Of her 1927 concerto for harp, the tonally indecisive first movement and the plaintive *Lento*, with its impressionist washes of orchestral colour, have nothing much to say but say it with *chic*: for the final rondo (which includes a fugato) the style completely changes to a happy quasi-rural diatonicism.

Taking a lead from the Concerto for piano and wind instruments by Stravinsky, that idol of the Parisian scene (a work which Koussevitsky had presented only two years previously), the Cello Concerto (1925) of **Jacques Ibert** (1890–1962) is scored for wind only—woodwinds in pairs, plus a single horn and trumpet—the basic distinction in timbre allowing the cello to come through without the difficulties usually encountered when accompanying it by a normally-constituted orchestra. If the thematic material is not intrinsically very striking, it is nevertheless an engaging work (particularly the charming polytonal initial *Pastorale* and the joyous concluding *Gigue*), inventive in texture, highly polished in craftsmanship and displaying a relaxed contrapuntal ease: its rarity of performance may be attributed to its brevity, which causes problems in concert programming. Ibert's most popular concerto, flawed only by a somewhat disproportionately long tarantella-like finale, is that for flute, composed nine years later. Again, the scoring is delightfully limpid, though the texture never sounds thin, and there is a constant flow of attractive and witty invention:

the graceful *Andante* is the very epitome of Gallic lyricism at its most coolly elegant. Ibert was also among the first composers (along with the much older Glazunov and the much younger Lars-Erik Larsson) to write a concerto—or at least a *Concertino da camera*—for saxophone (though Debussy had, with the greatest reluctance, sketched a Spanish-coloured *Rapsodie* for it which, after procrastinating for nine years, he had abandoned in 1911 and which had been completed by Roger-Ducasse). Unlike Debussy, who did not understand, nor want to understand, the instrument, Ibert exploits its potential to the full, and without recourse to the language of jazz (albeit the first movement does contain a broad Gershwin-type theme). The flavour is unmistakably French, with an alert and cheerful opening movement and a short languorous *Larghetto* that leads straight into a mercurial finale whose main subject is formed from the typical outlines of eighteenth-century violin *bariolage* technique.

Poulenc

The most extrovert of Les Six, and through his appearances as a performer more in the public eye than the others, was **Francis Poulenc** (1899–1963), whose music initially epitomized the new spirit of *gaminerie*, but before long, after he had experienced a spiritual crisis and returned to his religion, showed a deeper, more sweetly lyrical (but sometimes also a harsher) expression. An accomplished and exuberant pianist himself, all his five concertos are for keyboard instruments, though his first was not for the piano (at which he habitually composed) but for the harpsichord, which Wanda Landowska was then reviving after well over a century of desuetude. At the private first performance of Falla's *Master Peter's puppet-show* in 1923 she invited him to write a work for her, but not until five years later did he complete his *Concert champêtre* (by which time Falla had composed the first harpsichord concerto of modern times, prudently limiting the accompaniment to five instruments). The 'pastoral' part of Poulenc's title referred to Landowska's home in the country, though he himself declared that, as a dyed-in-the-wool townsman, bugles at a suburban barracks (suggested in the finale) 'heard from the neighbouring woods, are as poetical as hunting-horns in a vast forest were for Weber'. The concerto presents considerable problems in performance, not only of balance between soloist and the much too large orchestra (for Poulenc had had no experience of the harpsichord's limited sonority), but in the kaleidoscopic character of the first movement, whose capricious diversity of ideas, moods and speeds is held together only tenuously by a brief last-minute recapitulation. The second movement is more firmly organized, combining a placid *sicilienne* with something resembling an old French carol. The finale begins, like the main *Allegro molto* of the first movement, in breezy neo-Classical vein, with echoes of Scarlatti and Handel; a brisk march (hinting at that in Tchaikovsky's Sixth Symphony) intervenes before themes from the first movement are taken up with enthusiasm; but the work ends in unexpected melancholy. Themes very similar to those of its first *Allegro molto* also appear in *Aubade*, a 'concerto choréographique' designed for Nijinska, in which the piano is very much to the fore, introducing almost each new section of the work: in particular it has a lengthy *molto animato* solo in the opening *Toccata*, depicting the goddess Diana's rebellion against the eternal chastity to which she is committed. Without a knowledge of the ballet's plot, however, *Aubade* (which is scored for 18 instruments and is largely neo-baroque in idiom) makes a less than convincing entity.

Poulenc described his D minor concerto for two pianos, first presented at the Venice ISCM Festival of 1932, as 'gay and direct', and its spirit is purely that of a *divertissement*. There is no attempt at orthodox concerto structure in the first movement, which suddenly goes from a boisterous opening and a pert second subject to a Prokofievian *Lento*, only to bubble up again and as unpredictably pass into a quiet imitation of the Balinese gamelans Poulenc had heard at the previous year's Colonial Exhibition. The *Larghetto* that follows pays homage to Mozart, though its long middle section reverts to the Parisian suburbs: the finale starts with a headlong helter-skelter, introduces a theme which is blood-brother to that of No. 6 of his *Improvisations* (written in the same year), and ends with a brief backward glance at Bali. The Organ Concerto, Poulenc's last before the war, is a more dramatic and powerful work altogether, which though coldly received at first, in 1938, has since firmly established itself. Scored for strings and timpani, it is in seven continuous sections (rather in the manner of a Buxtehude or Bach toccata) with subtle thematic transformations. Bach is indeed recalled in the work's imperious opening gesture (though with harsher dissonances than he could ever have written); this is accompanied by a persistent minor third on the timpani of which much more is to be heard later; but after a tense, vigorously rhythmic theme (appearing in three keys) which belies its *giocoso* marking and an extended *Andante* in dotted rhythm for organ, there is constant alternation between outbursts of violence and passages of calm pathos. It is in a mood of quiet resignation that the concerto ends, with a measured tread foretelling the tragic procession to the scaffold of the *Dialogues des Carmélites* all but 20 years later.

Milhaud's Early Concertos

Far and away the most prolific French writer of concertos—as indeed of most other musical genres—was **Darius Milhaud** (1892–1974), who composed more than forty *concertante* works for a wide range of instruments. Even if less than half this number are performed other than rarely, this still represents an enormous contribution to the repertoire. In keeping with the iconoclastic tenets of Les Six, his early works showed a reaction against accepted norms by espousing the cause of brevity: by the mid-1920s he had composed six chamber symphonies and three *opéras-minutes*, and all his concertos written before the Second World War were likewise short. After four minor works for piano, including the entertaining suite *Le carnaval d'Aix* derived from his ballet *Salade*, his first declared concerto (1927)—for his own instrument, the violin—has a duration of only ten minutes, though in the orthodox three movements, with a solo cadenza in the last. Of ferocious technical difficulty, it is sunny in mood, the vigorously cheerful outer movements sandwiching a lulling monothematic *Romance* entirely free from the polytonality of the *Prélude* (in which Milhaud delights in sevenths and block chords moving in opposite directions). Polytonality even more uncompromising is found in the first two movements (particularly the linear *Lent*) of the Viola Concerto written a couple of years later for Hindemith to play; but after them the style changes abruptly: the relaxed third movement adopts a rustic idiom anticipating that of his *Concertino de printemps*, and the finale is diatonic and jazzily syncopated. Milhaud was anxious to avoid any jazz connotations in the Percussion Concerto composed at much the same time for a Belgian timpanist who had taken part in a performance of his music to the *Choëphores* (in which, as in his opera *Christophe Colomb*, solo percussion had been used as a background to actors' narration). Scored for strings, six wind instruments and a soloist surrounded by four kettledrums and 15 other percussion instruments, it consists of two short telescoped movements—the first, marked *rude et dramatique*, based on Stravinskian gestures, the second a quiet elegy in which the percussion adds exotically coloured rhythmic comments to the orchestral lament.

The period of intellectual experimentation through which Milhaud was then passing is exemplified in his most substantial and fully scored concerto so far, No. 1 for piano: its lack of popularity is due not so much to the rather ponderous, self-conscious jocularity of the outer movements as to the arid bitonal counterpoint of the central barcarolle. There was a bewildering change of persona for his next *concertante* work, the shortest of all these earlier compositions of his apart from the Percussion Concerto. The one-movement 1934 *Concertino de printemps* for violin and chamber orchestra does indeed convey a charming and airy vernal freshness. Set with an abundance of piquant syncopations and exhilarating cross-rhythms in a basically dance style resembling the *maxixe* (with which Milhaud had become acquainted during his time in Brazil), its appealing diatonic themes and its succinctness make it a most engaging miniature. He followed this up immediately with what is perhaps the most attractive of all his concertos, the light-hearted No. 1 for cello. A misleadingly stern unaccompanied cello recitative at the outset in fact prefigures the lilting subject of the monothematic first movement (aptly marked *nonchalant*), in whose last pages there is a momentary flicker of Brazilian dance rhythms. The melancholy slow movement, which contains some extremely original dark scoring, exploits the cello's lowest register (but also takes it up high in a passage of increased tension); but the finale is an uninhibited piece of carnival gaiety whose Cariocan flavour is underlined by one of its themes—identical in notes, though not in rhythm, with a theme in the *Concertino de printemps*— foreshadowing one in the *Dansa* of No. 5 of Villa-Lobos's *Bachianas Brasileiras*.

Roussel

However, the sheer number of works by Les Six, and the publicity they attracted, should not obscure the realization that other currents were also flowing in French music in this period. At the other extreme from the frivolity under whose banner that group had originally set out stood the figure of **Albert Roussel** (1869–1937), a d'Indy pupil of strong individuality, who has been called a 'connoisseur's composer'. Certainly, his 1927 Piano Concerto—more a *sinfonia concertante*, since the piano is but an element in the texture and the soloist is offered little in the way of precedence or any kind of brilliance—at first hearing makes a somewhat forbidding impression (not that Roussel sought popularity) by its severe and elusive substance and abrasive harmony: only in time does its power grow on the listener. As compared to its aggressive opening *Allegro* the finale is a little more unbending, but the core of the work is the heavily brooding *Adagio*, whose effect is deeply disturbing. Far more accessible is his 1936 Concertino for cello (his last orchestral composition), whose brevity, as with Ibert's Cello Concerto, has stood in the way of its more frequent performance. Cast in an unambiguous C major, with a number of easily recognizable themes, greater lyric expansion and refined craftsmanhip, it consists of an invigoratingly rhythmic first movement and a short, mainly calm *Adagio* of nobility which leads into a confident *Allegro molto* in which the soloist's cadenza attracts occasional contributions from other instruments. The work as a whole has a bracing quality that reflects the atmosphere of the Normandy coast where it was written.

Ravel

A local background is even more strongly to be sensed in what, without much question, are the finest and deservedly most successful of all twentieth-century French concertos—the two by **Maurice Ravel** (1875–1937). Himself a Basque by birth, he had originally set out to write a *Basque Rhapsody* for piano and orchestra for his own use on an American tour, but in fact its material was transferred to the G major Piano Concerto, work on which, however, was interrupted by a request for a piano concerto using the left hand alone from Paul Wittgenstein, a Leschetizky pupil who had lost an arm in the war. The technical challenge this presented inspired Ravel to one of his most imaginative, as well as most darkly dramatic, works, containing a nightmarish quality which links it to his *Scarbo*. Its unique opening, with a contra-bassoon snorting through a murk of bass strings, suggests the stirring of some primeval monster in the depths of the ocean: its theme awakens the response of a three-note falling figure from the horns and gradually rises to the surface, where it is met by an imperious assertion from the piano, which proceeds to develop it in a cadenza as a proud sarabande (Ex. 4), adding a

Ex. 4

challenging second idea. After a grandiose tutti complete with brass fanfares the piano muses on a plaintive new subject, but the initial theme returns almost at once on woodwind under decorative piano figurations, the speed increasing to an *Allegro*, when heavily accented beats and harsh descending block chords announce the start of a sardonic jazzy scherzo, of which Ravel himself said that 'only afterwards is one aware that it is actually based on the themes of the first section'. A pentatonic idea momentarily relaxes the tension, but the early horn motive makes a ghostly reappearance first on bassoon and then on muted trombone, and is developed to a massive climax in which the second sarabande theme is thundered out by the full (indeed very large) orchestra. A long cadenza, taking the piano to still further extremes of virtuosity, reviews previous material (concentrating at first on the hitherto neglected plaintive subject) and sweeps the work to a rowdy finish.

The mastery of orchestral colour displayed there is also very conspicuous in the untroubled, vivacious and brittle Piano Concerto in G, completed in that same year of 1931—Ravel's very last work but one. The first movement reveals its Basque origin by recalling a fife-and-tabor in the rhythm of a *bransle*: this dance tune (released by a whipcrack like a starting-pistol) is followed by four slower themes mingling Spanish characteristics with those of the blues. The last of these is the one chosen by the piano for its short cadenza. Ravel declared that the extended piano monologue in the style of a stately sarabande (though against a 3/8 accompaniment) which opens the second movement was inspired by Mozart's clarinet quintet, although its tranquil outline suggests the hieratic Grecian friezes which fascinated Satie. There is a gently dissonant episode with the piano weaving traceries above rising figures in the orchestra before the main theme returns on the cor anglais, the piano adding delicate filigree high above. The joyous and brilliant toccata-like finale is shot off the mark by four snapped-out chords: its hell-for-leather brief course is spurred on by screams from the E flat clarinet and piccolo, brays from the trombone and, every so often, bursts of fanfares from the brass. The original four chords finally stop the onrush.

In 1931 also, **Florent Schmitt** (1870–1958), who had been a fellow-pupil with Ravel of Fauré, completed, in the Pyrenees, his *Symphonie concertante* commissioned by Koussevitzky, which had been on the stocks for three years. It is described as 'for orchestra and piano', and the order is significant, since although the keyboard part (played by the composer at the Boston première) is of great complexity and difficulty, its role is that only of a first among equals. The work (which provoked an uproar at its first Paris performance) is characterized by richly sensuous post-impressionist harmony, often dense texture, and themes that all seem to be striving upwards to the light; and the central movement, which rises to a violent climax, at first appears to be echoing the insistent bell-tolling of Ravel's *Le gibet*.

The early 1930s saw the arrival of several piano concertos much less monumental than Schmitt's single venture into this terrain. One such was that in E minor by Ravel's contemporary **Reynaldo Hahn**, a Venezuelan by birth but brought as a child to Paris, where he studied with Massenet and became an intimate friend of Marcel Proust and a typical boulevard dandy. There is more than a whiff of the salons (where he was idolized) in its facile initial *Improvisation* (begun by the piano alone); but there is an angular originality in the brilliant *Danse* which succeeds it, and humour in the busy *Toccata* finale which grows out of a rather superficial *Rêverie*. Second only to Milhaud in the profusion of his *concertante* works (of which he has written about 20), but his junior by 20 years, is **Jean Françaix** (*b.* 1912), who has confessed to being a compulsive composer. He was only 20 years old and still a student of Nadia Boulanger when his pert eight-minute Piano Concertino proved an instant hit at a Lamoureux concert in Paris. Its material is in a line of descent from Chabrier and Poulenc, but is of the slightest, relying on deft neo-Classicism, side-slips of tonality and bright but delicate chatter to mask its use of essentially simple repetitive patterns; but there is wit in the 5/8 finale (whose erroneous time-signature of 5/4 in the published score has misled more than one distinguished commentator). Similar short-winded and patterned phrasing and unpretentious harmonic vocabulary but melodic grace, spontaneity and brilliance also characterize his Quadruple Concerto for woodwinds, the cello *Fantaisie* (later revised) and the 1936 Piano Concerto, whose naïvely charming *Andante* and sparkling *gamin* Scherzo earned it a huge success at the time (though the finale shows up Françaix's weaknesses). A striking contrast to his fashionable irreverence, produced in the same years as his cello *Fantaisie*, is the Piano Concerto No. 1 by **Henri Sauguet** (*b.* 1901), a composer content to write in an openly romantic style which, like his harmonic vocabulary and pianistic rhetoric, basically harks back half a century. His suave and sincere, if not very memorable, lyric gift is most in evidence in the first movement, which, however, suffers from too disparate a structure: there is greater subtlety in the nocturne-like central *Lento*.

The outbreak of war in 1939 and the occupation of France effectively silenced musical creativity there for some time, and almost the only composer to write a concerto was **Henry Barraud** (*b.* 1900), a patrician and somewhat reserved figure who had to wait six years for his 1940 piano concerto to be performed (in New York). His only further venture in this medium was a short concerto for flute and strings in 1963 whose textual strands are often highly elaborate and which adopts elements of Schoenbergian tone-row principles but ends on a plain C major chord: its progress was greatly impeded by the date of its première coinciding with that of President Kennedy's assassination.

Milhaud's Postwar Concertos

The standard-bearer for French concertos during the war was **Darius Milhaud**, who had fled to the USA in 1940 and taken up a teaching post in California: there he wrote half a dozen such works before returning to his homeland in 1947, thereafter commuting across the Atlantic and composing another dozen or so. The first-fruit of all these was his No. 2 for piano, a twelve-minute work written for himself to play in Chicago (though 'some of the passages were beyond me'): this is capable of being interpreted as autobiographical, the stressful, brittle first movement reflecting American city bustle, the languorous *Romance* recalling the sunshine of his native Provence, and the finale looking back to the lively rhythms of Brazil. In the same year of 1941 he also produced a vivacious concerto for two pianos and one for clarinet written for Benny Goodman (who, for some reason, never played it), manfully refraining from capitalizing on the latter's jazz eminence but unable to resist employing breezy South American rhythms in the second and fourth movements: perhaps most memorable, however, is the calmly lyrical third (slow) movement, which carries a suggestion of folk-song. The Second Cello Concerto composed four years later is one of Milhaud's cleanest and least complicated scores, at least in its insouciant first movement, lolloping along with an easy gait, and its tender, delicately instrumented second (which opens with the cello against four solo violins): only in the dance-like finale (with bagpipe-drone imitations), for much of which the cello has a busy *moto perpetuo* but which also contains a virtuoso cadenza, does the texture fill out. It might have been expected that the ending of the war would have stimulated the creation of a joyful work, but the Second Violin Concerto of 1946 is Milhaud at his most serious, apparently preferring to look back on the perils and tribulations of the preceding years. It begins with a dramatic recitative that leads to an *Animé* permeated with a sense of unease, after which the recitative returns; the sombre, dark-coloured slow movement is one of the composer's noblest and most profound; and not until the finale are spirits lifted, though even then, seemingly, only by a determined effort of will.

The melodic contours, syncopated rhythmic displacements and plethora of block sevenths of Milhaud's Concerto for marimba and vibraphone hark straight back to his *Concertino de printemps* of 13 years earlier, and the diatonic main subject of its finale—though not the more abrasive polytonality of the middle section—might well have come from the still earlier *Carnaval d'Aix* suite: only the somewhat long-drawn-out slow movement, with its self-conscious canons, lessens the work's sunny appeal. The contrast between the two solo instruments (the player frequently having to turn rapidly from one to the other) is heightened by Milhaud demanding five varieties of beaters—and in one place directing the marimba to be struck by the hands alone. (These nuances of timbre largely disappear in this concerto's alternative version as a piano *Suite concertante*.) The *Concertino de printemps* seems to have been in his thoughts around this time, for not long afterwards he wrote three more concertinos named for the other seasons of the year. That for summer is for violin accompanied by nine instruments (mostly wind): its lively central section and busy third part unfortunately do not live up to the promise of its charmingly lyrical 6/8 pastoral opening. Autumn is represented in changeable moods, from pensive to restlessly energetic, in some aggressively dissonant polytonality, and in the dark colour of the eight-instrument group (dominated by horns, violas and cello) that accompanies the two solo pianos. Winter, the last of this group to be written (during an Atlantic crossing in 1953), begins with an angular cheerfulness, its solo trombone hopping about briskly as if to keep out the cold, which is suggested in a slower middle section by close-muted tone and an occasional flutter-tongue shiver. That same year Milhaud composed a four-movement Harp Concerto for Zabaleta. Both the fresh-faced second movement (after the first's relaxed lilt) and the sprightly finale contain many of the composer's familiar fingerprints—a chirpy principal theme, cross-accents (often applied to ascending common chords in the bass) that stimulate the rhythmic impetus, and a fondness for sevenths and for canonic writing. Were it not for a less than convincing toying with tone-rows in the slow movement, the neglect of this work would be inexplicable. But several more postwar concertos by Milhaud are rarely, if ever, performed—his third and fourth for violin, the third, fourth and fifth for piano (1946, 1949 and 1955 respectively—the immense difficulty of the fourth, bristling as it does with bravura octave passages, possibly deterring prospective players) and that for harpsichord (1964). The 1957 Oboe Concerto is airy and transparent in texture, but overall it exudes a rather doggedly fabricated air. There is activity in plenty in the bustling outer movements, but their material (like that of the reflective slow movement also) is too lacking in character to sustain interest. Almost his last concerto, except for that for harpsichord and the *Music for Boston* (for violin and orchestra), was one for two pianos and percussion (1961) in which he was at pains to avoid any similarity to that by Bartók for the same combination. It is a cryptic but intriguing work, beginning with an elaborate luminous web of fragile tinklings. The percussion are all but silent in the grave slow movement, but come into their own in the finale, where alone some feeling of tonality, however free, is recognizable.

Martin

If Milhaud's concertos show a bewildering diversity of idiom, a remarkable consistency of style is apparent in the dozen or so *concertante* works written over a period of 35 years by **Frank Martin** (1890–1974), whom it may not be inappropriate to include in this survey. Though Swiss, he was of French descent, and his stylistic sympathies aligned him with the French rather than the Germans—despite having absorbed, from the early 1930s, some aspects of Schoenberg's techniques. These, however, he treated in a very personal way: he spoke of himself as employing a 'chromaticism in which many melodic elements from twelve-note series occur without ever adopting Schoenberg's dodecaphonic system in all its rigour or, above all, his principle of atonality'; and unlike many dodecaphonists, he laid much stress on rhythmic vitality (doubtless a legacy of his time as a teacher at the Dalcroze Institute). His works are characterized not merely by an overall elegance and lucidity, an imaginative ear for sonorities and a greater interest in texture than in form (though his forms are often interestingly unorthodox), but by certain individual fingerprints—a predilection for themes either of undulating close intervals or of a highly ornate nature, for sequential treatment, for note-groups that turn into *ostinatos*, and, surprisingly, for block triads. (All his concertos also end tonally, on an unequivocal common chord.)

Though he had already composed many fine works in various genres, his greatest popularity came with his 1945 *Petite symphonie concertante* for the novel and unique combination of harp, harpsichord and piano with double string orchestra. In many ways this could be regarded as a paradigm of his concertos—in its initial enigmatic atmosphere of quest, its use of sequence, the character of its themes, and their rhythmic transformation (as in the second of its two movements, where a dark-toned *Adagio* subject is transformed into a crisp march (Ex. 5)). Martin had, however, written several

Ex. 5

earlier *concertante* works: a piano concerto (originally designated *Concerto romantique*, beginning with a long flute solo over a persistent drum-beat, and its three movements connected by common material) which had been hailed as one of the outstanding successes of the 1936 ISCM festival in Barcelona, and four *Ballades*, respectively for saxophone, flute, piano and trombone. Those for flute (which sets out from a sinuous sequential pattern) and for trombone had been composed as test-pieces for Geneva international competitions: that for piano, more substantial and with a sizeable cadenza, is in the composer's words 'more epic than lyric' (which to some extent is true of the other *Ballades* also). The *Petite symphonie concertante* was followed up in 1949 by the masterly Concerto for seven wind instruments, which again exemplifies Martin's finesse in scoring: in the mordant but diverting first movement each solo instrument retains its individuality by there being only minimal sharing of material; the *Adagietto* (marked *misterioso ed elegante*) sets diverse melodic lines over a tick-tocking *ostinato* figure; and in the finale the soloists, treated more as a group (with occasional solo sorties) are interrupted by the timpani demanding their share of the limelight, after which a sardonic march (containing suggestions of Stravinsky's *Histoire du soldat*) takes over. The same year saw the appearance of the technically extremely demanding *Ballade* for cello (its declamatory introduction and cadenza entirely in double-stopping).

Martin produced two major concertos at the start of the 1950s, one for violin, the other for harpsichord. The first movements of both are largely built on not dissimilar six-note groups, the former restlessly exploring possible paths, the latter (which becomes an ostinato) allegedly representing 'the steady rocking of waves on the North Sea shore'. The violin work has two further movements, an intense elegiac *Andante* whose initial subject is more melodically introverted than ever, and a sinewy finale whose striding fourths are an unusual feature for Martin. In the Harpsichord Concerto there are strong family resemblances to the *Petite symphonie concertante*, alike in a rhapsodic first-movement theme for the soloist and in the triadic style of the curiously constructed only other movement, which begins slowly on woodwind but becomes increasingly lively, turning into a waltz (punctuated by a long cadenza). Neither the Cello Concerto of 1966 nor the Second Piano Concerto, composed three years later when Martin was 80, has yet established a foothold in the repertoire. The first movement of the latter is more spikily astringent, atonal and melodically disjoint than his previous works, but the subsequent *quasi-passacaglia* on a tone-row and, particularly, the stuttering-themed finale (with extensive use of triads) serve to soften this acerbity.

Retracing our steps to the end of the war, three more works by former members of *Les Six* are noteworthy. In his *Concerto da camera* (for flute, cor anglais and strings) of 1948, what Honegger himself referred to as the facetiousness of their early works has given way to a more mature, more pungent wit; and his declared predilection for polyphony finds expression in the plangent *Andante* (which gives the impression of a *passacaglia* without being one) and the coquettishly gay, tonally footloose finale; but its most endearing movement is the elegantly delicate initial *Allegretto amabile*, which at moments resembles Milhaud in his pastoral vein. Also turning his back on youthful frivolities, Ibert produced in his *Symphonie concertante*—over which, he declared, he had pondered unusually long—a sizeable, closely-knit work of Rousselian sinewy energy. As if to counterbalance his Cello Concerto, which had offset the cello with wind instruments only, here a solo oboe is partnered only by strings: indeed, it is in danger of being the junior partner, since the much divided strings carry on quite half of the complex contrapuntal arguments of the three ternary movements without it. In the first movement it is restricted mainly to providing lighter interludes, but it plays a more important role in the melancholy *Adagio*, and in the course of the work it is allowed several cadenzas. Poulenc, alone of the former Six, remained unregenerate in the Piano Concerto he himself premièred at the start of 1950. The work is little more than an agreeable series of ingenuous tunes strung together in inconsequential fashion, with virtually no development. Its moods constantly change abruptly, there are echoes from the *Concert champêtre*, and the finale, which quotes the folk-song *A la claire fontaine* but also seems to hint at *The old folks at home*, displays all Poulenc's old *gaminerie*.

Jolivet

A new and iconoclastic voice made itself heard from 1948 with the appearance of the first of what were to be a dozen concertos by **André Jolivet** (1905–1974). At the opposite pole from everything Poulenc and his circle stood for, Jolivet—who had been profoundly influenced by Varèse and Bartók—stated his aim as being 'technically to liberate myself totally from the tonal system, aesthetically to restore to music its primordial character as a magic, incantational expression . . . directly related to the universal cosmic system'. These beliefs and his eclecticism, embracing ingredients from various non-Western musics as well as from jazz, lend his works a strongly individual style, mostly atonal (though rarely serial) and often emotionally disturbing. His Ondes Martenot Concerto of 1948 is a violent work, the solo instrument pitting its remarkable dynamic range, flexibility and ability to soar to dizzy heights against elaborate orchestral turbulence (with savage *Sacre*-like rhythms in the second movement) but finally floating clear in the finale's rapturous serenity: after all the turmoil, the music ends in a radiant D major. The frenetic atmosphere is entirely absent both from the *Concertino for trumpet, strings and piano*—the piano in a subordinate role, reversing the relationship in Shostakovich's concerto for the same forces—which is a set of five variations (the last a slightly jazzy one) on a light-hearted theme featuring an augmented fourth, and from the short Flute Concerto of 1949 (also with strings only), which has two quick movements each preceded by the same gravely hieratic slow theme (Ex. 6b), the second further preceded by another thematic cell (Ex. 6a) which is

Ex. 6

transformed to become the main subject of the final *Allegro risoluto* section. Violence and intricacy of texture return with renewed vigour, however, in the Piano Concerto of the following year, whose first performance ended in a near-riot. Except for a brutalist cadenza at the start of its last movement, the piano's solo status is rivalled by that of a massive array of percussion (to membership of which it is often relegated); for exotic coloration is the work's outstanding feature, incorporating melodic and rhythmic elements from Central Africa, the Far East and Polynesia respectively in its three movements. Large claims have been made by French critics for the hypnotic quality and mystic cosmic vision of this concerto, though to others the purely musical value of its metaphysical concepts is more open to question. There is a more compelling sense of mystery in the reflective central *Andante cantabile* of the concerto for harp and chamber orchestra (1952), a work which involves the soloist in an unusual degree of chromaticism and keeps her almost continuously at full stretch in the outer movements.

Jolivet returned to his Flute Concerto pattern of two quick movements each preceded by a slow introduction (here the first is a recitative demanding the utmost virtuosity and extending over a range of $3\frac{1}{2}$ octaves) for his Bassoon Concerto, which like the Trumpet Concertino was designed for a Conservatoire competition and calls for a pianist as an auxiliary soloist. Along with the Concertino, it is one of his most immediately attractive compositions, alike in the lyric appeal of its *Largo* section and the outright joviality both of the first *Allegro* and of the final *Fugato*. The mixture of styles in a Second Trumpet Concerto, written in that same year of 1954, is as curious as its instrumentation—for eight wind (including two saxophones), string bass, harp, piano and 14 percussion (which play a major part throughout and have a passage to themselves in the finale). The first movement, after a brief wailing wa-wa-muted introduction, is a vehemently obsessive angular dance with Latin-American overtones; the central *Grave*, which sets out from the chord formed by the open strings of a guitar, is languidly Oriental; and the ebulliently jazzy finale, complete with trombone smears and 'dirty' tone and ending rowdily, is designated by the composer as a 'homage to Chabrier'.

Three late concertos by Jolivet—two for cello and one for violin—are more uncompromisingly atonal, luxuriate in complex and novel sonorities and push string virtuosity to its limits, as well as employing various original techniques. After the sombre expressive power of the 1962 First Cello Concerto's opening movement, exoticism raises its head in the second, with four timpani and 22 other percussion instruments helping to create an oppressive atmosphere of equatorial ritual; the finale, save for a restrained central episode, is one long burst of fantastic barbaric energy. The Cello

Concerto No. 2 of four years later is even more extreme in its technical demands (having been written for Rostropovich), but in it Jolivet tackles the difficult problem of making the cello stand out against an orchestra of strings only (including a solo quintet). The fevered intensity of the writing for both soloist and orchestra is maintained almost without respite, except momentarily in the anguished *Aria* that succeeds the long cadenza around which the work pivots. The starting-point of the 1972 Violin Concerto is a typical Jolivet thematic cell that gropes its way in minute intervals around a central note and gradually spreads upwards, rising in mounting passion; once again, percussion occupies a significant place in the scoring.

Olivier Messiaen (*b.* 1908), who before the war had been associated with Jolivet in the short-lived 'Jeune France' group, has composed no concertos in the strict sense of the term, though several of his works include very considerable, and immensely difficult, piano parts. Two works of the mid-1950s designated as 'for piano and orchestra' both illustrate his preoccupation with birdsong: *Le Réveil des oiseaux* and *Oiseaux exotiques*. The former subordinates orthodox musical structure to its aim of presenting a time-sequence, from midnight to noon, of birds' songs in the order of their awakening; the latter is a counterpoint of a wide variety of birds from different countries, partly grouped by their colours, but its percussion section also employs a number of esoteric Hindu and Greek rhythms. Novel and ingenious as are the sonorities and structures of these compositions, it is not unfair to say that they are of greater interest to analysts and ornithologists than to the musical public in general.

The advanced musical language of Jolivet and of Messiaen was by no means universal among French composers of concertos in the immediate postwar period. At much the same time as Jolivet's piano concerto, for example, and a world away from its stressful complexities, **Marcel Delannoy** (1898–1962), a largely self-taught musician who had been encouraged by Honegger and whose declared ideal was clarity, was producing his piano *Concerto de Mai* for the Jeunesses Musicales. Unpretentiously diatonic, optimistic and youthful in spirit, in places reminiscent of early Milhaud, its material unfortunately lacks sufficient distinction to support the weight of a full-length concerto. Despite a rapturously rhapsodic atmosphere and elegant craftsmanship, **Sauguet**'s 1953 *Concerto d'Orphée* (in three linked movements) for violin suffers from a similar handicap, in that its themes fail to stay in the mind. The poetic stimulus that brought it into being is also evident in his Piano Concerto No. 3 a decade later (No. 2 was merely an adaptation of a film score), inspired by the eerie, dank surroundings of an underground cave. Sauguet describes his *Mélodie concertante* for cello (commissioned by Rostropovich) which immediately followed, as an 'extended improvisation based on an introspective, melancholy theme', but this theme has not a great deal of character, and though the interval of the minor third which it features recurs repeatedly in the course of the work, continuity suffers from the incessant changes of mood every few bars (except in the penultimate *Con moto* section): only in an all too short central *Lento* does the composer's lyric gift find an opportunity to flower. His *Garden's concerto* of 1970 (named for the harmonica virtuoso Claude Garden) promises greater individuality in its romantic opening *Andantino*, but the fantasy of its middle movement lacks spontaneity: well-placed syncopations and delicate use of percussion contribute to the perkiness of its finale.

The stream of *concertante* works that Jean Françaix has poured out since the war includes *Divertissements* for flute, for horn and for bassoon, but in a sense nearly all his music could be so described: its aim is unashamedly entertainment, and basically ingenuous as are his melodies (and harmonies, though artfully and piquantly disguised), they are frequently beguiling and do at least impart to his works a personal flavour, in which mischievous humour, often manifested in quicksand-shifting tonal centres, is to the fore. Amongst his most disarmingly popular is the *Horloge de Flore* for oboe, a kind of counterpart to Messiaen's *Réveil des oiseaux* in that it consists of a series of linked movements representing seven flowers from Linnaeus's catalogue according to the hour (from 3 am to 9 pm) at which each blooms: there is a catchy finale, one exotic flower prompts a rumba, and a 5 o'clock flower is punningly presented in 5/4 time. A featherweight Harpsichord Concerto of the same year (1959), whose first movement is a curious portmanteau structure of two toccatas and an *Andantino* (mostly on a tonic pedal) with two interludes, pushes to the limits Françaix's penchant for *ostinato* patterns. A spirit of music-hall levity characterizes the bustling first movement of his somewhat over-long *Concerto for two pianos* (1965), though the remainder of the work, full of verve as it is, contains less impudent moments. His later concertos—which include those for flute, clarinet, bassoon, violin and double-bass—continue his individual combination of chirpy melodic invention (sometimes deliberately skirting the commonplace) and rhythmic zest with, for contrast, straightforward cantilena sections. The trouble with producing concertos as an apple-tree produces apples (to borrow Stravinsky's phrase) is that apples tend to resemble each other. Perhaps the most attractive of these more recent works is the 1968 Clarinet Concerto, which besides bubbling with vivacity and wit needs a soloist of exceptional virtuosity.

The works of two near-contemporaries of Françaix make it clear, however, that a civilized but easy-going, undemanding style, characteristically Gallic as it may be, by no means represents all that modern French concertos have to offer. **Jean Martinon** (1910–1976), best known as a distinguished conductor, had earlier composed a *Concerto grosso* for violin which he completed while a prisoner of war, but of altogether greater significance is his deeply impressive Second Violin Concerto of 1961. Cast in a free idiom (with occasional side-glances at tone-rows), its first movement is powerfully dramatic, even tragic, but also contains an impassioned lyrical passage that sounds like updated Walton (Ex. 7) and is obliquely hinted at later—one of several cross-references within the work. Its haunting second movement constantly alternates between a ghostly *pizzicato quasi-scherzo* and a mysterious, plangent *Adagio*. Martinon's Cello Concerto of two years later, which opens with an elaborate cadenza, shows an equal exuberance of rhythmic invention but a more overt acceptance of serial thinking, though still without abandoning a basic tonality.

Ex. 7

In 1970, when Martinon also wrote a Flute Concerto, **Henri Dutilleux** (*b.* 1916), a fastidious, supremely individualistic composer, produced (and had encored) his *Tout un monde lointain* for cello—the title of the work and each of its five sections (played without a break) coming from Baudelaire. Serial in technique, rhapsodic in character, and of transcendental difficulty, its thematic material undergoes constant subtle modifications, lending continuity to the structure; and though Dutilleux has expressed an aversion to all 'prefabricated formal scaffolding', the first movement consists of an atmospheric introductory cadenza (with soft cymbal strokes and string chord-clusters) followed by a theme and four variations. It is a work of the utmost imagination, scored with unusual and often beautiful sonorities (especially in the third and fourth movements, the latter spinning delicate marimba and harp contours), and the slow second movement (which takes the solo cello up into the highest possible register) displaying a sensuousness that even those out of sympathy with avant-garde techniques would find it hard to resist. The way it finally tails off into nothingness contrasts sharply with the paroxysmal ending of his 1985 violin concerto, entitled *L'arbre des songes*: both works, however, begin rather similarly, the latter starting off with the soloist musing against a background of vague orchestral sounds. Somewhat more consonant than its predecessor, the violin concerto consists of four main sections linked by interludes of differing character—respectively pointillistic, monodic and static: moods vary widely, ranging from hypnotically calm to violently frenzied. Although the composer has stated that he wanted to avoid bravura writing as such for the violin, its role is extremely exacting, with much interplay with the orchestra—notably in the slow movement, where its lines intertwine rapturously with those of an oboe d'amore. Dutilleux's fascination with exotic instrumental sonorities is again manifest in his profuse colourful invention: a cimbalom and a group of 'ringing percussion' (piano, celesta, chimes, vibraphone, etc.) make significant contributions. A passage in the last movement seems a curious (but very successful) attempt to reproduce the random polyphony of an orchestra tuning and limbering up on their instruments, before entering a voluptuously Szymanowskian mystic dreamworld. The work has not had time yet to establish itself in the repertoire, but it demonstrates that the day of impressive post-romantic concertos is by no means over.

CHAPTER 9

The Concerto in the Nordic Lands

Robert Layton

Although music flourished in the great courts of the Northern Kingdoms before the eighteenth century, neither Copenhagen nor Stockholm could claim to be remotely comparable with the great musical centres of Europe. Schütz and Dowland spent some time at the court of Christian IV of Denmark, and the King fostered Danish talent too, sending young musicians like Mogens Pedersøn and Borchgrevinck to study in Venice. But there was little that one could call distinctively Nordic about their work. Even the sinfonias and concertos of **Johan Helmich Roman** (1694–1758) do not differ stylistically to any marked extent from those of Geminiani, Handel or Pepusch whom Roman admired.

Roman, the 'Father of Swedish music'—the title was in currency long before it was used by his first modern biographer Patrick Vretblad—was a younger contemporary of Handel. He was not only a considerable composer but a formidable executant, and such hopes were entertained of his talent that the Swedish court, like Christian IV, paid for him to study abroad so as 'to perfect himself in the art of music'. To this end he spent five years in England (1716–21), where he probably studied under Pepusch and acquired his love of Handel. Roman's music is a compound of various stylistic traits. On his travels he readily absorbed Italian and English influences, and his enthusiasm for Handel left an indelible imprint on his style though he never attempted a set of *concerti grossi.* Even if it was Italian music that constituted the most potent factor in his stylistic make-up, he was thoroughly conversant with the French style and his library shows him to have been familiar with the North German tradition, so we can see that he was a composer of wide culture and a diversity of musical sympathies. The best of Roman's output is fully commensurate with, say, Geminiani or Telemann, and there are often unpredictable quirks of line or harmony that make him most appealing. Five violin concertos are attributed to him, and though Ingmar Bengtsson[1] voiced some doubts about them, the balance of evidence

---

1. Ingmar Bengtsson, *J. H. Roman och hans instrumentalmusik. Käll och stilkritiska studier,* Uppsala, 1955.

he adduces favours their authenticity. Both the D minor (BeRI 49) and F minor (BeRI 52) concertos have strong melodic appeal and their charms still remain considerable. Formally they are based on Italian models, and in particular, Vivaldi.

Crusell

Although there are interesting composers working in other fields, Agrell, Joseph Martin Kraus in Sweden, the first concertos to have entered the international repertoire are the three clarinet concertos of **Bernhard Crusell** (1775–1838), a virtuoso of Finnish origin though he moved to Stockholm when he as 15 and made a career for himself as a virtuoso. The concertos, all composed as a vehicle for his own prowess, are urbane and mellifluous, fertile of invention and fluent. It would seem that Crusell never played any of the concertos of Spohr and Weber, but his three examples well withstand comparison with these celebrated contemporaries. All three show him fully aware of contemporary developments: the E flat, Op. 1 (*c.* 1807–10) was published in 1811–12, No. 2 in F minor, Op. 5, was first performed in 1815 and published in 1818, No. 3 in B flat (*c.* 1807), was the first in order of composition but was subsequently revised and published in 1829, which explains its numbering. Probably the finest is the F minor, Op. 5, which he thought well enough of to dedicate it to Tsar Alexander I in 1818. There is little real development in the first movement of No. 1: ideas are presented rather than exploited. The rondo theme of the finale shows an affinity with Rodolphe Kreutzer whom Crusell had come to know in Paris, and the F minor concerto even shows some awareness of Beethoven. All three are attractive pieces much in the style of Spohr, Rode and Weber, but they are totally 'international' in idiom and without any individually 'nordic tone'.

Berwald

If in the beginning of the nineteenth century the Scandinavian countries, like Russia, had yet to discover a distinctive regional 'tone', there were still important native talents. Yet as far as the concerto is concerned, few contributions that are remotely commensurate with European models before we come to Grieg. **Franz Berwald** (1796–1868) produced two concertos, neither of which are fully characteristic. A violinist himself, Berwald had played a concerto by Giovanni Giornovichi as a child, and in 1811 gave the Edouard Du Puy concerto in public. His first concerto, for two violins (1816), does not survive though he is known to have performed it with his brother, in 1817[1]. His Violin Concerto in C sharp minor, Op. 2 (1820)[2] is a work of

1. See Robert Layton, *Franz Berwald*, London, 1959, p. 30.
2. Included in the Complete Edition, BwGA 5, Bärenreiter, Kassel, 1974.

more charm than depth. It was championed in the early years of the present
century by the French virtuoso Henri Marteau, but it is unlikely to gain more
than a peripheral place in the repertory. There is also a Konzertstück for
bassoon and orchestra (1827), to which Berwald inadvertently assigned the
same opus number as the Violin Concerto: it is barely credible that later in
life he called yet another piece, the Piano Quintet in A major of 1857, Op. 2!
His most substantial and original contribution to this genre is the much later
Piano Concerto (1855). A considerable fragment of an earlier slow
movement from 1854 also survives.[3] The piano plays throughout without a
bar's respite; indeed the score bears the legend that 'the work can be
performed without orchestra'. It was written for his pupil Hilda Thegerström
but was not performed until the present century when the composer's
granddaughter Astrid Berwald was the soloist in 1904. Although Berwald
himself was not a pianist of any distinction, his writing for the keyboard is
strangely personal and by no means ineffective. It is a concerto in the sense
that it is a display piece but the orchestra assumes an accompanimental role,
even more than is the case with the Chopin concertos and there is none of the
tension and interplay between soloist and orchestra that distinguishes the
classical concerto.

Grieg

Although it is agreeably fresh, the Violin Concerto of **Niels Gade**
(1817–1890) remains as Mendelssohnian in its speech as do his eight
symphonies, and neither of the piano concertos of Chopin's Norwegian
pupil, the Trondheim-born, **Thomas Dyke Ackland Tellefsen**
(1823–1874) nor the two concertos of **Johan Severin Svendsen**
(1840–1911) for violin, Op. 6, and cello, Op. 7, respectively are likely to
make inroads into the international repertoire. **Edvard Grieg** (1843–1907)
is, of course, another story. We tend to think of him primarily as a
miniaturist, and as a master of the keyboard rather than the orchestra. Indeed,
Grieg himself often complained that his studies at the Leipzig Conservatoire
left him with scant understanding of the orchestra. He withdrew his early
Symphony of 1864, though it was unceremoniously disinterred some years
ago. Even in its revised form of 1888, his Concert Overture, I Høst (In
Autumn) (1866) was not much more successful. In any event Grieg had not
fully mastered the orchestra by 1868, the year in which the concerto saw the
light of day. It was composed the year after his marriage while he was on
holiday in Søllerød in Denmark. He was still a young man of 25 and the
concerto was soon launched on its eventful career by its dedicatee, Edmund
Neupert. Thanks to Svendsen, a score was published only three years later,

3. Included in BwGA 6, Bärenreiter, Kassel, 1974.

but Grieg remained unhappy with both the solo and orchestral part throughout his life and constantly returned to the task of revision. (Plans in 1883 for a second concerto in B minor came to nothing.) The first published score, which already embodied some changes, gives the second subject to a solo trumpet and not to the cellos, a suggestion emanating from Liszt, whom Grieg met in Rome in 1870, a year after the first performance. The various stages of the changes which affected the piano part and the scoring are outlined in Gerald Abraham's *Symposium*[1]. Grieg made the final revision as late as 1906–7, the last year of his life, and the published piano part (Schirmer, 1919) also includes some minor alterations made by Percy Grainger, one of its most authoritative interpreters, which Grieg himself sanctioned in the summer of 1907.

Grieg included the Piano Concerto on many of his tours and the work has remained one of the most popular works in the repertoire, surviving unceasing exposure in the concert halls of the world only to emerge perennially and indestructibly fresh. Yet it is in the ideas themselves rather than the ingenuity of their development that its strength lies. Grieg was never to become a master of large-scale structures: his much underrated contemporary Svendsen, whom he greatly (and rightly) admired, had a much stronger feeling for form. The Grieg A minor is modelled on the Schumannesque concept of the concerto: during his Leipzig years, Grieg studied with E. F. Wenzel, one of Schumann's keenest advocates, and he had also heard Clara Schumann play her husband's concerto. Formally the work is almost perfunctory, and although the orchestra is not reduced to so subservient a role as it is in the Berwald, there is little real interplay between piano and orchestra in respect of the disposition of material. As Gerald Abraham puts it, Grieg 'cheerfully ignores all the subtle possibilities of the classical concerto and simply wrote a first movement in sonata form for piano and orchestra'. Yet if it is not innovative formally (the restatement mechanically traverses the same steps as the exposition), it is extraordinarily successful. There is the poetic ambience of Schumann and the keyboard bravura of Liszt, and yet every bar is suffused with Grieg's original voice. One has only to hear it in the hands of a Lipatti, Rubinstein or Perahia to realize its stature. Even at a time when the songs have fallen from the repertoire, the sure instinct of the public has never allowed the Piano Concerto to slip from view.

Sibelius

Apart from the Grieg, there is one other Nordic concerto that has attained classic status and universal popularity. Although **Jean Sibelius** (1865–1957)

1. Gerald Abraham, London, 1948, pp. 26–31.

was not as good a violinist as Grieg and Stenhammar were pianists, he was gifted enough to entertain youthful ambitions as a soloist and gave up the idea only in his mid-20s. By this time (1891) he was a pupil of Robert Fuchs and auditioned for the strings of the Vienna Philharmonic Orchestra. However, his mastery of the instrument is clearly evident from the kind of music he wrote for it: in particular the Concerto, the grievously neglected Serenades, Op. 69, and the wonderful Humoresques, Opp. 87 and 89, which may well have been afterthoughts of a second violin concerto that we know he was planning in 1915. This idea from the Sixth Symphony was at one stage intended for it (Ex. 1). The D minor Concerto is a superbly written piece, bristling with difficulties of the kind players enjoy overcoming. A measure of its strong hold over the affections of both players and public is the fact that it is the most recorded violin concerto written in the present century (there have been some 60 commercial recordings).

Ex. 1

The extraordinary genesis of the concerto is outlined in detail by Erik Tawaststjerna in his definitive study of the composer.[1] It was eventually finished in 1903, just over a year after the première of the Second Symphony and first performed in Helsinki the following year but Sibelius was far from happy with it and withdrew it for revision. It was eventually given in its definitive form in 1905 with the violinist Karl Halir as soloist and Richard Strauss, no less, conducting the Berlin Philharmonic. Sibelius's grip on his material is as firm as ever and the organic nature of his musical thinking is never in any doubt. Certainly, the very opening is one of the composer's most inspired and magical ideas. The first movement is far more closely argued than its outward appearance would suggest, and although its brilliant cadenza comes close to the language of the great virtuoso composers like Vieuxtemps, Sibelius breathes meaning into the empty rhetorical gestures they favour. He treats sonata form with great freedom and flexibility: none of the processes of the movement is handled mechanically. There are many flashes of real power in the orchestral writing that hint at the tough,

1. Erik Tawaststjerna, *Sibelius*, Vol. 1, London, 1976, pp. 273–87.

symphonic mind below the surface. Who would suspect on hearing its magical, other-worldly opening, surely one of the most inspired beginnings of any concerto, that the music was capable of such sinew (Ex. 2)?

Ex. 2

The slow movement is full of warmth: the paired woodwind in thirds, far from seeming cold, produce an atmosphere that seems almost lush by comparison with the slow movements of the Second and Third symphonies. If in this movement the solo writing is noble and eloquent, the finale offers a dazzling exhibition of virtuosity. Apart from the brilliance of the solo part, the pace never slackens from the very beginning until the last bar. The music carries all before it with an infectious and irresistible sense of momentum.

Nielsen

While the Sibelius concerto remains his only essay in the genre, his Danish contemporary, **Carl Nielsen** (1865–1931) composed three, one of which— the Clarinet Concerto (1928)—is surely the greatest example of its kind after Mozart and among his most mysterious utterances. His Violin Concerto, Op. 33 (FS63)[1] comes from the middle of Nielsen's creative career: he finished working on it in December 1911, some eight months after the *Sinfonia espansiva*. (Both Nielsen works have a geniality that is in marked contrast to the Sibelius of this period and to the bleak spiritual landscape of the Fourth Symphony and *The Bard*.) It has certainly not captured the public imagination in the way that the Sibelius concerto has. Yet in a way it had a strong initial advantage in that it enjoyed the advocacy of a major violinist. When it was first presented in February 1911, Nielsen's son-in-law, the celebrated Hungarian violinist Emil Telmányi, was the soloist. The Sibelius concerto was not taken up by the great players of the period, like Ysaÿe and Kreisler, and it was not until the 1930s that the championship of Heifetz turned the scales in its favour. The Nielsen, on the other hand, does not possess quite the outgoing virtuoso profile that distinguishes the Sibelius. Yet for all that, it is wonderfully fresh and has a strong appeal. It may not have the depth and vision of the Clarinet Concerto or the poignancy of its

1. FS refers to the catalogue compiled by two leading Danish scholars, Dan Fog and Torben Schousboe.

predecessor for flute, but it contains many beautiful things. The Intermezzo, which prefaces the last movement, is deeply felt, and much of the invention of the first movement itself is of a high order and deeply characteristic of its composer. Take, for example, the G major idea which emerges after the soloist's introductory cadenza, whose gentle, smiling character is quite captivating, as indeed is the second theme of the main part of the movement.

The work is unusual formally: there are two movements each preceded by a slow section: first, a Praeludium *(Largo)* which leads to the *Allegro cavalleresco*; and Intermezzo *(Poco adagio)* which leads into a final Rondo, marked *Allegretto scherzando*. As is so often the case in Nielsen's music, the concerto exhibits the principle of progressive tonality, that is to say that the music begins in one key and ends in another. The first movement opens in G minor and the Rondo finale is firmly in D major. The Praeludium opens with an explosive chord which leads to a cadenza. Then follows the gentle, reflective idea on the strings that holds the stage for a time though the music grows in vehemence until the *Allegro cavalleresco*. The opening chivalresque theme sets in motion a traditional sonata-form process that is easily followed by the listener. The second group, which begins on the woodwind and in which the soloist immediately joins, is a marvellous idea, as characterful and warm hearted as the first subject is relatively conventional. There is a long cadenza before the very end of the movement. The Intermezzo offers the most searching pages of the work: it opens by tracing the notes B A C H and is more chromatic in character than anything else in the work, yet there is not the slightest suspicion of sentimentality. Its mood strikes a deeper vein of feeling than the Rondo into which it leads. In his study of the composer, Robert Simpson says 'the more one appraises the work as a whole, the more characteristic it seems in the quiet purity of its chromaticism and the subtlety of its proportions'. The rondo theme is twice interrupted by contrasting episodes, and after the third apperance of the theme, there is a short development section and a cadenza for the soloist before the Rondo theme and the first episode are restated.

When Nielsen returned to the concerto medium it was after the Sixth Symphony and in a very different climate. Both he and Sibelius had ended their symphonic progress. For the former only *Tapiola* remained, and like the Nielsen Flute Concerto (1926), FS119, it was composed in Italy. Nielsen put the finishing touches to the work while he was staying in Florence in October 1926 and its dedicatee, Holger Gilbert-Jespersen, gave its first performance later the same month at an all-Nielsen concert in Paris at the Salle Gaveau, when the composer's son-in-law, the violinist Emil Telmányi conducted. Later, Nielsen revised the end of the second movement and it was in this form that its first Danish performance took place. Few concertos of modern times are so closely tailored to the personalities of their soloists as the two wind concertos Nielsen composed towards the end of his life. It is well known that in the early 1920s, after the completion of his Fifth Symphony, Nielsen had heard the Copenhagen Wind Quintet rehearsing some Mozart and resolved to compose a work for them: the result was the enchanting Wind Quintet of 1922. The members of the ensemble had all become his personal friends and in the next few years he planned to write each of them a concerto. Alas, he did not live long enough to compose more than two: the Flute Concerto (1926) and the Clarinet Concerto of 1928 (FS129). Holger Gilbert-Jespersen was by all accounts an artist of refined taste and strong Gallic sympathies (he made the first commercial recording of the work in the early 1950s) and much of the soloist's music was inspired by his temperament. The robust burlesque gestures of the trombone at the end are an affectionate joke at his expense.

The formal layout of the concerto is unusual. There are two movements only: the first, an *Allegro moderato*, is a sonata design of subtle and refined colouring. The work, incidentally, is scored for chamber orchestra (double wind, two horns, bass trombone, timpani and strings) and its texture is light and spacious. Yet for all its high spirits and good humour, there is an undercurrent of deeper concerns: the coda of the first movement sounds a note of gentle sadness, an expressive and wistful regret for a vanished world and lost innocence. In the *Allegretto*, this feeling invades the *Adagio ma non troppo* section (beginning at bar 62) where it becomes more intense and poignant. These moments of deep poetic feeling lend an added dimension to the good humour and mercurial vitality that are the hallmark of the concerto. Nielsen's use of key is as subtle as his instrumental characterization is well defined and like the symphonies exhibits the principle of 'progressive tonality'. However, it is the trombone and not the soloist that turns up with the right theme in the right key at the very end of the piece!

Although there are disturbing overtones in the Flute Concerto, its successor is even more remarkable. If ever there was music from another planet, this is surely it. Its sonorities are sparse and monochrome; its air rarified and bracing. As is the case in the Fifth Symphony, the side-drum is a leading protagonist in the argument though the orchestral forces Nielsen employs, are modest: two bassoons, two horns and strings. The concerto is in one continuous movement, though it undergoes changes of mood and tempo that are comparable with those of the four movements of a normal symphonic work, slow movement, scherzo and finale. So too does the Seventh Symphony of Sibelius, written four years earlier, though it, like the concerto, remains a one-movement structure. The opening idea is difficult to characterize verbally; it is fugal yet not tautly enough held together to be a proper fugue subject; it proceeds purposefully and deliberately, yet is not pregnant with feeling (Ex. 3). A contrasting idea from the soloist playing with a three-note figure can be thought of as a second group; it is highly expressive and not wholly free from the suggestion that Nielsen was responding to the wistful harmonic flavouring of some jazz, which was enjoying quite a vogue in the late 1920s with Martinů, Milhaud and

Ex. 3

Stravinsky. There is a brief development and a cadenza, and eventually another solo passage with comments from the side drum lead to a ruminative slow movement. There is a particularly imaginative episode where the soloist cries ecstatically over a sustained dotted rhythm on the strings. The longest section is the quicker, almost scherzo-like episode that follows, and this and the finale that follows embrace some of Nielsen's most powerfully original and thoughtful music. Not only does the Clarinet Concerto occupy a special position in Nielsen's output, it is also one of the most remarkable clarinet concertos ever written.

Stenhammar

Wilhelm Stenhammar (1871–1927) is without question the most important Swedish composer after Berwald, who occupies a not dissimilar place in Swedish music to that of Elgar in Britain, and underwent a comparable neglect in the 1950s. He was born into a musical family—his father Per Ulrik Stenhammar (1829–1875) was himself a composer—and after studies in his native Stockholm went to Berlin in the 1890s. Here he made quite a name for himself particularly as a pianist, and at the turn of the century was a noted interpreter of the Brahms D minor Concerto. He was only 21 when he composed his First Piano Concerto in B flat minor (1893) and it says much for his renown that its first performance took place in Berlin under the baton of Richard Strauss. Stenhammar's early music was much influenced by both Brahms and (in such pieces as *Florez och Blanzeflor*, Op. 3, and the opera, *Tirfing*) Wagner, but in his mature work there is something of the gentleness and reticence of Fauré and the dignity of Elgar. Yet his sensibility is distinctly northern, and his personality, though not immediately assertive, becomes more sympathetic, more strongly defined and compelling as one comes to grips with it.

The original score of the First Concerto does not survive and we know the work only in a reconstruction by Kurt Atterberg. After each performance the full score was apparently returned to his publisher in Breslau, but even when the orchestral parts disappeared in Norway in 1906 (they were later recovered) no steps were taken to make a copy. Stenhammar grew tired of playing it on his concert tours, and during the first decade of the century composed a Second, in D minor, with which he toured until his work as a conductor at the Royal Opera, Stockholm, and from 1910 onwards Gothenburg claimed more of his energies. The score of No. 1 languished unplayed and was destroyed in Breslau during the Second World War, though fortunately a piano reduction had been printed. It is about as long as the Brahms B flat and by far the most characteristic movements are the delightful scherzo and the pensive slow movement. The Second, in D minor, Op. 23, occupies a less peripheral place in the repertoire: its four movements are linked together and the opening betrays a distinct debt to Saint-Saëns (Ex. 4). Fresh though much of it is, the reliance on sequence in the scherzo and the somewhat naïve melodic ideas in the slow movement make it unlikely to take its place in the international concert hall. The Stenhammar of the Serenade for Orchestra, the Second Symphony and the later string quartets has a poetry and depth that elude him here.

Ex. 4

What concertos of note have appeared in the wake of Sibelius and Nielsen? None which have established themselves as firmly in concert halls outside Scandinavia. In Finland the five piano concertos of **Selim Palmgren**

(1871–1951) have never really established themselves outside Finland, though the Second (*The River*) did enjoy some exposure in the 1930s, nor has the violin concerto of **Erkki Melartin** (1875–1939); nor the two of **Uuno Klami** (1900–1961). Finland has made more of a mark after Sibelius with the symphonies of **Joonas Kokkonen** (*b*. 1921) and the operas of **Aulis Sallinen** (*b*. 1935). Indeed, as far as the wider public is concerned, the concerto has not enjoyed much representation until the last decade when the cello concertos of Kokkonen and Sallinen have taken the stage. **Aarre Merikanto** (1893–1958) belonged to an earlier generation, and was an exact contemporary of Kilpinen in Finland, and of Prokofiev, Martinů and Rosenberg beyond. His music is shrouded in mystery and neglect, yet what little has penetrated outside Finland reveals an extraordinarily vital imagination, which explored terrain over which Sibelius had not cast a shadow. There are moments that prompt one's thoughts to turn to Janáček and even Szymanowski: as a young man he studied with Reger in Germany and later with Sergei Vasilenko in Moscow, where he came into contact with Scriabin's music. A renaissance of interest in his music is a relatively recent phenomenon following the successful disinterment of his opera, *Juha*: the Second Piano Concerto (1937), and the Fourth Violin Concerto (1954) reveal an original voice and sensibility.

In Sweden there were a number of figures in the generation following Stenhammar and Alfvén, the most important of which was **Hilding Rosenberg** (1892–1985). However, he is best remembered for his powerful symphonies, in particular the Fourth (*Johannesuppenbarelse*) (The Revelation of St John the Divine) and the Fifth (*Örtragårdsmästaren*), rather than his contribution to this genre. His Violin Concerto No. 2 (1951) opens most imaginatively, and its delicacy almost calls to mind the Violin Concerto of Frank Martin. Dr John Yoell finds it 'Rosenberg in top form'[1], but to my mind it never really lives up to the promise of its opening: both here and in the Cello Concerto No. 2 (1954) there is some considerable resort to note-spinning. **Dag Wirén** (1905–1986) composed concertos for the violin, the piano and the cello, but as with his quartets the thematic ideas are short breathed and he seems unable to sustain long paragraphs. Yet he creates an atmosphere that is entirely his own, and there is no question either of the individuality or beauty of his sound world. Like his contemporary, **Lars-Erik Larsson** (1908–1986) his musical models were Mozart and Nielsen, and his ideals to produce music pure and simple. There is a stronger sense of line than in Wirén as one can see in the simple yet affecting slow movement of the Concerto for Alto-Saxophone and strings, Op. 14 (Ex. 5). But without

1. John Yoell, *The Nordic Sound*, Boston, 1974, p. 197.

Ex. 5

doubt it is the Violin Concerto, Op. 42 (1952) which has the most enduring appeal and the strongest chances of survival. This is a beautifully crafted three-movement work which inhabits much the same world as the violin concertos of Walton and Prokofiev, but its lyricism is tinged with an individual melancholy and gentle poetry that is characteristically Swedish. Larsson has composed twelve concertinos, Op. 45 (1953–7) intended for amateur musicians, all of them highly attractive and imbued with a 'musikantische' spirit. But both the Violin Concerto and the Saxophone Concerto are works of substance. Something of the warmth and romanticism of Larsson can be found in the Violin Concerto of **Bo Linde** (1933–1970), though it is less well proportioned—and ultimately less individual than the Larsson. All the same its craftsmanship is thoroughly assured, much of the invention is warmly lyrical, and his scoring is rarely less than expert. Although the closing pages do not have the resonance or the sweetness of the coda of Szymanowski's First Concerto, their melancholy is still poignant. The Estonian-born, **Eduard Tubin** (1905–1982) is a powerful symphonist and vastly superior to many more acclaimed figures: he has two violin concertos to his credit, No. 1 (1941), No. 2 (1944), but neither gives much idea of his very considerable stature, nor does his Balalaika Concerto (1964) written for the remarkable Nicolaus Zwetnow who combines a career as a soloist with that of professor of neuro-surgery at Oslo University Hospital! Of the 'Monday Group', so-called (not because they composed only on Mondays but rather because they met to study the modern music of the day—Bartók, Schoenberg, Webern and so on), **Karl-Birger Blomdahl** (1916–1968) and **Sven-Erik Bäck** (*b.* 1919) have produced concertos. Blomdahl's Violin Concerto (1946) is a rather Hindemithian piece, but the Chamber Concerto for piano and wind (1953) has that dark, austere intensity that marks his best music. However, it seems to have fallen from the repertoire; and Bäck's Violin Concerto (1960) has made little headway. Nor, despite the advocacy of Ida Haendel, did the Second Violin Concerto of **Allan Pettersson** (1911–1980).

Denmark after Nielsen

In his early work **Vagn Holmboe** (*b*. 1909) reflects an admiration for Nielsen as well as a preoccupation with the neo-Classical ideas of Hindemith, Toch with whom he briefly studied, and Stravinsky. From Nielsen he inherited clarity of line and a vital polyphonic sense. The assimilation of the rhythmic patterns and characteristic figures of neo-Classicism is evident in the series of twelve chamber concertos written in the 1940s. The Double Concerto for violin and viola (1946) and the Chamber Concerto No. 11 for trumpet and strings (1948) are among the most successful, and given the paucity of the repertoire for the trumpet, the Holmboe should enjoy wide currency. Generally speaking, Holmboe's music has a certain reserve. Its impact is not always immediate: he relies on the cumulative effect rather than on isolated details of colour. The finest of his works have a continuity of thought and an elevation of feeling that is unlikely to appeal to the vitiated palate. In his music it is the subtle shaping of thematic ideas and their organic transformation that constitute the basis of symphonic thought. The textures are transparent and luminous, and the music immediately establishes a distinctive sound world all its own. The Cello Concerto, Op. 120 (1974) is a remarkable piece: there are five short sections played without a break: the thematic substance heard at the outset provides the basis for the bulk of the subsequent ideas. There are two flute concertos of great character and brilliance from the 1980s. Hardly less impressive a symphonist in the early 1950s but far more uneven is his enormously prolific younger contemporary, **Niels Viggo Bentzon** (*b*. 1916). As a young man Bentzon was a formidable pianist so that it comes as no surprise there are seven piano concertos, the last, written in 1967–9, is Op. 243—that is at the last count; by now there are probably more! Perhaps his best-known work is the Chamber Concerto for three pianos and eleven instruments, a work bubbling over with ideas and full of energy. At this time his models were Stravinsky, Nielsen and Hindemith but there are distinctive accents here. A less familiar name outside Denmark is **Hermann D. Koppel** (*b*. 1908), who has made no mean contribution to the genre. He is a fine and fluent craftsman, less individual than Holmboe but a very imaginative composer. His Third Piano Concerto (1948) is neo-Classical in feeling but one is carried along by the invention. The Cello Concerto (1952) even reminds one of the Tippett Piano Concerto in its luminous textures and questing spirit. His music deserves a hearing even if his personality is not as strong as his immediate compatriots'.

Norway after Grieg

There was no immediate sucessor to Grieg in Norway: to take two almost random examples, both the D flat major Piano Concerto, Op. 6, of **Christian**

Sinding (1856–1941) and the Fourth Concerto of **Halfdán Cleve** (1879–1951) sound tired and conventional by comparison with his concerto, and the Violin Concerto of **Johan Halvorsen** (1864–1935) has remained in obscurity. On the other hand, the Violin Concerto of **Fartein Valen** (1887–1952), a work of strange beauty, enjoyed a brief vogue in the 1950s and deserves much wider exposure. Valen spent his childhood in Madagascar and studied philology and languages at Oslo University before becoming a pupil of Max Bruch. He was something of an outsider in Norwegian musical life, and as early as his Piano Trio, Op. 5 (1923) used a twelve-note technique, which he used for the rest of his creative life. His Violin Concerto (1940) is his masterpiece, a short intense work in one movement lasting about 13 minutes, and like the Berg, an outpouring of grief at the death of a young relative, Arne, three years earlier. It also ends, as does the Berg, by quoting a Bach chorale ('Jesus, meine Zuversicht'). Valen's music has a strong feeling of the open air, a keen sense of nature—indeed its textures almost call to mind Delius at his most transparent—but at the same time, there is a feeling of claustrophobia as if the fjords inhibit vision and light. The concerto is a haunting piece whose pale colours and powerfully distilled atmosphere reflect an almost neurasthenic world. The opening line is serial—yet the accompanying idea on flute and clarinets also plays an important part in the music's development (Ex. 6):

The Violin Concerto is strong in profile and powerfully concentrated in atmosphere. It is an intensely human piece, and such is its power that it renders the techniques and the means by which they are achieved seemingly irrelevant. But the most distinctly Norwegian of this generation is **Harald**

Ex. 6

Saeverud (*b.* 1897), best known for his post-war incidental music for Ibsen's *Peer Gynt*. He has written concertos for clarinet, piano, violin and oboe. His Oboe Concerto, Op. 12 (1938) was the first and the Piano Concerto, Op. 31 (1950) is among the most characteristic. It opens with a neo-Classical flourish that one might expect from Stravinsky had he been born a troll, and it has the kind of energy one finds in many works of this period all over the world (Lukas Foss's Second Concerto is not dissimilar). Saeverud's keyboard writing is naïvistic and simple in texture, but the invention has a gnarled, stubborn quality that is thoroughly individual and full of character. Although Saeverud has nine symphonies to his credit, he is not prolific, but the sheer volume of his output has told against **Geirr Tveitt** (1908–1981): his opus list extends to the three-hundreds though much is unpublished and much was destroyed in 1970 in a fire which consumed not only his house but much of his life's work. He was a pupil of Florent Schmitt, Honegger and Egon Wellesz, and when his Fifth Piano Concerto, Op. 156, was performed in Paris, a French critic spoke of him as 'a Norwegian Bartók'. He was absorbed in folk music and collected more than a thousand hardangar melodies, and there are two concertos for hardangar fiddle. His piano writing is quite forward-looking and the Piano Sonata No. 29, Op. 129 (1950) 'Sonata etere' makes use of chord clusters silently depressed but their overtones activated by staccato notes in the manner of Henry Cowell; but above all he had a real flair for the orchestra. His music is at times naïve, but there are flashes of colour and real inspiration that make his total neglect outside his native Norway regrettable.

Norway has no lack of creative talent though it has not greatly enriched the concerto repertoire. **Klaus Egge** (1906–1978), who has receded into obscurity since his death, wrote three piano concertos, though it is his Violin Concerto (1951), written like the Rosenberg Second for Camilla Wicks, that is most impressive. **Bjarne Brustad** (1895–1978), a prolific symphonist has written four violin concertos, but No. 4 (1963) strikes me as curiously manufactured given the atmosphere generated by the Second Symphony. There are figures such as **Johan Kvandal** (*b.* 1919), who has a fine concerto for the oboe (1977) and violin (1979) to his credit, **Arne Nordheim** (*b.* 1931), who has written a concerto for Rostropovich and a significant talent, **Ketil Hvoself** (*b.* 1939), one of the sons of Harald Saeverud. The Concerto for double bass that he wrote for Gary Kerr is thoroughly individual, refreshingly unpredictable and resourceful—and full of humour! Though one can recognize some of the characteristics of the father, the robust humour and the fresh tang of the northern seaboard, Ketil Hvoself is very much his own man and his music performs a function for which Handel strove—it makes one feel better!

CHAPTER 10

The Concerto in Modern Times

(i) Four Romantics: Reger, Pfitzner, Schmidt and Korngold

Harold Truscott

Few musicians have developed so fast and as early as did **Max Reger** (1873–1916). By 1900 he had completed roughly one third of his total output, in spite of a period of military service, for which he was unfitted and which left him ill and unhappy. That year saw the composition of two Romances for violin and orchestra which have strong hints of what is to come in the Violin Concerto, just as the two Beethoven *Romances* look forward to *his* Violin Concerto. The Reger pieces are larger than the corresponding slow movement of the Concerto. Each has the same reflective spirit, beautiful, solo decorative counterpoint covering an orchestral melodic framework that displays one of Reger's most characteristic yet frequently misunderstood methods of harmonic movement: this is elaborate chromatic decoration around a tonal centre without in the least disturbing it.

The two *Romances* form a fine intermediate platform to the two great concertos. These are among Reger's major achievements: both are large-scale works, the Violin Concerto in A, Op. 101 (1908) lasting almost an hour. The concertos are sharply contrasted, the violin work being a mainly smiling, optimistic affair, in a bright A major; the Piano Concerto dark and sometimes threatening in a stormy F minor. Nevertheless, the latter contains one of the most ethereal passages in the whole of his output. On the surface the Violin Concerto is one of his least complex works, tonally and harmonically. His habit of exploring, even establishing, his tonality by remote exploration often means that a movement will begin on some harmony other than the tonic chord, as, for example, in the *Larghetto* third movement of his E flat String Quartet, Op. 109, and perhaps even more strikingly at the outset of the Violin Sonata in C, Op. 72. The Concerto, on the other hand, begins directly with a large *ritornello*, in the tonic A major (Ex. 1). At first hearing it seems innocuous enough, even if there is a suggestion of something strange about it. But looking at it, and especially beyond it, someone unresponsive to Reger might say: 'See, he can't write a straight melodic phrase in A major; he has to bring in extraneous chords that disturb it.' And, on the surface, he might be right. I have taken the quotation beyond the covering phrase to show further alternations with our tonic

Ex. 1

chord. It would appear that Reger is putting the A major tonic chord into almost every conceivable harmonic context, and the result is that at the end of the phrase the A major chord we come to does not sound like the one we started from. At the end of the next two short phrases it sounds even less like it. Then the plunge on to C major initiates a large passage which has a momentary halt on G major, circles round an almost unrecognizable home dominant, comes to A minor, which now sounds a million miles away, with a development of the opening melodic line, and becomes quite excited as it leads to the opening melodic phrase in and on a full and easily recognizable A major.

There is method in Reger's madness, as anyone can hear who does not make up his mind too hastily. Reger's treatment of the tonic chord has now brought about a situation in which, since it has been heard in almost every guise, its personality is obvious, and can be recognized whenever and wherever Reger wants us to. At the same time he has given us a fascinating tour round aspects of A major not normally included in the price of admission! No better proof is needed of the solid stability of his tonal and harmonic methods.

Ex. 1 is followed by seven more major themes, making a *ritornello* on a very large scale (although not so large as in Joachim's *Hungarian* Concerto), and comes to rest eventually on a resounding chord of C sharp major. Here, the soloist makes a hesitant entrance giving the effect of finding his way, alighting at last on a sort of variation of the beginning of Ex. 1 on D major, expanding this and coming at last to Ex. 1 fully in A major. The solo part is a mixture of direct statement and brilliant and thoughtful counterpoint to orchestral thematic matter. When we come to the main second group idea, in E major, the orchestra again presents it first, in a fair-sized tutti. It begins with a rhythm, ♩· ♪ ♩ which the soloist, when he re-enters, alters to ♩ ♩· ♪. In the recapitulation these rhythms are reversed. The most interesting characteristic of this main second-group melodic line is that in the course of the movement it grows gradually closer to the first phrase of Ex. 1, eventually becoming a continuation of the latter, as well as making a bass on more than one occasion. The two are also heard in counterpoint. Reger writes a fairly full recapitulation, with much altered detail, the *ritornello* to the second group being much cut short. He also writes a large, very carefully thought out cadenza, which should not be cut (although one short cut is suggested) because it spoils the balance of this superb movement.

The slow movement, in B flat major, starting with one of Reger's most beautiful ideas, in another fairly large *ritornello*, pursues a quietly meditative path, with occasional moments of passion, on the lines of a somewhat more closely structured companion to the Romances, Op. 50. It has a moment of breathtaking harmonic beauty towards the end.

The finale begins in an audaciously Regerian vein with a rhetorical F minor outburst followed by a long pause. Then the movement proper begins at the other end of the harmonic universe, on F sharp veering to C sharp minor, which is briefly maintained until we are poised on the dominant seventh of A major. C sharp minor has a habit of deflecting A major throughout this high-spirited movement.

By contrast, the Piano Concerto in F minor, Op. 114 (1910) is stern and severe, with a strong tragic first movement. The orchestral *ritornello* occupies only 24 bars, but although it is not on the same scale as the Violin Concerto, it is every bit as weighty and deploys three distinct themes. The piano immediately asserts its independence in virtuoso octave passages (which betray a relationship to the initial *ritornello* theme) and with a theme of its own. The soloist then dwells on and illuminates the material of the *ritornello*, the orchestra giving him support. A great deal of ground is covered in a comparatively short space. The Violin Concerto is far from slack in its organization, but the concentration shown in this F minor work almost makes it seem so. Nor, when, through a number of further themes with the piano utilizing a wide range of sonorities, we come to the main idea of the second group, does that concentration relax. It effectively explodes the myth, still in currency, that Reger is heavy handed and ponderous (Ex. 2). For delicacy of expression this is hard to beat, but its concentration is complete. Its essence is contained in a very few bars.

Apart from this and its re-appearance later, the movement remains stormy

Ex. 2

and tragedy-laden to the end. One bass figure, descending in thirds, prominent towards the end of the movement, reappears in the middle of the slow movement, *Largo con gran expressione*, an instance of thematic transference rare in Reger. The movement is in F sharp minor, although characteristically it begins with the piano hovering round the dominant seventh of C sharp minor, in a three-chord theme that haunts this wispy, sadly brooding piece. The gentle contemplation brings one thematic fragment after another, each complementing the other, in a perfect balance between piano and orchestra. Apart from one very loud outburst midway, the markings are *pp, ppp, una corda* and so on. Reger rarely wrote a more quietly expressive movement. It ends on a chord of F sharp major, triple piano, with A sharp and F sharp prominent on flutes.

With the beginning of the finale there is another unusual instance of thematic transference. It begins with a loud three-chord gesture that is to play a large part in the piece. Tonally it is not remotely connected with F major, the key of the movement, although the music dutifully gets there by the end of the first sentence. The initial chord is of E flat, B flat, G flat, with a prominent octave C, and this is the hub on which the wheel turns. The quiet A sharp and F sharp at the end of the slow movement has become B flat and G flat, the nucleus of this new harmony, and the three-chord figure is a vigorous version of the theme that opened the slow movement.

The finale is a large sonata design, with a suggestion, which never becomes anything more, of rondo about it.

Pfitzner

Hans Pfitzner (1869–1949) was born in Moscow, and already while studying at the Frankfurt Conservatory he produced his fine Op. 1 Cello Sonata and the Cello Concerto in A minor (1890). A finely thought-out composition (this is a mark of Pfitzner's work in general), it was to linger in his memory. He did not return to the genre until he was in his 50s: the Piano Concerto in E flat, Op. 31 (1922) and the Violin Concerto in B minor, Op. 34 (1923). Pfitzner does not preface the first with a *ritornello* but builds up to a large orchestral section heralding the recapitulation. The tempo is a moderate *Allegro*, but there is plenty of power and energy and the movement has a fine swing to it. A jerky upward springing figure on the orchestra greets the piano, which turns it into a splendid theme (Ex. 3).

Ex. 3

The music sinks gradually to B minor, 12/8, and the second group begins, much slower. The strings lead to a long and expressive solo meditation. A woodwind interjection brings another longer solo comment. All the time the music is losing pace. And here we meet, not only one of Pfitzner's departures from the classical norm, but a feature that appears elsewhere in his work, notably in the first movement of the Piano Quintet. The music loses all momentum, and by the end of the exposition has virtually come to a standstill. This is not inadvertent but intentional, and one of the most thrilling and remarkable phenomena in all my experience of music is the regaining of that momentum. This process is gradual and subtle until eventually the orchestra bursts out in full original tempo, with a huge tutti, moving all round E flat, our home key, stringing up one's expectancy almost to breaking point, and arriving at last at the piano's opening theme on full orchestra, but moved at the last moment to E major instead of E flat. So skilfully has this been managed that the outburst in E comes as a real surprise, well worth waiting for. One full statement is succeeded by the piano breaking out almost angrily, as though very much put out by this independence on the part of the orchestra, and in a few bars E flat is restored. Again comes 12/8, much abbreviated, and the movement ends with slow repeated low E flats, scored as before.

These repeated E flats begin the second movement which transforms them into a 6/8 theme flying as though its feet barely touched the ground. The convolutions and variety of expression which Pfitzner extracts from his quite simple scherzo themes are astonishing.

The slow movement opens expressively, and when after this meditation the piano enters, it dreams on material of its own that responds to the orchestra's thinking. Towards the end a slow chorale emerges: there are hesitations and suddenly it launches us into a vigorous finale, slightly off-course harmonically but righting itself almost immediately. The finale culminates in a written-out 'cadenza in fugen-form' of phenomenal difficulty.

The Violin Concerto is like no other work of its kind in my experience; much of it could be described as majestic turbulence. Its shape is dictated entirely by its material. An explosive outburst, and the soloist is in, with a long outpouring almost savage in its intensity, punctuated at times by growls from violas and cellos in a figure of dotted quaver and two semiquavers. This has appeared already in the opening solo passage, and grows more and more into the work, becoming a dominating feature. The orchestra breaks into a tutti on this figure, but sets loose also a rolling triplet theme which takes the music to D flat, where the soloist, with the triplets as bass, plays another important theme, a sort of second subject, although this is hardly a normal sonata movement (Ex. 4). In the slow movement the soloist is silent; the piece is one of the grandest and most thrilling orchestral crescendos ever conceived, grief-laden though it is. A quiet reference to the beginning of the work lets the soloist in again, and a version of the soloist's initial material, differently conceived, leads to a long introduction by the

Ex. 4

soloist to the final part of the concerto, in D major. This introduction already hints at the figure with which the finale begins.

This is a sonata movement using a long, ambling melody marked *gemütlich*. As with movements which Schubert starts with a pretty tune, that turn out to be rather cataclysmic, we should be wary when Pfitzner writes in his *gemütlich* vein. The movement develops in an unforeseeable way: very simply at first, on strings, then with the soloist, and the orchestra enlarged to include oboe and horn. This long main tune shares with others Pfitzner's way of constantly altering elements yet allowing the material to remain recognizable.

Until now, all this and other turbulent music (witness the second act of *Palestrina*) had been written when Pfitzner's life was fairly straightforward. The death of his wife in 1926 had been a great grief, a personal tragedy, but that was part of the normal life cycle: the advent of the Nazi regime brought horror in its train. Yet as his life outwardly became more unbearable, he fell back on his inner life and his music assumed simplicity and serenity untroubled by the trauma of events. In this mood he wrote his last great series of works including the two cello concertos, the first of which, in G major, Op. 42, was written for Gaspar Cassadó in 1935. It is a single movement with roughly eight sections, each of which grows organically into the next. Mainly it is an elegiac work, dominated by the long-breathed tune played by the cello at the beginning, from which bits are broken off as woodwind echoes, but taking in more rapid music, including a brilliant *fugato*. The elegiac mood predominates, and it is on this note that the short work (about 16–17 minutes) ends.

With the Cello Concerto No. 2 in A minor, Op. 52 (1944) his work in this genre comes full circle. To make this even plainer he uses a theme from the early A minor concerto, and in a note in the score writes that it is his old age greeting his youth. It has four short movements: a happy brooding, with a cadenza for solo cello and clarinet; a quietly smiling scherzo; a slow meditation leading to the largest, a 6/8 finale. This does have a momentary uneasy outburst in the middle, which, however, is soon put to rout, leaving the way clear for a serene ending.

Schmidt

Franz Schmidt (1874–1939), whose music is gradually penetrating the musical consciousness of Britain and America, wrote two concerted works, both for left hand piano and orchestra. The Austrian pianist Paul Wittgenstein lost his right arm in the First World War, and there was in fact quite a lot of music already written for left hand alone, including some chamber music by Josef Labor, but only one concerto, that by Count Géza Zichy, in E flat (1902). So Wittgenstein began to commission works for piano and orchestra, and later chamber music as well. The first two composers he approached were Franz Schmidt and Erich Wolfgang Korngold. He was lucky: this brought him two masterpieces straight away. Schmidt's *Concertante Variations on a theme by Beethoven* (1923) are based on the complete scherzo *and* trio of Beethoven's Sonata in F major for violin and piano, Op. 24. It is a brilliantly conceived work, with an almost funereal introduction founded on the opening figure of the scherzo plus the beginning of the second part, followed by the complete statement of the scherzo and trio. The first four variations get one in the mood, sticking closely to the scherzo, using the trio as an intervening *ritornello*; Tovey described this use of the trio as a stroke of genius, and I agree with him. But with the fifth variation there comes a magical change. We are no longer in Beethoven's world, but in Schmidt's. He has cunningly taken the one *legato* phrase in the entire scherzo and trio (from the beginning of the second part of the trio) and transformed it into pure Schmidt.

And it is Schmidt who dominates the rest of the set of 14 variations and a large coda, which becomes more and more furious until it breaks off in mid-air and, after a pause, we hear the scherzo played in quiet *pizzicato*, with piano echoes. (Wittgenstein did once play this work at Edinburgh in 1927, with Tovey conducting.)

The Piano Concerto (1934) is a large three-movement work, with a full-sized opening tutti featuring an initial theme of upward and downward leaps which, like so many of Schmidt's themes, gains in power and meaning with each appearance, whether on orchestra or piano. There are a number of other themes, including the main second group tune (one of Schmidt's most personal and beautiful) on B flat, which never at this point sounds like a definite key. With a characteristic rush the orchestra stops in mid-air, and after a pause the soloist enters, on a long cadenza-like passage rising from the deep bass, gradually encompassing the orchestra's themes and adding one of its own. The movement is large and majestic, with a highly organized written out cadenza, a good deal of which extracts ever new matter from the second-group tune. As is a habit which Schmidt, it ends suddenly on a final chord. Rarely do we find any reiterated chords at the end of a Schmidt piece. The middle movement is a long-breathed song in G minor, on two melodies, the first stated by the soloist with a minimum of support, giving a suggestion of quiet chamber music. The other is more animated, bearing a relationship to the second-group tune in the first movement of Schmidt's Third Symphony. Such music is balm to the spirit, and there is little enough of this quality being produced today. The finale, a rondo, is a 6/8 romp, related in tempo, mood and style to the corresponding movement of, again, the Third Symphony; in fact, its first episode tune is own brother to one in the symphony finale.

Both the Variations and the Concerto have gained currency in editions for two hands made by Schmidt's pupil Friedrich Wührer, which unbalance the relationship between piano and orchestra; we badly need the originals.

the second-group tune in the first movement of Schmidt's Third Symphony.

Korngold

When Wittgenstein approached **Erich Wolfgang Korngold** (1897–1957), he was 26 and fresh from his triumph with the opera *Die Tote Stadt.* He worked on his Concerto for the Left Hand, Op. 17, at the same time as Schmidt was writing the *Concertante Variations,* though he did not complete the orchestration until 1924.

The main mood of this concerto is grim, in spite of its nominal key, C sharp major; this is contradicted to minor within the first few bars. The work is one of a number which share a rather hard outlook, and those who expect to find in it what they are pleased to call Korngold's 'lush' romanticism will be disappointed.

The concerto is a single large-span sonata movement, which yet takes in a good deal of territory normally well beyond such a structure. The key to the work is in the opening (Ex. 5).

Mässiges Zeitmaß heldisch, mit Feuer und Kraft

Ex. 5

The concerto is astonishingly difficult, although always possible for the left hand, and the orchestral writing shows all the mastery evident from Korngold's very first work, the *Schauspiel-Ouvertüre*, Op. 4, written when he was 14 years old.

The one thing that comes to most people's minds when Korngold is mentioned, is that he wrote film music, and for this he has often been condemned unheard. So did Vaughan Williams, Walton, Shostakovich and Prokofiev, but Korngold's crime, it would seem, is that he wrote for Hollywood where he went in 1935, remaining there until the end of the Second World War. At that point he turned to two works for the concert hall, the Third String Quartet, Op. 34, and the Violin Concerto, Op. 35, both of them in D major.

The concerto, which had obviously been forming in his mind, along with the quartet, was written for Huberman, but he was ill and, indeed, died in 1947. It was taken up by Heifetz, with brilliant results. It is a joyous, happy work, and there are not too many of those around today. Joy, happiness, was never far away in Korngold's music (I have mentioned certain exceptions and, indeed, even in those he could not entirely keep it out). This too helps to make him an unfashionable composer, as well as his inexhaustible gift of melody. But fashion changes; quality remains. The violin part throughout is brilliant, virtuosic to a degree, yet tellingly melodic at the same time. The second-group main theme comes from one of his finest film scores, *Juarez* (1939). There is no initial *ritornello*, but orchestral interjections grow throughout the movement, culminating in the largest, which presents most of the opening group, without the soloist, in a recapitulation. In this, no doubt unconsciously, Korngold is echoing Medtner's procedure in the first movement of his Second Piano Concerto.

The slow movement (G major) is a long-breathed song in which intense semitonal play, often with telling octave leaps, adds to its expressive power. With the finale Korngold gives virtuosity its head. It is a single-theme movement, the theme presented in number of variations which approximate to a sonata structure both in style and mood. The movement has given the impression that the soloist could scarcely go any faster, but the coda disproves this. It is a work to savour, to hear again and again. However, it is really also a work which requires a soloist who can do it justice and in Heifetz it found one.

Although with the end of the war and his return to writing concert music, Korngold's interest in film music was all but exhausted, he did remain long enough to provide some outstanding music for a 1946 film, *Deception*. The story involves a concert cellist, a composer and a cello concerto. Afterwards Korngold expanded the score into a twelve-minute single-movement concerto, highly melodious and with typical Korngoldian passion; one of the shortest cello concertos ever written, but one of the most pungent.

(ii) Central Europe in the Twentieth Century
Arnold Whittall

The concertos discussed in this section are as diverse in style and form as their composers are in personality. Late-Romantic, neo-Classical or avant-garde, tonal or atonal, concertos which exploit aspects of indeterminacy or electronics—all may be found. The spirit of experiment has touched this genre in the twentieth century, as it has all others, and can be traced not only through such obvious differences of style and technique as distinguish Szymanowski from Schoenberg and Bartók from Berio: there have been diverse and resourceful attempts to extend or modify the concerto principle itself, so that the solo concerto is just one of a whole range of formal types, many of which—not least that essentially twentieth-century phenomenon, the concerto for orchestra—relate to the Baroque *concerto grosso*, rather than to more immediate nineteenth-century models.

The characteristically modern spirit of experiment that seeks something new within an existing genre, rather than attempting to destroy the old and start again from scratch, can already be found in what is probably the only concerto by a central European composer written between 1900 and 1914 to embody ambitious innovation: the Piano Concerto with male chorus in the finale (1903–4) by **Ferruccio Busoni** (1866–1924), a more than worthy successor to his attractive Violin Concerto (1896–7). But this was a period of relatively little interest in the form. Mahler and the younger generation of Viennese radicals were preoccupied with issues to which such a prototypically Romantic genre, so often concerned more with instrumental display than symphonic substance, must have seemed peripheral. The more conservative late-Romantics in Austria and Germany like Reger, Pfitzner and Franz Schmidt, did not wholly reject it, but the greatest of them, **Richard Strauss** (1864–1949), was much more interested, first in the tone poem, then in opera: there is a remarkable gap of almost 60 years between Strauss's two early concertos—for violin (1880–2) and No. 1 for horn (1882–3) and his final pair, No. 2 for horn (1942) and for oboe (1945: finale revised 1948). The gap was bridged to some extent by four concertante works: *Burleske* for piano and orchestra (1885–6), *Parergon zur Symphonia domestica* (1924) and *Panathenäenzug* (1927)—both for piano left hand and orchestra—and Duett-Concertino for clarinet, bassoon, strings and harp (1947). But it is the horn and oboe concertos that are most often heard.

The Violin Concerto is a very early work, and for all its skilful treatment of the soloist and expert use of the orchestra, it is rather rambling in form. The

First Horn Concerto is better built, making up in thematic freshness and integration for what it (sensibly) shuns in adherence to full-scale symphonic structuring. Freshness, and with it a youthful vitality, are particularly attractive features of the Second Horn Concerto. Though written when Strauss was tired and anxious in war-torn Germany, the music wears its craftsmanship lightly, never getting bogged down by the prodigality of its thematic invention. Strauss's cogency and flexibility are especially evident in the way the initial *Allegro* yields to the central *Andante*, and this generally relaxed music is well complemented by the mercurial, often forceful final Rondo.

The three-movement Oboe Concerto is another work with winning ways, showing how the well-tried melodic and harmonic characteristics of Strauss's late manner, backward-looking but neither maudlin nor pretentious, can still inspire music whose charm and polish transcend mere superficiality. Not the least of this concerto's charms is the way the composer plays with our occasional suspicion that the melodically expansive solo is about to turn prolix and garrulous. It never does so, for Strauss knew exactly when to counter exuberance with restraint.

It was during the 1920s that the first great generation of modern masters born and working in central Europe began to employ the concerto as a medium for some of their most attractive and powerful music. Compared to the riches to appear after 1920 from Bartók, Berg, Hindemith and Schoenberg, the previous decade yielded a meagre harvest—not surprisingly, in view of the war. Nevertheless, there is one important, striking and forward-looking composition from this period: the First Violin Concerto, Op. 35 (1916) by **Karol Szymanowski** (1882–1937). Szymanowski's 25-minute single movement might best be regarded as a tone-poem in concerto form, since a poem—'May Night' by Tadeusz Miciński—lies behind what Jim Samson[1] has described as its 'extraordinary world of fantasy where nature is interpreted through a blend of classical, oriental and nordic mythologies'. As Samson has shown, there is no point in trying to relate the work's form to traditional schemes. What is nevertheless remarkable is the conviction of its continuity and shape, despite the many twists and turns, the sudden changes of character and direction, the powerful accumulations and rapid reductions of tension. It is as if the composer is demolishing the late-Romantic style from within, luxuriating in an extravagant fusion of impressionistic and expressionistic attributes. What is so strong in atmosphere may be less impressive in sheer substance, but even if the work's thematic ideas are not outstandingly memorable in themselves, the rich

1. Samson, *The Music of Szymanowski*, London, 1980, p. 114.

harmonies, poised between the worlds of tonality and atonality, and the sumptuous orchestral sonorities (which the soloist can nevertheless penetrate with ease) provide ample compensation. Brief quotation can convey little of the music's sustained energy or quicksilver shifts of atmosphere, but Ex. 1 does illustrate the fervent violin line, and the way in which the orchestral accompaniment can switch from density to evanescence in a moment.

Szymanowski's later concertos do not on the whole match the achievement of Op. 35. A piano concerto which he worked on in 1924–5 remained unfinished, and two works of the early 1930s—the Symphonie Concertante for piano and orchestra Op. 60 (1932) and the Violin Concerto No. 2 Op. 61 (1932–3)—confirm that something of the sheer poetry and compelling grasp of large-scale form evident in his earlier work had been lost. There remains keen interest in Szymanowski's personal brand of neo-Romanticism, yet a broadly comparable composer, **Ernest Bloch** (1880–1959), who was born in Switzerland but spent much of his working life in America, is currently rather out of fashion. One concertante work with a strong Jewish flavour—*Schelomo* for cello and orchestra (1915–16)—remains deservedly familiar, but his larger-scale Violin Concerto (1937–8) and Concerto Symphonique for piano and orchestra (1947–8) also have their devotees. The Violin Concerto is the finer of the two, an impassioned yet never rambling outpouring of considerable emotional force. Its expansive three-movement design is held together by clear thematic correspondences, and Bloch's own training as a violinist pays dividends in the skilful lay-out of the demanding yet rewarding solo part. It is none the less to composers of more progressive inclinations than Bloch that we must turn for the most significant exploitation of the concerto genre as artistic life began to recover in the years after 1918.

What gives particular richness to the new music of the 1920s, in central Europe above all, is the co-existence of and increasing interaction between two tendencies: the neo-Classicism associated primarily with Stravinsky and his preservation of certain features of tonal harmony, and the atonal, eventually twelve-note music of Schoenberg, Berg and Webern, which stemmed most directly from the late-Romantic and Expressionist world of prewar Vienna. The neo-Classical composers were the most numerous, and the most prolific. It is generally assumed that Paul Hindemith was unrivalled in his productivity, but as far as the concerto is concerned he is easily outstripped by **Bohuslav Martinů** (1890–1959).

Martinů

Martinů was Czech by birth, but spent long periods in Paris and America

Ex. 1

before returning to spend the last six years of his life in France and Switzerland. His contribution to the concerto genre spans more than 30 years, and comprises almost 30 different works, with a refreshing variety of titles: as well as concerto and concertino, we find *concerto grosso, suite concertante, sinfonia concertante, fantasia concertante, concerto da camera, sonata da camera,* rhapsody, and *sinfonietta giocosa.* Apart from five piano concertos, and two each for violin and cello, Martinů wrote for such unusual combinations as flute, violin and chamber orchestra: violin, piano and orchestra: and piano trio and strings. The image of amiable, often desultory note-spinning that easily attaches itself to such fertility is not always unjustified: works which begin in lively neo-Classical vein, like the large-scale *Sinfonietta giocosa* for piano and orchestra (1940), can grow rather anonymous in manner even if they sustain their energy throughout. At his best, however, Martinů can create strongly dramatic as well as memorably poetic music. The Double Concerto for two string orchestras, piano and timpani (1938), composed under the shadow of the Munich crisis, is one of his most weighty symphonic scores, and also a reminder of how flexible, or imprecise, the title 'concerto' had become: no-one would be too surprised if Bartók had called his work of the same period for strings, percussion and celesta 'Concerto' rather than 'Music'. As for Martinů's many solo concertos, one of the best and most interesting is the Piano Concerto No. 4 *(Incantation)* of 1955–6. As Brian Large[1] has pointed out, not only is this impressively exploratory in form, but it exploits the solo instrument with remarkable imagination and variety. Passages 'such as those in the first movement cadenza where piano and harp are combined, are anything but merely experimental—this is where Martinů is saying something completely new and important'. This cadenza, which ends the movement, is arresting not just for its unusual colour-combinations, but because it shows the composer using a well-tried toccata style in a lively, unhackneyed way. *Incantation,* cast unusually in just two movements, is memorable not only for the precision and diversity of its instrumental effects. Its form contrives to be both wide ranging and well focused, its material essentially economical, yet generating a great diversity of related ideas. In a note Martinů declared that *Incantation* was a protest against excessive mechanization in modern society, and it is indeed an angry as well as an exhilarating piece.

Hindemith

Like Martinů, **Paul Hindemith** (1895–1963) began and ended his career in Europe, with an extended period of residence in America in between.

1. Large, *Martinů*, London, 1975, p. 151.

Hindemith is most closely associated with the emergence of neo-Classicism in Germany in the 1920s, and his first concerto to exemplify this style is the second of his *Kammermusik* series, the Concerto for piano and twelve instruments (1924). Before discussing Hindemith in detail, however, it is worth mentioning two significant contributions to the genre by other Austro-German masters, not least because they could scarcely be more different in character from Hindemith himself: Alban Berg's Chamber Concerto for piano, violin and thirteen wind instruments (1923–5) and the Concerto for violin and wind of 1924 by Kurt Weill (1900–50). Berg's work is a remarkable fusion of urgent expressiveness and meticulously executed planning. The Weill concerto is an ambitious early work that embodies elements—from Weill's teacher Busoni as well as from Stravinsky and even Mahler—which were, when more fully developed, to become essential ingredients of Weill's most familiar manner, that of such theatre pieces as *Die Dreigroschenoper* and *Happy End*. Fascinating though it is, however, the Violin Concerto lacks the kind of direct appeal that was to make those later theatre pieces seem to a degree reactions against Weill's earlier style.

If Weill in 1924 was still on the way to finding his true musical self, Hindemith—five years Weill's senior—was already displaying the fruits of his triumphant, exuberant self-discovery. By the mid-1920s triumph and exuberance were not the most obvious qualities in Germany, as the Weimar Republic failed to solve the country's most severe postwar problems. Yet Hindemith turned his own by now aggressive anti-Romanticism into a positive neo-Classicism—or rather into an energetic and affirmative transformation of the contrapuntal style of the greatest of all German Baroque masters, J. S. Bach.

The solo concertos of 1924–7, *Kammermusiken* Nos. 2 to 7, are the first important examples of his new manner, and response to them has always been varied. Hindemith shares abundant energy, and explicit anti-Romanticism, with Stravinsky: yet his refractions of traditional, Baroque tonal counterpoint, often caricatured as 'wrong-note' harmony allied to 'sewing-machine' rhythms, can convey a dogged earnestness totally absent from Stravinsky's lithe, astringent idiom. At its best, however, Hindemith's mature music has a well-sculpted monumentality which can soften into tender, unsentimental lyricism. Only his most fanatical devotees would deny that his work is uneven. Yet no-one can dispute that Hindemith found in the concerto a particularly suitable genre for the projection of tensions between elements of bygone forms and styles and modern reactions to, or rethinkings of, those elements.

His first essay in the form was the Cello Concerto in E flat, Op. 3 (1915–16)—a student effort revealing his precocious gifts, but published only after his death. Then there was a gap until 1923, when he wrote a left-hand concerto, now apparently lost, for Paul Wittgenstein. In 1924 came the *Kammermusik* No. 2 and thereafter a steady flow of works for viola, viola d'amore, organ, violin, cello, piano, clarinet, horn, woodwinds and harp, and trumpet and bassoon. There is also *Der Schwanendreher* (The Swan-turner), a 'concerto after folksongs' for viola and small orchestra, a concerto for orchestra, and the so-called *Philharmonic Concerto*, a set of orchestral variations. Broadly speaking, these works chart a shift from the pervasively contrapuntal manner of the 1920s, in which the principal soloist tends to be first among equals, to a clearer distinction between the soloist or soloists and the accompanying orchestra, in forms closer to Classical or Romantic precedent, and with a less forceful, more harmonically centred style. Comparison of the two violin concertos—the *Kammermusik* No. 4 (1925) and the concerto of 1939—indicates that the later style is in some respects inferior in imagination and sheer vitality to the earlier. But the broader manner of the later concertos can also yield strongly characterized and convincingly developed materials. The Cello Concerto (1940) has been described by Ian Kemp[1] as 'exhilarating' and 'a concerto in the grand manner', and it displays as well as any of Hindemith's later compositions the musical virtues of the period when he was living in America and concerned, among other things, to reinforce his carefully argued and comprehensive theories of harmony.

The first of its three substantial movements opens with an abrasive tutti, and it soon becomes clear that although the soloist's initial function is to exercise a calming influence through the sheer poise of a well-sprung lyric line, his long-term role is to harness energy and project drama more effectively than the almost chaotic opening tutti can manage. Although, as usual with Hindemith, there is much quite conventional passage-work, and a devotion to counterpoint that produces a rather poker-faced *fugato* near the end of the first movement, the work as a whole demonstrates that such passage-work, and various kinds of contrapuntal combination, could still be used with vigour and wit. The second movement's eventual combination of its *Andante* and *Scherzo* elements (Ex. 2) and the finale's progressively more high-spirited embellishment of its March and Trio themes show the full strength of Hindemith's imagination, and there is nothing in the least grey or routine about it.

Bartók

Szymanowski, Martinů and Hindemith are most judiciously categorized as significant rather than incontestably great composers, and whatever claims

1. Kemp, *Hindemith*, London, 1970, p. 47.

Ex. 2

are made for them their concertos are not likely to be heard with any regularity in the concert hall, even though recording companies have been reasonably attentive to them. By contrast, the stature of **Bela Bartók** (1881–1945) is beyond dispute, and his seven concertos (eight, if we count the version for two pianos and orchestra of the Sonata for two pianos and percussion) are among the most highly regarded and frequently performed modern works.

Bartók's prominence has rather overshadowed his Hungarian forebear, **Ernö Dohnányi** (1877–1960), whose two violin and two piano concertos merit occasional hearing, not least as alternatives to his familiar Variations on a Nursery Song for piano and orchestra (1913). His first essay in the medium, the First Violin Concerto (1907–8), comes from the early period in which he was strongly influenced by the more radical tendencies of French and Russian music—Debussy and Scriabin—and by the great German late-Romantics, especially Richard Strauss. It was unknown until it became available after the death in 1956 of the violinist Stefi Geyer, with whom Bartók was in love when the concerto was composed. Its allusive, rather reticent Romanticism gives it the character of a secret, coded message. But Bartók did not suppress the music entirely. The first movement, slightly changed, became the first of the *Two Portraits* for orchestra, 'The Ideal', first performed in 1909. (As for Stefi Geyer, she later inspired two Swiss violin concertos, by Othmar Schoeck (1912) and Willy Burkhard (1943)).

The concerto was preceded by two single-movement works for piano and orchestra, Rhapsody and Scherzo, neither of great intrinsic interest, though useful preparations for the eventual development of a mature concerto style.

The musical world of Bartók's First Piano Concerto (1926) was radically different. It came after a long period of development in which he had produced many of his best works—the opera *Duke Bluebeard's Castle* (1911), the String Quartet No. 2 (1915–17) and the ballet *The Miraculous Mandarin* (1918–19), as well as the two violin sonatas, the Dance Suite for orchestra, and a large amount of piano music, culminating in the sonata and the suite *Out of Doors* which immediately precedes the concerto. Ever since the *Allegro barbaro* (1911) Bartók had made the insistent exploitation of the piano's percussive qualities the basis of a highly dramatic but intensely anti-Romantic language very much his own, and it was a language well suited to the rugged modality and angular rhythms which he brought from his folk-music studies into his own compositional style. The mid-1920s were the high point of that Bartókian anti-Romantic phase, when, without resorting to the kind of allusions and strategies found in wholeheartedly neo-Classical composers, Bartók was able to use traditional formal outlines to project a musical argument in which motivic economy and contrapuntal dexterity made a formidable combination, to the well-nigh total exclusion of gentler lyricism. There was clearly a danger that the slow movements of large-scale works in this manner might be dangerously austere, even arid, without the flow of lyric melody. Yet, as the central *Andante* of the First Piano Concerto shows, Bartók could provide a more than adequate contrast to the prevailing forcefulness of the outer movements in music that by no means shunned melodic breadth in the service of sustaining a serious, often sombre atmosphere of great intensity.

Even in this, his most radical concerto, Bartók never totally abandons tonality, although it is the kind of radically extended tonality that the modal characteristics of folk-music encouraged him to explore. The large-scale forms, relating in outline to those of the Classical tradition, are filled out by writing that frequently employs *ostinatos*, yet the music is dynamic and forward-moving, never static, and the solo writing is explicitly virtuosic, in dazzling passage-work and vertiginous leaps that triumphantly proclaim the adaptability of earlier notions of display to the modern style, as they did in contemporary concertos by Prokofiev and Stravinsky.

For many listeners the most radical aspect of Bartók's First Piano Concerto is his use of the orchestra. The strings are absent altogether in the middle movement, and throughout, in keeping with the style, wind, brass and—especially—percussion are given great prominence. This emphasis is less pronounced in the Piano Concerto No. 2 (1930–1), a work often felt to be more approachable, more genial yet no less powerful and original than

No. 1. Though like its predecessor in having three movements, No. 2 borrows from the Fourth String Quartet (1928) a formal scheme that became a crucial feature of Bartók's later manner. In Classical and Romantic symphonic music it was customary to regard the form of the whole work as progressive, whether or not the most weighty music came in first movement or finale. But Bartók began to employ a more explicit, arch-like correspondence between movements placed about a pivotal centre. This was prompted, perhaps, by the symmetrical properties of pitch modes that divide the octave into equal segments, pivoting on a central tritone, rather than by the unequal divisions of the usual major or minor scale, as well as by his awareness of the way in which the twelve-note composers, from the mid-1920s onwards, used a single intervallic sequence to generate all the thematic ideas of a work. This is clearest in his five-movement compositions (the String Quartets Nos 4 and 5) in which the materials of movements one and five, and of two and four, are closely related. But Bartók also establishes clear parallels between the first and final movements of the Second Piano Concerto and even closer ones, six years later, in the Second Violin Concerto. In both cases the finale is much more than a mere re-run of the first movement: it is more like a large-scale variation, with appropriate changes of character. Nevertheless, Bartók intensifies the overall symmetry of the Second Piano Concerto by dividing the central movement into three parts— Adagio, Presto, Adagio—and by making the finale a seven-section Rondo, pivoting on its central episode, even though the sixth section does not mirror the second: it has 'new' material, deriving from the first movement's main contrasting theme. As has often been noted, the style of this concerto's highly contrapuntal outer movements, and especially the first, is more overtly neo-Classical—Bach-like even—than anything Bartók had written previously. The force and originality of the music scarcely suffer from this association, however, and the more lyrical, atmospheric material of the Adagio with its string chorale, offset by the nocturnal mood-painting of the shadowy Presto, a feature of many of Bartók's mature compositions, also contributes to a wider variety of mood and expression than is found in the First Piano Concerto.

It is precisely the distinction and dynamism of its lyric melody that makes the Second Violin Concerto (1937–8) so memorable, and one of the best of all twentieth-century contributions to the genre. Although its reliance on symmetry is substantial, and its musical language is less astringent than that of the two earlier piano concertos, the result is never predictable or soft-centred. The quiet, repeated harp triads with which the work opens may in themselves seem almost daringly simple, but the alliance they embody between rhythmic purposefulness and harmonic richness, soon opening out the basic B major tonality to include a wide range of chromatic elements, splendidly displays the composer's confidence and control, even before the soloist enters with a melody whose strength is matched by its sweep. The most energetic material in the first movement is generally subordinate to this spacious lyricism—a quality sustained with special distinction in the early part of the development section, where the exchanges between the violinist and various woodwind soloists have a direct poetic appeal (Ex. 3). The extended tonality of the music even enables Bartók to include a twelve-note theme without lapsing into more than momentary atonality. This underlines his desire to diversify tonality in as many ways as seemed to him musically justified rather than engineering a negative confrontation between tonal and atonal elements. As already mentioned, the concerto's finale is a spirited

Ex. 3

rethinking of the first movement's form and materials, as complementary in mood as it is comparable in ideas and methods. The effect of the central *Andante tranquillo* is especially difficult to pin down in words. It is one of Bartók's most allusive and subtle compositions in that, although the formal outline of theme and variations is unambiguous, its details are delightfully delicate and mercurial. If a single, decisive factor has to be picked out, however, then it is surely the shifting relationship between the rhythm of the theme and the basic 9/8 metre, a relationship enabling Bartók to sustain a constant, teasing ambiguity between background and foreground. No less subtle is the use of the orchestra: the treatment of timpani and strings at the start of the first variation is one of many possible examples of such imagination.

While it would be incautious to declare that none of Bartók's compositions after the Second Violin Concerto equalled the genius of that work, it is quite safe to claim that neither of the solo concertos do so. The transcription of the Sonata for Two Pianos and Percussion for two pianos and orchestra (1940) though worth hearing, remains too deeply under the shadow of the very special and specific sound world of the original sonata to have a truly independent existence as a concerto. The Piano Concerto No. 3, despite the fact that the last 17 bars had to be filled out by Tibor Serly after Bartók's death, is a stronger work than its more voluble detractors have allowed. The haunting lyricism of its opening, while worlds away from the forceful launchings of the First and Second Concertos, is no less memorable, not least because Bartók's musical idiom is ideally suited to exploring the tonal—modal—shifts and inflections of the basic idea. Despite its marking, the *Adagio religioso* is not a mawkish lament by an ailing composer but a moving recreation of the world of Beethoven's 'Heiliger Dankgesang', to which it clearly alludes: and the finale, shunning, like all Bartók's late works, the arch-like symmetries common in the 1930s, has genuine vitality and good-humour, not least in the contrapuntal excursions that reinforce the composer's long-sustained independence of the more turgid manifestations of neo-Classicism. The Viola Concerto was completed by Tibor Serly from the composer's sketches. There is enough of Bartók in it to make occasional hearings welcome; nevertheless, for most music-lovers the concerto that best represents the strengths of Bartók's American years is the Concerto for Orchestra (1943). Here, reverting to a five-movement scheme but without the arch-form correspondences of the fourth and fifth quartets, Bartók creates a magnificently satisfying fusion of lively musical argument and sheer brilliance of instrumental colour. There is no shortage of deep and direct emotion, as the central *Elegia* reveals. But even if some of the work's ideas express longing for that prewar Hungary that was lost for ever, there is nothing in the least in-turned or melancholic about the dazzling contrapuntal textures and finely controlled harmonic processes that underpin and project the music's essential vitality.

Schoenberg

Bela Bartók was the central European composer of the first half of the twentieth century whose music most memorably reinvigorated those traditional values associated with 'well-made' forms in the symphonic tradition, and with harmony that communicates through essentially hierarchic modes of organization, even if the relationships involved are no longer those of the tonal system as understood in the eighteenth and nineteenth centuries. Furthermore, Bartók's concertos are the best sector of his output, after the string quartets, in which to observe the full results and rewards of that reinvigoration. The prospect then arises of a substantial if not complete contrast with that other great central European master **Arnold Schoenberg** (1874–1951), dedicated to rejecting what Bartók chose to retain, and whose concertos are of far less interest than his operas, chamber works or other symphonic music. But such an attempt at contrast soon collapses into implausibility. Although Schoenberg's musical language—atonal, twelve-note—was certainly not hierarchic to the extent that it retained clear and consistent links with fundamental features of tonal procedure, his forms and textures sound more like resourceful reshapings of traditional modes of organization than like wholesale rejections of them. As for whether or not his concertos are of lesser interest than other areas of his output: their interest is certainly great enough for them to enshrine much that is most representative of this troubling but major figure in modern music.

It was at the height of his most radical, Expressionist phase, in 1912, that Schoenberg earned some much needed money by providing continuo realizations for two concertos by the minor eighteenth-century composer M. G. Monn—one for cello in G minor and one for keyboard in D major. More than 20 years later Schoenberg returned to this keyboard concerto, recomposing rather than arranging it for cello and orchestra as an intended vehicle for Casals. That task occupied him from November 1932 to January 1933, and later the same year, between May and August, he transformed Handel's *Concerto grosso* Op. 6 No. 7 into a concerto for string quartet and orchestra. With such activities, Schoenberg might seem to have been trying to beat the neo-Classicists at their own game: rather than making his own music sound like 'wrong-note' Bach, he makes Monn and Handel sound like would-be Schoenbergs! He could do this without total loss of credibility because his transformations of eighteenth-century models used techniques of motivic elaboration comparable to those which provided the primary generative force for his own 'real' music: Schoenberg was not so much an atonal, or twelve-note composer, as a motivic composer dedicated to the idea that composition required the gradual wresting of stability and equilibrium from an initially unstable state. He therefore saw no inconsistency in replacing tonal harmony and retaining traditional formal outlines, since he felt that these still provided a valid basis for that exploration of motivic processes—imbalance progressing to balance—that constituted the true task of the composer. And Schoenberg's irritatingly arrogant belief in his own rightness—in a letter he talks of the 'defects of the Handelian style': excessive sequences, and the fact that 'the theme is always best when it first appears and grows steadily more insignificant and trivial in the course of the piece'[1]—does not mean that his own music is actually unsuccessful.

1. See Reich, *Schoenberg*, London, 1971, p. 185.

Schoenberg's own concertos—for violin (1935–6) and piano (1942)—were both relatively late works from his American years, which absorb and reflect the rich and varied experiences of more than three decades of symphonic and solo instrumental composition. Neither in any sense forgoes the immediate excitement of making virtuoso demands—the Violin Concerto, in particular, is of supreme technical difficulty—but both are firmly in the tradition of the Brahmsian symphonic concerto, with extended motivic development and elaborate thematic argument. The Violin Concerto is the larger of the two, in three substantial movements, each in the three principal parts conveniently termed 'exposition', 'development' and 'recapitulation'—and that convenience need not be rejected here, provided the overriding tendency to make development continuous and cumulative is acknowledged. As with Bartók's Second Violin Concerto, the first movement is the most expansive, the finale the most energetic, the central *Andante* (*grazioso* in Schoenberg, *tranquillo* in Bartók) the most reflective. The severe technical demands Schoenberg makes on his soloist are evident early in the first movement's triple stoppings and elaborate use of harmonics: the atmosphere soon becomes tense, but with that urgent sense of eloquence and aspiration that is typically Schoenbergian. The composer lightens the atmosphere by giving the central development section of the first movement a dance-like character—a nostalgic evocation of a Viennese waltz. The drama of the later stages of the movement is enhanced by making the start of the recapitulation a turbulent tutti, and before the coda there is a short, uncompromisingly concentrated cadenza.

After such a demanding first movement, the predominant delicacy and reticence of the *Andante* is welcome. Not that the movement is without its upheavals, or its contrapuntal enrichments, and there is a powerful climax before the restrained conclusion. But the mood is altogether less sombre and striving than that of the initial *Allegro*. The soloist then launches the finale in a determinedly cheerful frame of mind, and there is an early indication of the rhythmic verve that will sustain the movement to its end (Ex. 4). Even so, this is no lightweight *jeu d'esprit*: there is an abundance of contrapuntal detail, and the whole is shaped with great skill to provide an appropriately substantial conclusion. The Violin Concerto, it can be argued, is the most imposing instrumental composition of Schoenberg's twelve-note phase, more ambitious in form than the Variations Op. 31, and reflecting in its absorbing tussle between intellect and emotion the concerns of the unfinished opera *Moses und Aron*. The Piano Concerto is less monumental: more concise in form yet more relaxed in manner. The Violin Concerto consciously challenges and confronts its great Romantic predecessors. While the form of the Piano Concerto is inconceivable without the precedents of

Ex. 4

those nineteenth-century four-movements-in-one schemes that Schoenberg had already adapted in much earlier works, it achieves a completely personal fusion of old and new that is quite without the usual attributes associated with the label 'neo-Classical'.

Apart from the formal outline, and aspects of the piano writing, what is most evidently 'old' in this music are the hints of traditional, consonant harmony, especially towards the end. Schoenberg often allowed such 'anachronisms' into his atonal compositions, perhaps because—whatever their expressive effect—they can scarcely be said to establish tonalities: there are not enough of them, nor do they set up those types of relationship that would justify linking them to the harmonic schemes and chordal progressions of true tonality. But if the *Ode to Napoleon*, written immediately before this concerto, is Schoenberg's sincere, serious outburst against the follies and horrors attendant on the Second World War, the Piano Concerto itself is his stoic acknowledgement that all bad things, however horrible, eventually come to an end. The composer described the work's four linked movements in a wry stanza:

> Life was so easy;
> But suddenly hatred broke out:
> A serious situation was created:
> But life goes on.

The tone is set by the balanced, expressive phrases of the opening piano melody, which could convince as a waltz-like salon piece—until one hears how Schoenberg makes it justify its presence in symphonic music. Even in this first section textures often become intricate, the orchestra sharing fully in the thematic process, the soloist accompanying with figurations whose doublings and rhythmic dispositions betray a Brahmsian ancestry. With the *Molto Allegro* ('Hatred broke out') a more turbulent spirit comes to the fore, and one has the sense of Schoenberg using rhythm as a means of restraint, regular phrase patterns preventing the turbulence from becoming positively destructive. The third section is an *Adagio*, progressing expeditiously from refined orchestral writing to a grandiose declamation by the soloist of its principal thematic idea. This is the section in which Schoenberg's transformation—radical, yet still recognizable—of his Romantic heritage is most palpable: 'a serious situation'. But after an imposing climax, the piano responds with a brief, shrugging cadenza, and launches the finale, *giocoso*. This predominantly ebullient material ('life goes on') expands to embrace reminiscences of the *Adagio* theme and also, more prominently, of the concerto's first, lyrical melody. The ending is not exactly a throwaway, but it does sustain the general good humour of these final stages. On its own, very considerable merits, Schoenberg's Piano Concerto is a convincing refutation of the argument that serial music cannot express lighter moods. Moreover, taken with the Violin Concerto, it offers powerful support to the thesis that the concerto genre could be made compatible with more radical forms of musical expression—a thesis that would be argued even more determinedly after 1950.

As Schoenberg's best-known pupils, **Alban Berg** (1885–1935) and **Anton Webern** (1883–1945) reveal obvious and seemingly absolute differences. Berg never lost touch with late-Romanticism, whereas Webern's roots were in the polyphonic art of Medieval and Renaissance music. Berg wrote extended works for large forces, Webern highly concentrated compositions for small numbers of performers. Despite such contrasts, however, there was also common ground—notably the propensity both pupils shared with their master for the retention of traditional formal principles and textural features, despite the radically new possibilities offered by the twelve-note method. Of the two, however, it was Berg who contributed most significantly to the concerto: indeed, Webern's only composition with that title, his Op. 24, could just as well be called 'Nonet'. It offers a characteristically lucid motivic debate between piano and groups of wind and strings, and although at one stage in the work's evolution its title was indeed 'Piano Concerto', its essential ethos is the intimate interplay of chamber music.

The interplay between chamber music and full-scale concerto has proved to be one of the twentieth century's most fruitful developments, for while the title 'chamber concerto' tends to suggest soloist(s) accompanied by chamber orchestra, or else a concerto-style work for chamber orchestra, it can also imply a tension between large-scale concerto characteristics and the possibilities available within chamber groups. Such a tension is crucial to one of the modern period's most remarkable concerted works, the Chamber Concerto for piano, violin and thirteen wind instruments by Alban Berg. Written to honour Schoenberg on his fiftieth birthday in September 1924, but not actually completed until July 1925, this work consciously sets out to employ an elaborate (pre-) compositional scheme in the service of music that is deeply felt. What that scheme comprises stems from the score's epigraph: 'all good things come in threes'. There are three movements for 15 players, 960 bars in length, the first movement (240 bars) in six sections, the second (also 240 bars) again in six sections, and the finale—after a 54-bar cadenza—in three sections (426 bars, including repeats). At the outset a motto is heard in which Schoenberg (piano), Webern (violin) and Berg (horn, representing the accompanying ensemble) are evoked by the various musical letters from their names, and this material is developed with unflagging imagination as the concerto proceeds.

All this may suggest a self-defeatingly complex amount of purely intellectual contrivance, yet it is arguable that Berg would have been unable to create music which sounds so spontaneous without the stimulus of such schemes—schemes in which his own favourite numbers 23 and 10 are often conspicuous. What matters is the result, and in the Chamber Concerto we have an initial variation movement of uncommon elegance and drama, an eloquent *Adagio* (in which the piano is silent, save for marking the mid-point with twelve very soft, low C sharps), and a brilliantly witty finale, set in motion by a dazzling double cadenza. The Chamber Concerto is as rich in atmosphere as it is in ideas. Even so, it can seem, in comparison with other works of Berg, to be embracing elaboration and complexity at the expense of direct and fully focused emotional expression. Certainly, it is the sense of having penetrated to the very heart of an idea, and an emotion, which gives Berg's Violin Concerto (1935) an impact and an appeal which is arguably greater than that of any other twelve-note composition, and of most other twentieth-century concertos.

That impact and appeal may be profoundly direct, yet the concerto is the result of a typically Bergian complex of interacting, even conflicting ideas and intentions. Its most explicit purpose is to act as a requiem for Manon Gropius, the 'angel' referred to in the dedication—the daughter of Walter Gropius and Alma Mahler, who died at the age of 18 in April 1935. In these terms the two movements of the work function first as an evocation of the girl herself, then as a lament—at first impassioned, then (with the entry of Bach's harmonization of J. R. Ahle's chorale 'Es ist genug') resigned. And yet the concerto's principal musical idea—a twelve-note row whose triadic and whole-tone segments do not so much give the work a basis in traditional tonality as enable Berg to allude to tonal harmony (a Carinthian folk-song in the first movement, the chorale harmonization in the second) while leaving the relationship between those allusions and the predominant atonal serialism ambiguous and, ultimately, unresolved—is itself teasingly ambivalent, hinting at other levels of meaning. For many years the only other level was assumed to be Berg's fatalistic awareness of his own precarious hold on life. But it now seems clear that when he composed the concerto he was not so much expressing a premonition of his own imminent death as recalling an event from his past—his youthful relationship, in Carinthia, with a young woman, Marie Scheuchl. In particular, it was this relationship that motivated the inclusion of the folk-song in the first movement, rather than any associations with Manon Gropius, and it may also have something to do with that extraordinary combination of the expression-marks *religioso* and *amoroso* in the finale.

Whatever the autobiographical elements involved, however, Berg's Violin Concerto stands as an impressively original piece of musical architecture. Instead of a three-movement design, Berg devised a two-movement plan, each movement further divided into two, with all four main sections essentially arch-like in shape. So, the first movement's *Andante* and *Allegretto* are complemented in the second by an *Allegro* (primarily a large-scale cadenza) and an *Adagio* (the chorale variations). In mood as well as tempo, therefore, the second movement is more extreme than the first, and this reinforces the large-scale avoidance of symmetry, the music progressing from a relatively calm and carefree state through a catastrophe to an ending which is neither resolution nor dissolution but an appropriately ambiguous combination of the two. It is very much a solo concerto: the soloist is rarely silent, and Berg uses a large orchestra with great skill to solve potential problems of balance. The solo violin part may not be quite as taxing as that of Schoenberg's concerto, but it is superbly conceived for the instrument. From the haunting use of the open strings at the beginning to the celebrated canon of the cadenza (Ex. 5) and on to the final meditation on the chorale melody, the violin's ability to range from seductive sweetness to astringent declamation is explored with an imagination unsurpassed in the twentieth-century repertory.

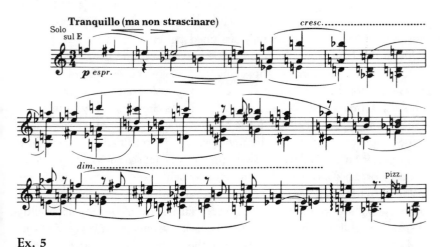

Ex. 5

Post-War Developments

It might occasionally be suspected that the solo concerto would not have survived the more radical musical developments of the second half of the twentieth century had it not been for a few enlightened virtuosi willing, even eager, to perform new and challenging works: Rostropovich is the pre-eminent example. But it is equally clear that the genre itself has remained a challenge, and an attraction, not least to composers who see themselves as reacting to conventions and traditions, from the earlier twentieth century as well as the more distant past, without wishing to reject them out of hand.

No central European composer of our time has shown a more remarkable and convincing stylistic transformation than the Polish-born **Witold Lutosławski** (*b.* 1913). He began his career within the relatively conservative framework of a cultural climate in which Shostakovich and Prokofiev (and by no means everything they wrote) represented the limits of what was acceptable. His Concerto for Orchestra (1950–4) is a good example of what could be achieved within such constraints. It is not flawless—the finale is too long and episodic—but it is none the less an imposing and brilliant score. Then, in the late 1950s, with the 'thaw' in the cold war affecting Poland no less than other Eastern European countries, Lutosławski was at last able to respond to avant-garde developments in Western Europe and America: to the greater range of harmonic possibilities that arose when all twelve notes were kept in play (though Lutosławski in general has shunned the rigours of serial pitch-ordering) and the stimulus to performers that became possible when the often frustrating demands of complex rhythmic notation was jettisoned in favour of something freer. Here too Lutosławski did not embrace thorough-going 'indeterminacy' of the kind John Cage and others were advocating; instead in what he termed 'aleatory counterpoint', he gave performers the freedom to play assigned patterns or groups of pitches without fixed durations, but in prescribed periods of time, usually marked in seconds and intentionally approximate. In 1969 he employed his new techniques for the first time in a concerto, composing a powerful and highly personal work for the cellist Rostropovich. As Steven Stucky points out, Lutosławski 'approached the form, as he had approached other large-scale closed forms before it, not to revive it but to reformulate its essential principles in an original way'.[1] That originality is not so much in the essential concept of the concerto, where an independent, capricious individual (the soloist) confronts and gradually learns to live with a 'society' (the orchestra), as in the skilful way the overall form accumulates from so many apparently disparate yet ultimately compatible episodes. The opening, an extended solo cadenza, could hardly be simpler. Yet the rewards of Lutosławski's new flexibility, in the way the attention of the interpreter is directed to characterization as much as to sheer technique, are abundantly evident. (As the notation makes clear, quarter-tones are an important part of the effect of this passage: Ex. 6.) The sheer variety of moods in this concerto makes for absorbing listening, but the process never seems arbitrary, the argument never becomes diffuse. Above all, by allowing the final section to embody the most dramatic confrontation between soloist and orchestra, Lutosławski ensures that the whole structure achieves its culmination in the most satisfying and, in the event, quite traditional way. Whether or not the ending represents the individual triumphing over an unfeeling environment, or learning to live with hostile forces, and even converting them to his will, it is a positive, invigorating conclusion.

Despite some mellowing in recent years, Lutosławski has remained faithful to the hard-won technical innovations of his most visionary phase. By contrast, his younger Polish contemporary **Krzysztof Penderecki**

---

1. Steven Stucky, *Lutosławski and his Music*, Cambridge, 1982, p. 172.

Ex. 6

(*b.* 1933) has on the whole abandoned the rather modish avant-gardisms of his youth for a more traditional, neo-Romantic manner. Of his concertos, that for violin, written for Isaac Stern in 1976, is ambitious and wholehearted in its embrace of this new conservatism. But a more imaginative exploration of the genre will be found in the music of the Hungarian-born **György Ligeti** (*b.* 1923). Like Lutosławski, Ligeti benefited from close contact with the radical music of the late 1950s, though unlike Lutosławski he now lives in the West. The Cello Concerto (1966), the Chamber Concerto for thirteen players (1969–70) and the Concerto for flute, oboe and orchestra (1972) all display Ligeti's ability to animate quite simple processes of textural change in ways that productively set off mysteriously still and manically active ideas against one another. Ligeti's concern to probe the possibilities of instrumental sonority is reflected in his often fanatically detailed notation, intended to inspire as much as to instruct the player: the eight *pianos* at the start of the Cello Concerto (quadruple *pianissimo*) is perhaps the most extreme example! The whole work, written not for Rostropovich but for Siegfried Palm, explores the complementary relationship between the very slow, soft music of the first movement, which tests technical control and concentration, and the much more actively virtuosic second movement in which elaborate, often wild, roulades predominate. Such contrasts also underpin the four movements of the Chamber Concerto, which can oscillate quite naturally between beguiling, impressionistic colour-washes like that of the opening, and vehement expressionistic assertions where warring rhythmic patterns fight it out in music of tremendous dynamic force. Like Lutosławski, Ligeti is able to find strong points of focus while employing the total chromatic, and so his music, while theoretically 'atonal', offers the listener easily detectable reference-points—the sense of an elaborate surface activating quite simple basic outlines which expand and contract organically. In his more recent music, including a piano concerto that has been performed in an incomplete version, there are signs that Ligeti's interest in building up forms from intriguing polyrhythmic processes is achieving a positive rapprochement with a style that appears on the surface more traditional in harmony and melody, though the effect is no less personal.

Henze

Ligeti is a Hungarian who has written most of his best music in Germany and Austria: but the leading contemporary German composer of concertos, **Hans Werner Henze** (b. 1926) has lived for many years in Italy. Henze's first essays in the form date back to 1947: that is, before Richard Strauss's last concerto was completed. Henze's Chamber Concerto for piano, flute and strings, and the Concertino for piano, wind and percussion are both student works, conservatively neo-Classical. And while the First Violin Concerto is both more ambitious and more forward-looking, in its musical language it is essentially another preliminary, with more than a nod to Hindemith. Henze first found his fully personal voice in vocal music, especially opera, and when he returned to the concerto form in the mid-1960s he not only used the medium to chart a crucial development from lyrical to more abrasive music: he used it as a vehicle for drama.

In 1966, after the *Concerto vocale e strumentale* 'Muses of Sicily' for chorus and orchestra, came two relatively small-scale but finely crafted works, the Double Concerto for oboe, harp and strings, and the Double-bass Concerto. Both intentionally embodied the 'characters' of the virtuosi for whom they were written: Heinz and Ursula Holliger, and Gary Kerr: both were unashamedly up-to-date in exploiting the latest playing techniques, notably oboe multiphonics. Then came the large-scale Piano Concerto No. 2 (1968) in which the central character is Henze himself. With its use of the piano to project long, rhythmically supple paragraphs this is very much a concerto in the grand manner, its 45-minute single movement leading to a final section inspired by Shakespeare's Sonnet No. 129—'The expense of spirit in a waste of shame/Is lust in action'. Henze himself has described the work as one 'in which the antagonism between strict form and formlessness, compulsion and freedom, moderation and excess, is resolved in various frames of reference.[1] It remains a matter of opinion as to how successful—how conclusively audible—this resolution is. But in exploring these various antagonisms Henze confronts some of modern music's most profound and challenging features with flair as well as seriousness.

The Second Piano Concerto may be problematic music: emotionally outgoing yet elusive in thematic shape and harmonic logic. After it, Henze tended to make the literary and dramatic connotations of his concertos more explicit, most notably in the Violin Concerto No. 2 for solo violin, tape, voices and 33 instrumentalists (1971), which is as much music theatre as concert work, and shares the fashion of the time for making reference to older music by means of literal quotations. The soloist, who appears 'wearing a tricorn hat with feather, and a flowing red-lined cape', is required to act in the spirit of Baron Munchhausen, a character celebrated in German literature as a resourceful teller of tall stories. The concerto's more immediate literary source is a poem by Hans Magnus Enzensberger about Gödel's theorem: 'in any sufficiently rich system of axioms, propositions exist that have a meaning which within the system itself cannot be proved nor refuted, unless, of course, the system is inherently inconsistent'. As the poem bluntly puts it, by way of elucidation: 'freedom from contradiction is a defect, or else a contradiction in terms'. Henze's own intention is to link a Munchhausen-like relish for fantasy to a Gödel-like acknowledgement that apparent contradictions, like that between the style of the *Lachrymae Pavan* and his own music, which are superimposed at various points, are to be exploited and enjoyed. The result—provided it is not taken too seriously—is an entertaining diversion, that needs to be seen as well as heard, and it contains much arresting musical invention, not least a cadenza for solo violin and trombone, whose free rhythmic notation is typical of much of this score.

Two years after the second violin concerto Henze composed what might be designated his Third Piano Concerto—*Tristan*, preludes for piano, electronic tapes and orchestra (1973); a mesmeric meditation in which elements of Wagner's *Tristan* and other musical found-objects are transformed and confronted by aspects of Henze's own life and thought at the time, as he has explained in one of his fascinating essays. As with the Second Piano Concerto, the result is possibly too personal to make for easy listening: the composer wants to communicate, and yet his need seems to be as much to understand himself as to reach out to other listeners. A more recent *concertante* composition, *Le Miracle de la Rose* for clarinet and thirteen

1. Hans Werner Henze, *Music and Politics. Collected Writings 1953–81*, London, 1981, p. 159.

players (1981), makes a stronger impression in purely musical respects, and this helps to justify its function as 'imaginary theatre'—Henze's term—and its links with a literary programme involving the writings of Jean Genet.

Berio

Though Italian composers are considered in the following section, it seems appropriate here to discuss the cosmopolitan figure of **Luciano Berio** (*b.* 1925). Of Henze's near-contemporaries, Berio has made the most significant contribution to the repertory of concertos and *concertante* compositions. The concerto principle is crucial to the series of chamber works called *Chemins*, elaborations of some of the solo *Sequenze*. Berio has also paid his own tribute to Rostropovich in *Ritorno degli snovidenia* (1977), for cello and orchestra. The Italian/Russian title means 'the return of dreams', and the music reflects in elaborate, allusive fashion on Russian folk materials that are never heard as such. As much as any of these post-war masters, Berio adopts the concerto principle only to challenge it. In a note written for the New York première of his Concerto for two pianos and orchestra (1972–3) he declared that 'the relationship between soloist and orchestra is a problem that must ever be solved anew, and the word "concerto" can be taken only as a metaphor'. Exactly how 'new' such a very basic relationship can be made is a moot point: after all, even to use the soloists as accompanists to members of the orchestra, as Berio does here, is hardly unprecedented. What seems clear is that, provided the musical material is characterful, memorable and suitable for development or elaboration, then any unavoidable lack of novelty in the relationship between soloist and orchestra will matter little. Berio's two-piano concerto is an intriguing demonstration of unfailing textural imagination allied to formal control, the potentially forbidding richness of the musical materials held in check by clearly prepared and presented points of focus. At the end, when the two solo pianos finally shake off the orchestral pianist to conclude the work on their own, there is even an allusion to consonant harmony, though in view of the superimpositions involved this can hardly be said to turn the concerto into a 'tonal' composition.

If an exhaustive listing of all concertos by central European composers in the past quarter-century were attempted, the full extent of the medium's persistence and adaptability would undoubtedly emerge. But the examples discussed here should already have provided significant evidence, not only of that persistence and adaptability, but of the likelihood that the concerto will survive developments even more radical and challenging than those that have formed twentieth-century music: survive, and remain a source of fascination and enjoyment in the future.

(iii) Italy, Spain and Latin America
Christopher Headington

Italy

Although the concerto was born in Italy and flourished with such masters as Vivaldi and his contemporaries, the nineteenth century and the early twentieth saw that country's leading composers preoccupied with opera, while the major concertos of the time came from elsewhere. However, **Giuseppi Martucci** (1856–1909) was a contemporary of Elgar and Janáček who turned his back on opera. He composed two piano concertos, in D minor (1878) and B flat minor (1885), but despite the advocacy of Toscanini, his music maintains a peripheral hold on the repertoire. 'La generazione dell'80', inspired by Torrefranca, who published a polemic on Puccini[1] were united in their belief that Italian opera had run out of steam and that a 'risorgimento', a renaissance of Italian instrumental music was the only way forward. The three commanding figures of this generation were **Ildebrando Pizzetti** (1880–1968), **Gian-Francesco Malipiero** (1882–1973) and **Alfredo Casella** (1883–1947). Martucci, Leone Sinigaglia (1868–1944) and others had laid the foundations for this reaction against the domination of opera, but the renaissance of Italian instrumental music began with Pizzetti. Yet, it must be admitted, few of his orchestral works or, for that matter, those of Malipiero and Casella have made much headway outside Italy. Pizzetti's *Concerto dell'estate* (1928) is a concerto in name only; the composer himself described it as a 'sinfonia pastorale' but his Cello Concerto (1934) and a Violin Concerto (1945) show fastidious craftsmanship and fine sensibility though their inspiration flows less abundantly than that in the concertos of Malipiero and Casella. Ironically his reputation now rests on his operas such as *Fedre* (1909–12), *Fra Gherardo* (1925–7) and *L'assasino nella cattedrale* (1959) after T. S. Eliot. While Pizzetti soon became a 'conservative' figure in Italian life, Malipiero remained a considerable force in the new music, and an active figure in the ISCM and it is to his pioneering editorial work that we owe the Monteverdi revival. The Violin Concerto No. 1 (1932) has the energy of the neo-Classical composers, the idiom is diatonic with some element of the modal thinking, which permeates much of his music. There is a genuine vein of lyrical feeling, and the work is refreshing and carefree.

His list of works is dauntingly long and includes no fewer than six piano concertos written between 1934 and 1964, two violin concertos (1932; 1963), a cello concerto (1937), a triple concerto for piano trio and orchestra

1. Fausto Torrefranca, *Giacomo Puccini e l'opera internazionale*, Turin, 1912.

(1938) and—written in his late 80s—a flute concerto (1968). There is also a *Concerto di concerti* for baritone, violin and orchestra (1960); this latter work is in six continuous movements and bears witness to the composer's skilful and inventive idiom. The voice (with various texts) is used only intermittently, as in the second movement and the fourth; indeed it is rare for the baritone and violin to be heard together although they are coupled near the end of the rather wistful *Lento* second movement. The impression of a thoroughly competent craftsman who perhaps goes little further is reinforced by a perusal of the Cello Concerto. Its initial *Allegro moderato* has the soloist entering at once with a 'Mannheim skyrocket' upward rush spread over three bars from his low open C through three and a half octaves to treble top G, and this momentum is carried on with a good variety of thematic material, key and texture, while the orchestra too has a positive contribution to make throughout the movement. The central *Lento* has the cello entering with a contemplative yet eloquent 13-bar melody.

This movement builds to a climax *(Molto largo)* but ends as quietly as it began. The finale is an *Allegro* in 4/4 with a bravura cello opening against side-drum/bass-drum accompaniment; much of the writing is cadenza-like in its demands although remaining metrical, and this very forceful movement, with the solo often in the treble clef, ends triple *forte*.

The same kind of effective instrumental writing is also a feature of Malipiero's Triple Concerto written a year later. Here a busy *Allegro* in 3/4 introduces the soloists at once, entering in turn in a resolute C major before the orchestra speaks in bar 13. The strong diatonicism is carried on into the following *Lento*, which has as its main material a kind of archaic chorale. The finale *(Allegro, non troppo mosso)* is again vigorous and chunky. Bravura also plays its part in the Fifth Piano Concerto (1958); but this three-movement work at times gives the impression of being conceived intellectually rather than as effective sound, as in its quasi-atonal harmony and the peculiar final chord for the soloist in the slow movement *(Non troppo lento)*, consisting of the notes G flat, D flat, G natural, C and F. In the Allegro finale 3/4 and 4/4 often alternate, a device also used in the same movement of the Triple Concerto: towards the end a long solo passage is followed by a coda marked *Gaio* that begins with a string fugato.

Alfredo Casella was undoubtedly the most influential musical figure between the two world wars, and of the three composers of 'La generazione dell'80' the most individual. Play the opening of any of his major works, including the Violin Concerto (1928), and a real personality immediately announces itself—neo-Classical, slightly Hindemithian but with a distinctive, Latin face, and a dry ebullient wit. The pastoral central movement of the concerto has great eloquence and nobility. For many years it was championed by Szigeti, who gave the first performance. Yet Casella was an eclectic figure who found his musical nourishment in such disparate figures as Strauss, Albéniz, Debussy and Stravinsky. Strangely enough, for he was a formidable pianist, he wrote no piano concerto; however there are concertos for the organ, and the cello (1935)—and like Milhaud, he wrote a Percussion Concerto (1943). Far better known thanks to his sumptuous Roman trilogy, **Ottorino Respighi** (1879–1936) composed two concertos of note: the Violin Concerto *(Concerto Gregoriano)* (1922) and the *Concerto in modo misolidio* for piano and orchestra (1925). The renaissance of interest in Respighi has revealed some surprises, such as the quality of his opera, *La fiamma*, and the tone-poem *Belkis*. The *Concerto Gregoriano* is an inventive piece, whose neglect will one day surely be rectified. Tovey called it 'a subtle and intimate work', and although the last two movements are inspired by the two Gregorian melodies, they are treated in an individual and unfailingly imaginative way. Nor should we forget **Mario Castelnuovo-Tedesco** (1895–1968), whose Guitar Concerto, Op. 99, written for Segovia, still holds the stage—and so it should, for it is charming, fluent and melodious.

The generation which followed turned away from the neo-Romanticism of Respighi and the modality of Malipiero. **Goffredo Petrassi** (*b.* 1904) began in the neo-Classical style favoured by his mentor, Casella, and his Piano Concerto (1936–9) shows distinctly Hindemithian overtones. (It is difficult to associate Gieseking with it, yet it was he who gave its first performance.) It is powerfully constructed, and there are moments of real vision in the first movement. Its neo-Classical stance does not preclude a high personal voice. There is a flute concerto (1960) but his postwar output is dominated by his eight concertos for orchestra. But as is the case with his contemporary, Luigi Dallapiccola (1904–1975) the solo concerto was not a central concern in his output.

Spain

Although the tradition of the concerto in Spain goes back to Soler, music in modern Spain began with the generation of **Felipe Pedrell** (1841–1922). Neither he nor Enrique Granados embraced the genre, though there is a piano concerto (1887) by **Isaac Albéniz** (1860–1909). It is an early and derivative piece, modelled on Liszt, whom he had met in 1880, and offers little hint of the mature keyboard composer. Better known is the Rapsodia sinfonica of **Joaquin Turina** (1882–1949) for piano and strings. The work is laid out in a clear two-part structure in which a ripe *Andante* bordering on the harmonically commonplace leads to an *Allegro vivo*.

The *Nights in the Gardens of Spain* by **Manuel de Falla** (1876–1946) was originally laid out for piano alone, but Falla recast it most successfully in its present form with orchestra on the suggestion of Ricardo Viñes. Dating from 1915, it is not called a concerto but bears the subtitle 'symphonic impressions': the three movements are called *En el Generalife*, *Danza lejana* and *En los jardines de la Sierra de Cordoba*. What has been called 'the shimmer of an Andalusian night' is a feature throughout and the work begins and ends quietly, but the composer avoids monotony by varying pace, dynamics, texture and colour throughout. The *bisbigliando* (whispering) opening has rapid repeated notes for the soloist that spell out a Moorish-sounding melody hovering hypnotically around D sharp; at figure 5 a *Poco più animato* brings a stamping dance-like vigour, while later another 'Moorish' tune for the soloist (figure 10) has the same two-bar figure repeated three times (Ex. 1).

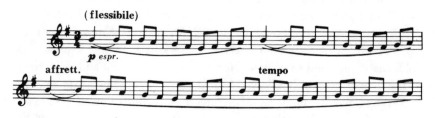

Ex. 1

A near-inversion of this played by the orchestra leads us back to the not dissimilar opening theme, with an 'augmented-triad' harmonization reminding us, as does the instrumentation, of the composer's debt to Debussy; but more material intervenes before the real reprise in the home key of C sharp minor at figure 20. The movement ends *sempre tranquillo* and poetically. It is the longest of the three: the *Distant Dance*, marked *Allegretto giusto*, is about half the length, crisper in style and clearer in outline. Here a rhythm of a minim plus two quavers in 3/4 time is prominent at first, but gives way to another tune at figure 7 introduced by the orchestra and then played *forte*, *molto marcato* by the solo piano. This is developed and then calms to a *pianissimo* restatement which combines the first tune on woodwind with the first phrase of the second, given to the piano. The movement appears to be heading for a quiet end, but instead an upward rush from the soloist leads into the brilliant finale, marked *Vivo*. Its stamping rhythms and blazing instrumentation have been thought to suggest a gipsy festival, and even the somewhat slower sections do not really relax the tension: rather, the piano, playing in octaves at the top of its compass (at figure 28), seems to become a *flamenco* singer of immense charm and presence. Another melody, once again revolving around one note in Moorish manner, is prominent later and highly seductive (Ex. 2). The end of the work, now finding a home key of D major, is quieter but does not lose the intensity of feeling that characterizes the whole work; it seems to tie all the melodic threads together into a sultry and reluctant farewell.

Ex. 2

Falla's other 'concerto' dates from 1926 and represents a move away from the rich impressionism of *Nights in the Gardens of Spain*: it is a chamber piece scored for harpsichord (or piano) with flute, oboe, clarinet, violin and cello. Yet its vigour prevents it from sounding small scale, and the composer's designation of it as a concerto is fully justified. He sought the rehabilitation of the harpsichord which has since taken place, in part thanks to the Polish player Wanda Landowska for whom this concerto was written. Though this instrument has the chief role, each of the other players also has something individual to contribute and in this sense there is less effect of an instrumental 'body' than of a conversational exchange among soloists. There are therefore echoes of the Baroque *concerto grosso* and of the Bach Brandenburg concertos, and in this way the work partakes of the neo-Classicism of its time. However, it seems that Falla's inspiration was also that of old Spain, and in particular its folk, religious and courtly styles: thus the opening *Allegro* alludes to a renaissance madrigal, the *Lento* to a modal *Tantum ergo* and the final *Vivace* with its harpsichord mordents to Scarlatti in his most brilliant keyboard vein. The first movement is in D major, *toccata*-like, lively and alert with various changes of metre that contribute to a general exhilaration. The *Lento* has something of the feverish joy of a Spanish religious procession; marked *giubiloso ed energico*, it includes a kind of march of which this example shows just the top notes of the soloist's richly chordal texture (Ex. 3). The finale of this Harpsichord Concerto makes great play

Ex. 3

with the rhythmic device of hemiola and is in the flexible 3/4 = 6/8 metre of the Andalusian dance called the *polo*; not surprisingly, this is the most brilliant movement of a sparkling work.

The veteran **Joaquín Rodrigo** (*b.* 1901), blind from childhood, is the best known among living Spanish composers, and his Guitar Concerto (*Concierto de Aranjuez*) (1939) probably receives more performances than any other Spanish concerto. This is not surprising, for the work is extremely well written for the instrument and abounds in Spanish colour, being irresistibly dance-like in its outer movements and sounding a movingly elegiac note in its long central *Adagio*, which is evidently a passionate lament for the events of the Civil War, newly ended at the time of its composition, which drove Rodrigo into self-exile. This movement begins with six-note guitar chords against a grave yet ornate melody for cor anglais, then echoed by the soloist with even more passionate melodic elaboration.

Although he has written several other concertos for piano, harp, violin and other concerted guitar pieces, none breaks new ground. The *Concierto de Aranjuez* remains his most personal and eloquent work. There are, of course, other Spanish concertos including guitar concertos by **Ernesto Halffter** (*b.* 1905) and **Antonio Ruiz-Pipo** (*b.* 1933) but the strongest artistic personality to have contributed to that genre is undoubtedly **Maurice Ohana** (*b.* 1914). He was born in Gibraltar of Spanish parents, but settled in Paris and is a French national. A student of Casella, his music conveys a strong sense of Spain and his Concerto (*Tres Graficos*, 1950–7) is full of the atmosphere of Andalusia, the colours strong and the images powerful.

Latin America

Among the Latin American musicians of this century, the chief composers of concertos are the Brazilian **Heitor Villa-Lobos** (1887–1959) and the Argentine **Alberto Ginastera** (1916–1983). Villa-Lobos was enormously prolific and his output encompasses everything from Bachian counterpoint to popular guitar idioms. One may question the judgement and powers of selection that he applied to his teeming ideas. He composed no fewer than 21 works for solo instrument(s) and orchestra including two for bassoon, one for harmonica and one for soprano- or tenor-saxophone, and any survey of them must be selective. The five piano concertos were written between 1945 and 1954 and are thus all fairly late works; each lasts between 20 and 30 minutes and is cast in four movements, the third of Nos 3 and 4 being labelled as a scherzo. The orchestra is frequently on a big scale to match, with four trumpets in the First Concerto and a vibraphone in the Second. The writing itself also incorporates grandiose elements, so that the soloist's first entry in the First Concerto is *forte pesante* and laid out on three staves and the rest of the movement (despite quieter music in G sharp minor at figure 18) is rather busy and noisy. Both this movement and the next are marked *Allegro*, and the second really has too much more of the same kind of writing, with big chords and register changes emphasizing the piano's power and compass. The third movement *(Andante)* is in the manner of a *passacaglia* beginning triple *piano* in the bass, but here too we soon come to more soloistic splashing and banging: a big cadenza (some seven pages of score) needs four staves for its notation. An *Allegro non troppo* finale in 2/4 time has *toccata*-like semiquavers and triplet semiquavers, with many accents, and ends triple *forte*. One cannot help wondering after all this whether the whole work is not too undisciplined in form and unvaried in style. The same doubts persist with the Fifth Piano Concerto.

Villa-Lobos's Second Cello Concerto and Harp Concerto also are late; both come from 1953. The cello work begins *Allegro non troppo* with rising orchestral figures that recur in the other movements, and the soloist enters *impetuoso*: this is a vigorous movement with cross-rhythms, several tempo changes and rather thick scoring—the big orchestra includes a bass clarinet, contrabassoon, tuba and xylophone. The slow movement gives the solo cellist a rich cantilena at his first entry, marked *Largo* (à 6). A middle section to this movement is in duple time and *più mosso*. The third movement is a *Vivace* (Scherzo) that dances along in 6/8 with much ricochet bowing for the soloist; a lengthy cadenza takes the cello to the B over an octave above the treble clef. As for the finale, this is a rough dance, perhaps deliberately primitive in effect. The Villa-Lobos Harp Concerto was created for Nicanor Zabaleta and the very nature of the instrument precludes excessive orchestral sonority. This also holds true of the Guitar Concerto (1951) a work which has found its way into the still small concerto repertory not least because the composer played the guitar and wrote sympathetically for it. The orchestra in this work is in any case of a suitably reduced size: the *Andantino* is perhaps the movement that has most charm and purpose.

Ginastera belongs to a later generation than Villa-Lobos and though also relatively prolific, is a very different kind of artist. He was something of a prodigy and established himself early as a major figure in Argentine music, not least in the theatre. His dramatic gift is reflected also in his concertos: these amount so far to two for piano (1961, 1972) and one each for harp, violin and cello. His First Piano Concerto was commissioned by the Serge Koussevitzky Foundation and is in four movements marked *Cadenza e varianti, Scherzo allucinante, Adagissimo* and *Toccata concertata*. This work has a big orchestra including five percussion players and a brilliant solo entry in double octaves. The scherzo is fragmentary, starting with muted cellos *pppp*; then comes a slow movement that alternates *piano dolcissimo* and *fortissimo appassionato*; finally, we have a movement that is powerful indeed, a kind of primitive romp with thumping *martellato* piano and ending with *ffff* tone-clusters.

The Violin Concerto of 1963, dedicated to its first performers Ruggiero Ricci, Leonard Bernstein and the New York Philharmonic Orchestra, is a work of great intellectual force and imagination. The orchestra includes six percussionists playing (among other things) temple blocks, crotales, bongos, the scrapers called güiro and reco-reco, three 'timbaletas' (small drums) graded in pitch, three tom-toms and three tam-tams similarly graded, a xylophone, marimba and glockenspiel. One would think that left little for the soloist to do, but in fact his part is exceedingly taxing, not merely technically but intellectually. Indeed, this concerto with its deliberate quotations from Paganini's caprices aims at a certain violinistic transcendentalism. The first movement, *Cadenza e Studi*, follows the solo cadenza with a group of 'studies' on a basic note row: for chords, for (double-stopped) thirds, for other intervals, for arpeggios, for harmonics (a fiendish display here) and 'for 24 quarter-tones', carefully notated. There is a coda, 'providing the whole piece with a symmetrical structure', as the composer puts it in his analysis in the score which he asks to be included in concert programmes. In his own words once again, the second movement (called '*Adagio* for 22 soloists') is 'full of poetic concentration and exalted lyricism . . . a developed Lied in five sections . . . the soloist integrates the whole'. There follows a *Scherzo pianissimo e perpetuum mobile*, with an opening *ppp* for percussion at a flying pace; at one point echoes of the Paganini caprices are heard 'as if the shadow of this great violinist were passing through the orchestra'. The Concerto has been called 'an exploration of colour and of mood—from festive to elegiac—of clusters, densities, microtonal complexes and aleatory structures'.

Inevitably, Ginastera's Harp Concerto (1956, then revised after its première in 1965) explores a different world. Nevertheless, this work written for Nicanor Zabaleta (and given its first performance by him with Ormandy and the Philadelphia Orchestra) still uses a surprising degree of chromaticism as well as the *arpeggio* and *glissando* passages that are only to be expected in such a piece. (There are some key signatures for the soloist, but not many.) The orchestra still plays an important role, and the percussion section is again large, four players. The first movement is an *Allegro giusto*, which relaxes at one point for a gentle tune in G minor from the soloist (bar 73); then comes a *Molto moderato* that has been called 'evocative and atmospheric' and an energetic finale introduced by a passage for the soloist marked *Liberamente capriccioso*. It is full of imaginative and individual sonorities.

CHAPTER 11

The American Concerto

Peter Dickinson

The study of the concerto in the work of American composers reveals fascinating dichotomies and polarities. The development of the concerto has reflected European hierarchies, but in the United States it has continued its history in a democratic society. The relation between the soloist and the orchestra, frequently viewed in terms of the individual versus the mass, ought to be differently perceived in North America, where the existence of European, African and Indian traditions offers the potential for a new fusion. But Afro-American music hardly affected so-called serious composers until well into the twentieth century. As in so many ways, **Charles Ives** (1874–1954) was the exception: but he completed no concertos. Just as American as Ives's unique mixture of different types of music is the figure of George Gershwin, starting in tin-pan-alley and conquering the concert hall with all the confidence of successful business on Broadway. Before that the Irish-born Victor Herbert had composed successful orchestral works before turning to the American musical theatre—the opposite of Gershwin's journey from pop to art—and after both of them came Kurt Weill (1900–1950), whose only concerto was written before he emigrated to the USA in 1935.

Consideration of the American concerto ought to begin with **Alexander Reinagle** (1756–1809) and his *Concerto on the Improved Pianoforte with the Additional Keys* (1794), but this work by the English-born disciple of C. P. E. Bach is presumed lost. Judging by Reinagle's four piano sonatas, it must have been a major example of American instrumental music in the eighteenth century. A work from the mid-nineteenth century, which could have occupied a similar position there, is also missing: the Piano Concerto in F minor (1856) by **Louis Moreau Gottschalk** (1829–1869). If the New Orleans-born, French-speaking, travelling virtuoso's Concerto showed the skill of his best solo works in integrating Creole syncopations with European forms, we might have had a precursor of Gershwin's. As it is, the last decade of the nineteenth century contains the first American concertos to have achieved wide currency. Their language reflects the European romanticism of Liszt, Grieg, Wagner and Brahms, much as later generations of American composers would respond to the mainstream of modernism through Stravinsky, Bartók, Hindemith and the Second Viennese School.

Edward MacDowell (1860–1908) was regarded for almost half a century as the first major American composer. Afterwards that position was conceded to Ives. MacDowell went to Europe to learn all the conventional skills that Ives stayed at home to do without. at the age of 15 MacDowell was taken to Paris, where he gained a scholarship at the Conservatoire as a pianist. He was composing all the time but he was fluent in the other arts too. He was offered free tuition as a painter there, and later on wrote poems and memoirs showing the literary bent to be found in other Romantics like Schumann, Berlioz and Wagner.

MacDowell failed to settle in Paris—unlike so many later American writers and composers—but found what he wanted at the Hoch Conservatory in Frankfurt where he studied composition with Joachim Raff. MacDowell played his Piano Concerto No. 1 to Liszt in 1882, who accepted the dedication. The key of A minor seems to be an immediate nod to Grieg's famous example, but the whole work is polished and satisfying in layout. The two concertos deserve their popularity, but it is in the second (1889) that MacDowell uses his strengths and weaknesses to best advantage. He is expert at decoration and, like Mendelssohn, can turn a deft scherzo. He also handles textural contrast dramatically. The opening of the first movement is soft until the shattering solo entry. The brooding chromatics may seem Wagnerian, but they have individual touches (Ex. 1).

Ex. 1

The resolution of the dominant thirteenth created by the melody in bars 4 and 5 on the first beats is not exactly what would have been expected, and the B flat in bar 7 creates a false relation of a kind which, in later American music, would be considered a blue note. The scherzo second movement contains rhythmic patterns which suggest syncopation, but their roots must be nearer to Beethoven's *Leonora* Overture than anything Afro-American. The finale, in its *largo* introduction, makes use of the question-and-answer technique of Beethoven's Fourth Piano Concerto, which also produced a response in Bartók's Third. Overall, MacDowell's concertos are a celebration of technical proficiency in both composer and performer. That gave audiences what they wanted, and was an achievement in the New World at this stage.

MacDowell's teacher was the Venezuelan pianist Teresa Carreño, a pupil of Gottschalk, and he dedicated his Second Concerto to her. Another work dedicated to the same performer was the Piano Concerto in C sharp minor (1899) by **Mrs H. H. A. Beach** (1867–1944), who gave the première herself. Amy Cheney was a child prodigy, well taught in Boston, who was married young to a distinguished physician. Most of her large works were written before her husband died in 1910, and after that she energetically promoted her own music by performing it in Europe, until the First World War, and in the USA. Her performance of the Piano Concerto with the Boston Symphony in 1917 seems to have been the last until Mary Louise Boehm revived it in 1976. The music is full-blooded, virile—if that is not a sexist way to refer to America's answer to Dame Ethel Smyth—and idiomatic. The themes have a disturbing way of recalling other composers and the passage-work is sometimes merely conventional rather than integral. But this does not detract from the accumulating power of the long first movement which, although diffuse, eventually reaches a high level. Greater concentration throughout would have been an advantage.

An earlier concerto which has both the conventional polish and concision of MacDowell is the Second Cello Concerto (1894) by **Victor Herbert** (1859–1924). The Irish-born composer, who was largely brought up in Stuttgart, was a professional cellist and gave the premières of both concertos himself. The second one was performed in New York just as Herbert embarked on his long run of successful operettas. Dvořák was present and admired the work, as well he might since Herbert was a master of all the elements of the Romantic concerto, and Dvořák was yet to write his own Cello Concerto. Herbert was a contemporary of Elgar, responding to some of the same continental influences, and Herbert's work in E minor is at times an uncanny anticipation of Elgar's written in the same key 25 years later. The problem which faced all these composers was how to use the framework of an overwhelmingly Austro-German tradition as the basis for their own national or personal individuality.

There are links with Elgar and with England in another American concerto from the turn of the century. **Horatio Parker** (1863–1919) was an industrious church musician, composer and academic in a typical late Victorian mould. As Professor at Yale he taught Ives, who respected his high principles more than his music. Parker's oratorios were a success at the Three Choirs Festivals, he was awarded an honorary doctorate of music by Cambridge University, and his Organ Concerto (1902) was dedicated to G. R. Sinclair, the organist of Hereford Cathedral portrayed in Elgar's eleventh *Enigma* Variation. Parker studied composition with Rheinberger in Munich and, as with MacDowell, the German model shows through. But the Concerto in E flat minor, scored for an orchestra of strings, brass, harp and timpani, has many imaginative touches. The opening theme of the first movement has a Brahmsian sweep as it rises in unison strings over the sustained tonic chord in the organ. The first movement ends with a self-contained *Andante* in B major, which opens with violin and horn solos and features a harp part throughout, lending traces of Impressionism. The second movement is a tranquil *Allegretto* on a dotted rhythm, where the soloist is in dialogue with the strings neatly unified with timpani figures. The tritone fanfare motif of the finale promises a new range of expression, but soon gives way to a rumbustious fugal exposition for the soloist. Parker sets the traditional personality of the organ against the strings or brass used in blocks with exhilarating if sometimes obvious effect. The ending has a romantic afflatus also found in Parker's oratorio *Hora Novissima* and indeed other religious works of the period such as Ives' cantata *The Celestial Country*.

In his *Memos*, Ives refers to the earlier stages of the Emerson movement in the Concord Piano Sonata (1911–15):

> It grew into more of a piano concerto, opening with several cadenzas, and gradually becoming more and more unified. The Emerson movement is a partial reduction for piano from the sketch of this concerto. I can't now find all of this concerto sketch ... but it was originally in three movements ...

Another lost link in the saga of the American concerto, but there were other composers looking for American sources of inspiration. In 1915 **John Alden Carpenter** (1876–1951) wrote his Concertino for piano and orchestra, which anticipates Gershwin and Copland in forming a style coloured by Latin and Afro-American elements. Carpenter was a well-equipped musician although, like Ives, he earned a living in business after studying with J. K. Paine at Harvard and even managing to get some lessons with Elgar in Rome in 1906. The Concertino's first movement suggests the Latin-American tradition of Gottschalk, but the *Lento Grazioso* responds to Dvořák's interest in indigenous American sources in a surprising way: superficially a pentatonic spiritual, it also sounds like a swung version of the slow movement of the *New World Symphony*. Altogether the designation of concertino is correct since the music's manner is informal and has been compared by the composer to casual and relaxed conversation in a pleasant atmosphere—quite different from the discussions represented in the second string quartets of either Ives or Carter.

Gershwin

Gershwin's *Rhapsody in Blue* (1924) was a landmark of successful communication in the idiom of what came to be called symphonic jazz. The eight years since Carpenter's Concertino and similar works by Henry F. Gilbert had witnessed the epoch-making birth of jazz from pre-jazz forms such as ragtime and blues. Gershwin came from a completely different background in popular music and was thus able to view both jazz and symphonic music as an outsider. This new injection into the mainstream of concert music gave rise to Gershwin's Piano Concerto (1925), commissioned by Walter Damrosch and the New York Symphony Orchestra. *Rhapsody in Blue* drew on jazz mannerisms, the romantic piano concerto, and above all characteristic and memorable melodies. The fact that these ingredients are not completely integrated has never bothered the public. But it is true that the *Rhapsody* works best if its passage-work is played by the soloist with a hard-edged unsentimental treatment typical of Gershwin and his pop background. Gershwin may have realized the formal problems of the *Rhapsody*, in spite of its enormous popularity, since he took more trouble to make a convincing structure out of the Piano Concerto. Even if it proceeds by chunks, the sections are carefully planned to succeed each other dramatically: an opera composer in the making. Gershwin has seldom been given credit for this, so it is a new departure to find Richard Crawford in the *New Grove Dictionary of American Music* (1986) concluding that 'the Concerto forms a convincing organic whole whose impact derives as much from its entire structure as from its separate parts'.

The evidence is that the different styles and sources of the Concerto are carefully selected and controlled. In the first movement, after four bars of percussion fanfare, the important Charleston rhythm is introduced and the following four bars outline another primary motif, a pentatonic figure in dotted rhythm. These two motifs interact to form the movement's introduction to the solo entry with the Concerto's motto theme. Gershwin knew enough about Liszt's cyclic forms to bring all three of these motifs back into the final stages of the finale. There the Charleston cunningly underpins the penultimate piano solo; the final climax is the motto in the grand manner, too often preceded in performance by a feeble rather than a shattering gong stroke; and the piano's last four bars are a reference to the pentatonic figure. The motto (Ex. 2) itself has many original features.

The *glissando* opening is clearly a reflection of the clarinet slide in *Rhapsody in Blue*, an accidental trademark that history has made seem inevitable, and the constant melodic syncopation reflects the black music which Gershwin heard regularly. The harmony is based on major seventh

Ex. 2

chords for the first four bars, then ninth chords. The melodic syncopation is already restless, and the harmonic aspect is disturbed too by the changing chromatic inner voices. The same effect is produced, more obviously, in the E major *Andantino* of the Rhapsody, and also in the accompaniment figure of the second Prelude for piano. If the seventh between melody and bass in bar 1 owes something to Debussy and Ravel—the former's *La plus que lente*, for example—as a sensuous dissonance, then the extension up a minor third in the next bar is a blue note. In the following bar the seventh enters the melody, and again in the next phrase. After such concentration, the theme turns legitimately to sequence for extension and the orchestra returns with a counter-melody for cor anglais and viola, which is only one example of ingenious scoring. Another is the layout of the motto in the strings with the counter-melody in the piano, which is the next event, prepared for by a snappy transition leading to the Charleston motif.

The *Alla breve* section can be regarded as development and variations followed by a suave self-contained 32-bar popular song, the *Moderato Cantabile*. The same thing happens with the *Espressivo con Moto* melody in the slow movement, except that this tune has been anticipated long before, in the early bars of the *Più Mosso* of that movement. The switch from the *Moderato Cantabile* in the first movement to the *Allegro Molto* is abrupt and expertly judged for contrast, as a deliberate crisis. The new texture is rooted in a primitive *ostinato* and both the Charleston and the pentatonic figure are worked out above it. For the *scherzando* variations *(Pochissimo Meno Mosso)* the popular song returns in the orchestra, up tempo, with aspects of the snappy transition contributing towards the final lyrical climax with the motto. The interaction of all these elements is complex. At the final *Allegro con Brio*, the piano has the Charleston plus the snappy transition, and the bass has the pentatonic figure, all simultaneously. Even the piano's last rising flourish (Ex. 3) is related to this figure.

If the first movement exudes the jazz age through dance-hall rhythms and Hollywood lyricism, then the second movement, *Andante con Moto*, is a cross between a nocturne and a blues. This populist concerto democratically shares the honours between a trumpet soloist and the piano, which is silent during the first section. When the piano enters, it takes its cue from a repeated-note figure in the earlier trumpet solo and both before and after the first appearance of the popular song *(Espressivo con Moto)* there is a feeling of improvization, the amiable conversational style suggested by Carpenter in his Concertino. The final surprise is the return of the opening trumpet melody for flute and piano, after the climactic version of the popular song is cut off in full flood.

The finale's *ritornello* sections are based on repeated notes, speeded up

Ex. 3

from those in the work's motto, and a blue-note component related to the snappy transition from the first movement as well as the motto itself. The contrasting episodes also hark back: the first *(Marcato)* is the motto itself, introduced by a quick piano *glissando*, and another is the popular song from the second movement. The trumpet theme (just before *Poco meno con Grazia*) is a new element replete with blue-note inflections which (at figure 16) gives rise to a fugato which would not sound out of place in *The Rite of Spring* (Ex. 4). Further examination provides more detail to support Crawford's assessment of the Concerto's impact as an organic whole.

Ex. 4

Copland

Gershwin's Piano Concerto was written following the success of *Rhapsody in Blue*, and so was Copland's, as the composer confirmed to me in conversation in 1982. Like Gershwin, **Copland** was interested in the symphonic treatment of jazz, but they approached it from different traditions. Of the first movement of his Piano Concerto (1926) Copland says, in *Copland Volume I 1900–1942* (1984), 'the melodic material . . . is taken from a traditional blues, one also used by Gershwin at about the same time in his Prelude No. 2 for piano.' The connection is clear, but Copland's concerto was finished before Gershwin premièred his Preludes in December 1926.

In the earlier part of its life Copland's Piano Concerto was controversial and it nettled the conservative critics. It was commissioned by Koussevitsky, the conductor who did so much for Copland and for American music, and the composer played it himself. Now the work seems typical of both Copland and the 1920s approach to jazz manners by composers such as Milhaud, whose *La Création du Monde* (1923) was a pioneering achievement from a non-American. Copland's Piano Concerto is in two movements: the first exploits what he called the slow blues and the second the snappy number. This pattern was one he followed again in the Clarinet Concerto (1948) with harp, piano and strings. The difference is that the Clarinet Concerto uses an unaccompanied cadenza to change from the slow manner to the fast one, and in the later work the opening slow music seems closer to Satie's *Gymnopédies* than any blues.

The Piano Concerto opens in Copland's fanfare manner, but when the strings enter spaciously the melody rises in Debussian whole-tones securely underpinned with the tonic E major (Ex. 5).

Ex. 5

After this expansive statement recurs at the end of the first movement, it gives way to reminiscences of the first piano solo on a handful of woodwind instruments, leading straight into the brittle honky-tonk piano world of the second movement. The piano even seems to be out of tune, and it would be impossible to guess the length of the commas in the first bars if the composer had not recorded the work himself. Copland thought he was not influenced by Gershwin's concerto, but Charleston rhythms certainly enter into this finale, helping to create the final crisis before the spacious music (Ex. 5) from the first movement recurs. Sometimes the barring is not the same for the solo piano as it is for the orchestra: this creates the impression of free ragging in performance, within obvious limits.

The Clarinet Concerto, written for Benny Goodman, was admired by Stravinsky. It shows the older composer's ability, as in the Symphonies of Wind Instruments, to move deliberately from one type of texture to another. After the placid opening movement—eventually a perfect fusion of Satie and Mahler into pure Copland—the intervening cadenza inclines increasingly to high spirits. The return of the orchestra—harp, piano and strings *col legno* or harmonics—is magical. The plot is dominated by *ostinato*, boogie bass, and fragments of the cadenza in new contexts. At its most serious (Figures 285 and 430), the declamatory style of the Piano Sonata (1939–41) reappears and leads in each case to a crisis, after which the music lightens to jazz-based riffs propelling things further. These junctions form the kind of culture shock which Gershwin manipulated in his concerto. Four years after *Appalachian Spring*, the Clarinet Concerto effects a comparable balance between Apollonian calm and Dionysiac frenzy, reliving the original impact of early jazz at a crucial moment in the development of the most characteristic American composer of the middle twentieth century.

In the concerto the American Romantics of the late nineteenth century set themselves to meet the Europeans on their ground. By the 1920s, supported by the explosion of American popular music and jazz, new means became available if composers wanted them. Gershwin and Copland integrated these with nineteenth- and twentieth-century European traditions as a hybrid source of strength. Other Americans were anxious to use their own resources as exclusively as possible. Most of these did not write concertos— the very word had undesired implications—but some did. **Henry Cowell** (1897–1965) pioneered tone-clusters in piano writing and promoted his own work in five successful European tours between 1923 and 1933. His Piano Concerto (1928) exploits these discoveries in a three-movement work which would have seemed novel in the 1960s. Cowell, soon after writing it, turned his attention to folk-music and non-Western musics. His book *New Musical Resources* (1919, but not published until 1930), gave a technical dimension to his rhythmic, interval and cluster theories, but the later works often seem naïve and casual. In fact, they can be seen as a contribution to a world culture rather than merely Western music. European notions of order do not always maintain. This has been a recurring aspect of the American scene, developed especially in composers such as **Harry Partch** (1901–1974) who did not write for conventional instruments.

Cowell's Piano Concerto is thus a long way both from the American romantics and the jazz age. The work paid for its remoteness by scanty performances in bizarre circumstances. In 1930 the conductorless Beethoven Orchestra could manage to play only the first two movements in New York; the first complete performance was in Havana later that year—both of these with the composer as soloist; but it was apparently not heard complete in the USA until 1978, or at all in Europe until 1987, even though the score had been published in France in 1931. Wilfrid Mellers, in *Music in a New Found Land* (1964), refers to the Concerto as relying on 'percussive violence unrelated to line and structure, grotesque rather than sublime'. In fact, the clusters usually outline melodies, and can often be regarded as accompaniments rather than a continuous assault in Cowell's pugilistic approach to the keyboard.

The first movement is called Polyharmony, a term Cowell used to apply to a type of polytonality comparable to Milhaud's earlier development. The strings are mostly lyrical in this movement: only the soloist remains untamed. (Cowell's solo piano work, *Tiger*, dates from the same period.) The second movement, although called Tone Cluster, is more melodic and it is clear that the clusters are being used as a textural colouring in conjunction with lines and chords. This is a particularly individual technique, at its clearest in the cadenza from this movement.

The last movement, Counter Rhythm, contains massed percussive effects, but also motifs and chords buried amongst the clusters. The last sixteen bars seem to introduce the *Dies Irae* and, as if to avoid retribution for such vandalistic treatment of an instrument which has been a monument of Western music, ends with an overlaid perfect cadence in C major.

Cowell's informal relationship with the musical cultures of the whole world is matched by the cultivation of the commonplace by **Virgil Thomson** (*b*. 1896). The finest expression of this aspect of Thomson is in his operas based on texts of Gertrude Stein. In fact I have claimed, in the *Musical Quarterly* (No. 3, 1986), that Thomson created an exact counterpart to Stein's literary techniques in his music. This colloquial, improvisatory approach is productive in shorter pieces, such as Thomson's long series of *Portraits Drawn from Life*, but is also the rationale behind longer structures such as the Cello Concerto (1950). There are three movements with titles: *Rider on the Plains*, *Variations on a Southern Hymn-Tune* and *Children's Games*. John Cage, in his book on Thomson's music, finds the work to be a kind of self-portrait where 'the most conventional aspects of Western musical structure'—thematic repetitions and the establishment of a single tonality—'do not successfully engage the intellect'. A comparison between Thomson's work and Cage's Concerto for Prepared Piano and Chamber Orchestra (1951) shows that the absence of these same elements can, paradoxically, have the same result. Thomson's concerto, however, belongs in the tradition of Ives's Third Symphony and the less adventurous works of Cowell. The Ives connection is through quotation—the Sunday school hymn-tune and the *Presto* from Beethoven's Piano Sonata, Op. 10, No. 2, in the last movement—and Thomson, in spite of his sophisticated training at Harvard and with Boulanger in Paris, shares Cowell's affection for the simplest materials.

Cowell's unorthodox use of the piano influenced **John Cage** (*b*. 1912) who took these procedures further in his invention of the prepared piano in 1940. In the *Sonatas and Interludes* (1946–8) Cage wrote a set of miniatures based on the binary sonata form of Domenico Scarlatti. With the Concerto, as in the String Quartet just before it, the time-scale is considerably extended. Just as Cowell belongs to world music, so Cage is bound up with oriental philosophy, especially Zen. Cage's position is consistent and disciplined. He felt the need to remove his own personality from his work by accepting the results of processes derived from using the charts in the ancient Chinese Book of Changes, the *I Ching*. The Concerto is a transitional moment in Cage's development. In the first section—'a drama between the piano, which remains romantic, expressive, and the orchestra, which itself follows the principles of oriental philosophy'—there is some freedom. By the last of the three sections, which are played continuously, both soloist and orchestra parts are strictly derived from the charts, and Cage had arrived at the philosophical position which determined the rest of his output. But at this stage, and later, there are still countless personal touches. The prepared piano to start with and, in the percussion section, the water gong, fragments of radio sound, and the amplified coil of wire. The way in which pointillist gestures such as trombone or harp *glissandi* recur in slow motion is a Cage fingerprint: the Concerto is the heir both to Webern's *Klangfarbenmelodie* and Satie's measured phrase-lengths. In the third section Cage is moving towards his silent piece, 4′ 33″, the following year as there are long gaps where silence takes over. This may tire an unprepared audience, but the Concerto is poetic and discerning, unique both in Cage's output and concerto literature. The notorious Concert for Piano and Orchestra (1957–8) is quite different, an indeterminate work with parts but no score, and with elements of theatre.

Cowell, Thomson and Cage have pursued their notions of style as a discipline achieved through a deliberate limitation, which thereby became a liberating force. This approach provided the background for the later minimalists, who did the same thing but went much further. The early repetitive works of **Philip Glass** (*b*. 1937) possessed an exhilaration as a result of emanating from a closely knit group under the composer-performer's own direction. The restriction of means, backed by a firm beat, electronic gadgetry and powerful promotion, nevertheless secured a wide international audience. After a decade of fame, Glass returned to the orchestra via his success in the opera house. Orchestral works such as *Light* and the Violin Concerto (1987) are based on a minimalism of intention, ideas and result, although the technique goes back to Gertrude Stein and Andy Warhol. Lacking the distractions of the opera house or the accoutrements of the rock concert, the concert hall is the most exposing of arenas.

It has been possible to follow a distinctively American strand in the development of the concerto by turning from the jazz-inspired Gershwin and Copland to the pioneering figures of Cowell and Cage. These were the exceptions. Far more concertos written during this century show American composers aware of European master such as Schoenberg, Stravinsky, Bartók and Hindemith: all of them lived in the USA and all wrote concertos. So did other immigrants such as Ernest Bloch and Ernst Křenek. Stravinsky and Hindemith served as models for the young **Lukas Foss** (*b.* 1922), himself an immigrant whose finely crafted Second Piano Concerto (1951, revised 1953) is rarely heard. Later he turned away from neo-Classical models to explore improvisation, indeterminacy and collage. Trends in the arts are often complemented by opposites. The urge towards reduction and simplification, either by the use of a vernacular or concentration on a limited area, was matched by an even stronger one towards complexity. In the concerto medium this may have reflected the increasingly complicated and confused relation between the individual and his society in a technological age.

The work of **Roger Sessions** (1896–1985) is a calculated response to the predicament of contemporary music largely without any recourse to Americanism. Like Ives he studied at Yale with Parker, then with Bloch, and from 1926 to 1933 lived in Europe, mostly in Italy. The Violin Concerto (1935) was begun in 1930 but not performed with an orchestra until 1940, because of its many difficulties. When it was revived in New York in 1959, Elliott Carter reviewed the performance in the *Musical Quarterly* and admired the way Sessions came to grips with 'the most serious and important issue that has faced contemporary music . . . the task of finding new forms for the new material'. Sessions anticipated Carter in defining a magisterial, internationally grounded approach to new music, but there are times when the Violin Concerto comes near to the energetic free counterpoint of later Carter. The work uses an orchestra without violins, like Stravinsky's *Symphony of Psalms*, and there are four movements taking some 35 minutes owing to the extended finale. The opening *Largo e Tranquillo* is sober and constantly melodic through the personality of the soloist. The texture thins to the soloist alone in double-stopping just before the end and here, as elsewhere, there is little of the redundant contrivance of most twentieth-century cadenzas. The *Scherzo* matches the neo-Classicism of the first movement with something close to expressionism: the rhythm may be derived from Baroque models, but the harmonic and contrapuntal freedom changes the context. The third movement, the *Romanza*, opens with a two-part texture for the soloist and a bassett horn alternating with clarinet— Sessions both melodic and uncomplex, but an individual mind in every bar (Ex. 6).

This movement leads straight into the finale, which is a wild jig or tarantella. It sounds as if the Gigue movement from Stravinsky's Duo Concertante has been inflated to a gigantic scale, but there are also expressionist waltzes in the tradition of Berg, whose Violin Concerto was completed in the same year.

Ex. 6

Elliott Carter

Sessions returned to the concerto medium in the work for violin, cello and orchestra (1970–1) and wrote a Concerto for Orchestra in 1981, but before this **Elliott Carter** (*b.* 1908) had achieved his own more personal continuity in his Double Concerto (1961) for harpsichord, piano and two chamber orchestras. His previous orchestral work, the *Variations* (1954–5) was heavily Schoenbergian, but with the Second String Quartet (1959) Carter, partly following Ives, was thinking dramatically about the separate performers and their materials. This provided a new injection with the notion of a concerto with two protagonists, each with his own orchestra. The result was a new musical language re-exploring continuity and metrical relationships. The Double Concerto is music of acknowledged difficulty for both performers and listeners, but it ushered in a series of major works which brought Carter immense international prestige and Stravinsky considered it a masterpiece.

Like Copland, Carter studied with Boulanger in Paris and his early works are both neo-Classical and related to American vernacular sources. After the Second World War this began to change, and Carter's involvement with the Second Viennese School, always latent, now emerged. His individual type of expressionism sometimes comes close to the predicament of a message swamped by its own energy. The Double Concerto began with the notion of a work for harpsichord and piano, and Carter decided to use pitchless percussion as a way of bridging the gap between their disparate sound characteristics. Thus the Concerto starts where some of the percussion episodes in Varèse leave off, a deceptive opening to a work where regular pulse is unusual, or disguised in cross-rhythm and groups of five and seven. As in later Carter—and more crudely in Ives, whom Carter met when he was 16—developments proceed simultaneously and are superimposed. This makes for a sound-palette which is kaleidoscopic rather than dense, full of energy and constantly evolving spatially—the score provides a seating plan for the performers. There is even a sense of role parody in the juxtaposition of keyboard instruments—the harpsichord (in effect amplified) largely concerned with early music, but here forced to come to terms in a dissonant style with the modern grand piano in a varied set of relationships between soloists and their respective ensembles. Carter found a literary analogue for this hectic striving in the imagery of parts of Pope's *Dunciad*, based on Lucretius, showing how the composer's imagination functions on several levels, each capable of fertilizing the others.

Carter's Piano Concerto (1964–5) was dedicated to Stravinsky for his 85th birthday and premièred in 1967. The composer has described the solo piano as 'in dialogue with the orchestral crowd, with seven mediators—a concertino of flute, cor anglais, bass clarinet, violin, viola, cello and double bass'. The work lacks the sparkle of the Double Concerto and seems aurally cluttered and unrelieved by comparison with the scintillating Concerto for Orchestra (1968–9). Charles Hamm, in *Music in the New World* (1983), felt that Carter's career 'underlines the fact that the gulf between audiences and certain types of contemporary music has grown even wider in the second half of the twentieth century, despite the work of the most talented and highly praised composers'. John Rockwell, in *All American Music* (1983), was worried about the 'too ready equation in our culture between complexity and excellence'.

Carter returned to the field with his oboe concerto (1986–87) written for Heinz Holliger. The soloist is part of a *concertino*, along with percussion and four violas, and interacts dramatically with the main orchestra. The two groups are concerned with different musical materials throughout the work's single movement.

The intellectuals amongst American composers have increasingly been employed by universities, where they have been able to compose with few responsibilities to a wider public. The expansion of such academic opportunities enabled composers such as **Milton Babbitt** (*b*, 1916), whose Piano Concerto (1985) was premièred in New York in 1986, to preoccupy themselves to a greater degree than ever before with mathematical aspects. The works of Babbitt, who studied with Sessions, are more complex even than those of Carter and strain the apparatus of the orchestra to breaking point. It is no wonder that such composers have preferred chamber groups specializing in contemporary works or electro-acoustic media. Charles Wuorinen (*b*. 1938), who set up the Group for Contemporary Music in New York, has written several concertos, some for amplified soloist. His First Piano Concerto (1965) is a post-Webern exercise in extending *Klangfarben-melodie* to a single movement of 20 minutes, employing a kind of moment form in a rich but ventilated orchestral texture requiring nine percussion players.

Ironically, some of the composers best equipped to attempt a synthesis of American music's disparate traditions have not always chosen to do so. Babbitt, for example, had an early career in jazz and popular music. **William Schuman** (*b*. 1910) wrote between 60 and 100 popular songs as a young man and worked in jazz. His tough, economical style, with rapt lyrical moments, is at its finest in his symphonies rather than the Piano Concerto (1938) or Violin Concerto (1947), but Schuman's *Concerto on Old English Rounds* (1974) for viola and women's chorus is one of the most unusual examples in the repertory. Like Schuman, **Walter Piston** (1894–1976) is at his most impressive in his eight symphonies but he has composed two violin concertos, a concerto for flute (1971) and a concerto for two pianos (1964). The First Violin Concerto (1939) has the same powerful lyrical impulse as the Second Symphony (1943), the same sense of logic and movement. The melodic lines are characteristically shaped and there is the organic inevitability about its musical processes that informs the finest of the symphonies.

Gunther Schuller (*b*. 1925) is an authority on jazz, a versatile musician, a tireless campaigner for higher standards and a greater commitment to contemporary music, and an extremely prolific composer. His first concerto was for his own instrument, the horn, in 1944 and another followed in 1978; he floated Third Stream in 1957—a new attempt to fuse jazz and modern music; and overall has almost a score of works involving the title of concerto. Many of these are for instruments not normally accorded the concerto treatment—the Concertino for jazz quartet (1959), the Double Bass Concerto (1968), the Contrabassoon Concerto (1978), probably the first written for this instrument, and the Alto Saxophone Concerto (1983). In a sense Schuller's works reflect the fashions through which he has lived and by 1978, in an article called 'Towards a New Classicism', he was protesting about the aridity and abstraction of much contemporary music. 'When have we had music that gave you goose pimples, that made you choke with emotion, that brought tears to your eyes?' Something of this sense of ecstasy comes across in the opening of the Violin Concerto (1975–6), whose opening recalls Szymanowski. Schuller's four-movement Trumpet Concerto (1979) is a polished and fluent example of his beliefs at this stage in a style close to neo-Classicism. The first movement is an introduction and allegro: the fast music establishes the trumpet's personality and the whole work has barely a suggestion of jazz.

Schuller's interests have largely been kept in separate compartments, as with the British composer Richard Rodney Bennett, also a skilled jazz musician. John Rockwell regretted this as a 'sad bifurcation of sensibility' arising because 'musicians of talent like Babbitt and Schuller' had not 'found a way to make a more successful fusion of their instincts'.

Other American composers—some of the most successful—simply wrote for the audience and regarded communication as part of the composer's task. **Gian Carlo Menotti**, born in Italy in 1911, perfected his approach in the theatre. His Piano Concerto (1945) has the same effortless expression in a refreshing but over-extended framework based on traditional tonality. Compare Menotti's debt to Scarlatti in the work's first movement with Cage's different one in Sonatas and Interludes. Menotti's almost lifelong friend **Samuel Barber** (1910–1981) throughout his career was one of the most regularly performed American composers. His Brahmsian Violin Concerto (1939) has become a classic, the Cello Concerto (1945) not far behind, and the Piano Concerto (1962) is a powerful extension of Barber's tonal romantic language.

Barber's Piano Concerto was written for John Browning, who played many works out of his own repertoire for Barber when he was contemplating the new one. The composer was responsive to his performers as well as to his public. Browning told me in 1982 that he and Leinsdorf suggested that Barber's original soft ending to the first movement might be better loud so that 'the slow movement might come out of nowhere'. Barber agreed and recast the passage. As a whole, the Concerto reflects Barber at his highest level, with each movement precisely judged in every way. Thematic invention is strong and Barber knew, like Gershwin who learnt it from Tchaikovsky, that good tunes need to be heard often enough to gain their effect. The second movement, the *Canzone*, is a poised lyric, with each appearance of the main theme differently laid out. A similar but weaker movement, a *Canzonetta*, is all that Barber was able to complete of his projected late Oboe Concerto. The inevitability of the Piano Concerto comes from the fact that Barber has selectively assimilated the main stream of European modernism in a way which suited both him and his public—and originally his teacher at the Curtis Institute, the Italian traditionalist Rosario Scalero. It hardly matters that the music is more European than American and composed a year after Carter's Double Concerto. The consistent quintuple metre of the finale is carried off with such dazzling effect that its sources seem as irrelevant as Brahms's debt to Beethoven. This is a work which connects, in the sense that E. M. Forster used the term, and its success is comparable to that of MacDowell. Both composers were conservatives and wrote concertos for the existing orchestral medium and its audience. It is not easy to find equally successful counterparts in the 1980s.

One later composer who has shown a concern for the public is **John Corigliano** (*b.* 1938), as an interview in the *New York Times* (1982) made clear: 'Audiences pay money to see or hear something that will move them, excite them, interest them or in some form involve them. If a composer has something important to say, it is his obligation to find a way of saying it that fulfills these basic requirements without compromising his standards in any way.' These were almost exactly Copland's sentiments in his autobiographical sketch, Composer from Brooklyn (1939). Corigliano studied with **Paul Creston** (1906–1985), another romantic who wrote many concertos, and his background includes a formal musical training followed by work in television, films and rock as a background to his concert music. A composer with this diversity ought to be equipped to heal the 'sad bifurcation of sensibility' which Rockwell complained about. Concertos can be a dramatic way of exploiting such conflicts. Corigliano's Piano Concerto (1968), with its echoes of composers from Mahler to Shostakovitch, is a parallel to the rejection of serialism in mid-career by **George Rochberg** (*b.* 1918) which led to his tonal works such as the Violin Concerto (1974). Rochberg is usually more consistent, whereas Corigliano modulates from style to style. His Oboe Concerto (1975) takes as its point of departure the instrument's tuning-up function in the orchestra, and its five movements cover a wide range of roles for the soloist. Another eclectic composer who has specialized in concertos is **Donald Erb** (*b.* 1927), whose jazz background fuses with an expressionist intensity in the Clarinet Concerto (1984).

Corigliano's Clarinet Concerto (1977), written for Stanley Drucker and Leonard Bernstein, is a spectacular vehicle for virtuosity and made a considerable impact at the New York Philharmonic. The concept is Ivesian, with instruments spread around the hall, a second movement—the Elegy— in a much simpler style, and quotation from Gabrieli as a basis for the

Antiphonal Toccata which acts as finale. The whispering effect from the soloist is a subtle start to the first to the first movement, Cadenzas (Ex. 7)—deceptive too, since there are theatrical exchanges between soloist and orchestra to come. The rapid passagework unifies the outside movements, where the atmosphere of nervous intensity is impressively sustained, enclosing the Elegy, an oasis of calm.

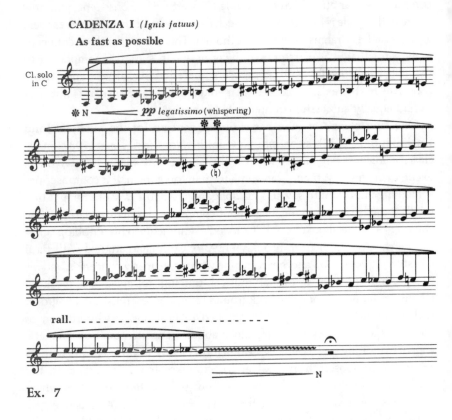

CADENZA I (*Ignis fatuus*)

Ex. 7

Corigliano's Clarinet Concerto was one of a number of commissions in an enterprising series for the principal players within the New York Philharmonic. Others included the Flute Concerto (1977) by Andrew Imbrie (*b.* 1921), his sixth concerto; the Concerto for English Horn and strings (1977) by **Vincent Persichetti** (1915–1987); and the Viola Concerto (1979) by **Jacob Druckman** (*b.* 1928). That three new concertos can be launched inside three years by only one American orchestra indicates the continuing vitality of the medium and of the orchestral culture which supports it. During the 1980s, reflecting prevailing aesthetic trends, the diversity of concertos—from Babbitt to Glass—seems more extreme than at any other period.

Between these poles an increasing number of American composers has come to realize that the public still views the concerto relationship in the Hollywood image. This implies the thrills of romanticism, effectively purveyed in piano concertos by MacDowell, Gershwin and Barber, and kept alive by the epic film scores of **John Williams** (*b.* 1932), who has written concertos for violin and for flute. Some of this fits in well with the so-called new tonality, or new romanticism. But finally, the heterogeneity which Ives—in almost complete isolation—was the first to recognize as the unique material of American music, and which Cage celebrated in *Musicircus*, is itself the orchestra against which each composer must perform his own concerto.

CHAPTER 12

The Concerto in Britain

Michael Kennedy

By the end of the eighteenth century, the improvements in the pianoforte led to the development of the virtuoso solo-instrument-and-orchestra concerto as a leading feature of the Romantic era. Early examples by English composers, such as the seven piano concertos of **J. B. Cramer** (1771–1858) and the three of **Cipriani Potter** (1792–1871), are interesting for their historical position, but are musically of less consequence than the seven by the Irishman **John Field** (1782–1837), a Clementi pupil. These contain fascinating pointers to the future where not only Chopin but Liszt and Brahms waited. Still of interest today are the four piano concertos of **Sterndale Bennett** (1816–1875), youthful essays which combine the fluency of a Mendelssohnian devotee with the Classical sharpness of Mozart and the Romantic poise that commended this composer to Schumann. No. 4 in F minor (1838) in particular deserves re-entry into the repertoire of pianists anxious to show that Mozart and Weber had a follower who was more than a clone.

One of the first string concertos by a recognized British composer was that for cello by **Arthur Sullivan** (1842–1900), written in 1866 for the virtuoso Alfredo Piatti, who gave the first performance at the Crystal Palace on 24 November of that year. There was a second performance a month later and only one more in Sullivan's lifetime. The concerto remained unpublished and has attracted only sporadic interest. In 1964 the autograph score and all the orchestral parts were destroyed in a fire. A copy of the solo cello part, with some indication of orchestral cues, survived in New York and another was found in Britain. From these scores, and from his memory of conducting the concerto in a BBC studio in 1953, Sir Charles Mackerras reconstructed the score for performance and recording in 1986. Whether the music deserves all this effort is debatable. Sullivan himself did not seem to care much for the concerto's fate. It is pleasant but lightweight and unsatisfactory in design.

Hubert Parry (1848–1918), a principal architect of the late nineteenth century revival of various aspects of English musical life including composition, wrote a piano concerto in F sharp in 1878–9 which his teacher

Edward Dannreuther introduced to London in 1880 with some success. Yet though Parry composed five symphonies he never returned to concerto form, unlike his friend **Charles Villiers Stanford** (1852–1924) who composed three concertos for piano, two for violin, and one for clarinet. This last, written in 1902, is the most successful of his works in this form, but even this suffers from garrulity and too slavish a dependence on a curious mixture of Brahms and Irish jig. In one movement, it was composed for Brahms's clarinettist Richard Mühlfeld, who rejected it. Charles Draper gave the first performance, but it was his pupil Frederick Thurston who championed it for many years. Lately, British solo clarinettists have renewed interest in it and it has twice been recorded.

Another major personality of the Parry-Stanford generation was **Alexander Mackenzie** (1847–1935), who played the violin in a German orchestra and in chamber concerts in his native Edinburgh. His Violin Concerto was written for the 1885 Birmingham Festival, where it impressed the young orchestral violinist Edward Elgar, but it was overshadowed by the *Pibroch* for violin and orchestra at the Leeds Festival of 1889. Both these works were written for Sarasate. A *Scottish Concerto* for piano followed in 1897 and was first performed in Leipzig two years later. Of the three works, the *Scottish Concerto* is the liveliest and most deserving of revival, though it was not only out of friendship for a fellow-composer that Elgar put pressure on Adrian Boult in 1932 to revive the Violin Concerto with the BBC Symphony Orchestra.

The unpopularity of British concertos, or the lack of enterprise among soloists and concert managements, may be gauged from a glance at the programmes of the Royal Philharmonic Society for the first nine years of the twentieth century. Three only were performed, Stanford's for clarinet and, in 1907 and 1908 respectively, **York Bowen**'s (1884–1961) for piano, with himself as soloist, and for viola, which served to introduce Lionel Tertis to the Society's audience. Bowen's position in British music today is epitomized by the brevity of his entry in *The New Grove Dictionary of Music and Musicians*, but not every musician would hold this to be a just estimate. His concertos were also championed by Henry Wood at his Promenade Concerts. They have, however, found no champion in the modern recording studio, unlike those by **Hamilton Harty** (1879–1941), whose fame as a conductor and, before that, an accompanist, overshadowed his gifts as a composer. These were by no means negligible, as can be heard from the lyrical, tuneful and skilfully constructed Violin Concerto (1908), written for Joseph Szigeti. Like Stanford, Harty found it difficult to keep his Irish background out of his music, but in the Violin Concerto he came nearer to the European idiom of Dvořák and, inescapably, Brahms, whose influence is all to the good in the poignancy of the second subject of the first movement. Harty's lyrical gift was individual and sustained, as can be heard in the slow movement, where the violin's ornate and long-breathed melody creates a memorable atmosphere. The finale, too, is unusually successful—one says unusually because in many British concertos it is the last movement which lowers the music's quality through forced and unnatural attempts at humour or gaiety. Harty's capacity for wit and burlesque, alternating with a poetic meditation, achieves a splendid climax to the concerto. He followed it in 1922 with a Piano Concerto, which is less successful than its predecessor only because the influences of Rachmaninov and Chopin have been less fully absorbed. That said, it is another attractive work and one can only wonder why so many concertos markedly its inferior are included in concert-programmes while it languishes almost unheard.

Elgar

However devotedly one may champion the cause of English music, there is no denying that until 10 November 1910 no British composer had written a concerto which could be claimed with confidence as the equal of those by the great European masters. All that changed on that evening in Queen's Hall, London, when Fritz Kreisler gave the first performance of the Violin Concerto in B minor by **Edward Elgar** (1857–1934). So great was the interest that hundreds of would-be listeners had to be turned away. 'The ovation at the end was tremendous', Elgar's friend Dora Penny (Mrs Richard Powell) remembered. It was the last major work by Elgar to enjoy an immediate popular success. Other performances rapidly followed and leading violinists quickly added it to their repertory.

Its success is easy to explain. First, it is immediately accessible yet there is no impression of glib popularity-seeking. It is obvious that the music is on a lofty plane and that it makes demands of concentration on the part of the listener almost as arduous as those it makes both technically and interpretatively on the soloist. It is a long work, spaciously planned, yet it has an elusive intimacy which is an integral part of its spellbinding appeal. Elgar regarded it as part of an autobiographical trilogy, with the Second Symphony of 1911 and the choral ode *The Music Makers* of 1912. 'I have written out my soul . . . in these three works I have *shewn* myself', he wrote in 1912 to his friend and confidante—and perhaps more—Alice Stuart-Wortley. Audiences can and do enjoy this concerto purely as music, but (as with so much of Elgar) they are also conscious of a personal drama, a hidden programme, yet another enigma. On the score he inscribed a quotation in Spanish from Lesage's *Gil Blas: Aquí está encerrada el alma de . . . . .* ('Here is enshrined the soul of . . . . .'). The five dots represent a name, feminine so

Elgar is said to have told his biographer Basil Maine. Who, then, is the heroine of this concerto? Almost certainly Mrs Stuart-Wortley: in their correspondence to the end of his life he referred to it as 'your concerto' or 'our concerto' and called some of its themes 'Windflower themes', Windflower being his nickname for her. Yet, music being what it is, perhaps some long-lost love of his youth is remembered here—for it is love music, beyond doubt—and of course there is Elgar himself, painting yet another self-portrait in sound and disguising himself as seen through another's eyes.

It is a concerto on the largest scale, which makes its emotional intimacy all the more remarkable an achievement. It opens with an extensive orchestral tutti ranging through several keys and containing at least six relatively short themes, the first of which (Ex. 1) is a kind of Elgarian *Ur-Thema*, since he used it as the start of the overture to his boyhood *Wand of Youth* music, which he converted into two orchestral suites in 1907–8. What is to develop into the 'Windflower' second subject is introduced at this point almost casually. (Ex. 2). The first of several structural surprises in the concerto comes with the soloist, who enters liks a great actor in a play. The strings play a wistful version of Ex. 1, which is now completed *(nobilmente)* by the violin to show that the answer to most of the questions posed lies with the soloist. The violin reviews and revises the themes of the tutti, leading to a G major expansion of the second subject (Ex. 2) which is now fully characterized as an expression of 'what might have been'. This theme may seem almost fragile in its tenderness but it is strong enough to withstand impassioned orchestral treatment and it is the lynchpin of the extraordinarily original development section, in effect a free fantasia, when it becomes the orchestral underpinning to the soloist's meditative and ornate rhapsodizing. Later it recurs in sequences and is eventually recapitulated in D major, from which it reaches B minor, the tonic, with dramatic emphasis. Yet it is Ex. 1 which dominates the coda.

Ex. 1

Ex. 2

Just as the soloist in the first movement never plays Ex. 1 as we first hear it from the orchestra, so in the slow movement, in a remote B flat, he or she never plays the principal theme, which is first introduced by the orchestra. When the solo violin enters, it is with a counterpoint of the theme. Twice the movement is brought to a climacteric where some peaceful resolution is expected; twice it is frustrated. Only at the third attempt does the soloist provide the answer that turns away wrath, with this panacea which has been offered earlier (Ex. 3). Some of the scoring in this movement is unusually

Ex. 3

daring—solo violin and trombones, for example, is worthy of Berlioz. The finale is the longest movement and the most surprisingly ambitious in design and scope. It opens with the most exhibitionist violin music in the work, rapid and brilliant ascending passages which serve eventually to re-establish B minor before a swaggering D major march theme bursts forth on the orchestra. This precipitates a lengthy episode of extrovert and pyrotechnic music which calls on all the soloist's technical virtuosity. Part of this episode, once B major is reached, involves the return of a theme from the slow movement, now in the tempo of the finale. By now the concerto is on course for a conventional ending, or so we think. But suddenly Elgar takes us back into B minor and thins down the orchestra to nothing but a muted horn. What mysterious world are we about to enter? Certainly one where no concerto has been before, for this is to be the long, accompanied cadenza in which the work's principal themes are passed in review, mused upon, elaborated and bidden a tender, tragic farewell. The soloist's entry is preceded and accompanied by Elgar's invention of a *pizzicato tremolando,* or 'thrumming', by the orchestral strings—suggested to him, it is believed, when he heard an Aeolian harp. Other instruments are added as the cadenza grows more impassioned and elaborate, although its central passage is a long solo passage for the violin, its poignant expressiveness left in no doubt from the copious markings in the score. This cadenza is the work's feature of high genius. There is no question of seeing through a glass darkly, for we are brought face to face with Elgar's transparent deepest feelings. It culminates in the soloist's first full statement of Ex. 1, now transformed from question to answer and invested with a finality and weight of emotion from which Elgar rapidly escapes into the romping brilliance of the coda.

That Elgar's is one of the half-dozen indisputably great violin concertos is no chauvinistic belief, for leading violinists from Ysaÿe to Heifetz recognized it as such from the start and in recent years a new generation of international soloists has revelled in its difficulties and glories. His only other concerto, for cello (1918–19), was slower to achieve proper recognition, although today it is perhaps cherished even more than the Violin Concerto. It was composed at the end of the First World War while Elgar was living for a large part of the year in a Sussex cottage, which he preferred to his Hampstead mansion. He had been ill, and was deeply depressed by the war and its blight on the world as he had known it. The music is autumnal in feeling, its scoring subdued compared with that of the Violin Concerto and the symphonies, but one must be careful not to equate these facets with a lack of vitality. Elgar, whose own description of the Violin Concerto was 'It's *good!* awfully emotional! too emotional but I love it', said the Cello Concerto was 'a real large work & I think *good* & alive'.

What is especially good is the subtlety and beauty of the orchestration so that the cello, always a problematical concerto instrument, is never obscured. Yet one cannot say the work is *lightly* scored: double woodwind, four horns, two trumpets, three trombones and optional tuba, with timpani and strings, is no chamber ensemble. In the first of the four movements the full orchestra is used for only six bars and without the soloist. The soloist's dramatic opening flourish is supported by lower strings, clarinets and bassoons, and the violas' hazy-lazy unharmonized *moderato* theme is reinforced by cellos, the soloist, clarinets and horns. Apart from a bar or two of horns, the soloist is usually accompanied by strings and woodwind. In the mercurial scherzo, where the cello part is *leggierissimo* and *brillante*, the accompaniment consists mainly of flecked-in points of colour in the shape of woodwind, a chord from horns and trumpets and the lightest of support from divided and often *pizzicato* strings. In the song without words that is the soulful *adagio*, the orchestra is reduced to strings, clarinets, bassoons and horns. For the finale, in which the glittering pre-war Elgar briefly shines out again, the full orchestra is called upon only when the cellist is silent. When, after an introductory recitative, the cello assists in the exposition of the robust first subject, Elgar allows only a solo horn from the brass section. As in the Violin Concerto, there is an accompanied cadenza, not as elaborate as in the earlier work. Like Dvořák's concerto at the same point, high spirits are abandoned as the strings cry out in chromatic anguish and the cellist plays a new and impassioned theme (Ex. 4) a heart cry that merges into a consolatory memory from the slow movement. From there it is no emotional distance to a recall of the concerto's opening flourish, heavy now with regret, and a hasty and brisk eight bars of coda in which soloist and full orchestra combine for the first time.

Ex. 4

In its conciseness, formal mastery and poetical expressiveness, the Cello Concerto ranks high among Elgar's major works, and its reticence commends it to the taste of many for whom the Elgar of the symphonies proves too rich. Its subdued mood—even the scherzo is in half-lights—is a lament not so much for the dead of the First World War as for the end of a way of life, a civilization, in which Elgar's music had blossomed and flourished. In his personal list of his works, Elgar entered the details of the Cello Concerto and added: 'Finis. R.I.P.' Prophetic words, for in the 15 years that remained to him he composed nothing on a scale or of a quality to compare with what had gone before. Sadly, at the first performance Queen's Hall was sparsely filled; Elgar's rehearsal-time had been selfishly eroded by Albert Coates, who was conducting the rest of the concert, so that the work was not well played and was generally not well received by critics and public. In spite of the advocacy of Beatrice Harrison during the 1920s, the concerto was not welcomed by cellists until Pablo Casals took it up and revealed its stature. Elgar himself also approved and conducted a transcription of the work for viola by Lionel Tertis. His only other work for solo instrumentalist and orchestra is the *Romance* for bassoon, a brief miniature of exquisite fancy nestling between the giants Op. 61 and 63, the Violin Concerto and the Second Symphony. It exists also in a cello arrangement made by Elgar. Sketches for a piano concerto were made over several years, but came to nought.

Delius

It is perhaps surprising that **Frederick Delius** (1862–1934), among English composers, should have four concertos to his name and Elgar only two. Superficially one might expect the tone-poet of nature and lost love, the composer of *Sea-Drift, Appalachia, In a Summer Garden* and *Song of the High Hills*, to be alien to the restrictions of concerto-form. But while it is true that Delius's concertos are like few others, the theory that he could not discipline his wayward art into such structured designs is a myth effectively exploded by the late Deryck Cooke in a famous detailed exposition of the Violin Concerto's form.[1] In any case, a rambling rose can be trained to take its place in a formal garden.

1. D. Cooke, 'Delius and Form: a Vindication', *Musical Times*, June and July 1962, reprinted in *A Delius Companion*, London, 1976.

Delius, like Elgar, was a violinist, probably a better one, certainly good enough to play Mendelssohn's concerto in public. Yet his first concerto was for piano. This has a complicated history. It began in 1897 as a one-movement *Fantasy* and may have been performed in this form in a Paris salon, though no one knows for sure. Someone then persuaded him to convert the work into the conventional three-movement concerto form. In this version it was played by Julius Buths and conducted by Hans Haym at Elberfeld on 24 October 1904. The third movement, only part of which survives in a two-piano arrangement, bears no resemblance to the definitive version known today. This began to evolve in 1906. Delius reconstructed the work into one movement of three sections, and it was played in London by Theodor Szántó at a Henry Wood Promenade Concert on 22 October 1907. But this was not the end. In June 1908 Szántó prepared a version incorporating what he regarded as improvements. Delius agreed to some but not all of them and allowed only two public performances of this revision. Eventually pianist and composer agreed on the changes and the score was published. In 1951 a score revised and edited by Sir Thomas Beecham was issued (Beecham had recorded the work in his own edition in 1946). Although some passages are characteristic of Delius, the Piano Concerto is not one of his strongest compositions. It bears the imprint of Grieg, particularly in the slow movement, and for all Szántó's assistance the piano part is not particularly effective. Yet such an ardent Delian as Cecil Gray regarded it and other early works as 'much more accomplished' than the later ones—an extraordinary judgement, I am bound to say.

One of Delius's objections to Szántó's revisions was that he had made his concerto into a 'spectacular' piece. Display for its own sake was never his aim, and the difficulties of his concerto lie in the demands on musicianship rather than on technical virtuosity (though that is required). His second concerto was composed in 1915 and was for the problematical medium of two soloists—violinist and cellist—and orchestra. It was inspired by a performance of Brahms's concerto for the same combination which Delius heard at a Hallé concert on 3 December 1914 in Manchester conducted by Beecham, with May and Beatrice Harrison as soloists. He completed it within a year. Beatrice Harrison has said[1] that 'it was written in unison and technically was almost impossible to play, but with Delius himself and Philip Heseltine at the piano, we rewrote the cello part and made it playable . . . All this took weeks'. The first performance was not given until 21 February 1920 when the Harrison sisters, its dedicatees, played it with Sir Henry

1. P. Cleveland-Peck (ed.), *The Cello and the Nightingale, the Autobiography of Beatrice Harrison*, London, 1985.

Wood conducting. Like all Delius concertos, it is in one continuous movement binding together the normal three-movements. Repetition—but what magical repetition—is preferred to development. The first section is virtually a sonata design, with a march as the second subject, a possible reference to the war. In the second section the cello's main theme bears a distinct and probably deliberate resemblance to the baritone solo in *Appalachia* ('O honey, I am going down the river in the morning'). The introductory theme to the whole work, cursorily dismissed at the outset, returns here on the flute as a prelude to the very Delian *molto expressivo* melody for the violin on which the final part of the work is based. The solo instruments are poetically intertwined or contrasted throughout and the principal reason for the work's neglect must be that it is melodically undistinguished compared with many of Delius's compositions. In 1935 Tertis's version for violin and viola was performed and published.

Delius's third concerto, but the second to be performed, was for violin, composed in 1916 and first performed by its dedicatee Albert Sammons in London on 30 Janury 1919, with Adrian Boult conducting. (Sammons was a wonderful exponent of Elgar's concerto, but he once told me he preferred the Delius.) It is among Delius's finest works, an outpouring of song-like melody in which the soloist is hardly silent throughout its nearly half-hour's duration. Deryck Cooke, in his classic essay, demonstrated beyond argument that the work is not a formless, waffling piece of pastoral 'cowpat' music but a highly organized structure which can be dissected into exposition—development (slow movement)—accompanied slow cadenza—recapitulation—scherzo—finale. Not only that, but themes cross-relate and cross-refer and the whole piece grows from the two-bar motto with which it opens (Ex. 5). But surely the sensitive listener scarcely needs Cooke's tour of the score to *hear* the organic nature of the music and to sense its formal mastery. At no point does Delius's concentration slacken, so neither does the listener's. Not only is there the most sensuous lyricism, the nature-poetry of which Delius was master, but also the contrasts of drama—brass fanfares and a full orchestral outburst—and of the light fantastic dance. Most of all, the melodic invention is of high quality.

Ex. 5

Whereas many regard the Violin Concerto as Delius's finest work in the medium, I believe that his last concerto, for cello, claims that position. It was written at the insistence of Beatrice Harrison in 1921, although the first performance was given in Vienna in January 1923 by the Russian cellist Alexandre Barjansky. Miss Harrison gave the first London performance seven months later. It explores and exploits one mood, that is true, but what a variety is contained within it. It is a meditation, but strong, heroic, passionate and never enervating. Again it is in one linked movement with no cadenza and no conflict between soloist and orchestra. It follows an A–B–A scheme, but in the recapitulation of A the material is suddenly abandoned and a new *allegramente* section begins, an exalted D major melody for the soloist with accompaniment by the orchestral strings (Ex. 6). When Elgar

Allegramente

Ex. 6

and Delius met shortly before they died, Elgar told his colleague how much he loved and wanted to conduct this concerto. Beatrice Harrison has described it, in non-technical language, as well as anyone:[1]

> ... The soloist has to realise that his part does not predominate but should weave its way through the exquisite harmonies of the orchestra, almost like a beautiful river passing through a lovely landscape, ever flowing on, sometimes clear and sometimes in shadow, but ever conscious of the rhythm of the work which seems in the end to vibrate into eternity. The artist's conception of this concerto must be an emotional one. Joy and sadness are so intermingled and the moods vary so exquisitely that it is only by understanding these transcending beauties that Delius's music can be interpreted.

The three concertos by Delius's exact contemporary **Arthur Somervell** (1863–1937) are never played today, but were admired by Sir Donald Tovey, who wrote extensive programme-notes on two of them. *Normandy* is not strictly a piano concerto, being described as symphonic variations on a French folk-song, but concerto-form can be discerned in it. The variations are better described as free fantasias and the music is clear and easily accessible.

1. B. Harrison, 'From the Performer's Point of View', *Musical Bulletin*, August, 1927.

Somervell's finale adopts a procedure of which Britten was to become a master: variations (11 in this case) on a ground. *Normandy* dates from 1912. A piano concerto, the 'Highland', followed in 1921 and in 1932 a violin concerto in G minor, described by Tovey as having an 'abundance of melodies and rhythmic invention'.

Ethel Smyth (1858–1944) wrote only one concerto, for violin and horn, which Boult premièred in Birmingham in 1927. **Samuel Coleridge-Taylor** (1857–1912) wrote a violin concerto, shortly before he died, for performance at the Norfolk Festival in Connecticut, the philanthropic founder of which—Carl Stoeckel—had suggested the work to him, proposing the African slave-song 'Keep me from sinking down, good Lord', as the theme of the slow movement. The first version of the work was based wholly on African melodies, but Coleridge-Taylor scrapped it and rewrote the concerto. It is almost never heard now, but the score is there, awaiting the violinist courageous enough to reveal its merits anew. Coleridge-Taylor's fellow-student at the Royal College of Music (RCM) as a Stanford pupil was **William Hurlstone** (1876–1906), who died at the age of 30. His Piano Concerto in D, rescued from total neglect in 1979 by a recording, was written for himself to play in 1896. Its three big movements—four in effect since the long *adagio* which introduces the rondo-finale is virtually a movement on its own—substantiate the claim that Hurlstone, with Butterworth, was one of the most promising of talents snuffed out too soon.

Holst and Vaughan Williams

Early death cut short the achievements of Coleridge-Taylor and Hurlstone, but two of their RCM friends went on to occupy honoured and special places in the English music of the first half of the twentieth century, **Ralph Vaughan Williams** (1872–1958) and **Gustav Holst** (1874–1934). Both were men for whom a Lisztian virtuosity in music was anathema, so it is surprising to find that between them they composed six concertos and a host of shorter work for instrumentalist and orchestra. None of their concertos is in any way conventional and all—except perhaps Vaughan Williams's Oboe Concerto—remain on the outer fringe of soloists' repertoires. Holst's *Fugal Concerto* of 1923 is one of the works which earned him an unjustified reputation as a 'dry' and 'cold' composer. Because he was so preoccupied with the solution of technical problems, he himself came to feel that his later music lacked 'warmth'. Even his daughter Imogen found that the *Fugal Overture* of the preceding year 'gives the impression that he had deliberately set out to write an intellectual exercise', but that is not the impression received today from this witty, sparkling piece. Similarly, the *Fugal Concerto* for flute, oboe and strings, while in the neo-Classical or neo-Baroque style popular in the 1920s, succeeds because Holst, in common with Stravinsky, imposes his own personality on the borrowed eighteenth-century conventions. If 'warmth' is to be equated with melodic lyricism, then what complaints can there be about this work's slow movement? The Concerto for two violins of 1929 is also fugal and bitonal, with its three interlinked movements played without a break. It begins with a Scherzo, with a fugal subject to which the countersubject ingeniously inverts the opening and fills in the rests. The world of *Mercury* and *Uranus* from *The Planets* is not far away, nor the more richly expressive style of Holst's earlier compositions. In one episode he borrows a section from the slow movement of his *Terzetto* for flute, oboe and viola (1925). The Scherzo is followed by a *Lament*, mainly for the soloists unaccompanied, and a finale in the form of variations on a ground—in which the *Lament* and *Terzetto* are both quoted. The Holst of the 1920s is overdue for searching reappraisal. The tag of 'cold' has been attached to him too long.

An indication of the sort of 'warm' romantic concerto that Holst might have written is given in his *Invocation* for cello and orchestra of 1911, a 'dry run' for *Venus* in *The Planets*. This attractive and passionate work was withheld for many years but was resurrected in 1983 in an edition by Colin Matthews and was recorded. It is the Holst one also hears in his *Hymn to Dionysus* of 1913 and the Holst who was re-surfacing in the *Lyric Movement* for viola and orchestra composed shortly before he died.

Vaughan Williams's first concerto belongs, like Holst's *Fugal Concerto*, to the neo-Classical phase of the 1920s. The Concerto in D minor of 1925, for violin and strings, was originally known as the *Concerto Accademico* when it was first performed by its dedicatee, Jelly d'Arányi, and for some years afterwards. 'Back to Bach' was the slogan of the first movement, and the title referred to eighteenth-century procedures rather than to any pedagogic rules (the concerto contains far too many consecutive fifths for the latter ever to have been a believable allusion). It is a lightweight piece, with a memorable opening theme and a jig as Finale which borrows a theme from the composer's opera *Hugh the Drover*. The deepest music is contained in the Dorian slow movement, where a solo cello is prominent.

The Piano Concerto was begun in 1926, when the first two movements were written. The third movement was added in 1930–1 and the completed work was first performed in 1933. The work thus belongs to a peak and prolific period in Vaughan Williams's career, being contemporary with the short oratorio *Sancta Civitas* and the cantata *Benedicite*, the operas *Sir John in Love* and *Riders to the Sea* and the masque for dancing *Job*. The concerto forms a bridge between *Job* and the F minor Symphony (begun in 1931). Its restless and turbulent first movement, entitled *Toccata*, based on a principal subject of rising fourths, should have alerted contemporary listeners to the direction the composer was taking so that they might have been less surprised by the 'violence' of the symphony. Echoes of folk-music here are ironic, whereas in the symphony they were to extend to self-parody. In the slow movement, a *Romanza*, there is no Rachmaninovian lusciousness, but in its place a cool elegance, not excluding sentiment, which belong to the music of Fauré and Ravel. This is one of Vaughan Williams's most intimate movements, almost a confessional. It ends with a short phrase for oboe and viola over a drum-roll which has been related to the music for the hypocritical Comforters in *Job*. It serves as a prelude to the trombones' statement of the *Fuga Chromatica*, tough angular music which reflects the works's admitted inspiration from Busoni's transcriptions of Bach. (Like the violin concerto, but how unlike, this is also a 'Back to Bach' work.) A formidable cadenza intervenes, after which the Finale becomes a waltz *(alla Tedesca)* based on the fugue theme, but a waltz with sinister overtones (Liszt's *Mephisto Waltzes* have been plausibly suggested as a model). This episode is followed by another cadenza containing quotations from the first and second movements. Originally this was succeeded by a few bars of curt orchestral tutti in G major, but Vaughan Williams revised the ending by prolonging the reflective mood of the cadenza's B major for nine bars of quiet lilting *pizzicato* and a final radiance.

This revised ending was the best feature of the otherwise regrettable 1946 conversion of the concerto into one for two pianos, made because of criticisms that the orchestral score was too powerful for one pianist (it undoubtedly was for the first soloist, Harriet Cohen). By adding a higher octave in the second piano part, the composer (or his accomplice, Joseph Cooper) merely lessened the effectiveness of the upper registers of the accompaniment. But the new ending, though perhaps less logically convincing than the original, is undoubtedly more poetic and visionary and therefore perhaps more in keeping with the psychological complexity of one of Vaughan Williams's greatest and least appreciated works. That it has an autobiographical significance is confirmed by the existence in the original version of the second cadenza of a quotation from Bax's Third Symphony, 'added according to my promise'. Harriet Cohen was, of course, Bax's mistress. The quotation was removed after the first performance. The Fourth Symphony, it will be recalled, was dedicated to Bax.

Though not a concerto, attention must be called to Vaughan Williams's other work involving solo piano with orchestra, the *Fantasia on The Old 104th* (1949), involving chorus also in the manner of Beethoven's *Choral Fantasia*. It is an eccentric piece, but the writing for the piano is fluent and massive and the work as a whole leaves a deeper impression than might be expected. Only two other 'official' concertos followed that for piano, the

Oboe in 1944 and the Tuba in 1954. The Oboe Concerto, with accompaniment for strings, was a response to the artistry of Leon Goossens and used material discarded from the Fifth Symphony of 1938–43. It is written awkwardly for the soloist, but is none the less challenging and rewarding to play, and for the listener it is a charming *mélange* of pastoral musing, skittish display and, in the finale, a nostalgic yearning rarely found so overtly expressed in this composer's music. The Tuba Concerto has become a favourite. Regarded at first as an old man's whim, it was soon realized that he had paid the instrument the compliment of taking it seriously, especially in the beautiful and shapely slow movement, and his concern to discover the tuba's capabilities resulted in a mini-masterpiece.

Considering what a major role the solo viola plays in many of Vaughan Williams's orchestral works, it is strange that he never wrote a concerto for it. *Flos Campi* (1925) and a *Suite* (1934) feature it prominently but are not concertos. He contemplated a cello concerto for Casals; his 1930 *Fantasia on Sussex Folk Tunes*, written for the Spanish virtuoso, was withdrawn but has been re-released and recorded. There is also the brief but haunting *Romance* for harmonica (1951). But Vaughan Williams's most frequently played work for solo instrument and orchestra is his violin romance *The Lark Ascending* (1914, rev. 1920), the music of an age beyond recall yet speaking of the eternal spell of nature and landscape. It is a work that one takes for granted, but its distillation of poetry in sounds exerts a unique spell, more powerful than could be expected from such slight resources.

Vaughan Williams's Piano Concerto is not the only great work of the 1930 period to have suffered an unjust neglect only partially assuaged by the existence of a splendid recording. The 'concerto elegiaco' for cello and orchestra entitled *Oration* by **Frank Bridge** (1879–1941) was composed in 1930 as a requiem for the dead of the First World War. Bridge was a pacifist and several of his works reflect his anguish and horror about the war. The effect on his music, which up to 1914 had been colourfully romantic in a Baxian way, was to toughen and radicalize it. His harmony became more astringent, with a marked dependence on bitonality. Almost alone among English composers of his time, he was aware of what Schoenberg and Berg were achieving. He did not follow them, but his music, while keeping its strong individuality, recognizes their existence. *Oration* is in one movement, in the form of an arch. Its subdued, elegiac, processional opening belies the title, for this is private grief, but as the work progresses the cello, as orator, seems to speak for all humanity as it and the orchestra project images of war such as the quasi-Mahlerian funeral march 'as of platoons of the dead', in Anthony Payne's memorable phrase. There is no 'programme' and the work is a finely constructed cello concerto, scored with immense skill and colour. At no point does it sound remotely like Schoenberg and Berg. The end is deeply impressive. The processional opening returns and seems to complete the arch-like symmetry. Then the cello begins a long and sparse epilogue over an *ostinato* on the harp; the private, inconsolable grief returns. In 1931 Bridge wrote a piano concerto called *Phantasm*, itself a powerful work, but it is *Oration* that grips the imagination.

Bax

Bridge was four years older than **Arnold Bax** (1883–1953). Bax composed several works in concerto form. He was himself a splendid pianist and had a long association with the pianist Harriet Cohen, but he did not write a piano concerto so called. However, his *Symphonic Variations* (1916–18) can easily pass as one, though the piano part is co-operative rather than in opposition. It was first performed in 1920 and then revised and cut because Cohen found it too difficult, but K. S. Sorabji still described it as 'the finest work for piano and orchestra ever written by an Englishman'. During the Second World War the score was partially destroyed, but was reconstructed in the 1960s when a complete set of parts was found. It is an autobiographical work— love and war, general and personal, are its themes—and it quotes from a Bax song 'Parting' and his first violin sonata. Each of its six linked movements has a descriptive title such as 'Strife', 'Enchantment' and 'Play' and the style is near to the concertos of Grieg and Delius. The impassioned coda of the work is certainly Delian in its expression of doomed passion.

Sorabji notwithstanding, Bax's finest and strongest work for piano and orchestra is, in my view, *Winter Legends* of 1929, composed just after the Third Symphony and originally intended to be dedicated to Sibelius because the music, in Bax's words, deals with 'heroic tales of the North—of the far North, be it said'. Symphonic in scale, it is often harsh and angry music, opening with a rhythm on the side-drum and 'a kind of whirlwind' (Bax) on the piano which leads into an emphatic theme. The work is in three movements, and while there are passages of Baxian dreaming and soliloquy, the predominant impression is one of virile muscular energy. It is one of those works that makes the fashionable wholesale castigation of British music in the 1930s as 'parochial' or 'pastoral' and out of touch with reality so ridiculous and ill-informed an assessment. Like most of Bax, it is a crucial few minutes too long, but such prodigality of creativity is not really to be deplored.

Bax's Cello Concerto was written for Gaspar Cassadó in 1932 at the prompting of Harriet Cohen, who had toured with him in the previous year. Cassadó gave the first performance, but the work was played most often by

Beatrice Harrison. Its central *Nocturne* is extremely beautiful, but the outer movements lack a genuine impulse, rather as if Bax had found the commission interesting rather than inspiring. On the other hand, the Violin Concerto of 1937 is wholly successful—and rare among Bax's works in having, apparently, no programmatic genesis. It is also rare in its lightness of texture—Mendelssohn rather than the late Romantics, although it quotes from Elgar's concerto. The first of the three movements is in three parts (Overture, Ballad and Scherzo), attractively scored and very tuneful. The *adagio* borrows as its second subject (Ex. 7) a theme Bax had composed for a

Ex. 7

projected pastiche eighteenth-century sonata. There is thus a factual basis for William Mann's comparison of its 'near-Mozartian' flavour with the late concertos and sonatinas of Strauss. The concerto was finished in 1938, but Bax did not release it until asked for a work for the BBC's St Cecilia's Day concert in 1943. Originally planned for Heifetz, it was played by Eda Kersey, whose early death was a tragic loss. Those fortunate enough to have heard her in this concerto cannot forget the easy grace of her playing. The concerto enjoyed a short burst of popularity, to the chagrin of Bax, who resented that it was preferred to his symphonies, though it soon came to share their neglect.

The Concertante for Piano (left hand) was composed for Harriet Cohen after she had cut her right wrist after falling while carrying a tray of glasses in 1949. It is a patchy work, a generous gesture that lacked the spark from heaven. There is also a viola concerto, re-titled *Phantasy*, written for Tertis in 1920. It is a modal, Celtic work, joyous in melody and spirit but now almost forgotten. Another pity.

Walton

The name of Lionel Tertis has occurred several times in this chapter as a great violist whose personal crusade on behalf of his instrument led several English composers to write works for him. Ironically, he at first refused to play the finest viola concerto of them all, that by **William Walton** (1902–1983). This was composed in 1928–9 at Beecham's suggestion, Walton having earlier written a Sinfonia Concertante for piano and orchestra. When Tertis rejected the Viola Concerto, Paul Hindemith gave the first performance, a rescue act which led to a lifelong friendship. Walton's achievement in this concerto, which is his most successful work taken as an artistic entity, is that while making it a concerto worthy of a virtuoso instrumentalist he also retained the viola's reticent character in music of deeply poetic import. Not that the music lacks drama—it is so dramatic that Tovey astutely observed that here was a composer born to write an opera. The essence of the drama is the rising interval heard at the start of the viola's entry in the first movement with the long principal theme and present in other themes too (Ex. 8). In addition, the

Ex. 8

music sways back and forth from major to minor. The development section of the first movement grows more and more agitated as the rhythms become syncopated and the themes are converted from cantilena to impetuous argument, but once this is exhausted by the orchestra the viola leads the way back to a poignant calm. Having placed his slow movement first, Walton then provides a scherzo full of electric discharge and marvellously constructed from germ-like ideas, restless and volatile, invoking jazz rhythms. The finale begins with a bassoon solo that has a touch of the grotesque about it. But, like a similar theme in Elgar's First Symphony, this is later broadened and enriched and the movement ends with the recall of Ex. 8 as the viola muses over the past with a faint suspicion of sourness. This coda has, however, lost that astringency in the 1961 revision of the orchestration, where Walton has added a harp, with consequent mollifying effect. He also reduced the woodwind to double and deleted double bassoon and tuba. The original score is preferable.

The Violin Concerto of 1938–9 *is* a display piece, commissioned by Jascha Heifetz and first played by him in Cleveland, Ohio, in December 1939. It is in B minor, like Elgar's, and its unforgettably Romantic—almost aromatic— first subject, marked *sognando* (dreaming) also contains rising intervals, an octave for the soloist's entry but a seventh thereafter (Ex. 9). As in the Viola Concerto, this movement proceeds to an excitable climax before calming down, but the solo part is extremely ornate and pyrotechnical, as it is also in

Ex. 9

the scherzo—*presto capriccioso alla napolitana*—where Walton's unusual treatment of tonality is again the cause of the music's spicy flavour, particularly in the trio section *(Canzonetta)* where the C major theme is harmonized over A flat and B flat. Walton's finale is a grand spacious movement, combining brilliance and deeper feeling. One of its main themes (Ex. 10) has a family kinship with the concerto's opening theme (Ex. 9) and it is no surprise when the latter is recalled to give the work a satisfying structural and emotional completeness.

Ex. 10

Nearly 20 years passed before Walton's last concerto, for cello, was written for Gregor Piatigorsky in 1956. The design is that of the first two concertos, with the beginning recalled at the end, but it is no formula-concerto, nor is it fair to say that Walton had nothing new to say by then. The concerto is softer in its harmonic idiom than its predecessors and has obvious links with the love-music of the opera *Troilus and Cressida*. Rising intervals are again common to many of the themes, giving the music its yearning, aspiring passion. This time the finale is a set of variations—*Tema ed improvvisazioni*—two of which are for cello alone and serve also as elaborate cadenzas. The sound of the music is throughout exotic and sultry, with much use of shimmering *tremolandi* for strings *sul ponticello* and of vibraphone, celesta, xylophone and harp. Walton had been living for nearly a decade in Ischia when he wrote this concerto, and the Italian sun which illuminates the scherzo of the Violin Concerto here suffuses the whole work with its light.

Walton's Viola Concerto was the music of a man of 27. Its success established him in the forefront of his contemporaries. One of the few English concertos of the same period to encounter a comparable welcome was **John Ireland**'s (1879–1962) for piano, composed in 1930, a beautifully wrought work in E flat, Schumannesque in mood, with thematic interlinking of movements. The writing for the piano, as might be expected from the composer of the sonata and the fine Legend for piano and orchestra shows an intimate and intuitive understanding of the instrument which has kept the work in the repertoire while other 'profound and significant' concertos have come and gone. An epic British concerto of the 1930s is **Alan Bush**'s (*b.* 1900) for piano, his Op. 18, in four movements with a baritone soloist and male chorus in the Finale. Its adherents rightly deplore the neglect of a strong, dramatic and above all pianistic work, which has never recovered from hostility to the text of the Finale, a poem by Randall Swingler which was regarded in 1938 as being dangerously Communistic but today seems merely a piece of wide-eyed idealism unlikely to precipitate revolution. Bush's Violin Concerto (1948) was written for Max Rostal, who introduced it at a Promenade Concert in August 1949. The soloist, the composer says in the score, 'represents the individual, the orchestra human society'. That may be so, but the work is a fine piece of pure music, more classical in style than the Piano Concerto and more economically scored. The solo instrument is treated lyrically and although a note-row can be traced in the slow movement, the work is essentially tonal and deserved to be accepted with the Walton and Britten as outstanding examples of mid-twentieth-century violin concertos.

Walton's other near-contemporaries, among them **E. J. Moeran** (1894–1950), **Gerald Finzi** (1901–1956), and **Edmund Rubbra** (1901–1986), did not produce concertos until the Second World War or after. Moeran's Violin Concerto (1937–41) was first heard at a wartime Promenade concert, its Irish-inspired lyricism and, especially, its long serene epilogue seeming out of key with world events but looking beyond them to the deeper affairs of the spirit. It pays tribute in form and sometimes in direct quotation to the concertos of Mendelssohn, Elgar and Walton, but this is not to say that Moeran's individuality is smothered by their influence. It is the homage of one composer to others who meant much to him. Even finer is the Cello Concerto of 1945, Moeran's best work and one of the most beautiful written for this instrument since Elgar's; also one of the most skilfully written, for the balance between soloist and orchestra is ideally held.

Moreover, in both his concertos Moeran achieved structural unity through compelling use of interrelated fragments of economical material, while in no way sacrificing his melodic breadth. Finzi's Cello Concerto (1951–5) also has the lyricism to be expected of its composer. The slow movement is most affecting and the finale has a catchy and uncharacteristic theme, but it is hard to evade the judgement that he was not at his happiest handling this scale of music. His shorter Clarinet Concerto (1948–9), with string accompaniment, is more successful as a composition and has had a deserved success.

Rubbra's concertos at present languish in obscurity, though if some enterprising pianist were to revive the Piano Concerto (1956), he or she would find it not only well written—Rubbra was an excellent pianist—but strikingly good music. The Viola Concerto (1952) and Violin Concerto (1959) both belie Rubbra's undeserved reputation as a composer with no feeling for colour and contrast. No such criticism would be made of the music of **Arthur Bliss** (1891–1975). His Piano Concerto (1938–9) was written for the New York World Fair and is a rare example of a British bravura concerto, written on a Lisztian-Brahmsian scale, with bold melodies, vigorous orchestration and a transatlantic breeziness that came easily to Bliss, who was half-American. Bliss's Violin Concerto (1955) is on a similar scale, though it carries less conviction, whereas the Cello Concerto of 1970 is more restrained. There is also a two-piano concerto from 1924, twice revised, the second time as late as 1950.

The four piano concertos and two violin concertos of **George Lloyd** (*b.* 1913) have their champions, the fourth piano concerto having been recorded. They endure the neglect which has all but enveloped the two splendid piano concertos by **Alan Rawsthorne** (1905–1971). Of these, the four-movement second, composed for the Festival of Britain in 1951, is still occasionally played and enjoyed a burst of popularity when it was new. Like Walton, Rawsthorne imparts a sub-stratum of tension to his music by ambivalent use of keys, evidenced by the flute melody which begins the second concerto. There is a tranquil *adagio* and a finale in which the Latin-American rondo theme is used as the text for a most witty display. It is an invigorating work, but its predecessor is better. This was composed in 1939 for strings and percussion and revised in 1942 for full orchestra. It is the piano concerto Walton did not write, having the same electric rhythms and alternations of irony and romance. The three movements are called *Capriccio*, *Chaconne* and *Tarantella*, sufficient pointers to the character of the music. The *Chaconne* is extraordinarily imaginative, one of the most haunting slow movements of its era, with each variation in a different key. In the finale, a song associated with the Republicans in the Spanish Civil War is quoted, giving the work, as will be seen, an affinity with Britten's Violin Concerto.

Rawsthorne also wrote a two-piano concerto, two violin concertos and one apiece for cello, oboe and clarinet.

Britten

Benjamin Britten (1913–1976) was a pianist of amazing subtlety and refinement, yet his Piano Concerto (1938, revised 1945) is the least successful of his concertos and is not yet regarded as among his best works. Yet of course it is entertaining music, a compendium of Britten's youthful skill in matching parody to originality in an individualistic way. He himself gave the first performance, at a 1939 Henry Wood Prom. Its four movements—*Toccata, Waltz, Recitative and Aria* and *March*—indicate a line of thinking astonishingly close to Rawsthorne's first concerto. The opening *Toccata* is a complex sonata-form structure, impressively through-composed, which tends in performance to overshadow the subsequent three movements and which betrays the influence of Prokofiev. The *Waltz* was probably inspired by the Nazi annexation of Austria and the final *March* belongs to the era of the Peace Pledge Union and anti-war demonstrations in Trafalgar Square. The *Recitative and Aria* was replaced in 1945 by an *Impromptu*—a *passacaglia* and seven variations—which used music written in 1938 but still belongs to the Britten of *Peter Grimes* rather than the pre-war composer. Walton later took the theme as the basis of his *Improvisations on an Impromptu of Benjamin Britten* (1969). The Violin Concerto (1939) was for long overshadowed by its exact contemporary, Walton's, and the two works have much in common, being difficult show-pieces and at the same time passionate emotional outpourings. Britten even challenged Beethoven by starting the concerto with a motto on timpani. The first movement, a threnody for someone or something, is constructed from this drum-motto and its various manifestations in other themes. In the scherzo, Britten gives demoniac scope to the soloist's virtuosity while indulging in eccentric excursions into orchestral contrasts, such as an *ostinato* for two piccolos as support for a tuba solo. The cadenza is the bridge between scherzo and finale, a *passacaglia* ending with a moving lamentation for—what? Almost certainly the dead of the Spanish Civil War. The concerto's first player was the Spanish violinist Antonio Brosa, who perceived a definite Spanish flavour in the motto-rhythm of the first movement. Curiously, the Spanish-born Roberto Gerhard's Violin Concerto, written in 1942–3 after he had settled in England, also has no acknowledged programme and resembles Britten's in its lyrical profusion. The finale juxtaposes quotations from 'La Marseillaise' with a Spanish idiom, but the overall effect is less tragic than Britten's. A splendid concerto, though, requiring an agile soloist.

Britten wrote a concerto, which he called *Diversions*, for the one-armed pianist Paul Wittgenstein in 1941. Some of the material derives from incidental music written for J. B. Priestley's play *Johnson over Jordan* in 1938, and it reverts to the vignette-variations of which Britten had shown himself a master in the *Variations on a Theme of Frank Bridge* (1937). Parody, epigrammatic wit and satire abound in a fertile score that contains many anticipations of works by Britten which have obtained wider currency. If one excepts the brief *Scottish Ballad* for two pianos of 1941, there was to be no work in concerto form until 1963 when the artistry of Rostropovich brought forth the Cello Symphony (although I suppose the orchestral song-cycles for Pears could in a sense be regarded as concertos for voice and orchestra). As I have written elsewhere, this great work is neither cello concerto nor symphony with cello obbligato but a kind of cello sonata for orchestra. Indeed, the first movement is Britten's most orthodox use of sonata-form and the spare, angular orchestration intensifies the sense of tragedy which is never far away. Mahler would certainly have recognized the techniques of the nightmarish scherzo and the *Nachtmusik* of the *adagio* with its timpani punctuations of the cello's theme (Ex. 11). The finale is again a passacaglia preceded by a cadenza. But this time there is to be no elegiac ending. A trumpet brightly re-establishes the tonic D major and over the six variations that follow, the music emerges into the light and to a peroration based on the adagio's first subject. If by 1963 people had forgotten what a good composer of orchestral works Britten was, this Cello Symphony was a formidable reminder.

No British composer of the past 30 years, since roughly 1960, has been more popular as a writer of concertos than **Malcolm Arnold** (*b.* 1921). Organ, oboe, harmonica, horn (two), guitar and clarinet (two) are among the instruments which have benefited from his adroit craftsmanship and fertile melodic imagination. Several other British composers—Lennox Berkeley, Stephen Dodgson, Richard Rodney Bennett among them—have written guitar concertos for Julian Bream and John Williams, while the revival of interest in Baroque music has led to the apparent anachronism of harpsichord concertos composed by twentieth-century composers Walter Leigh, John McCabe and Richard Rodney Bennett (taking a hint from Falla in 1923–6). McCabe has also written concertos for piano and for violin. Like John Ogdon and Britten, he can play his own piano concertos. The organ concerto, has been revived with conspicuous success by Kenneth Leighton, Peter Dickinson, Michael Berkeley and Michael Ball, while Walton's and Constant Lambert's use of jazz-rhythms in their concertos is made to look merely tentative by Peter Dickinson in his piano and violin concertos. Peter Maxwell Davies's gradual metamorphosis from shock-tactics to neo-

Ex. 11

Romantic was carried an important stage further in his Violin Concerto of 1985. With the increasing versatility and virtuosity of individual British instrumentalists—the artistry of a Tertis or a Goossens is no longer an isolated phenomenon—we may expect that concertos galore will continue to flow from the pens of our composers.

Yet it is typical that a concerto for a combination of instruments for which no other British composer has written, so far as I can discover, should have been composed as he approached the age of 75 by the inexhaustibly innovative and inventive **Michael Tippett** (b. 1905). His Concerto for violin, viola and cello (1978–9), risky as it may be to say so, seems like a summing-up of the phase in his work which began with the Third Symphony and resulted in a re-flowering, more profuse and exotic, of the earlier lyricism of the *Midsummer Marriage* period during which his Piano Concerto was also composed. The Triple Concerto is in a continous span, but the outlines of the customary three movements are easily discerned. It begins with what Tippett calls a 'birth-motif' on the orchestra. The soloists introduce themselves with individual cadenzas and then come together in a theme derived from the coda of Tippett's Fourth String Quartet. Nothing like sonata-form follows, rather a kind of free fantasia based on five principal motifs varied and transformed in the movement's second, slower, half in which the soloists find increasing lyrical rapport with one another.

Linking the first two movements is an interlude for tuned percussion, horns and harp, a preparation for the Javanese gamelan characteristics of the accompaniment to the soloists' intense and seductive melody. The soloists are now heard as duettists—cello with bass oboe, violin with alto flute, violin and viola in canon. There are two orchestral interludes in this movement, one in gamelan style, the other nearer to Western Jazz. The Finale opens with a slow introduction in which each soloist in turn is heard. Strings have a melody marked in the score as 'singing, rich and golden'. Themes from the preceding movements are recalled, the music becoming more effulgent as it nears the final short flourish on the orchestra.

There have been criticisms that Tippett's restless, inquiring mind has allowed him to be sidetracked from this concerto's main path into irrelevant excursions into the gamelan and jazz interludes. But that is Tippett's way, and one must accept the questing spirit and mind that can draw such influences into their orbit and absorb them so convincingly. This concerto stretches back across the century to link itself to Elgar's for violin. Both works have an unquenchable radiance and serenity of spirit. Both are 'full of romantic feeling'. Both are landmarks in the progress of the English concerto.

Bibliography

General studies

Arthur Hutchings, *The Baroque Concerto*. London, 1961
Charles Rosen, *The Classical Style*. London, 1971
Sir Donald Tovey, *Essays in Musical Analysis*. Vol. III. Concertos. London, 1936, new edn. 1981
Antonio Veinus, *The Concerto*. London, 1948

Specific studies

Gerald Abraham ed., *Schumann—A Symposium*. London, 1952
Friedrich Blume, H. C. Robbins Landon, 'The Concertos' (*Mozart Companion* ed. Mitchell, Landon). London, 1956
David Brown, *Tchaikovsky*. 3 vols to date: London 1978; 1982; 1986
Joan Chissell, *Schumann*. London, 1949 rev. 1988
Martin Cooper, *French Music from the Death of Berlioz to the Death of Fauré*. London, 1951
Ronald Crichton, *Falla*. London, 1981
Roger Fiske, *Beethoven Concertos and Overtures*. London, 1970
Denis Forman, *Mozart's Concerto Form*. London, 1971
C. M. Girdlestone, *Mozart's Piano Concertos*. London, 1948
John Horton, *Brahms Symphonies and Concertos*. London, 1969
Alec Hyatt King, *Mozart's Wind and String Concertos*. London, 1978
Wolfgang Kolneder, *Vivaldi*. London, 1970
Robert Layton, *Dvořák Symphonies and Concertos*. London, 1978
Geoffrey Norris, *Rachmaninov*. London, 1976
Philip Radcliffe, *Mozart Piano Concertos*. London, 1978
Stanley Sadie, *Handel Concertos*. London, 1972
Michael Talbot, *Vivaldi*. London, 1978
John Warrack, *Tchaikovsky Symphonies & Concertos*. London, 1969

Select Discography

Robert Layton

Discographies are out-of-date almost before they are compiled, and in these days of a rapidly burgeoning CD catalogue and the imminent disappearance of LP, there are inevitable gaps. At the time of writing, there is no CD representation of the concertos of J. C. Bach, for example, or the piano concertos of Martinů. Nor are the classic accounts of the Beethoven concertos by Gilels or Solomon available in the new medium. I have attempted in the limited space available to include at least one recommendation for each major work discussed in the book. In this context I have where possible given preference to records which offer other concertos of interest rather than miscellaneous or symphonic repertoire. In some instance I have included the most recently available LP where no alternative is to be found, but generally speaking I have confined the list to records that are in present currency. Needless to say it is (and can only be) highly selective. CD numbers are indicated in heavy type; LP are placed before cassette numbers though where numbers are identical they do not have a separate listing. (The suffix for LP is 1 and that for the cassette is 4.)

ALBINONI   *Concertos Op. 9, Nos. 2, 3, 5, 8, 9, 11.* Holliger, I Musici. Philips **420 255-2PH**

MALCOLM ARNOLD *Guitar Concerto, Op. 67.* Bream, ECO, Gibson. RCA **GL/GK13883**
   John Williams, ECO, Groves-Brouwer. CBS **MK36680**

JOHANN SEBASTIAN BACH *Violin Concertos in A minor, BWV1041; E major, BWV1042; for two violins in D min., BWV1043; Concerto in C minor for violin, oboe and strings, BWV1060.* Perlman, Zukerman, Black, ECO, Barenboim. HMV EG290530-1/4
   Sitkovetsky, Garcia, Black, ECO. ASV/Novalis **150017-2**

Violin Concertos in A minor, BWV1041; E major, BWV1042; for two violins in D minor, BWV1043.
   Mutter, Accardo, ECO, Accardo. EMI **CDC7 47011-2**
   Accardo, Chamber Orchestra of Europe. Philips **416 142-2PH**
   Standage, Wilcock, English Concert, Pinnock. DG **410 646-2AH**
   Menuhin, Enesco, Paris Cons. Enesco, Monteux. EMI **CDH7 61082**

Brandenburg Concertos Nos. 1–6, BWV1046–51. English Concert, Pinnock. Archive **410 500/1-2AH**
   Bath Festival Orchestra, Menuhin. ED290374/5-1/4
   Busch Chamber Players. COLH13-14

Clavier Concertos BWV1052–7. Pinnock (hp), English Concert. **413 634-2AH3**
   Gavrilov (pf), ASMF, Marriner. EMI **CDS7 47629-8** EX2707470-3/8

Clavier concertos: in D min., BWV 1052; in G min., BWV1058; in F min., BWV1056. Katsaris, Franz Liszt CO, Rolla. Teldec. **8.43208** 6/4.43208
Steuerman, COE, Judd. Philips **420 200-2PH**

Concertos for two and three claviers, BWV 1060–4. Pinnock, Gilbert, Mortenson, (harpsichords), English Concert. Archive **413 634-2AH3**

Concertos for two claviers, BWV1060–2. Kocsis, Schiff, Franz Liszt Academy, Simon. Hungaroton **HCD12926-2**

CARL PHILIPP EMANUEL BACH *Clavier Concertos, Wotq. 43, Nos. 1–6.* Bob van Asperen, Orchestra Melante 81, EMI SLS1434863

Flute Concertos, Wotq. 166–69. Nicolet, Netherlands CO, Zinman. Philips 412 043-1/4

Harpsichord concerto in A, Wotq. 29. Ton Koopman, Amsterdam Bar. O. Philips **416 615-2** 416 615-1/5

Double concerto in F, for two harpsichords and orchestra, Wotq. 46. Staier, Hill, Musica Antiqua Köln, Goebel. Archive **419 256-2AH** 416 615-1/4

WILHELM FRIEDMANN BACH *Concerto in E flat for two harpsichords, F46.* Staier, Hill, Musica Antiqua Köln, Goebel. Archive **419 256-2AH** 416 615-1/4

BARBER *Violin Concerto.* Silverstein, Utah SO, Ketcham. **CDD245** PAD/PCD245
Cello Concerto. Wallfisch, ECO, Simon-Shostakovich No. 1. **CHAN8322** ABRD/ABTD1085
Piano Concerto. Joselsson, LSO, Schenck ASV **CDDCA 534** DCA/ZCDCA 534

BARTÓK *Piano Concertos Nos. 1–3.* Zoltan Kocsis, Budapest Festival, Ivan Fischer. Philips **416 531-2PH3**

Concertos 1 & 2. Pollini, Chicago SO, Abbado. DG **415 371-2GH**

Violin Concerto No. 1. Chung, Chicago SO, Solti—Berg. Decca **411 804-2DH**

Violin Concerto No. 2. Perlman, LSO, Previn. HMV EG290322-1/4
Menuhin, Philharmonia, Furtwängler. EMI 2C051-01322

ARNOLD BAX *Winter Legends.* Fingerhut, LPO, Bryden Thomson. Chandos **CHAN8484** ABRD/ABTD1195

Symphonic Variations. Fingerhut, LPO, Bryden Thomson. Chandos **CHAN8516** ABRD/ABTD1226

BEETHOVEN *Piano Concertos Nos. 1–5.* Schnabel, LSO or LPO, Sargent. Arabesque **Z6549-51**
Ashkenazy, VPO, Mehta. **411 900/3-2DH** 411 988-1/4DH
Serkin, Boston SO, Ozawa. **CD80061**

Piano Concerto No. 1 in C major. Perahia, Concertgebouw, Haitink—No. 2. CBS **MK42177**
Kempff, Berlin Philharmonic, Leitner. DG **419 856-2GGA**
Glenn Gould, Columbia SO, Golschmann. CBS I3M/I3T390936

Piano Concerto No. 2 in B flat. Perahia, Concertgebouw, Haitink—No. 1. CBS **MK42177**
Kempff, Berlin Philharmonic, Leitner. DG **419 856-2GGA**
Rubinstein, Boston SO, Leinsdorf—No. 3. RCA **RD85675**
Pollini, VPO, Jochum—No. 4. DG **413 445-2GH**

Piano Concerto No. 3 in C minor. Brendel, LPO, Haitink—No. 4. Philips **420 861-2**
Perahia, Concertgebouw, Haitink—No. 4. CBS **MK39814**
Kempff, Berlin Philharmonic, Leitner—No. 4. DG **419 086-4**
Rubinstein, Boston SO, Leinsdorf—No. 2. RCA **RD85675**
Richter, Philharmonia, Muti—Mozart K482. EMI **CDM7 69103-2**

Discography

Piano Concerto No. 4 in G major. Perahia, Concertgebouw, Haitink—No. 3. CBS **MK39814**
Pollini, VPO, Böhm—No. 2. DG **413 445-2GH**
Kempff, Berlin Philharmonic, Leitner—No. 3. DG **419 086-2**
Brendel, LPO, Haitink—No. 3. Philips **420 861-2**
Rubinstein, Boston SO, Leinsdorf—No. 5. RCA **RD85676**

Piano Concerto No. 5 in E flat. Arrau, Staatskapelle Dresden, Sir Colin Davis. Philips **416 215-2**
416 214-1/4
Edwin Fischer, Philharmonia, Furtwängler. **CDH7 61005-2** HLM7027
Perahia, Concertgebouw, Haitink. CBS **MK42330**
Brendel, LPO, Haitink. Philips **412 917-2**
Kempff, Berlin Philharmonic, Leitner. **419 468-2GGA**
Rubinstein, Boston SO, Leinsdorf—No. 4. RCA **RD85676**

Violin Concerto in D major. Heifetz, Boston SO, Munch—Brahms. RCA **RD85402**
Menuhin, Berlin Philharmonic, Furtwängler—Mendelssohn. EMI **CDC7 747119-2**
Perlman, Philharmonia, Giulini. EMI **CDC7 47002-2** ASD/TCC-ASD4059
Mutter, Berlin Philharmonic, Karajan. DG **413 818-2**
Grumiaux, Concertgebouw, Sir Colin Davis. Philips **420 348-2**
Szeryng, Concertgebouw, Haitink. Philips **416 418-2**

Triple Concerto in C major. David Oistrakh, Rostropovich, Richter, Berlin Philharmonic, Karajan. EMI **CDM7 69032-2**
Zimmermann, Cohen, Manz, ECO, Saraste. CFP 41 4495-1/4

ALBAN BERG   *Violin Concerto.* Perlman, Boston SO, Ozawa—Stravinsky. DG **413 725-2GH**
Chung, Chicago SO, Solti—Bartók No. 1. Decca **411 804-2DH**

BERWALD   *Violin Concerto in C sharp minor* (1821); *Piano Concerto in D* (1855). Tellefsen, Migdal, RPO, Björlin. EMI 7C 061 34571

BLOCH   *Violin Concerto.* Menuhin, Philharmonia, Kletzki. EMI EX290864-3/9
Schelomo Rostropovich, FNO, Bernstein—Schumann. EMI **CDC7 49307-2**

BRAHMS   *Piano Concertos Nos. 1–2.* Gilels, Berlin PO, Jochum. DG **419 158-2GH2**

No. 1 in D minor. Curzon, LSO, Szell. Decca **417 641-2DH**
Arrau, Philharmonia, Giulini. EMI **CDC7 69178-2**
Rubinstein, Chicago SO, Reiner. **RD85668**

No. 2 in B flat. Rubinstein, RCA Victor SO, Krips. **RD85671**
Gilels, Chicago SO, Reiner, RCA **RD85406**

Violin Concerto in D. Heifetz, Chicago SO, Reiner—Beethoven. RCA **RD85402**
Oistrakh, Leipzig Gewandhaus, Konwitschny.
Neveu, Philhamonia O, Dobrowen—Sibelius. EMI **CDH 7610112**

Double Concerto in A minor. Heifetz, Piatigorsky, RCA Victor SO, Wallenstein. RCA **GD86778**
Mutter, Meneses, Berlin PO, Karajan. DG **410 603-2GH**

FRANK BRIDGE   *Oration (Concerto elegiaco).* Isserlis, City of London Sinfonia, Hickox—Briten. **CDC7 4916-2** EL749716-1/4

BRITTEN   *Piano and Violin Concertos.* Richter, Lubotzky, ECO, Britten. Decca 417 308-1/4LE

Symphony for cello and orchestra. Isserlis, City of London Sinfonia, Hickox—Bridge. **CDC7 49716-2** EL749716-1/4

Companion to the Concerto

BRUCH *Violin Concertos Nos. 1–3.* Accardo, Leipzig Gewandhaus, Masur. Philips 6768 065

No. 1 in G minor. Heifetz, NSO, Sargent. RCA **RD861214**
Cho-Liang Lin, Chicago Symphony Orchestra, Slatkin. **MK42315** IM/IMT42315
Perlman, Concertgebouw, Haitink. EMI **CDC7 47074-2**
Chung, RPO, Kempe. Decca **417 707-2DM**
Mintz, Chicago SO, Abbado—Mendelssohn. DG **419 629-2**
Shizuka Ishikawa, Brno PO, Belohlavek—Sibelius. Supraphon **2SUP002**

CASELLA *Violin Concerto.* Gertler, Prague SO, Smetácek. Supraphon 110 1838

CHAUSSON *Poème.* Perlman, Paris, Martinon. **CDC7 27745-2**
Dumay, Monte Carlo, Plasson. EMI **CDC7 47544-2**

CHOPIN *Piano Concertos Nos. 1–2.* Krystian Zimerman, Los Angeles PO, Giulini. DG **415 970-2GH**
Rubinstein, New SO, Skrowaczewski. RCA **RD85612**

No. 1 in E minor. Argerich, LSO, Abbado—Liszt No. 1. DG **415 061-2**
Perahia, NYPO, Mehta. CBS **MK42400**
Krystian Zimerman, Concertgebouw, Kondrashin. DG **419 054-2GGA**

No. 2 in F minor. Haskil, Lamoureux, Markevich—Falla. Philips **416 443-2PH**

COPLAND *Clarinet Concerto.* Benny Goodman, Columbia SO, Copland. CBS **MK42227**

CORELLI *Concertos Op. 6.* Franz Liszt CO, Rolla. **HCD12376-6** SLPD/MK12376-8
La Petite Bande, Kuijken. EMI **CDS7 47919-8**

JOHN CORIGLIANO *Clarinet Concerto.* Drucker, NYPO, Mehta—Barber, Essay No. 3. **NW309-2** NW309

CRUSELL *Concertos Nos. 1–3.* Karl Leister, Lahti SO, Vänskä. BIS **CD345**

No. 2. Thea King, LSO, Francis, Hyperion **CDA66088** A66088 KA66088

DELIUS *Violin Concerto.* Ralph Holmes, RPO, Handley. Unicorn-Kanchana **DKPCD9040** DKP9040 DKPC9040

Cello Concerto. Lloyd Weber, Philharmonia O, Handley. RCA **RD70800** RL/RK70800

PETER DICKINSON *Organ Concerto* (1971). *Piano Concerto* (1984). Bate, Shelley, BBC SO, Atherton. **CDC7 47584-2** EL270439-1/4

DOHNÁNYI *Variations on a Nursery Song.* Dohnányi, LPO, Boult. HMV ED291275-1/4
Schiff, Chicago SO, Solti—Tchaikovsky No. 1. **417 294-2**

DUTILLEUX *Violin Concerto (L'arbre des songes).* Stern, RPO, Previn. CBS **MK24429** IMT24429

Cello Concerto ('Tout un monde lointain . . .'). Rostropovich, Orchestre de Paris, Baudo—Lutoslawski. HMV **CDC7 49304-2**

DVOŘÁK *Violin Concerto.* Perlman, LPO, Barenboim. EMI **747 168-2**
Menuhin, Paris Cons., Enescu—Mendelssohn. EH7 49394-1/4

Cello Concerto in B minor.—Tchaikovsky. Rostropovich, Berlin Philharmonic, Karajan. DG **413 819-2GH**
Rostropovich, LPO, Giulini—Saint-Saëns. EMI **CDC7 49036-2** EG749036-1/4

Piano Concerto. Richter, Bavarian Radio Symphony, Kleiber—Schubert 'Wanderer' Fantasy. EMI **CDC7 47967-2**

ELGAR *Violin Concerto.* Kennedy, LPO, Handley. **CDC7 47210-2** EMX412058-1/4

Discography

Cello Concerto. Du Pré, NPO, Barbirolli. EMI **CDC7 47329-2**
Yo-Yo Ma, LSO, Previn. CBS **MK39541** IM/IMT39541

FALLA *Nights in the Gardens of Spain.* Rubenstein, Philadelphia, Ormandy. RCA **RD85666**
Larrocha, LPO, Fruhbeck de Burgos. Decca **410 289-2DH**
Haskil, Lamoureux, Markevich—Chopin No. 2. Philips **416 443-2PH**
Harpsichord Concerto. Veyron-Lacroix, Ens. Willemoes. Erato STU/NME70713

FAURÉ *Ballade, Op. 19; Fantaisie, Op. 111.* Collard, Orchestre du Capitole de Toulouse, Plasson. EMI **CDC7 47932-2**

JEAN FRANÇAIX *Concerto for two pianos* (1965). Jean & Claude Françaix, Sudwestfunk, Baden-Baden, Stoll. Wergo 60087
Piano Concerto (1937). Claude Françaix, Radio Luxembourg, Jean Françaix. TVS34552

FRANCK *Symphonic Variations.* Larrocha, LPO, Fruhbeck de Burgos. Decca **410 583-2DH**
Rubinstein, Philadelphia, Ormandy—Falla. RCA **RD85666**
Collard, Orchestre de Capitole, Toulouse, Plasson. **CDC7 47547-2**

GEMINIANI *Concerti Grossi, Op. 3.* La Petite Bande. EMI **CDC7 47656-2**

GERSHWIN *Piano Concerto: Rhapsody in Blue.* Werner Haas, Monte Carlo Op. de Waart. Philips **420 492-2** 420 492-1/4
Previn, LSO. EMI **CDC7 47161-2** EG 290849-1/4
Daniel Blumenthal, ECO, Bedford. CFP **CFPD9012** 4413-1/4

GLAZUNOV *Violin Concerto in A minor, Op. 82.* Heifetz, RCA Victor SO, Hendl. RCA **RD87019** GL/GK83833
Amoyal, RPO, Scimone. STU/NME71164
Saxophone Concerto in E flat, Op. 109. Savijoki, Stockholm New CO, Panula. BIS **CD218**

GLIÈRE *Horn Concerto, Op. 91.* Baumann, Leipzig Gewandhaus, Masur. Philips **416 380-2PH**
Concerto for coloratura and orchestra, Op. 82; Harp Concerto, Op. 74. Joan Sutherland, Ossian Ellis, LSO, Bonynge. Decca SXL6406

GRIEG *Piano Concerto in A minor.* Bishop-Kovacevich, BBC SO, Davis—Schumann. Philips **412 923-2**
Lupu, LSO, Previn—Schumann. Decca **417 728-2DM**
Curzon, LSO, Fjeldstad. Decca 417 676-4DC

HANDEL *Concerti Grossi, Op. 3.* Linde Consort—Alexander's Feast. EX270245-3/5
Concerti Grossi, Op. 6. ASMF, Iona Brown. Philips **410 048-2PH3**
ASMF, Marriner. Decca 414 260-1/4DM3
Opp. 3 & 6. English Concert, Pinnock. Archive **423 149-2AX6**
Organ Concertos, Op. 4. Simon Preston, English Concert, Pinnock. **419 634-2AH2**
Organ Concertos, Op. 7. Simon Preston, English Concert, Pinnock. **419 468-2AH2**

HAYDN *Trumpet Concerto in E flat.* Håkan Hardenberger, ASMF, Mariner. Philips **420-302-2PH**
Marsalis, National PO, Leppard—Hummel. CBS **MK37846**
Clavier Concerto in D. Pinnock (harpsichord), English Concert. Archive **415 518-2AH**
Violin Concerto in C. Lin, Minnesota, Marriner—Vieuxtemps No. 5. CBS **MK37796**

Cello Concertos in D and C. Coin, AAM, Hogwood. Oiseau-Lyre **414 615-2**
Yo-Yo Ma, ECO, Garcia. CBS **MK36674**
Lloyd-Weber, ECO. Philips **412 793-2**

HENZE *Piano Concerto No. 2.* Eschenbach, LPO, Henze. DG 2740 150
Double Concerto for oboe, harp and strings. Holliger, Collegium Musicum, Sacher. DG 139 396
Violin Concerto No. 2. Langbein, London Sinfonietta, Henze. Decca HEAD5

HINDEMITH *Horn Concerto.* Brain, Philharmonia, Hindemith. EMI **CDC7 47834-2** EG291173-1/4
Violin Concerto. Oistrakh, LSO, Hindemith. Decca 414 437-1/4E
Viola Concerto (Schwanendreher). Benyamini, Orch de Paris, Barenboim. DG **423 241-2GG**

VAGN HOLMBOE *Cello Concerto, Op. 120* (1974)—Koppel. Ehrling Blondahl Bengtsson, Danish Radio SO, Janos Ferencsik. BIS-LP78

HONEGGER *Concerto da camera for flute, cor anglais and strings.* Shostac, Vogel, Los Angeles CO, Schwarz—Strauss. Nonesuch **CD79018**
Cello Concerto (1929). Sadlo, Czech PO, Neumann. Supraphon 110 0604

HUMMEL *Piano Concertos in A minor, Op. 85; B minor, Op. 89.* Stephen Hough, ECO, Bryden Thomson. **CHAN8507** ABRD/ABTD1217
Trumpet Concerto in E flat. Marsalis, National PO, Leppard. CBS **MK37846**

JOHN IRELAND *Piano Concerto.* Tozer, Melbourne SO, Measham—Rubbra Violin Concerto. **DKPCD9056**

JOLIVET *Concerto for trumpet* (1954); *Concertino for trumpet and strings.* Marsalis, Philharmonia, Salonen—Tomasi. CBS **MK42096**

KHACHATURIAN *Piano Concerto.* Mindru Katz, LPO, Boult. PRT **PVCD8376**
Violin Concerto. David Oistrakh, USSR SO, Khachaturian—Kabalevsky. Chant du Monde **LDC278 883**

LALO *Cello Concerto in D minor*—Saint-Saëns. Yo-Yo Ma, French Nat. O, Maazel. CBS **MK35848**
Symphonie espagnole. Perlman, Orchestre de Paris, Barenboim. DG **400 032-2GH**
Grumiaux, Lamoureux, Rosenthal. Philips **416 886-2PH**

LARS-ERIK LARSSON *Violin Concerto; Concertino for violin and strings.* Leo Berlin, Stockholm Philharmonic, Westerberg. Swedish Society **SCD1004**
Saxophone Concerto. Christer Johnsson, Swedish Radio SO, Segerstam. Caprice CAP1242

LISZT *Piano Concertos Nos. 1 & 2.* Richter, LSO, Kondrashin. Philips **412 006-2PH**
Bolet, LSO, Ivan Fischer. Decca **414 079-2DH**
Arrau, LSO, Davis. Philips **412 926-2PH**
No. 1 in E flat. Argerich, LSO, Abbado—Chopin No. 1. DG **415 061-2**

LUTOSŁAWSKI *Cello Concerto.* Rostropovich, Orchestre de Paris, Lutosławski—Dutilleux. HMV **CDC7 49304-2**

MALIPIERO *Violin Concerto No. 1.* Gertler, Prague SO, Smetacek—Milhaud. Supraphon **110 1120**

FRANK MARTIN *Piano Concertos Nos. 1 & 2. Ballade.* Antonioli, Rurin SO, Votti. Claves **CD8509** D8509
Violin Concerto. Schneiderhan, Luxembourg Radio, Martin. Vox STGBY661

Discography

PETER MAXWELL DAVIES *Violin Concerto.* Stern, RPO, Previn—Dutilleux. CBS
MK24429 IMT24429

MENDELSSOHN *Violin Concerto in E minor.* Cho-Liang Lin, Philharmonia, Michael Tilson
Thomas—Saint-Saëns. **MK39007** IM/IMT39007
  Menuhin, Paris Cons., Enescu—Dvořák. EH7 49395-1/4
  Menuhin, Berlin Philharmonic, Furtwängler—Beethoven. EMI **CDC7 747119-2**
  Mintz, Chicago SO, Abbado—Bruch No. 1. DG **419 629-2**
  Mutter, Berlin PO, Karajan—Mozart No. 5. DG **423 211-2**
Piano Concertos Nos. 1 in G minor; 2 in D minor. Perahia, ASMF, Marriner. CBS **MK42401**
  Schiff, Bavarian Radio SO, Dutoit. Decca **414 672-2**

MIASKOVSKY *Cello Concerto.* Rostropovich, Philharmonia, Sargent—Prokofiev.
CDC749 548-2

MILHAUD *Cello Concertos Nos. 1 & 2.* Apolin, Brno PO, Waldhans. Supraphon
SUAST50864

Piano Concerto No. 2. Johannesen, Radio Luxembourg, Kontarsky. TV34496S

Violin Concerto No. 2. Gertler, Prague SO, Smetacek—Malipiero. Supraphon 110 1120

Concertino de printemps. Goldberg, Lamoureux, Milhaud. Philips 6527 221

MOZART *Piano Concertos (Complete).* Perahia, ECO. CBS **M13K 42055**

Piano Concertos Nos. 5 in D, K175; 25 in C, K503. Perahia, ECO. CBS **37267**

Piano Concertos Nos. 8 in C, K246; 22 in E flat, K482. Perahia, ECO. CBS **76966**

Piano Concertos Nos. 9 in E flat, K271; 11 in F, K413. Bilson (fortepiano), E.Bar., Gardiner.
Archive **410 905-2AH**

Piano Concertos Nos. 11 in F, K413; 16 in D, K451. Brendel, ASMF, Marriner. Philips **415 488-
2PH**

Piano Concertos Nos. 12 in A, K414; 13 in C, K415. Ashkenazy, Philharmonia. Decca **410 214-
2DH**

Piano Concertos Nos. 14 in E flat, K449; 11 in F, K413; 12 in A, K414. Perahia, ECO, CBS
MK42243

Piano Concertos Nos. 15 in B flat, K450; 16 in D, K451. Ashkenazy, Philharmonia. Decca **411
612-2DH**

Piano Concertos Nos. 15 in B flat, K450; 16 in D, K451. Perahia, ECO. CBS **MK37824**

Piano Concertos Nos. 17 in G, K453; 26 in D (Coronation), K537. Barenboim, ECO. HMV **CDC7
47968-2**

Piano Concertos Nos. 17 in G, K453; 18 in B flat, K456. Perahia, ECO. CBS **MK42442**

Piano Concertos Nos. 20 in D Minor, K466; 21 in C major, K467. Uchida, ECO, Tate. Philips **416
281-2PH**

Piano Concertos Nos. 20 in D minor, K466; 21 in C major, K467. Bilson, E Baroque Sol. Gardiner.
Archive **419 609-2AH**

Piano Concertos Nos. 20 in D minor, K466; 27 in B flat, K595. Curzon, ECO, Benjamin Britten.
Decca **417 288-2DH**

Piano Concertos Nos. 20 in D minor, K466; 27 in B flat, K595. Perahia, ECO. CBS **MK42241**

Piano Concertos Nos. 20 in D minor, K466; 24 in C minor, K491. Haskil, Lamoureux, Markevich.
Philips **412 254-2PH**

Piano Concertos Nos. 20 in D minor, K466; 24 in C minor, K491. Brendel, ASMF, Marriner.
Philips **420 867-2PH**

Piano Concerto No. 22 in E flat, K482. Richter, Philharmonia, Muti—Beethoven No. 3. EMI **CDM7 69103-2**

Piano Concertos Nos. 22 in E flat, K482; 24 in C minor, K491. Perahia, ECO. CBS **MK42242**

Piano Concertos Nos. 23 in A, K488; 27 in B flat, K595. Brendel, ASMF, Marriner. Philips **420 487-2PH**

Piano Concerto No. 27 in B flat, K595; (i) Concerto for two pianos, K365. Gilels, VPO, Böhm. (i) w. Elena Gilels. DG **419 059-2GC**

Piano Concerto No. 27 in B flat, K595; (i) Concerto for two pianos, K365. Brendel, ASMF, Marriner. (i) w. Imogen Cooper. DG **416 364-2PH**

Violin Concertos Nos. 1–5. Perlman, VPO, Levine. DG **419 184-2GH(3)**

Violin Concertos Nos. 1 in B flat, K207; 2 in D, K211, 4 in D, K218. Grumiaux, LSO, Davis. Philips **416 633-2PH**

Violin Concertos Nos. 1 in B flat, K207; 4 in D, K218. Zimmermann, Württemburg CO, Faerber. HMV **CDC7 47431-24**

Violin Concertos Nos. 3 in G, K216; 5 in A, K218. Perlman, VPO, Levine. DG **410 020-2GH**
   Zimmermann, Württemburg CO, Faerber. HMV **CDC7 47426-2**
   Mutter, Berlin PO, Karajan. DG **415 327-2GH**
   Grumiaux, LSO, Davis. Philips **412 250-2PH**
   Cho-Liang Lin, ECO, Leppard. **MK42364**

Sinfonia concertante in E flat, K364. Grumiaux, Pelluccia, LSO, Colin Davis. Philips **412 244-2PH**
   Kremer, Kashkashian, VPO, Harnoncourt. DG **413 461-2GH**

Bassoon Concerto in B flat, K191. Brooke, RPO, Beecham—Clarinet. HMV **CD7 47864-2**

Flute Concerto No. 1 in G, K313; Oboe Concerto in C, K314. Tripp, Turetschek, VPO, Böhm. DG **413 373-2GG**

Flute & Harp Concerto in C, K299. Zabaleta, Schulz, VPO, Böhm. **413 552-2GH**

Clarinet Concerto in A, K622. Brymer, RPO, Beecham—Bassoon. HMV **CD7 47864-2**
   Prinz, VPO, Böhm—Flute & Harp. DG **413 552-2GH**

Horn Concertos Nos. 1–4. Brain, Philharmonia, Karajan. EMI **CDH7 61013-2**
   Civil, ASMF, Marriner. Philips **420 709-2**
   Högner, VPO, Böhm. DG **413 792-2**
   Seiffert, Berlin Philharmonic, Karajan. DG **419 097-2**
   Tuckwell, ECO. Decca **410 284-2**

NIELSEN   *Clarinet Concerto.* Cahuzac, Royal Orchestra, Copenhagen, Frandsen—Symphonies 2, 4, 5. HMV EM290443-3/5
   Schil, Gothenburg SO, Chung. BIS **CD321**

Violin Concerto. Dong-Suk Kang, Gothenburg SO, Chung. BIS **CD370**

Flute Concerto. Nicolet, Leipzig Gewandhaus, Masur. Philips **412 728-2GH**

PAGANINI   *Violin Concerto No. 1.* Perlman, RPO, Foster. **CDC7 47101-2**

Nos. 1 & 2. Accardo, LPO, Dutoit. DG **414 378-2GH**

Nos. 3 & 4. Accardo, LPO, Dutoit. DG **423 370-2GH**

No. 5. Accardo, LPO, Dutoit. DG **423 578-2GH**

POULENC   *Concert champêtre for harpsichord and orchestra; Organ Concerto in G minor.* Koopman, Alain, Rotterdam PO, Conlon. Erato **ECD88141** NUM/MCE75210

Piano Concerto; Concerto in D minor for two pianos; Aubade (Concert choréographique). Duchable, Collard, Rotterdam PO, Conlon. Erato **ECD88140**

Discography

Concert champêtre for harpsichord and orchestra; Concerto in D minor for two pianos; Aubade (Concert choréographique). van de Wiele, Poulenc and Fevrier, Tacchino, Paris Cons, Prêtre. ESD/TC-ESD7165

PROKOFIEV *Violin Concertos.* Mintz, Chicago SO, Abbado. DG **410 524-2GH** 410 524-4GH 410 524-1GH

Perlman, BBC Symphony Orchestra, Rozhdestvensky. EMI **CDC& 47035-2**

No. 2 in G minor—Glazunov; Sibelius. Heifetz, Chicago SO, Hendl. **RD87019.** Sibelius only—GL/GK89833

Szeryng, Bamberg SO, Krenz—Szymanowski, Wieniawski, LSO, Rozhdestvensky. Philips **410 106-2**

Piano Concertos Nos. 1, 4 & 5. Béroff, Leipzig Gewandhaus, Masur. HMV EG290326-1/4

Piano Concertos Nos. 2 & 3. Béroff, Leipzig Gewandhaus, Masur. HMV EG290261-1/4

Piano Concerto No. 1. Gavrilov, Philharmonia, Rattle. EMI **CDM7 69026-2** EG 290325-1/4

No. 3. Argerich, Berlin Philharmonic, Abbado—Tchaikovsky No. 1. DG **415 062-2GH**

No. 5. Richter, Warsaw Philharmonic, Rowicki—Rachmaninov No. 2. **415 119-2GH**

Sinfonia concertante for cello and orchestra. Rostropovich, RPO, Sargent—Miaskovsky **CDC749 548-2**

RACHMANINOV *Piano Concertos Nos. 1, 4, Paganini Variations.* Rachmaninov, Philadelphia, Ormandy. RCA **RD86659**

Concertos Nos. 2 (Stokowski) & 3 (Ormandy). RCA **RD85997**

Piano Concerto No. 1. Paganini Variations. Mikhail Pletnev, Philharmonia, Pesek. Virgin **VCO 790717/2**

No. 2. Richter, Warsaw Philharmonic, Wislocki—Prokofiev No. 5. **415 119-2GH**

Nos. 1 & 3. Jean-Philippe Collard, Orch de Capitole, Toulouse, Plasson. EMI **CDM7 69115-2**

No. 4 in G minor. Michelangeli, Philharmonia O, Gracis—Ravel in G. EMI **CDM7 49326-2**

RAVEL *Piano Concertos.* Jean-Philippe Collard, Orchestre National de France, Maazel. EMI **CDC7 47386-2**

Argerich, Berlin Philharmonic, Abbado. DG **419 062-2GG**

Pascal Rogé, Montreal SO, Dutoit. Decca **410 230-2DH** 410 230-4DH 410 230-1DH

Michelangeli, Philharmonia, Gracis—Rachmaninov No. 4. EMI **CDM7 49326-2**

REGER *Piano Concerto in F minor.* Serkin, Philadelphia, Ormandy. CBS 72402

RODRIGO *Concertio de Aranjuez.* John Williams, Philharmonia, Frémaux. CBS **MK37848**

JOHAN HELMICH ROMAN *Violin Concertos in D minor, BeRI 49; E major, BeRI 50, F minor, BeRI 52.* Sparf, Orpheus Ch Ensemble. BIS **CD284**

SAINT-SAËNS *Piano Concertos 1–5.* Pascal Rogé, LPO/RPO, Dutoit. Decca **417 351-2DH2**

Nos. 2 in G minor, 4 in C minor. Jean-Philippe Collard. EMI **CDC7 47816-2**

No. 2 in G minor. Rubinstein, Philadelphia, Ormandy—Falla; Franck. RCA **RD85666**

Violin Concerto No. 3 in B minor. Cho-Liang Lin, Philharmonia, Michael Tilson Thomas—Mendelssohn **MK39007** IM/IMT39007

Cello Concerto No. 1 in A minor. Rostropovich, LPO, Giulini—Dvořák. EMI **CDC7 49036-2** EG749036-1/4

Yo-Yo Ma, French Nat. O, Maazel—Lalo. CBS **MK35848**

SCHUMANN *Piano Concerto in A minor.* Lupu, LSO, Previn. Decca **417 728-2DM**

Bishop-Kovacevich, BBC SO, Davis—Grieg. Philips **412 923-2**

Cellos Concerto in A minor. Rostropovich, FNO, Bernstein—Bloch. Schelomo. EMI **CDC7 49307-2**

Violin Concerto in D minor. Kremer, Philharmonia, Muti—Sibelius. **CDC7 47110-2**

SCHOENBERG *Violin Concerto, Op. 36; Piano Concerto, Op. 42.* Pierre Amoyal, Peter Serkin, LSO, Boulez. Erato **ECD99175** NUM/MCE75263

SCHNITTKE *Violin Concerto No. 2.* Kremer, Basle SO, Holliger. Philips 411 107-1/4

SCRIABIN *Piano Concerto in F sharp minor.* Ashkenazy, Cleveland O, Maazel. Decca 417 242-1/4LE

SHOSTAKOVICH *Violin Concerto Nos. 1 & 2.* Oistrakh, Leningrad Philharmonic, Mravinsky; (2) Moscow PO, Kondrashin. DC 278 882

Cello Concertos Nos. 1 & 2. Schiff, Bavarian Radio SO, Maxim Shostakovich. Philips **412 526-2PH** 412 526-4PH 412 526-1PH

SIBELIUS *Violin Concerto in D minor.* Heifetz, Chicago SO, Hendl—Glazunov; Prokofiev. **RD87019**
Neveu, Philharmonia, Susskind—Brahms. EMI **CDH 7610112**
Shizuka Ishikawa, Brno PO, Belohlavek—Bruch No. 1. Supraphon **2SUP002**
Amoyal, Philharmonia, Dutoit—Tchaikovsky. Erato **ECD88109**

RICHARD STRAUSS *Horn Concertos Nos. 1 & 2.* Brain, Philharmonia, Sawallisch—Hindemith. EMI **CDC7 47834-2**
Baumann, Leipzig Gewandhaus, Masur. Philips **412 237-2PH**

Duet Concertino for clarinet, bassoon, strings and harp. Shifrin, Munday, Los Angeles CO, Schwarz—Honegger. Nonesuch **CD79018**

Oboe Concerto. Boyd, COE, Berglund—Mozart. ASV **CDCOE808**
Holliger, NPO, de Waart. Philips **6500 174**

STRAVINSKY *Violin Concerto in D.* Perlman, Boston SO, Ozawa. DG **413 725-2GH**

SZYMANOWSKI *Violin Concertos Nos. 1 & 2.* Kulka, Polish Radio SO, Maksymiuk. HMV ED291214-1/4

Violin Concerto No. 2. Szeryng, Bamberg SO, Kren—Wieniawski. Prokofiev No. 2. Philips **420 106-2**

TCHAIKOWSKY *Piano Concerto No. 1 in B flat minor.* Argerich, RPO, Dutoit—Prokofiev No. 3. DG **415 062-2GH**
Richter, Vienna SO, Karajan. DG **419 068-2GGA**
Gilels, NYPO, Mehta. CBS **MK36660** IM/IMT36660

Piano Concerto No. 2 in G major. Donohoe, Bournemouth SO, Barshai. **CDC7 49124-2** EL749124-1/4

Violin Concerto in D. David Oistrakh, Leipzig Gewandhaus, Konwitschny. DG mono **423 399-2GD**
Heifetz, Chicago SO, Reiner. GL/GK85264
Amoyal, Philharmonia, Dutoit—Sibelius. Erato **ECD88109**

TELEMANN *Concertos for winds.* Musica Antiqua Köln, Goevel. Archive **419 633-2AH** 419 633-4AH

Oboe Concertos in E minor, D minor, C minor, F minor, D major. Holliger, ASMF, Brown. Philips **412 879-2**

TIPPETT *Triple Concerto.* Pauk, Imai, Kirshbaum, LSO, Davis. Philips 6514/7337 209

Discography

FARTEIN VALEN *Violin Concerto.* Tellefsen, Bergen SO, Andersen. Philips 6507 039

VAUGHAN WILLIAMS *Concerto for two pianos.* Vronsky, Babin, LPO, Boult. HMV EL290653-1/4

Oboe Concerto. Theodore, LSO, Bryden Thomson. Chandos **CHAN8594** ABRD/ABTD1260 Winfield, Northern Sinfonia, Hickox. EMI **CDC7 49745-2**

Concerto accademico. Creswick, Northern Sinfonia, Hickox. EMI **CDC7 49745-2**

VIEUXTEMPS *Violin Concerto Nos. 4 in D; 5 in A minor.* Perlman, Paris, Barenboim. EMI **CDC7 47165-2**

No. 5. Cho-Liang Lin, Minnesota, Marriner—Haydn. CBS **MK37796**

VILLA-LOBOS *Concerto for guitar and orchestra.* John Williams, ECO, Barenboim— Castelnuovo-Tedesco. CBS IMT39017
Moreno, Mexico City SO, Batiz—Castelnuovo-Tedesco. EL1270330-1/4
Moreno, Mexico City SO, Batiz—Bachianas Brazilieras cpte. **CDS7 47901-8** EX270580- 3/5
Bream, LSO, Previn. RCA **GD86525**

VIVALDI *Op. 3 ('L'Estro Armonico').* The English Concert, Pinnock. Archive **423 094- 2AH**
Carmirelli, I Musici. Philips **412 128-2PH**

Op. 4 ('La Stravaganza'). Huggett, AAM, Hogwood. Oiseau-Lyre **417 502-20H2**

Op. 8 ('Il cimento dell'armonia e dell'inventione'). Pongracz, Liszt CO, Rolla. Hungaroton **HCD 12465/6-2**
Hirons, Holloway, AAM, Hogwood. Oiseau-Lyre **417 515-20H**

Op. 8, Nos. 1–4: 'The Four Seasons'. Standage, English Concert, Pinnock. Archive 00 045-2AH
Nils-Erik Sparf, Drottningholm Bar. Ens. BIS **CD 275**
Carmirelli, I Musici. Philips **410 001-2PH**
Kremer, LSO, Abbado. DG **413 726-2GH**

Op. 9 ('La Cetra'). Huggett, Raglan Baroque, Kraemer. EMI **CDC7 47829-2** EX270557-3 ED270557-5

Flute Concertos, Op. 10, Nos. 1–6. Stephen Preston, AAM. Oiseau-Lyre **414 685-2**

Concertos for flutes or recorders, RV435, 442, 90, 98, 101, 104 (original versions of Op. 10). Bruggen, Orchestra of the 18th century. RCA **RD70951** GL/GK 70951

Concertos for bassoon, RV473, RV483, RV485, RV497, RV503. Thunemann, I Musici. Philips **416 355-2PH**

Concertos for strings in D, RV121; D min., RV127; E min., RV133; F major, RV142; G major, RV145; G major, RV151; G min., RV152; A min., RV161; B flat, RV166. I Musici. Philips **411 035-2PH**

Violin Concertos in D minor (Senza cantin), RV243; E major (Il Riposo), RV370; E minor (Il Favorito), RV277; F major (Per la solennita di San Lorenzo), RV286. Accardo, I Solisti delle Settimane Musicali. EMI **CDC7 49320-2** El270133-1/4

WALTON *Cello Concerto.* Yo-Yo Ma, LSO, Previn—Elgar. CBS **MK39541** IMT39541 IM39541

Violin and Viola Concertos. Kennedy, RPO, Previn. EMI **DCD7 46928-2** EL746928-1/4

WEBER *Clarinet Concertos.* Hilton, CBSO, Järvi. Chandos **CHAN8305**

No. 1. Johnson, ECO, Tortelier. ASV **CDDCA585**

No. 2. Thea King, LSO, Francis. Hyperion **CDA66088** A66088 KA66088

KURT WEILL *Concerto for violin and winds.* Nona Liddell, London Sinfonietta, Atherton. DG **423 455-2GC**

WIENIAWSKI *Violin Concerto No. 2*—Szymanowski, Prokofiev No. 2. Szeryng, Bamberg SO, Krenz. Philips **420 106-2**

Index

Index

Index

Index

Index

Index

Index

Wirén, Dag 256
Wittgenstein, Paul 207, 233, 267–8, 278, 347
Wolf, Hugo 101
Wood, Sir Henry 327, 333–4
Wührer, Friedrich 269
Wuorinen, Charles 321

Yoell, John 256

Zabaleta, Nicanor 237, 303–4
Zichy, Count Géza 267–8
Zwetnow, Nicolaus 257